COLLINS GEM

WINE

A CONSUMER'S GUIDE

Anthony Lamont

COLLINS
London and Glasgow

The publishers are grateful to Robert Erskine for
his assistance in compiling entries in the Glossary.

First published 1988
Reprint 10 9 8 7 6 5 4 3 2 1

ISBN 0 00 458864 9

INTRODUCTION

Wine, A Consumer's Guide is exactly what the title says: a Tasting Guide to 535 of the wines available for under £5.00 at 21 of the country's supermarket and High Street wine chains; and a useful Glossary of terms used to describe wines and of names found on labels from around the world. It is a practical book for the consumer who would like to know more about wine but has been daunted by books which require an expensive depth of knowledge to be understood.

Wine consumption is growing rapidly as more and more people enjoy the delights of the vine. The Tasting Guide on page 11 will help you, as a wine buyer, to select for everyday quaffing from the vast array of wines now available on the shelves of supermarket and off-licence chains. At the same time, you will learn more about your palate and develop your knowledge of what is essentially a pleasant and sociable pastime open to everyone.

Thousands of wines are now available at under £5 a bottle. Our selection here concentrates on the best table wines from 21 major outlets. Each wine has been tasted and is described in language in which jargon has been kept to a minimum. Terms that are used are fully described in the Glossary. The prices of the wines for the winter of 1988 are included, but it should be borne in mind that these may rise a little. The wines are arranged by colour and by price in the order white, red, rosé and sparkling, with the lowest-priced wines first. The names of the wines follow as closely as possible the wording on the labels and include suppliers' names where these are useful. Own-brand wines do not have the supplier's name.

I am grateful to the individual outlets represented in the Tasting Guide for supplying samples of their wines and information on them. Because the chain of Safeway, Presto and Galbraith supermarkets is completely revamping its range of wines I have been unable to include these wines here, but I hope to be able to do so in the next edition of this book. The Peter Dominic chain of wine merchants has chosen not to be included in this edition as it publishes its own explanatory guide to its wines.

I was impressed by the overall standard of the wines submitted, and only regret that because of lack of space not all the wines submitted could be reviewed.

The Glossary exists not only to explain terms in the Tasting Guide but to help you decipher and read any wine label. There is also information on grapes, wines and wine-producing countries and regions.

Anthony Lamont
October 1988

4

TASTING GUIDE

EVALUATION OF WINES

We evaluate wines to assess quality, which, until a machine is invented to do this task for us, is where the human senses of sight, smell and taste reign supreme. And by assessing the quality of a wine we can decide whether or not it represents value for money. The amateur wine enthusiast, following a few basic guidelines, can quickly raise his or her level of appreciation of wine and gain even more pleasure from imbibing. Like riding a bicycle, once learned the technique is never forgotten.

Quality in wine is complexity and balance of colour, smell and flavour. Such a wine continually reveals different odours and flavours which come from the various chemical constituents. It is the infinite combination of these nuances of colour, aroma, taste and texture which makes wine so pleasurable and interesting.

Wine evaluation is a three-step process involving assessment of the colour and condition of a wine by sight, its nose by smell and its palate by taste. By analysing the impressions imparted to these senses you will soon be able to make your own more experienced judgements according to the requirements of your particular palate and pocket. When evaluating a wine remember that the ability to do so can be affected by the setting. A noisy party or poor lighting, for example, will make evaluation more difficult and less reliable than quiet surroundings in a well-lit room.

Colour and Condition

Colour and condition are assessed by filling a clear, thin, plain glass one-third full with wine and observing its colour against a white background, say a piece of paper, angled in such a way that it reflects as much light as possible from an overhead source. When the glass is tilted, the wine travels up the side and the reflected light will shine through the wine, allowing you to judge its colour and clarity. Concentrate on the change of colour, from the deepest colour in the centre to the palest in the curved upper surface (meniscus). The colour should be attractive, and the wine should have no haze or floating particles. Any cloudiness or suspended material is both visually unappealing and may also indicate a faulty wine, possibly from poor filtration technique, an unwanted second fermentation, or from microbiological activity in the bottle. The correct colour for the style of wine is described in the entry on colour in the Glossary.

Nose

'Nosing a wine' is the term used to describe smelling it. The sense of smell is used by humans less and less, although when developed it is far more acute than the sense of taste. First and foremost, an unpleasant odour tells us there is a strong possibility that the wine will be just as unpleasant to taste. But more enjoyably, nosing a wine allows us to smell all the lovely fruity aromas of the grape combined with the bouquet which originates from the wine's fermentation and ageing.

Begin nosing by swirling a glass to aerate and agitate the wine in it. This intensifies and lifts the fruit aromas and bouquet out of the glass. Then smell the wine with quick full sniffs, putting your nose deep in the glass. Do not do this for long as the sense of smell is easily fatigued and may become confused.

Wine should have an appealing bouquet, full of lovely fruity aromas combined with the more complex smells which are imparted during winemaking and maturation.

Palate

The most important aspect of wine evaluation is the palate, which in essence is the sensation of taste on the mouth, tongue and throat. To evaluate the palate, which is most sensitive approximately one hour before meals, first take some wine into your mouth and swirl it about. Next, draw air through the wine and bubble it over the tongue. This aerates the wine and assists in 'opening' it up for assessment. Take a small sip and swallow. This helps to evaluate the finish (the flavour remaining in the mouth and throat). Look for fruitiness, depth of flavour and the balance of acid to sweetness. The flavour should be pleasant and persistent and be consistent with the style or type of wine you are tasting. For example, a rosé should look, smell and taste like a rosé. Balance, harmony and integration of all constituents results in complexity. In a wine of complex make-up, different flavours will constantly compete for the attention of the taste buds. A balanced wine is one in which the fruit, body and acidity (also tannin in reds) are in proportion to each other, resulting in a full, rounded feel in the mouth.

Vintages and Vintage Charts

A point worth mentioning is that of vintages and vintage charts. These are a guide only and are generally of relevance only for higher priced wines. As winemaking techniques improve, the gap between the better and lesser years is narrowing, and wines from a particular producer may be of very good quality in a year which is not held in high regard. Yet many people will discredit a wine of a particular vintage without bothering to taste it, simply saying it's of a poor vintage. It is the contents of the bottle which are important, not the year on the label. By trying out the wines of lesser years good value can often be found, so rather than include a very generalized chart covering the different regions, each wine has been individually tasted regardless of whether it comes from what is held to be a good year or a bad one.

Wine and Food

For centuries wine has been served with food to enhance enjoyment and aid digestion. For millions, food without wine does not constitute a meal, it is sustenance only. Good food deserves good wine, and their successful marriage makes a magnificent repast, but food prepared with effort and love can be let down by a poorly chosen wine. Choosing the right wine does not necessarily require great expense. As good food can be prepared cheaply, so too can good wine be found at relatively low cost. The secret for both is care and imagination in selection. Tremendous enjoyment can be had from the discovery of new tastes in both food and wine. Be prepared to experiment and look forward to the myriad flavours awaiting you.

The old rule says white wine with white meat and red wine with red meat for the good reason that these are the best combinations overall. If you feel like breaking the rule, then go ahead and enjoy it to the full.

Here are a few suggestions as a guide to which wines suit each course. Aperitifs should be fairly dry wines to clean and stimulate the palate. This is the domain of dry Sherry or sparkling wines, but also suitable are dry, light and crisp white wines such as German Cabernets, Soave or Frascati from Italy, Sherry or white Rioja from Spain, Vinho Verde from Portugal, and Chablis and Muscadet from France. Riesling and Sauvignon Blanc from almost every region that produces them could also be tried. For soup, try medium-dry Sherry or Sercial Madeira. With fish, try to match the body or depth of flavour of the wine with the strength of flavour of the fish. For delicate white fish try light German wines. Strongly flavoured fish can carry a full-bodied Chardonnay from France, Australia or California. For oily fish try crisp, fairly acidic wines such as Muscadet or Sauvignon Blanc. For white meats almost any white wines will suffice. Again, try to match the body of the wine with the depth of flavour of the food. Strongly flavoured white meats are well matched with rich full-bodied white wines and also red wines. Red meat allows a wide choice of red wines, but as a general rule try to find where the recipe for the dish originated and match the wine style to that which would be used within the region. Desserts call for sweet wines or sparkling wines.

An excellent each-way bet to satisfy a diverse range of tastes is a refreshing rosé. Similarly, champagne or sparkling wine will accompany almost any dish. Ultimately it is up to the individual to decide on the tipple as it is his or her palate which seeks stimulation.

When you have decided whether or not you like a wine, stick to your opinion but do not condemn a wine simply because you do not like the type or style it presents, as it may be of good quality although not your preferred style.

Enjoy - in your good health.

ASDA

WHITE WINES

WINE: **VIN DE PAYS DES CÔTES DE GASCOGNE**
COUNTRY: France
PRICE: £1.99 (70cl)
COLOUR: Pale straw with green tints.
NOSE: Very impressive for a wine at this price, with attractive fruity aromas and yeast character.
PALATE: Medium-bodied, rounded and flavoursome, with soft fruit and a crisp finish.
SWEETNESS: 2.   Excellent value for money.

WINE: **CÔTES DE DURAS**
COUNTRY: France
PRICE: £2.19 (70cl)
COLOUR: Very pale straw.
NOSE: Reasonable intensity of aroma of the Sauvignon Blanc and Semillon grapes; some stalkiness;
PALATE: Medium/full-bodied, with light fruit flavours, crisp acidity and some stalkiness showing on the finish.
SWEETNESS: 2.

WINE: **BADEN (QBA)**
COUNTRY: Germany 1986
PRICE: £2.29 (75cl)
COLOUR: Pale/mid straw with green tints.

NOSE: Very floral, fruity bouquet.
PALATE: Medium-bodied, medium dry. A soft easy drinking style.
SWEETNESS: 3.   Value for money.

WINE: **WILTINGER SCHARZBERG Kabinett, Mosel**
COUNTRY: Germany 1983
PRICE: £2.45 (70cl)
COLOUR: Straw in colour.
NOSE: Excellent intensity of the aromas of the Riesling grape.
PALATE: Medium-bodied, with very intense, tangy Riesling fruit flavour and a crisp fruity finish.
SWEETNESS: 5.   Excellent value for money.

WINE: **SAUVIGNON DE BORDEAUX**
COUNTRY: France 1986
PRICE: £2.45 (70cl)
COLOUR: Very pale straw.
NOSE: Delicate, grassy Sauvignon Blanc character.
PALATE: Medium-bodied, with soft, delicate, grassy fruit and a crisp palate; cleansing finish.
SWEETNESS: 2.   Excellent value for money.

WINE: **CHARDONNAY ALTO ADIGE (DOC)**
COUNTRY: Italy
PRICE: £2.99 (70cl)
COLOUR: Pale straw.
NOSE: Lightly perfumed bouquet with some stalkiness.

PALATE: Medium-bodied, with pleasant combination of fruit and vinosity. Very soft texture and pleasant lingering finish.

SWEETNESS: 2. Value for money.

WINE: **PINOT D'ALSACE (AC)**
SUPPLIER: Meirerheim
COUNTRY: France 1985
PRICE: £2.75 (70cl)
COLOUR: Pale/mid straw.
NOSE: Appealing, fragrant fruitiness.
PALATE: Medium-bodied, soft and rounded. Good balance of fruit and vinous flavours on the finish. Good food wine.

SWEETNESS: 3. Value for money.

RED WINES

WINE: **VALDEPEÑAS (DO)**
COUNTRY: Spain 1985
PRICE: £1.79 (70cl)
COLOUR: Light mid/red.
NOSE: Good depth of light, ripe fruit.
PALATE: Medium-bodied, with ripe fruit and old oak flavours.

TASTE: B. Very good value for money.

WINE: **VIN DE PAYS DU GARD**
COUNTRY: France
PRICE: £1.85 (70cl)
COLOUR: Light/mid red.
NOSE: Attractive, with a spicy fruity bouquet.

PALATE: Medium-bodied, soft and very fruity, with tannin and oak in harmony. Pleasant finish. Good quaffer!

TASTE: B. Very good value for money.

WINE: **CÔTES DU VENTOUX (AC)**
COUNTRY: France
PRICE: £1.95 (70cl)
NOSE: Spicy with peppery fruit aromas.
PALATE: Full-bodied, with rich, spicy fruit flavour and a crisp finish.
TASTE: D. Very good value for money.

WINE: **CÔTES DE DURAS (AC)**
COUNTRY: France
PRICE: £2.19 (70cl)
NOSE: Good depth of Cabernet Sauvignon fruit with its characteristic grassy bouquet.
PALATE: Medium/full-bodied, soft, fruity and flavoursome; strong tannin and some astringency.
TASTE: C. Value for money.

WINE: **DÃO (RD)**
COUNTRY: Portugal 1982
PRICE: £2.19 (75cl)
COLOUR: Red/brown.
NOSE: Very appealing, showing spicy fruit enhanced by oak.
PALATE: Light/medium-bodied, with spicy fruit flavours and a pleasantly astringent, oaky finish.
TASTE: D. Excellent value for money.

WINE:	**PENEDÈS (DO)**
COUNTRY:	Spain
PRICE:	£2.19 (70cl)
COLOUR:	Red.
NOSE:	Bouquet of lifted, ripe fruit.
PALATE:	Medium-bodied, soft and rich with very ripe fruit. Persistent finish, with good tannin and crisp acidity.
TASTE:	D. Very good value for money.

WINE:	**CLARET (AC)**
COUNTRY:	France
PRICE:	£2.25 (70cl)
COLOUR:	Deep red/ruby.
NOSE:	Excellent grassy Cabernet fruit with some blackcurrant character.
PALATE:	Medium/full-bodied, fruity and rounded, with smooth texture. Finish has lingering tannin and oak flavours.
TASTE:	C. Excellent value for money.

WINE:	**SYRAH, VDP DES COLLINES RHODANIENNES**
COUNTRY:	France
PRICE:	£2.45 (70cl)
COLOUR:	Ruby red.
NOSE:	Exhibits the peppery characteristics of the Syrah grape.
PALATE:	Full-bodied, rounded with very peppery flavour. Smooth, soft, fruity finish.
TASTE:	D. Excellent value for money.

WINE:	**RIOJA (DO)**
COUNTRY:	Spain 1984
PRICE:	£2.69 (70cl)
COLOUR:	Red.
NOSE:	Lovely oaky/fruit fragrance which defines the Rioja style of wine.
PALATE:	Medium/full-bodied, very smooth and rich, with strong oaky/fruity flavours. Pleasant oaky finish.
TASTE:	C. Good value for money.

WINE:	**CHIANTI CLASSICO (DOCG)**
COUNTRY:	Italy 1985
PRICE:	£2.79 (75cl)
COLOUR:	Red.
NOSE:	Very subtle fragrance of fruit and oak in good harmony.
PALATE:	Medium/full-bodied, with good balance of fruit/tannin/oak/acidity, resulting in wine with complexity of flavours.
TASTE:	D. Good value for money.

WINE:	**MÉDOC (AC)**
COUNTRY:	France
PRICE:	£2.99 (70cl)
COLOUR:	Dark red.
NOSE:	Very appealing, with a classic claret bouquet that would normally only be found on a far more expensive wine.
PALATE:	Full-bodied, smooth and fruity, with tasty oak flavours and a fruity finish.
TASTE:	D. Excellent value for money.

WINE:	**RED BURGUNDY (AC)**
COUNTRY:	France 1984
PRICE:	£3.49 (70cl)
COLOUR:	Red with brown tints.
NOSE:	Excellent bouquet showing what Pinot Noir can achieve if well made. Earthy, strawberry/raspberry fragrance.
PALATE:	Medium-bodied, very soft and smooth, with distinct varietal character of Pinot Noir. A bargain!
TASTE:	B. Excellent value for money.

WINE:	**ST EMILION (AC)**
COUNTRY:	France
PRICE:	£3.75 (70cl)
COLOUR:	Dark red.
NOSE:	Good depth of fruit and oak.
PALATE:	Medium/full-bodied, with good balance of fruit/oak/acidity. Finish is flavoursome with soft tannin.
TASTE:	C. Value for money.

WINE:	**FITOU**
SUPPLIER:	Les Caves de Tuchan
COUNTRY:	France
PRICE:	£4.79 (150cl)
COLOUR:	Dark red/ruby.
NOSE:	Complex spicy/peppery bouquet.
PALATE:	Full-bodied, with rich, peppery fruit and integrated oak. Very long finish. A robust wine which raises the standards of Fitou.
TASTE:	D. Value for money.

ROSÉ WINES

WINE:	**CABERNET DE SAUMUR (AC)**
COUNTRY:	France
PRICE:	£2.45 (70cl)
COLOUR:	Pink/amber.
NOSE:	Delicate, fruity bouquet.
PALATE:	Light/medium-bodied, medium dry, with very soft fruity flavours.
SWEETNESS:	3. Value for money.

SPARKLING WINES

WINE:	**CRÉMANT DE BOURGOGNE BRUT (AC)**
COUNTRY:	France 1985
PRICE:	£4.99 (75cl)
COLOUR:	Straw/deep straw.
NOSE:	Very attractive with delicate, toasty, appleish bouquet.
PALATE:	Full-bodied, creamy, soft and flavoursome. Some complex toasty flavours on the finish. Made using the traditional Champagne Method. Well-made sparkling wine.
SWEETNESS:	2. Very good value for money.

AUGUSTUS BARNETT

WHITE WINES

WINE:	**VIVAL D'ORO**
SUPPLIER:	Vinival
COUNTRY:	Spain
PRICE:	£2.19 (70cl)
COLOUR:	Mid/dark straw.
NOSE:	Strong aroma of the Moscatel grape.
PALATE:	Light/medium-bodied, with fruity Moscatel/grapey flavour. Finish is slightly sweet.
SWEETNESS: 3.	Value for money.

WINE:	**BERGERAC BLANC (AC)**
SUPPLIER:	Mau
COUNTRY:	France
PRICE:	£2.29 (75cl)
COLOUR:	Pale/mid straw.
NOSE:	Light, fruity bouquet with aroma of the Sauvignon Blanc grape slightly overshadowing the other varieties in this blended wine.
PALATE:	Light/medium-bodied, with delicate fruit flavour, good balance and a crisp finish.
SWEETNESS: 1.	Value for money.

WINE:	**CÔTES DE DURAS SEC (AC)**
COUNTRY:	France 1987
PRICE:	£2.29 (75cl)
COLOUR:	Pale/mid straw.

NOSE: Light, mainly vinous bouquet, with underlying aroma of Semillon fruit.

PALATE: Medium-bodied, rounded with good depth of vinous flavour. Pleasant finish.

SWEETNESS: 1.   Value for money.

WINE: **CÉPAGE COLOMBARD CÔTES DE GASCOGNE (VDT)**

COUNTRY: France

PRICE: £2.29 (70cl)

COLOUR: Pale/mid straw.

NOSE: Attractive, floral/fruity bouquet with slight nutty aroma.

PALATE: Medium/full-bodied, very fruity and flavoursome. Easy drinking wine with a fruity, dry finish.

SWEETNESS: 2.   Good value for money.

WINE: **BULGARIAN SAUVIGNON BLANC**

SUPPLIER: Vinimpex

COUNTRY: Bulgaria

PRICE: £2.39 (70cl)

COLOUR: Pale/mid straw.

NOSE: Vinous with some aroma of Sauvignon Blanc and slight stalkiness.

PALATE: Medium-bodied, soft and smooth, with reasonable depth of fruit flavour and a tangy finish.

SWEETNESS: 2.   Value for money.

WINE: **CORBIÈRES BLANC (AC)**

COUNTRY: France 1987

PRICE: £2.39 (75cl)

COLOUR: Pale/mid straw.
NOSE: Light yeasty bouquet with good underlying fruit.
PALATE: Medium-bodied, crisp and fruity, with strong yeast character. Pleasant finish. Easy drinking wine.
SWEETNESS: 2. Value for money.

WINE: **MOSEL TAFELWEIN**
SUPPLIER: Zentralkellerei
COUNTRY: Germany
PRICE: £2.45 (70cl)
COLOUR: Pale/mid straw.
NOSE: Light vinous bouquet with some stalky character.
PALATE: Light/medium-bodied, with very fruity flavour and a crisp finish.
SWEETNESS: 5.

WINE: **BADEN Qualitätswein**
SUPPLIER: ZBW
COUNTRY: Germany
PRICE: £2.79 (75cl)
COLOUR: Straw.
NOSE: Very floral/fruity bouquet.
PALATE: Medium-bodied, with delicate fruity flavour and well-balanced acidity. Fruity finish.
SWEETNESS: 4. Value for money.

WINE: **LE CHARDONNAY (VDP)**
SUPPLIER: Boutinot
COUNTRY: France 1987

PRICE: £2.99 (75cl)
COLOUR: Straw.
NOSE: Pleasant fruity bouquet with slight fruit salad aroma.
PALATE: Medium/full-bodied, with good depth of flavour. Finish is persistent.
SWEETNESS: 2.   Value for money.

WINE: **ORLANDO JACOB'S CREEK**
COUNTRY: Australia 1987
PRICE: £2.99 (75cl)
COLOUR: Straw.
NOSE: Attractive fruity bouquet with slight yeast character.
PALATE: Medium/full-bodied, with good depth of fruit flavour and well-balanced acidity. Flavoursome finish.
SWEETNESS: 2.   Good value for money.

WINE: **DOM DES ROSIERS, MUSCADET SÈVRE ET MAINE (AC)**
COUNTRY: France 1987
PRICE: £3.09 (75cl)
COLOUR: Pale/mid straw.
NOSE: Good combination of vinous/Muscadet grape aroma.
PALATE: Medium-bodied, with delicate fruit flavour and a crisp, lingering finish.
SWEETNESS: 1.   Value for money.

WINE: **MARQUÉS DE CACERES RIOJA (DO)**
COUNTRY: Spain 1987

PRICE:	£3.29 (75cl)
COLOUR:	Straw.
NOSE:	Mainly vinous with some underlying fruit aromas.
PALATE:	Full-bodied, with good depth of vinous/fruit flavour. Finish is very persistent.
SWEETNESS: 2.	Value for money.

WINE: GEWÜRZTRAMINER ALSACE (AC)

COUNTRY:	France 1986
PRICE:	£3.89 (75cl)
COLOUR:	Straw.
NOSE:	Excellent bouquet which exhibits the spicy/grapey aroma of the Gewürztraminer grape.
PALATE:	Medium-bodied, with strong, spicy fruit flavour. Easy drinking.
SWEETNESS: 4.	Very good value for money.

WINE: PINOT GRIGIO ALTO ADIGE (DOC)

SUPPLIER:	Lageder
COUNTRY:	Italy 1986
PRICE:	£3.99 (75cl)
COLOUR:	Pale straw.
NOSE:	Attractive bouquet of delicate fruit.
PALATE:	Medium/full-bodied, soft and rounded, with good depth of fruit flavour. Finish is slightly honeyed.
SWEETNESS: 2.	Value for money.

WINE: BROWN BROS. DRY MUSCAT BLANC

COUNTRY:	Australia 1987

23

PRICE: £4.59 (75cl)
COLOUR: Straw, with green tints.
NOSE: Excellent intensity of fruity/grapey Muscat aroma.
PALATE: Medium/full-bodied, with strong grapey flavour and a crisp fruity finish.
SWEETNESS: 3.

RED WINES

WINE: **BERGERAC (AC)**
SUPPLIER: Mau
COUNTRY: France
PRICE: £2.29 (75cl)
COLOUR: Red with blue tints.
NOSE: Attractive bouquet with Cabernet Franc, Malbec and Merlot grapes all contributing aroma in harmony.
PALATE: Light/medium-bodied, very soft and fruity, with light tannin and a delicate, fruity finish which is persistent.
TASTE: C.   Value for money.

WINE: **CÔTES DE DURAS (AC)**
SUPPLIER: UPD
COUNTRY: France 1985
PRICE: £2.29 (70cl)
COLOUR: Red.
NOSE: Light, fruity bouquet.
PALATE: Medium-bodied, with good fruit flavour and firm tannin. A rounded and well balanced wine.
TASTE: C.   Value for money.

WINE:	**CORBIÈRES (AC)**
SUPPLIER:	Pre-La-Reine
COUNTRY:	France
PRICE:	£2.39 (70cl)
COLOUR:	Red with blue tints.
NOSE:	Light fruity bouquet.
PALATE:	Medium/full-bodied, with slightly raisined/spicy fruit with strong tannin and a slightly astringent finish.
TASTE:	C. Good value for money.

WINE:	**BULGARIAN CABERNET SAUVIGNON**
SUPPLIER:	Vinimpex
COUNTRY:	Bulgaria 1984
PRICE:	£2.39 (75cl)
COLOUR:	Red with brown tints.
NOSE:	Intense bouquet of ripe, raisined fruit and oak.
PALATE:	Full-bodied, with rich, raisined fruit and soft tannins. Finish is oaky and lingering.
TASTE:	C. Excellent value for money.

WINE:	**DOM DE L'AMEILLAUD (VDT)**
SUPPLIER:	Herail
COUNTRY:	France 1987
PRICE:	£2.59 (75cl)
COLOUR:	Light/mid red with blue tints.
NOSE:	Delicate fruity bouquet.
PALATE:	Medium-bodied, with delicate, spicy fruit flavour and light tannin. Good balance.
TASTE:	B. Value for money.

WINE:	**FITOU (AC)**
SUPPLIER:	Mont Tauch
COUNTRY:	France 1986
PRICE:	£2.69 (70cl)
COLOUR:	Dark red with purple tints.
NOSE:	Ripe, slightly spicy/cinnamon fruit bouquet.
PALATE:	Full-bodied, with pleasant flavour of slightly raisined fruit. Subtle oak flavour on finish.
TASTE:	D. Excellent value for money.

WINE:	**CH DU GRANDE-MAINE (AC)**
SUPPLIER:	Lichine
COUNTRY:	France 1986
PRICE:	£2.99 (75cl)
COLOUR:	Dark red.
NOSE:	Excellent stalky/Cabernet Sauvignon aroma. Good claret nose.
PALATE:	Full-bodied, with attractive stalky fruity flavour and pleasant tannin. Good balance of oak/fruit/acidity.
TASTE:	C. Excellent value for money.

WINE:	**ORLANDO JACOB'S CREEK DRY RED**
COUNTRY:	Australia 1985
PRICE:	£2.99 (75cl)
COLOUR:	Mid/dark red.
NOSE:	Intense bouquet of buttery, vanillan oak and fruit.
PALATE:	Full-bodied, with excellent depth of fruit flavour enhanced by oak maturation. Persistent, flavoursome finish.
TASTE:	D. Excellent value for money.

WINE:	**RIOJA (DO) MARQUÉS DE CACERES**
COUNTRY:	Spain 1983
PRICE:	£3.69 (75cl)
COLOUR:	Dark red/ruby.
NOSE:	Very dominant oaky bouquet with underlying fruit aromas.
PALATE:	Full-bodied, with good depth of tarry fruit and oak flavour. High tannin and acidity will help carry this wine in the cellar. Needs 12 months or so to begin to show its potential.
TASTE:	C. Good value for money.

WINE:	**PENALBA DUERO (DO)**
SUPPLIER:	Lopez
COUNTRY:	Spain 1985
PRICE:	£3.89 (75cl)
COLOUR:	Dark red with blue tints.
NOSE:	Very attractive bouquet of vanilla/buttery oak and underlying fruit aromas.
PALATE:	Full-bodied, smooth and supple, with ripe fruit and strong oak flavour.
TASTE:	D. Excellent value for money.

WINE:	**CROZES-HERMITAGE (AC)**
SUPPLIER:	Delas
COUNTRY:	France 1986
PRICE:	£3.99 (75cl)
COLOUR:	Dark red with purple tints.
NOSE:	Excellent peppery/fruity bouquet.
PALATE:	Full-bodied, with intense peppery fruit flavour and a lingering, slightly astringent finish.
TASTE:	D. Excellent value for money.

WINE: **PENFOLDS KOONUNGA HILL**
COUNTRY: Australia 1986
PRICE: £3.99 (75cl)
COLOUR: Dark red with purple tints.
NOSE: Excellent complexity of aromas in good harmony. Lovely buttery/vanilla oak with spicy/peppery Shiraz fruit and stalky/berry/Cabernet Sauvignon fruit competing for attention.
PALATE: Full-bodied, silky smooth and wonderfully palatable, with excellent balance of lovely fruit and oak flavours.
TASTE: E.   Excellent value for money.

WINE: **CH TIMBERLAY (AC)**
SUPPLIER: Giraud
COUNTRY: France 1985
PRICE: £4.79 (75cl)
COLOUR: Dark red.
NOSE: Pleasing combination of oak and fruit aromas.
PALATE: Full-bodied, with rich, ripe Cabernet fruit flavour. Firm tannin and a fruity finish.
TASTE: C.   Value for money.

WINE: **VINO NOBILE DI MONTEPULCIANO (DOCG)**
SUPPLIER: Polizano
COUNTRY: Italy 1983
PRICE: £4.99 (75cl)
COLOUR: Dark red with brown tints.
NOSE: Strong bouquet of ripe, tarry fruit and oak.

PALATE: Full-bodied, robust, with good depth of tarry fruit and firm tannin. Finish is oaky with pleasant astringency.

TASTE: D.   Very good value for money.

ROSÉ WINES

WINE: **LISTEL GRIS DE GRIS (VDT)**
COUNTRY: France
PRICE: £2.95 (70cl)
COLOUR: Salmon pink.
NOSE: Slight, lively, fruity bouquet.
PALATE: Medium-bodied, with delicate fruit and crisp finish.
SWEETNESS: 8.

BEJAM

WHITE WINES

WINE:	**VIN DE PAYS DE L'HERAULT**
SUPPLIER:	Doury
COUNTRY:	France
PRICE:	£1.69 (70cl)
COLOUR:	Straw.
NOSE:	Fruity/stalky bouquet.
PALATE:	Medium/full-bodied, with attractive fruity flavour and balanced acidity.
SWEETNESS:	2. Very good value for money.

WINE:	**LIEBFRAUMILCH Qualitätswein**
SUPPLIER:	Brems
COUNTRY:	Germany 1986
PRICE:	£1.89 (70cl)
COLOUR:	Straw.
NOSE:	Attractive, floral, fruity bouquet.
PALATE:	Light/medium-bodied, with strong, floral, fruity flavour. Easy drinking style.
SWEETNESS:	5. Very good value for money.

WINE:	**BEREICH BERNKASTEL Qualitätswein**
SUPPLIER:	Brems
COUNTRY:	Germany 1987
PRICE:	£1.99 (70cl)
COLOUR:	Pale/mid straw.
NOSE:	Bouquet of floral fruit and chalky overtones.

PALATE: Medium-bodied, fruity and flavoursome.
SWEETNESS: 3.   Very good value for money.

WINE: **VINHO VERDE (RD)**
SUPPLIER: Fonseca
COUNTRY: Portugal
PRICE: £1.99 (75cl)
COLOUR: Straw with green tints.
NOSE: Attractive fruit aromas and some straw character.
PALATE: Medium-bodied, with good depth of vinous flavour and crisp acid.
SWEETNESS: 2.   Very good value for money.

WINE: **PIESPORTER MICHELSBERG Riesling Qualitätswein**
SUPPLIER: Brems
COUNTRY: Germany 1987
PRICE: £2.29 (70cl)
COLOUR: Pale straw.
NOSE: Delicate bouquet with some light fruit-salad aromas.
PALATE: Medium-bodied, soft and smooth, with good depth of Riesling fruit flavour. Very easy drinking.
SWEETNESS: 3.   Good value for money.

RED WINES

WINE: **DOMAINE DES TOURELS (VDP)**
SUPPLIER: Bessière
COUNTRY: France 1987

PRICE: £1.69 (70cl)
COLOUR: Red with purple tints.
NOSE: Very fruity with slightly jammy character.
PALATE: Medium-bodied, very soft and fruity. Easy drinking style with soft tannin.
TASTE: B.   Value for money.

WINE: **CLARET (AC)**
SUPPLIER: Rocheau
COUNTRY: France
PRICE: £1.99 (70cl)
COLOUR: Red with brown tints.
NOSE: Strong, fruity bouquet showing some bottle-aged development.
PALATE: Medium/full-bodied, very soft with good claret flavour.
TASTE: C.   Very good value for money.

WINE: **BEAUJOLAIS (AC)**
SUPPLIER: Martin
COUNTRY: France 1987
PRICE: £2.49 (70cl)
COLOUR: Red with blue tints.
NOSE: Delicate aroma of the Gamay grape with a slightly jammy character.
PALATE: Light/medium-bodied, soft with delicate fruit flavour. Easy drinking style.
TASTE: A.   Value for money.

BLANEY

WHITE WINES

WINE: **FRANCISCO DRY WHITE (DO)**
SUPPLIER: Vinival
COUNTRY: Spain
PRICE: £1.95 (70cl)
COLOUR: Deep straw with faint brown tinges.
NOSE: Very distinctive, with strong vanillan overtones and light fruity fragrance.
PALATE: Medium-bodied, with light fruit and some Sherry-like flavour. Crisp acidity.
SWEETNESS: 2.

WINE: **TREBBIANO DI ROMAGNA (DOC)**
SUPPLIER: Ravenna Antica
COUNTRY: Italy
PRICE: £2.19 (70cl)
COLOUR: Very pale straw with green tints.
NOSE: Good intensity of attractive fruit aromas.
PALATE: Medium/full-bodied, very soft and mouth-filling, with very agreeable fruit flavours.
SWEETNESS: 2.   Good value for money.

WINE: **BEREICH BERNKASTEL Qualitätswein**
SUPPLIER: Koch
COUNTRY: Germany 1987
PRICE: £2.29 (70cl)
COLOUR: Straw.
NOSE: Fragrant, floral bouquet.

PALATE: Medium-bodied and very soft with delicate fruit.

SWEETNESS: 3.   Good value for money.

WINE: **SAUVIGNON**
SUPPLIER: Kressmann
COUNTRY: France
PRICE: £2.49 (70cl)
COLOUR: Pale straw with green tints.
NOSE: Light, earthy fruit with some character of the Sauvignon Blanc grape.
PALATE: Medium-bodied, with earthy fruit flavour and good balance of acidity.
SWEETNESS: 1.

WINE: **GLORIA LIEBFRAUMILCH**
Qualitätswein
SUPPLIER: Schmitt
COUNTRY: Germany 1987
PRICE: £2.49 (70cl)
COLOUR: Straw.
NOSE: Light with delicate fruity fragrance.
PALATE: Medium-bodied, soft and rounded, with delicate fruit flavour - not simply sugary sweet.
SWEETNESS: 5.

WINE: **PIESPORTER MICHELSBERG**
Qualitätswein
SUPPLIER: Schmitt
COUNTRY: Germany 1987
PRICE: £2.55 (70cl)
COLOUR: Pale straw.

NOSE: Fruity bouquet with some chalky character.
PALATE: Medium-bodied, crisp, fruity and pleasantly rounded. Finish is clean and fruity.
SWEETNESS: 3.

WINE: **NIERSTEINER SPIEGELBERG Kabinett (QMP)**
SUPPLIER: Schmitt
COUNTRY: Germany 1986
PRICE: £2.99 (70cl)
COLOUR: Straw/deep straw.
NOSE: Strong bouquet of tropical fruits.
PALATE: Medium-bodied with very distinctive tropical fruit flavour. Soft easy-drinking wine.
SWEETNESS: 4.   Good value for money.

WINE: **VOUVRAY CH DE VALMER (AC)**
SUPPLIER: Besombes
COUNTRY: France 1986
PRICE: £3.29 (70cl)
COLOUR: Pale/mid straw.
NOSE: Pleasing intensity of the aroma of the Chenin Blanc grape.
PALATE: Medium-bodied, soft and mouth-filling and displaying well the flavour of the Chenin Blanc grape.
SWEETNESS: 3.   Very good value for money.

WINE: **MUSCADET, CH DE LA BOURDONNIER (AC)**
COUNTRY: France 1986
PRICE: £3.75 (75cl)

COLOUR:	Straw.
NOSE:	Pleasant bouquet of well-made Muscadet wine.
PALATE:	Medium/full-bodied, with strong fruit flavour and crisp acidity. Finish is fruity and lingering.
SWEETNESS:	1. Value for money.

WINE:	**NUMERO UNO BIANCO**
SUPPLIER:	Rocca delle Macie
COUNTRY:	Italy 1986
PRICE:	£4.15 (75cl)
COLOUR:	Straw.
NOSE:	Attractive with good intensity of fruit.
PALATE:	Medium/full-bodied, soft and fairly fruity with well-balanced acidity and a persistent finish. Well-made wine.
SWEETNESS:	2.

WINE:	**MÂCON-VILLAGES DOMAINE MICHEL (AC)**
SUPPLIER:	Loron
COUNTRY:	France 1986
PRICE:	£4.39 (70cl)
COLOUR:	Straw/deep straw with green tints.
NOSE:	Attractive honeyed fruit character and slight stalkiness.
PALATE:	Full-bodied with nutty fruit flavour and crisp acidity. Finish is persistent and very slightly coarse.
SWEETNESS:	2.

WINE:	**MONTANA CHARDONNAY**
COUNTRY:	New Zealand 1987
PRICE:	£4.59 (70cl)

COLOUR: Deep straw with green tints.

NOSE: Excellent Chardonnay fruit character, with strong bouquet of fruit salad and guava. Yeast character and oak add to complexity.

PALATE: Crisp, clean and fruity with excellent mouth-filling fruitiness and tasty oak flavours. Finish is very fruity, crisp and persistent.

SWEETNESS: 2.   Excellent value for money.

WINE: **GERWÜRZTRAMINER KUEHN (AC)**

COUNTRY: France 1985

PRICE: £4.95 (70cl)

COLOUR: Deep straw/light gold.

NOSE: Excellent intensity of the aroma of the Gewürztraminer grape, a very spicy bouquet.

PALATE: Medium-bodied, with wonderful soft, spicy, fruity flavours. Very slight coarseness on the finish (common characteristic of many wines made from this variety) does not greatly detract from this well-made wine.

SWEETNESS: 4.   Good value for money.

RED WINES

WINE: **FRANCISCO DRY RED (DO)**

SUPPLIER: Vinival

COUNTRY: Spain

PRICE: £1.95 (70cl)

COLOUR: Red.

NOSE: Ripe, raisined fruit with a hint of vinegar.

PALATE:	Medium-bodied, with light fruit, nice tannin and a crisp fruity finish.
TASTE:	B. Value for money.

WINE:	**CÔTES DE GASCOGNE ROUGE (VDP)**
SUPPLIER:	Mau
COUNTRY:	France
PRICE:	£1.99 (70cl)
COLOUR:	Red/ruby.
NOSE:	Very appealing, with intense grassy fruitiness.
PALATE:	Medium-bodied with grassy fruit flavours and soft tannin. A touch of oak comes through on a tangy finish.
TASTE:	B. Good value for money.

WINE:	**LA NAVETTE ROUGE Vin de Table**
SUPPLIER:	Mau
COUNTRY:	France
PRICE:	£1.99 (70cl)
COLOUR:	Deep red.
NOSE:	Quite unusual, with very ripe fruity bouquet showing strong overtones of caramel.
PALATE:	Medium-bodied, with toasty fruit flavours and light tannin.
TASTE:	A. Value for money.

WINE:	**SANGIOVESE DI ROMAGNA (DOC)**
SUPPLIER:	Ravenna Antica
COUNTRY:	Italy
PRICE:	£2.19 (70cl)
COLOUR:	Deep red.
NOSE:	Pleasant bouquet of rich, ripe fruit.

PALATE: Medium/full-bodied, with strong blackcurrant flavour and a crisp, fruity finish.

TASTE: C.   Very good value for money.

WINE: **CHIANTI CAMPELLI (DOCG)**
COUNTRY: Italy 1985
PRICE: £2.49 (70cl)
COLOUR: Red.
NOSE: Strong bouquet of crushed flowers.
PALATE: Medium/full-bodied with crushed flower flavour and pleasant tannic astringency on a crisp finish. Unusual style, but one of merit and some complexity.

TASTE: D.   Value for money.

WINE: **CH DE BEAUREGARD Coteaux du Languedoc (AC)**
SUPPLIER: Bonfils
COUNTRY: France 1986
PRICE: £2.69 (70cl)
COLOUR: Red with blue tints.
NOSE: Bouquet of ripe, raisined fruit and some caramel character.
PALATE: Medium/full-bodied, rich, ripe and rounded. Very fruity flavoursome wine.

TASTE: B.   Value for money.

WINE: **CÔTES DU RHÔNE (AC)**
SUPPLIER: Prieure
COUNTRY: France 1986
PRICE: £2.69 (70cl)
COLOUR: Light/mid red.

NOSE:	Very attractive, with a light, spicy, peppery fruit bouquet.
PALATE:	Full-bodied, with soft, peppery fruit flavour. Mouth-filling quaffing wine.
TASTE:	C. Very good value for money.

WINE:	**FITOU (AC)**
SUPPLIER:	Parmentier
COUNTRY:	France
PRICE:	£2.99 (70cl)
COLOUR:	Red/dark red.
NOSE:	Pleasantly fruity.
PALATE:	Full, soft, smooth and mouth-filling, with some complexity.
TASTE:	D. Value for money.

WINE:	**RIOJA SEÑOR BURGUES (DO)**
SUPPLIER:	Martinez
COUNTRY:	Spain 1985
PRICE:	£2.99 (70cl)
COLOUR:	Red/deep red.
NOSE:	Lovely vanillan oak odours and pleasant underlying fruit. Very attractive bouquet.
PALATE:	Medium/full-bodied, silky smooth in texture with strong oak and pleasing fruity flavours on the finish.
TASTE:	C. Excellent value for money.

WINE:	**CH LA BORIE Côtes du Rhône (AC)**
SUPPLIER:	Chauvenet
COUNTRY:	France 1986
PRICE:	£3.25 (75cl)

COLOUR:	Red.
NOSE:	Light, spicy fruit aromas.
PALATE:	Full-bodied, with strong tannin and mouth-filling fruit flavours. Oak is well integrated and the finish is persistent, showing some complexity of flavours.
TASTE:	C. Good value for money.

WINE:	**DOURO RESERVA (DO)**
SUPPLIER:	Caves Acacio
COUNTRY:	Portugal 1980
PRICE:	£3.29 (75cl)
COLOUR:	Red/ruby.
NOSE:	Strong vinegar odour, with tarry fruit and oak also evident.
PALATE:	Full-bodied with spicy peppery fruit and oak. Very flavoursome wine with good tannin and a fruity finish.
TASTE:	D. Good value for money.

WINE:	**CH DE FONSCOLOMBE (AC)**
COUNTRY:	France 1986
PRICE:	£3.29 (75cl)
COLOUR:	Red with blue tints.
NOSE:	Unusual but very attractive floral, fruity bouquet.
PALATE:	Medium/full-bodied, floral and fruity with soft tannin. Easy drinking style.
TASTE:	C. Very good value for money.

WINE:	**CH DE PARAZA (AC)**
SUPPLIER:	Girard
COUNTRY:	France 1986

PRICE:	£3.29 (75cl)
COLOUR:	Red/ruby.
NOSE:	Rich ripe bouquet of jammy fruit.
PALATE:	Medium/full-bodied, with good balance of fruit flavour and acidity. Strong tannin on finish.
TASTE:	C. Good value for money.

WINE:	**TEROLDEGO (DOC)**
SUPPLIER:	Donini
COUNTRY:	Italy 1986
PRICE:	£3.59 (75cl)
COLOUR:	Red with purple tints.
NOSE:	Attractive fruity bouquet.
PALATE:	Full-bodied, soft and rounded, with pleasant fruit and well-balanced oak and acidity.
TASTE:	D. Good value for money.

WINE:	**MÉDOC (AC)**
SUPPLIER:	Kressmann
COUNTRY:	France
PRICE:	£3.59 (70cl)
COLOUR:	Red with purple tints.
NOSE:	Excellent intensity of the aroma of Cabernet fruit.
PALATE:	Full-bodied and very fruity, with good balance of tannin, oak and acidity.
TASTE:	D. Excellent value for money.

WINE:	**BEAUJOLAIS-VILLAGES RÉGNIÉ**
COUNTRY:	France 1986
PRICE:	£3.69 (70cl)
COLOUR:	Red.

NOSE: Light, delicate, fruity fragrance.

PALATE: Medium/full-bodied, with velvety smooth texture. A flavoursome wine with a lingering fruity finish.

TASTE: B.   Very good value for money.

WINE: **BROWN BROS. CABERNET SAUVIGNON**

COUNTRY: Australia 1985

PRICE: £4.95 (75cl)

COLOUR: Deep red/ruby.

NOSE: Good intensity of the aroma of Cabernet Sauvignon enhanced by buttery oak odours.

PALATE: Full-bodied, with silky texture and mouthfilling fruit flavour. High acidity will enable further cellaring for 1-2 years.

TASTE: D.   Good value for money.

SPARKLING WINES

WINE: **ASTI SPUMANTE SAN CARLO (DOC)**

COUNTRY: Italy

PRICE: £3.95 (75cl)

COLOUR: Straw.

NOSE: Very intense grapey bouquet.

PALATE: Full-bodied, with intense grape flavour and balanced acidity. Very flavoursome wine.

SWEETNESS: 7.   Value for money.

BUDGEN

WHITE WINES

WINE:	**LIEBFRAUMILCH Qualitätswein**
COUNTRY:	Germany 1986
PRICE:	£1.99 (70cl)
COLOUR:	Straw.
NOSE:	Attractive floral, fruity bouquet.
PALATE:	Medium-bodied, crisp with lovely, light fruit flavour.
SWEETNESS:	5. Very good value for money.

WINE:	**MOSCATEL DE VALENCIA (DO)**
SUPPLIER:	Augusto Egli
COUNTRY:	Spain
PRICE:	£2.49 (75cl)
COLOUR:	Straw.
NOSE:	Intense, raisined Moscatel fruit aroma.
PALATE:	Full-bodied, rich and luscious, with strong fruity flavour of Moscatel.
SWEETNESS:	8. Excellent value for money.

WINE:	**COLOMBELLE VDP DES CÔTES DE GASCOGNE**
COUNTRY:	France 1987
PRICE:	£2.49 (75cl)
COLOUR:	Pale straw with green tints.
NOSE:	Floral/fruity/earthy bouquet with some stalky character.

PALATE: Medium-bodied, rounded and fruity, with good balance and crisp acidity.

SWEETNESS: 2.

WINE: **KLÜSSERATHER ST MICHAEL KABINETT**

SUPPLIER: Mertes

COUNTRY: Germany 1986

PRICE: £2.59 (70cl)

COLOUR: Pale/mid straw.

NOSE: Light, delicately fruity nose with some grassy character.

PALATE: Medium-bodied, with good depth of fruit flavour and a crisp finish.

SWEETNESS: 4.   Good value for money.

WINE: **MONTANA SAUVIGNON BLANC**

COUNTRY: New Zealand 1987

PRICE: £3.99 (75cl)

COLOUR: Straw with green tints.

NOSE: Excellent grassy/gooseberry aromas.

PALATE: Medium/full-bodied, with grassy/gooseberry flavours. Soft texture, with a crisp fruity finish.

SWEETNESS: 1.   Excellent value for money.

WINE: **ORLANDO RF CHARDONNAY**

COUNTRY: Australia 1987

PRICE: £3.99 (75cl)

COLOUR: Mid/deep straw.

NOSE: Very oaky bouquet with strong aroma of the Chardonnay grape.

45

PALATE: Full-bodied, with fruit-salad Chardonnay fruit and strong oak flavour.

SWEETNESS: 2.   Excellent value for money.

WINE: **SANCERRE (AC)**
SUPPLIER: Cherrier
COUNTRY: France 1986
PRICE: £4.99 (75cl)
COLOUR: Pale/mid straw.
NOSE: Subtle, grassy, fruity bouquet.
PALATE: Full-bodied, with very pleasant, crisp Sauvignon Blanc fruit flavour and good balance of acidity.

SWEETNESS: 1.   Excellent value for money.

WINE: **CH LA NERE, LOUPIAC (AC)**
SUPPLIER: Dulac et Seraphon
COUNTRY: France 1983
PRICE: £4.69 (75cl)
COLOUR: Deep straw/golden.
NOSE: Rich, sweet-smelling bouquet.
PALATE: Full-bodied, rich and luscious. Very fruity, sweet dessert style of wine.

SWEETNESS: 8.   Value for money.

WINE: **SAINT-VÉRAN, LES MONTS (AC)**
COUNTRY: France 1986
PRICE: £4.99 (75cl)
COLOUR: Straw with green tints.
NOSE: Complex bouquet of fruit with strong toasty character.

PALATE: Full-bodied, soft with good balance of toasty fruit/oak acidity.

SWEETNESS: 2.   Value for money.

RED WINES

WINE: **MINERVOIS, CH DE RUSSOL**
COUNTRY: France 1986
PRICE: £2.29 (75cl)
COLOUR: Dark red with purple tints.
NOSE: Bouquet of ripe, raisined fruit.
PALATE: Medium/full-bodied, with good depth of spicy, ripe fruit and tannin. Persistent finish with slight astringency.
TASTE: C.   Excellent value for money.

WINE: **CLARET (AC)**
PRICE: £2.49 (70cl)
COLOUR: Ruby/red.
NOSE: Light bouquet with slight stalky character.
PALATE: Light/medium-bodied, fruity and flavoursome with light tannin and a crisp finish.
TASTE: C.   Value for money.

WINE: **CÉPAGE SYRAH (VDP COLLINES RHODANIENNES)**
PRICE: £2.59 (75cl)
COLOUR: Red with purple tints.
NOSE: Excellent intensity of peppery fruit.

PALATE:	Medium/full-bodied, with spicy, peppery fruit and good balance of tannin.
TASTE:	D. Very good value for money.

WINE:	**ABBAYE ST HILAIRE (VDQS)**
SUPPLIER:	C.S.M.
COUNTRY:	France 1985
PRICE:	£2.79 (75cl)
COLOUR:	Dark red with purple tints.
NOSE:	Attractive fruity bouquet.
PALATE:	Full-bodied, soft and rounded, with mouth-filling fruit flavour. Pleasant oak and tannin on the finish.
TASTE:	C. Very good value for money

WINE:	**CÔTES DU RHÔNE VILLAGES (AC)**
SUPPLIER:	Dauphins
COUNTRY:	France 1986
PRICE:	£2.89 (75cl)
NOSE:	Light peppery bouquet.
PALATE:	Medium/full-bodied, soft, smooth and fruity. Finish is fruity and slightly astringent.
TASTE:	C. Good value for money.

WINE:	**CH CANON MONSÉGUR (AC)**
SUPPLIER:	Lovato
COUNTRY:	France 1983
PRICE:	£3.99 (75cl)
COLOUR:	Dark red.
NOSE:	Light fruity bouquet.

PALATE: Full-bodied, soft with light fruit and firm tannin. Slight astringency on the finish.
TASTE: C.

WINE: **BOURGOGNE PINOT NOIR (AC)**
COUNTRY: France 1985
PRICE: £3.99 (75cl)
COLOUR: Light/mid-red with brown tints.
NOSE: Strong aromas of the Pinot Noir grape and oak.
PALATE: Medium/full-bodied, with strong oak flavour and subtle strawberry/raspberry fruit flavour in good balance. Good tannin and some astringency on the finish. Will keep 12-24 months.
TASTE: B.   Excellent value for money.

WINE: **BAROLO TERRE DEL BAROLO (DOCG)**
COUNTRY: Italy 1983
PRICE: £4.39 (75cl)
COLOUR: Red/brown.
NOSE: Complex bouquet, with excellent tarry/liquorice fruit and oak aroma.
PALATE: Full-bodied, rich and robust, with strong flavour of tarry fruit and oak.
TASTE: E.   Very good value for money.

WINE: **MONDAVI CABERNET SAUVIGNON**
COUNTRY: California, US 1985
PRICE: £4.39 (75cl)
COLOUR: Red/ruby.
NOSE: Excellent intensity of the stalky/berry aromas found in well-made Cabernet Sauvignon wines.

PALATE: Full-bodied, with intense, spicy blackcurrant fruit which has been aged in oak. Finish is crisp and astringent. Cellaring potential 12-24 months.

TASTE: B.   Excellent value for money.

ROSÉ WINE

WINE: **LAMBRUSCO ROSÉ**
COUNTRY: Italy
PRICE: £2.19 (75cl)
COLOUR: Cherry/pink.
NOSE: Very grapey/appleish bouquet.
PALATE: Light/medium-bodied, with crisp grapey/appleish flavour.
SWEETNESS: 6.

WINE: **LISTEL GRIS DE GRIS (VDT)**
COUNTRY: France
PRICE: £2.29 (70cl)
COLOUR: Salmon pink.
NOSE: Light, lively, fruity bouquet.
PALATE: Medium-bodied, with delicate fruit and crisp finish.
SWEETNESS: 8.   Good value for money.

CO-OP

WHITE WINES

WINE: **BEREICH NIERSTEIN (QBA)**
SUPPLIER: Lohengrin
COUNTRY: Germany 1986
PRICE: £1.95 (70cl)
COLOUR: Straw with green tinges.
NOSE: Very floral with grapey fruit.
PALATE: Medium-bodied, sweet and rounded, very fruity and with good balancing acidity.
SWEETNESS: 4.   Value for money

WINE: **LAMBRUSCO BIANCO**
SUPPLIER: Carissa
COUNTRY: Italy
PRICE: £1.99 (70cl)
COLOUR: Pale straw and semi-sparkling.
NOSE: Pleasing combination of clean fruit and vinosity.
PALATE: Light/medium-bodied, clean, with good balance of fruit and acidity. Well made.
SWEETNESS: 6.   Value for money.

WINE: **VIN DE PAYS DES CÔTES DE GASCOGNE**
COUNTRY: France
PRICE: £1.99 (70cl)
COLOUR: Pale/mid straw.

NOSE:	Reasonable depth of clean fruit, with slight grassy character.
PALATE:	Medium-bodied, clean and fruity with a crisp finish.
SWEETNESS:	1. Good value for money.

WINE:	**OPPENHEIMER KRÖTENBRUNNEN (QBA)**
SUPPLIER:	Lohengrin
COUNTRY:	Germany
PRICE:	£2.15 (70cl)
COLOUR:	Straw.
NOSE:	Very floral and fruity.
PALATE:	Medium-bodied and very fruity. Balance is good.
SWEETNESS:	4. Good value for money

WINE:	**MOSELTALER (QBA)**
SUPPLIER:	Lohengrin
COUNTRY:	Germany
PRICE:	£2.25 (70cl)
COLOUR:	Pale straw with green tinges.
NOSE:	Attractive fruit and some grassy aromas.
PALATE:	Medium-bodied with reasonable fruit. Finish crisp, clean.
SWEETNESS:	4. Value for money.

WINE:	**PIESPORTER MICHELSBERG (QBA)**
SUPPLIER:	Lohengrin
COUNTRY:	Germany 1986
PRICE:	£2.35 (70cl)
COLOUR:	Straw with green tinges.

NOSE:	Very attractive, lifted fruit.
PALATE:	Medium/full-bodied, soft and rounded, with good depth of fruit and well-balanced acidity. Well-made wine.
SWEETNESS:	4. Good value for money.

WINE:	**MUSCADET (AC)**
SUPPLIER:	Pierre Chaumont
COUNTRY:	France
PRICE:	£2.39 (70cl)
COLOUR:	Pale straw.
NOSE:	Reasonable depth of Muscadet fruit.
PALATE:	Light/medium-bodied, soft and rounded, with crisp acidity and a clean finish. Good summer quaffing.
SWEETNESS:	1. Value for money.

WINE:	**PREMIÈRÈS CÔTES DE BORDEAUX (AC)**
SUPPLIER:	Pierre Chaumont
COUNTRY:	France
PRICE:	£2.39 (70cl)
COLOUR:	Straw with green tinges.
NOSE:	Intense fruit and a hint of noble rot.
PALATE:	Full-bodied and luscious, with well-balanced acidity.
SWEETNESS:	8. Very good value for money.

WINE:	**SAUVIGNON BLANC (AC)**
SUPPLIER:	Pierre Chaumont
COUNTRY:	France
PRICE:	£2.49 (70cl)

COLOUR:	Pale/mid straw.
NOSE:	Reasonable depth of grassy fruit.
PALATE:	Medium-bodied, clean, well balanced and with reasonable Sauvignon Blanc fruit and a crisp finish.
SWEETNESS:	1. Value for money.

WINE:	**ORVIETO SECCO (DOC)**
SUPPLIER:	Carissa
COUNTRY:	Italy
PRICE:	£2.55 (70cl)
COLOUR:	Pale straw with green tinges.
NOSE:	Pleasing combination of fruit and vinosity.
PALATE:	Medium/full-bodied and vinous with good underlying fruit. Well balanced with a clean, persistent finish.
SWEETNESS:	2. Good value for money.

WINE:	**VERDICCHIO CLASSICO (DOC)**
SUPPLIER:	Carissa
COUNTRY:	Italy
PRICE:	£2.85 (75cl)
COLOUR:	Straw with green tinges.
NOSE:	Very attractive, lifted fruit and some stalkiness.
PALATE:	Light/medium-bodied, with good balance of fruit and acidity and a clean finish.
SWEETNESS:	1. Good value for money.

WINE:	**GEWÜRZTRAMINER ALSACE (AC)**
SUPPLIER:	Pierre Chaumont
COUNTRY:	France

PRICE: £3.75 (70cl)
COLOUR: Deep straw with green tinges.
NOSE: Good intensity of spicy Gewürztraminer fruit.
PALATE: Medium-bodied, crisp, with very spicy fruit and good acidity.
SWEETNESS: 2.

WINE: **BOURGOGNE BLANC (AC)**
SUPPLIER: Pierre Chaumont
COUNTRY: France
PRICE: £4.29 (70cl)
COLOUR: Straw.
NOSE: Very honeyed bouquet.
PALATE: Medium/full-bodied, soft with balanced acidity.
SWEETNESS: 2.

RED WINES

WINE: **VIN DE PAYS DES CÔTES CATALANES**
COUNTRY: France
PRICE: £1.79 (70cl)
COLOUR: Red with purple tinges.
NOSE: Pleasant light fruit, with hints of pepper and raisined fruit.
PALATE: Medium/full-bodied, with spicy, peppery fruit and good tannin. Balance of fruit, tannin and acidity on finish.
TASTE: B.   Excellent value for money.

WINE:	**LAMBRUSCO ROSSO**
SUPPLIER:	Carissa
COUNTRY:	Italy
PRICE:	£1.89 (70cl)
COLOUR:	Light red with orange tints. Semi-sparkling
NOSE:	Light, spicy fruit with plummy, liquorice characters.
PALATE:	Light/medium-bodied, with spicy fruit and a clean finish. Good quality for this style.
TASTE:	B. Good value for money.

WINE:	**CÔTES DU ROUSSILLON (AC)**
SUPPLIER:	Pierre Chaumont
COUNTRY:	France
PRICE:	£2.29 (70cl)
COLOUR:	Red with purple tints.
NOSE:	Fruity, with slight raisined character.
PALATE:	Full-bodied, rich and fruity, with good acidity and slight astringency.
TASTE:	B. Good value for money.

WINE:	**CORBIÈRES (AC)**
SUPPLIER:	Pierre Chaumont
COUNTRY:	France
PRICE:	£2.29 (75cl)
COLOUR:	Light/mid red.
NOSE:	Clean, light scented fruit.
PALATE:	Medium/full-bodied, very clean and fruity. With excellent balance of fruit/tannin/oak and acidity. A bargain.
TASTE:	C. Excellent value for money.

WINE:	**COTEAUX DU TRICASTIN (AC)**
SUPPLIER:	Pierre Chaumont
COUNTRY:	France
PRICE:	£2.29 (70cl)
COLOUR:	Light red.
NOSE:	Light, faintly spicy/peppery fruit.
PALATE:	Light/medium-bodied, with light spicy fruit.
TASTE:	B.

WINE:	**MINERVOIS (AC)**
SUPPLIER:	Pierre Chaumont
COUNTRY:	France
PRICE:	£2.39 (70cl)
COLOUR:	Red with purple tinges.
NOSE:	Reasonable fruit and slight volatility.
PALATE:	Medium-bodied, with reasonable fruit/tannin/acid/oak balance.
TASTE:	C.

WINE:	**CÔTES DU VENTOUX (AC)**
SUPPLIER:	Pierre Chaumont
COUNTRY:	France
PRICE:	£2.39 (70cl)
COLOUR:	Red.
NOSE:	Attractive, lifted Grenache fruit.
PALATE:	Medium-bodied, fruity and spicy, with good tannin and acidity. Good quaffing wine.
TASTE:	C. Value for money.

WINE:	**CÔTES DU RHÔNE (AC)**
SUPPLIER:	Pierre Chaumont
COUNTRY:	France

PRICE:	£2.39 (70cl)
COLOUR:	Mid/dark red.
NOSE:	Good, with very spicy fruit and oak.
PALATE:	Medium/full-bodied, with soft, peppery fruit and oak. Some complexity. Worth cellaring for 12 months.
TASTE:	C. Very good value for money.

WINE:	**CHIANTI (DOC)**
SUPPLIER:	Carissa
COUNTRY:	Italy 1985
PRICE:	£2.45 (70cl)
COLOUR:	Deep red.
NOSE:	Good Chianti character, with good depth of fruit and oak.
PALATE:	Medium/full-bodied, with tarry fruit and pleasant oak. Finish is crisp, clean and persistent
TASTE:	D. Excellent value for money.

WINE:	**CLARET (AC)**
SUPPLIER:	Pierre Chaumont
COUNTRY:	France
PRICE:	£2.55 (70cl)
COLOUR:	Deep red with purple tints.
NOSE:	Very attractive Cabernet fruit and a touch of volatility.
PALATE:	Medium-bodied, with good Cabernet fruit. Balance of fruit/acid/oak/tannin is good
TASTE:	C. Very good value for money.

WINE:	**BERGERAC ROUGE (AC)**
SUPPLIER:	Pierre Chaumont

COUNTRY:	France
PRICE:	£2.65 (70cl)
COLOUR:	Red with purple tints.
NOSE:	Very attractive, intense Cabernet Sauvignon fruit and some oak.
PALATE:	Full-bodied with excellent Cabernet Sauvignon fruit. Good balance of tannin and oak on a crisp, clean finish. Some complexity. Worth cellaring for six months.
TASTE:	C. Very good value for money.

WINE:	**BEAUJOLAIS (AC)**
SUPPLIER:	Pierre Chaumont
COUNTRY:	France
PRICE:	£2.75 (70cl)
COLOUR:	Red.
NOSE:	Reasonable Gamay fruit.
PALATE:	Medium-bodied, with light spicy fruit and good acidity.
TASTE:	A.

WINE:	**RIOJA, VIÑA VALDUENGO**
COUNTRY:	Spain
PRICE:	£3.19 (70cl)
COLOUR:	Red/brown.
NOSE:	Very oaky and has good depth of fruit. Slight volatility lifts fruit.
PALATE:	Medium/full-bodied, oaky, with good depth of tarry fruit and balanced acidity. Worth keeping 12-24 months.
TASTE:	C. Good value for money.

WINE:	**RIOJA RESERVA, REMELLURI**
COUNTRY:	Spain 1980
PRICE:	£4.09 (75cl)
COLOUR:	Red/brown.
NOSE:	Excellent vanillan oak and fruit bouquet.
PALATE:	Medium/full-bodied and very oaky. Good depth of subtle, tarry fruit and slight volatility. Good finish. Some complexity.
TASTE:	C. Value for money.

WINE:	**CHÂTEAU GRIMONT (AC)**
SUPPLIER:	Pierre Chaumont
COUNTRY:	France 1985
PRICE:	£4.15 (75cl)
COLOUR:	Mid-red.
NOSE:	Very aromatic, with spicy Cabernet fruit, enhanced by oak.
PALATE:	Full-bodied, with good depth of Cabernet fruit and soft tannin. Oak and acidity are well balanced. Worth keeping 12-24 months. Quite a complex wine.
TASTE:	C. Good value for money.

WINE:	**BOURGOGNE ROUGE (AC)**
SUPPLIER:	Pierre Chaumont
COUNTRY:	France
PRICE:	£4.15 (70cl)
COLOUR:	Mid-red.
NOSE:	Good combination of Pinot Noir fruit and oak aromas.

PALATE:	Medium-bodied, with light Pinot Noir fruit. Fruit, oak and acidity are well balanced. Slightly astringent. Well made.
TASTE:	B. Value for money.

ROSÉ WINE

WINE:	**ROSÉ D'ANJOU (AC)**
SUPPLIER:	Pierre Chaumont
COUNTRY:	France
PRICE:	£2.15 (70cl)
COLOUR:	Excellent pink/amber.
NOSE:	Vinous and clean with some underlying fruit.
PALATE:	Medium-bodied, medium-sweet, fruity and rounded with a clean finish.
SWEETNESS:	4. Good value for money.

SPARKLING WINE

WINE:	**SPUMANTE**
SUPPLIER:	Ponti
COUNTRY:	Italy
PRICE:	£3.09 (75cl)
COLOUR:	Deep straw
NOSE:	Great depth of Muscat fruit. Very grapey aroma.
PALATE:	Medium-bodied with intense, sweet Muscat fruitiness. Clean, well made, for those who love the taste of grapes.
SWEETNESS:	7. Excellent value for money.

DAVISONS

WHITE WINES

WINE: **PAMPETTE DRY (VDT)**
SUPPLIER: Davies
COUNTRY: France
PRICE: £2.09 (70cl)
COLOUR: Straw.
NOSE: Pleasing combination of vinosity and stalky character.
PALATE: Medium-bodied, with good depth of agreeable fruit flavour and a clean finish.
SWEETNESS: 2.   Good value for money.

WINE: **PAMPETTE MEDIUM (VDT)**
SUPPLIER: Davies
COUNTRY: France
PRICE: £2.09 (70cl)
COLOUR: Straw.
NOSE: A vinous bouquet with some floral character.
PALATE: Medium-bodied, soft and fruity with good balance of acidity.
SWEETNESS: 4.   Good value for money.

WINE: **CÔTES DE GASCOGNE, CÉPAGE COLOMBARD (VDT)**
COUNTRY: France 1986
PRICE: £2.55 (70cl)
COLOUR: Pale, mid straw.

NOSE: Vinous/stalky bouquet with underlying fruit aroma.

PALATE: Medium-bodied, with tangy/fruity flavour and a crisp finish.

SWEETNESS: 2.   Value for money.

WINE: **BEREICH BERNKASTEL Qualitätswein**
SUPPLIER: Hahn
COUNTRY: Germany 1986
PRICE: £2.55 (70cl)
COLOUR: Straw with green tints.
NOSE: Attractive fruity/floral bouquet.
PALATE: Light/medium-bodied, soft with fruity/floral flavour.

SWEETNESS: 2.   Value for money.

WINE: **VIN BLANC DE TABLE**
SUPPLIER: Duboeuf
COUNTRY: France
PRICE: £2.55 (70cl)
COLOUR: Pale straw.
NOSE: Mainly vinous, with some underlying fruit aroma.
PALATE: Medium/full-bodied, with good depth of vinous flavour. Soft, smooth persistent finish. Easy drinking style.

SWEETNESS: 2.   Value for money.

WINE: **CH TERTRE DE LAUNAY, ENTRE DEUX MERS (AC)**
COUNTRY: France 1987
PRICE: £2.99 (75cl)

COLOUR:	Pale straw with green tints.
NOSE:	Vinous with underlying fruit aroma.
PALATE:	Medium-bodied, with good depth of vinous/fruit flavour.
SWEETNESS: 1.	Value for money.

WINE:	**CH DE LA JANNIÈRE, Muscadet de Sèvre et Maine (AC)**
SUPPLIER:	Lusseaud
COUNTRY:	France 1987
PRICE:	£3.49 (75cl)
COLOUR:	Straw with green tints.
NOSE:	Attractive fruit/celery aroma.
PALATE:	Medium/full-bodied, very flavoursome with good depth of flavour of the Muscadet grape. Soft finish.
SWEETNESS: 1.	Value for money.

WINE:	**JOÃO PIRES Dry Muscat**
COUNTRY:	Portugal 1986
PRICE:	£3.89 (70cl)
COLOUR:	Dry straw.
NOSE:	Lovely honeyed Muscat/grapey bouquet.
PALATE:	Medium/full-bodied, with excellent flavour of the Muscat grape and balanced acidity. Lingering, grapey finish.
SWEETNESS: 3.	

WINE:	**GEIERSLAY KABINETT, WINTRICH**
SUPPLIER:	Huesgen
COUNTRY:	Germany 1985
PRICE:	£3.99 (75cl)

COLOUR:	Very pale straw with green tints.
NOSE:	Delicate Riesling grape aroma.
PALATE:	Medium-bodied, with delicate Riesling flavour and good balance of acidity. An elegant style with persistent flavour.
SWEETNESS: 4.	Value for money.

WINE:	**GERWÜRZTRAMINER (QMP)**
SUPPLIER:	Cave Ingersheim
COUNTRY:	France 1986
PRICE:	£4.29 (70cl)
COLOUR:	Straw with green tints.
NOSE:	Excellent intensity of the spicy aroma of the Gewürztraminer grape.
PALATE:	Medium-bodied, with very spicy/fruity flavour and a soft, smooth finish.
SWEETNESS: 4.	Value for money.

WINE:	**NIERSTEINER SPIEGELBERG KABINETT (QMP)**
SUPPLIER:	Guntrum
COUNTRY:	Germany 1985
PRICE:	£4.29 (70cl)
COLOUR:	Straw with green tints.
NOSE:	Very fruity and floral.
PALATE:	Medium/full-bodied, with intense fruity flavour and a soft, fruity finish.
SWEETNESS: 4.	

WINE:	**MÂCON PRISSÉ (AC)**
SUPPLIER:	Duboeuf
COUNTRY:	France 1986

PRICE:	£4.95 (75cl)
COLOUR:	Straw/dark straw,
NOSE:	Complex smokey/fruity bouquet with slight honeyed character.
PALATE:	Full-bodied, smooth and rounded, with excellent depth of fruit flavour and some nutty character. Very persistent, flavoursome finish.
SWEETNESS: 2.	Value for money.

RED WINES

WINE:	**PAMPETTE ROUGE (VDT)**
SUPPLIER:	Davies
COUNTRY:	France
PRICE:	£2.09 (70cl)
COLOUR:	Red.
NOSE:	Spicy, ripe, slightly raisined fruit aroma.
PALATE:	Medium-bodied, with a spicy/cinnamon/fruit flavour.
TASTE:	A. Value for money.

WINE:	**DOM ST ANDRÉ LA COTE, COSTIÈRES DU GARD (VDQS)**
SUPPLIER:	Davies 1986
COUNTRY:	France 1986
PRICE:	£2.35 (70cl)
COLOUR:	Red.
NOSE:	A bouquet of ripe, raisined fruit.

| PALATE: | Medium-bodied, with ripe fruity flavour and soft tannin. Finish is crisp with spicy flavour. |
| TASTE: | B. Good value for money. |

WINE:	**CABERNET SAUVIGNON, PLOVDIV**
COUNTRY:	Bulgaria 1983
PRICE:	£2.45 (70cl)
COLOUR:	Dark red.
NOSE:	Very ripe/raisined character and strong aroma of the grape.
PALATE:	Medium/full-bodied with strong raisined/fruity flavour and good balance of tannin/fruit/oak/acidity.
TASTE:	C. Good value for money.

WINE:	**CÔTES DU ROUSSILLON VILLAGES (AC)**
SUPPLIER:	Davies
COUNTRY:	France
PRICE:	£2.45 (70cl)
COLOUR:	Dark red.
NOSE:	Light fruit aroma.
PALATE:	Medium-bodied, with slight peppery flavour and firm tannin. Finish is slightly astringent.
TASTE:	B.

WINE:	**LATURCE RIOJA RED**
COUNTRY:	Spain 1985
PRICE:	£2.99 (70cl)
COLOUR:	Dark red with blue tints.
NOSE:	Excellent bouquet of vanilla/buttery oak with strong underlying fruit.

67

PALATE:	Medium/full-bodied, smooth with lovely warm flavours of fruit and oak. Very persistent finish.
TASTE:	C. Excellent value for money.

WINE:	**BEAU-RIVAGE, BORIE-MANOUX (AC)**
SUPPLIER:	Davies
COUNTRY:	France 1983
PRICE:	£2.99 (70cl)
COLOUR:	Dark red with brown tints.
NOSE:	Good depth of Cabernet fruit aroma and a slight crushed flowers character.
PALATE:	Medium/full-bodied with good balance of fruit/acid/oak/tannin. Flavoursome finish with slight astringency.
TASTE:	C. Very good value for money.

WINE:	**ORLANDO JACOB'S CREEK**
COUNTRY:	Australia 1985
PRICE:	£3.25 (75cl)
COLOUR:	Mid/dark red.
NOSE:	Intense bouquet of buttery, vanillan oak and fruit.
PALATE:	Full-bodied, with excellent depth of fruit flavour enhanced by oak maturation. Persistent flavoursome finish.
TASTE:	D. Very good value for money.

WINE:	**PARADOR NAVARRA RESERVA**
SUPPLIER:	Chivite
COUNTRY:	Spain 1983
PRICE:	£3.35 (75cl)
COLOUR:	Dark red with blue tints.

NOSE: Attractive vanilla/buttery oak and strong fruit aroma.

PALATE: Medium/ full-bodied, with excellent depth of fruity/oaky flavour. Good balance and crisp flavour.

TASTE: B. Excellent value for money.

WINE: **VACQUEYRAS, CÔTES DU RHÔNE-VILLAGES (AC)**

SUPPLIER: Pascal

COUNTRY: France 1985

PRICE: £4.15 (75cl)

COLOUR: Dark red.

NOSE: Spicy, slightly peppery bouquet.

PALATE: Full-bodied, robust, with good depth of fruity flavour. Firm tannin on a very flavoursome finish.

TASTE: C. Good value for money.

WINE: **ORLANDO RF CABERNET SAUVIGNON**

COUNTRY: Australia 1985

PRICE: £4.39 (75cl)

COLOUR: Dark red.

NOSE: Excellent bouquet of Cabernet Sauvignon fruit enhanced by buttery oak.

PALATE: Full-bodied, silky smooth and very flavoursome. Good balance of fruit/oak/acidity.

TASTE: D. Very good value for money.

WINE: **MACHIAVELLI CHIANTI CLASSICO RISERVA (DOCG)**

COUNTRY: Italy 1982

PRICE:	£4.75 (75cl)
COLOUR:	Dark red with brown tints.
NOSE:	Excellent combination of tarry fruit and oak aromas.
PALATE:	Full-bodied, with complex tarry fruit and firm tannin. Finish has pleasant, lingering fruit and oak flavour.
TASTE:	D. Very good value for money.

WINE:	**LA TOUR ST BONNET, MÉDOC (AC)**
SUPPLIER:	Merlet-Lafon
COUNTRY:	France 1981
PRICE:	£4.75 (75cl)
COLOUR:	Red/brown.
NOSE:	Good claret bouquet with some stalky character.
PALATE:	Medium/full-bodied, smooth with good tannin and a warm slightly astringent finish. Ready for drinking.
TASTE:	D. Value for money.

WINE:	**BOURGOGNE ROUGE, TASTEVIN**
SUPPLIER:	Boisset
COUNTRY:	France. 1985
PRICE:	£4.95 (75cl)
COLOUR:	Dark red.
NOSE:	Lively strawberry/raspberry aromas.
PALATE:	Medium/bodied, soft, smooth and very fruity with slight earthy flavour.
TASTE:	B. Good value for money.

WINE:	**CH ROQUETAILLADE LA GRANGE, GRAVES (AC)**
SUPPLIER:	Guignard
COUNTRY:	France 1982
PRICE:	£4.99 (75cl)
COLOUR:	Dark red with brown tints.
NOSE:	Very attractive bouquet of stalky, Cabernet fruit.
PALATE:	Full-bodied, very smooth, with good depth of fruit and oak flavour. Firm tannin on a slightly astringent finish.
TASTE:	C. Excellent value for money.

ROSÉ WINE

WINE:	**ROSÉ D'ANJOU (AC)**
SUPPLIER:	Gouin
COUNTRY:	France 1986
PRICE:	£2.39 (70cl)
COLOUR:	Pink/amber.
NOSE:	Very pleasant with a stalky/fruity bouquet.
PALATE:	Medium-bodied, soft and fruity. Easy drinking style.
SWEETNESS:	4. Very good value for money.

71

FULLERS

WHITE WINES

WINE: **VIN DE PAYS DE VAUCLUSE (VDT)**
COUNTRY: France 1986
PRICE: £1.99 (70cl)
COLOUR: Straw.
NOSE: Vinous/straw bouquet with underlying fruit aroma.
PALATE: Medium-bodied, rounded with good depth of flavour and good balance of fruit/acidity on the finish.
SWEETNESS: 2.   Good value for money.

WINE: **VIN DE PAYS CHARANTAIS**
SUPPLIER: St André
COUNTRY: France 1986
PRICE: £2.09 (70cl)
COLOUR: Pale/mid straw.
NOSE: A bouquet of stalky fruit and very earthy/chalky character.
PALATE: Medium/full-bodied, with soft texture and rounded fruit flavour. Finish is a touch coarse.
SWEETNESS: 2.

WINE: **LE GASCONY BLANC DE BLANCS (VDT)**
COUNTRY: France 1987
PRICE: £2.19 (70cl)
COLOUR: Pale straw.

NOSE: Very aromatic with strong yeast/fruit.

PALATE: Medium-bodied, soft and very fruity, with a crisp, lingering finish. Easy drinking wine.

SWEETNESS: 2. Good value for money.

WINE: **MOSELTALER Qualitätswein**

SUPPLIER: Zimmermann-Graeff

COUNTRY: Germany 1986

PRICE: £2.19 (70cl)

COLOUR: Pale straw.

NOSE: Intense floral/fruity bouquet.

PALATE: Light/medium-bodied, soft and very fruity with a hint of fruit salad flavours. Soft, fruity finish.

SWEETNESS: 3. Value for money.

WINE: **SOAVE (DOC)**

SUPPLIER: Girelli

COUNTRY: Italy 1987

PRICE: £2.39 (70cl)

COLOUR: Very pale straw.

NOSE: Vinous with slight boiled-sweet aroma.

PALATE: Light/medium-bodied, with reasonable depth of vinous flavour. Finish is crisp. Food wine.

SWEETNESS: 2.

WINE: **CH DES VERGNES (AC)**

SUPPLIER: Univitis

COUNTRY: France 1987

PRICE: £2.85 (75cl)

COLOUR: Pale/mid straw with green tints.

NOSE: Excellent bouquet of grassy Sauvignon Blanc fruit with slightly honeyed character.

PALATE: Medium/full-bodied, soft in texture with grassy fruit flavour and a crisp, slightly stalky finish.

SWEETNESS: 1.   Very good value for money.

WINE: **ALSACE PINOT BLANC ST ODILE (AC)**
COUNTRY: France 1985
PRICE: £2.99 (70cl)
COLOUR: Straw.
NOSE: Strongly vinous with underlying fruit aroma.
PALATE: Medium/full-bodied, very fruity and flavoursome. Soft, straightforward style.
SWEETNESS: 3.   Value for money.

WINE: **BIANCO SAN PIETRO**
SUPPLIER: Rizzardi
COUNTRY: Italy 1987
PRICE: £2.99 (75cl)
COLOUR: Very pale straw.
NOSE: Strong vinous character.
PALATE: Medium-bodied, with good depth of vinous flavour. Well-balanced wine with a crisp finish.
SWEETNESS: 2.

WINE: **DIRMSTEINER MANDELPFAD GEWÜRZTRAMINER Kabinett**
SUPPLIER: Schlossgut Janson
COUNTRY: Germany 1986
PRICE: £3.75 (70cl)
COLOUR: Straw.

NOSE: Excellent bouquet of spicy Gewürztraminer fruit with strong honeyed overtones.

PALATE: Medium/full-bodied, with complex fruit and honey flavour. Soft in texture and well balanced.

SWEETNESS: 4. Value for money.

WINE: **CH LA JAUBERTIE (AC)**
SUPPLIER: Ryman
COUNTRY: France 1987
PRICE: £3.95 (75cl)
COLOUR: Very pale straw.
NOSE: Excellent intensity of grassy Sauvignon Blanc aroma and some yeast character.
PALATE: Medium/full-bodied, with very grassy fruit flavour and some yeast character on a crisp, balanced finish.
SWEETNESS: 1. Good value for money.

WINE: **COSTEGGIOLA SOAVE CLASSICO (DOC)**
SUPPLIER: Rizzardi
COUNTRY: Italy 1987
PRICE: £3.95 (75cl)
COLOUR: Pale straw with green tints.
NOSE: Strong vinous bouquet.
PALATE: Medium/full-bodied, with very good depth of vinous flavour and a crisp finish.
SWEETNESS: 2.

WINE: **SAUVIGNON DE ST BRIS (VDQS)**
SUPPLIER: Sorin
COUNTRY: France 1986

FULLERS

PRICE: £3.99 (75cl)
COLOUR: Straw with green tints.
NOSE: Strong honeyed/fruity bouquet with delicate grassy stalky character.
PALATE: Full-bodied, rounded, with grassy fruit flavour and honeyed overtones. Wine of good balance and style.
SWEETNESS: 1.   Excellent value for money.

WINE: **ERBACHER STEINMORGEN RIESLING SPÄTLESE (QMP)**
SUPPLIER: Wagner-Weritz
COUNTRY: Germany 1985
PRICE: £4.65 (75cl)
COLOUR: Pale/mid straw.
NOSE: Very delicate bouquet of spicy/floral fruit.
PALATE: Medium/full-bodied with excellent depth of subtle mouth-filling fruit flavour and a crisp, fruity finish.
SWEETNESS: 6.   Good value for money.

RED WINES

WINE: **VIN DE PAYS DE VAUCLUSE**
COUNTRY: France 1987
PRICE: £1.99 (70cl)
COLOUR: Light red with blue tints.
NOSE: Lively scented bouquet with some jammy/stalky characters.

PALATE:	Medium-bodied, with delicate fruit flavour, light tannin and crisp acidity. Easy drinking style.
TASTE:	B. Value for money.

WINE: **CABERNET SAUVIGNON VDP DES COTEAUX DE L'ARDÈCHE**
SUPPLIER: St Didier
COUNTRY: France 1986
PRICE: £2.35 (70cl)
COLOUR: Mid/dark red.
NOSE: Good depth of the aroma of raisined Cabernet Sauvignon fruit with slight stalky character.
PALATE: Medium-bodied, with good depth of flavour, light pleasant tannin and a very crisp finish.
TASTE: D.   Good value for money.

WINE: **CÉPAGE GAMAY VDP DES COTEAUX DE L'ARDÈCHE**
SUPPLIER: St Didier
COUNTRY: France 1986
PRICE: £2.35 (70cl)
COLOUR: Red.
NOSE: Earthy/fruity bouquet.
PALATE: Medium-bodied, rounded with mouth-filling fruit flavour and good balance of tannin and acidity.
TASTE: B.   Value for money.

WINE: **CASTILLO DE ALMANSA (DO)**
SUPPLIER: Bonete
COUNTRY: Spain 1982

PRICE: £2.85 (75cl)
COLOUR: Dark red with blue tints.
NOSE: Excellent vanillan/buttery oak bouquet with underlying fruit.
PALATE: Full-bodied, rich and flavoursome, with tarry fruit and a soft oaky finish. Good style.
TASTE: C.   Excellent value for money.

WINE: **CÔTES DU VENTOUX (AC)**
SUPPLIER: Jaboulet Ainé
COUNTRY: France 1985
PRICE: £2.99 (75cl)
COLOUR: Dark red.
NOSE: Ripe, raisined, fruity bouquet.
PALATE: Full-bodied, very robust, with mouth-filling fruit flavour. Good balance of tannin and acidity.
TASTE: D.   Good value for money.

WINE: **BOURGOGNE GRAND ORDINAIRE (AC)**
SUPPLIER: Labouré-Roi
COUNTRY: France 1985
PRICE: £2.99 (75cl)
COLOUR: Red with blue tints.
NOSE: An attractive, lively bouquet of honeyed fruit with some earthiness.
PALATE: Medium-bodied, with soft, spicy fruit flavour. Crisp finish with a hint of oak.
TASTE: B.   Good value for money.

WINE:	**CH DE PARAZA (AC)**
SUPPLIER:	Girard
COUNTRY:	France 1986
PRICE:	£3.25 (75cl)
COLOUR:	Red/ruby.
NOSE:	Rich ripe bouquet of jammy fruit.
PALATE:	Medium/full-bodied, with good balance of fruit and acidity. Strong tannin on finish.
TASTE:	C. Good value for money.
WINE:	**CH GRAND MAZEROLLES (AC)**
SUPPLIER:	Rigal
COUNTRY:	France 1985
PRICE:	£3.65 (75cl)
COLOUR:	Dark red.
NOSE:	Very intense bouquet of stalky fruit with slight earthy character.
PALATE:	Full-bodied with robust, fruity flavour and firm tannin. Finish has slight tannic astringency and oak.
TASTE:	C. Value for money.
WINE:	**SAUMUR CHAMPIGNY (AC)**
SUPPLIER:	Carre
COUNTRY:	France 1985
PRICE:	£3.69 (75cl)
COLOUR:	Light red with blue tints.
NOSE:	Very attractive bouquet of stalky/Cabernet fruit.
PALATE:	Medium-bodied, soft with delicate fruit flavour and good tannin.
TASTE:	B. Good value for money.

WINE:	**VALPOLICELLA CLASSICO**
SUPPLIER:	Rizzardi
COUNTRY:	Italy 1987
PRICE:	£4.95
COLOUR:	Light red with purple tints.
NOSE:	Light delicate fruity bouquet.
PALATE:	Medium-bodied, with delicate spicy fruit flavour and light tannin. Subtle lingering finish.
TASTE:	B. Good value for money.

ROSÉ WINE

WINE:	**CH DE TIGNE (AC)**
SUPPLIER:	Lalanne
COUNTRY:	France 1986
PRICE:	£2.75 (75cl)
COLOUR:	Amber/pink.
NOSE:	Excellent lively aroma of the Cabernet grape.
PALATE:	Medium/full-bodied with excellent depth of very fruity flavour and a lingering fruity finish.
SWEETNESS:	4. Excellent value for money.

GATEWAY

WHITE WINES

WINE: **VIN DE PAYS DES COTEAUX DE L'ARDÈCHE**

SUPPLIER: U.C.O.V.A.

COUNTRY: France

PRICE: £1.85 (70cl)

COLOUR: Pale straw.

NOSE: Attractive honeyed character with underlying fruit aroma.

PALATE: Medium-bodied, with a pleasing combination of vinosity and fruit flavour. Finish is crisp and slightly honeyed.

SWEETNESS: 2.   Value for money.

WINE: **MUSCADET DE SÈVRE ET MAINE (AC)**

COUNTRY: France 1987

PRICE: £2.15 (70cl)

COLOUR: Pale straw.

NOSE: Attractive stalky/Muscadet fruit aroma and slight chalky/earthy character.

PALATE: Medium-bodied, crisp with strong flavour of the Muscadet grape. Good balance of fruit/acidity.

SWEETNESS: 1.   Good value for money.

WINE: **BORDEAUX BLANC DE BLANCS (AC)**

COUNTRY: France

PRICE: £2.19 (70cl)

COLOUR: Pale straw.

NOSE: Fruity bouquet with some bottle-age development.

PALATE: Medium-bodied, with good depth of pleasant fruity flavour. Lingering, fruity finish.

SWEETNESS: 4. Value for money.

WINE: **HALLGARTEN'S KABINETT**

SUPPLIER: St Gangolf

COUNTRY: Germany 1986

PRICE: £2.35 (70cl)

COLOUR: Straw with green tints.

NOSE: Excellent, lively fruity/floral bouquet.

PALATE: Medium/full-bodied, with excellent fruit flavour and a soft, smooth, fruity finish.

SWEETNESS: 4. Excellent value for money.

WINE: **SAUVIGNON DE TOURAINE (AC)**

COUNTRY: France

PRICE: £2.35 (70cl)

COLOUR: Straw/dark straw.

NOSE: Delicate, grassy Sauvignon Blanc aroma with some bottle-age development.

PALATE: Medium-bodied, with pleasant bottle-age character and a crisp, fruity finish.

SWEETNESS: 1. Good value for money.

WINE: **CH DE LA MOUCHETIERE, MUSCADET DE SÈVRE ET MAINE.**

SUPPLIER: Sourice

COUNTRY: France 1986

PRICE: £2.79 (75cl)

COLOUR: Straw.

NOSE: Attractive stalky/Muscadet grape aroma and slight chalky character.

PALATE: Medium/full-bodied, very fruity and rounded, with good balance of fruit/acidity and a fruity finish.

SWEETNESS: 1.   Good value for money.

WINE: **GEWÜRZTRAMINER, ALSACE (AC)**

SUPPLIER: Simon

COUNTRY: France 1985

PRICE: £3.75 (70cl)

COLOUR: Straw with green tints.

NOSE: Very aromatic, with strong, spicy Gewürztraminer grape character.

PALATE: Medium-bodied, smooth, with delicate fruit flavour and a soft smooth finish.

SWEETNESS: 4.   Value for money.

WINE: **BOURGOGNE CHARDONNAY (AC)**

SUPPLIER: Cave des Vignerons

COUNTRY: France 1986

PRICE: £3.85 (70cl)

COLOUR: Straw with green tints.

NOSE: Attractive bouquet of smokey oak and honeyed fruit.

PALATE: Full-bodied, with very pleasant balance of honeyed fruit/oak/acidity. Lingering finish showing some bottle-aged development.

SWEETNESS: 2.   Good value for money.

RED WINES

WINE: **CH DES VIGNERONS, BERGERAC (AC)**
COUNTRY: France 1986
PRICE: £1.99 (75cl)
COLOUR: Dark red with purple tints.
NOSE: Rich, ripe, fruity bouquet.
PALATE: Medium/full-bodied, with slightly raisined fruit flavour and firm tannin. Lively, fruity finish.
TASTE: C.   Good value for money.

WINE: **CH QUILHANET, CORBIÈRES (AC)**
SUPPLIER: Durand
COUNTRY: France 1987
PRICE: £1.99 (70cl)
COLOUR: Red with blue tints.
NOSE: Light, lively, fruity bouquet.
PALATE: Medium-bodied, with very spicy fruit flavour and light tannin. Easy drinking style.
TASTE: C.   Very good value for money.

WINE: **CÔTES DU RHÔNE (AC)**
COUNTRY: France
PRICE: £2.19 (70cl)
COLOUR: Red with blue tints.
NOSE: Spicy/peppery bouquet.

PALATE: Full-bodied, robust, with good depth of peppery/fruity flavour. Slightly astringent finish.

TASTE: C. Excellent value for money.

WINE: **CLARET (AC)**
COUNTRY: France
PRICE: £2.25 (70cl)
COLOUR: Red.
NOSE: Attractive bouquet of Cabernet fruit with some stalkiness.
PALATE: Full-bodied, with good depth of the flavour of the Cabernet grape and firm tannin on the finish.

TASTE: C. Good value for money.

WINE: **CHIANTI (DOCG)**
COUNTRY: Italy 1986
PRICE: £2.49 (70cl)
COLOUR: Red with blue tints.
NOSE: Excellent bouquet of tarry fruit and strong oak character.
PALATE: Full-bodied, rich and robust, with excellent depth of tarry/liquorice/oaky flavours.

TASTE: C. Excellent value for money.

WINE: **LISTEL ROUGE (VDT)**
SUPPLIER: C.S.M.
COUNTRY: France 1983
PRICE: £2.85 (75cl)
COLOUR: Dark red with brown tints.
NOSE: Strong bouquet of rich, ripe fruit.

PALATE: Full-bodied, smooth and robust, with excellent depth of flavour and firm tannin.
TASTE: B.   Very good value for money.

WINE: **RIOJA CAMPO VIEJO**
COUNTRY: Spain 1984
PRICE: £2.99 (70cl)
COLOUR: Dark red with brown tints.
NOSE: Lovely bouquet of buttery/vanillan oak and fruit.
PALATE: Full-bodied, velvety smooth, with good depth of fruity/oaky flavours.
TASTE: C.   Excellent value for money.

WINE: **RIOJA BANDA AZUL (DO)**
SUPPLIER: Paternina
COUNTRY: Spain 1984
PRICE: £3.25 (70cl)
COLOUR: Red with brown tints.
NOSE: Pleasantly fruity and less oaky than most Riojas.
PALATE: Full-bodied, with light oak and cinnamon/fruity flavour. Firm tannin on the finish.
TASTE: C.   Value for money.

WINE: **BAROLO (DOCG)**
SUPPLIER: Fontanafredda
COUNTRY: Italy 1983
PRICE: £4.99 (75cl)
COLOUR: Red/brown.
NOSE: Strong bouquet of tarry fruit and oak.

PALATE: Full-bodied, smooth, with rich, robust flavour. A complex wine with excellent bottle-age development. Very flavoursome, lingering finish.

TASTE: E.   Excellent value for money.

SPARKLING WINE

WINE: **MARQUÉS DE MONISTROL, CAVA MÉTHODE CHAMPENOISE**

COUNTRY: Spain

PRICE: £3.99 (75cl)

COLOUR: Straw with small bead (bubbles).

NOSE: Pleasant, with a toasty, fruity bouquet.

PALATE: Full-bodied, very fruity and flavoursome, with a crisp fruity finish.

SWEETNESS: 2.   Very good value for money.

LITTLEWOODS

WHITE WINES

WINE: **LIEBFRAUMILCH (QBA)**
SUPPLIER: Sprendlingen
COUNTRY: Germany 1986
PRICE: £1.69 (70cl)
COLOUR: Pale straw.
NOSE: Pleasant fruity bouquet.
PALATE: Light, fruity, with slight honeyed character.
SWEETNESS: 5.   Good value for money.

WINE: **VIN DE TABLE BLANC Carcassonne**
COUNTRY: France
PRICE: £1.79 (70cl)
COLOUR: Straw.
NOSE: Slight boiled-fruit character.
PALATE: Medium-bodied, with subtle fruit flavour.
SWEETNESS: 3.

WINE: **BORDEAUX BLANC**
COUNTRY: France
PRICE: £2.39 (70cl)
COLOUR: Pale straw.
NOSE: Light, grassy/fruity bouquet.
PALATE: Light fruit, good acidity and persistent finish.
SWEETNESS: 2.

WINE: **MUSCADET DE SÈVRE ET MAINE (AC)**
SUPPLIER: Celliers de la Loire
COUNTRY: France 1986

PRICE: £2.39 (70cl)
COLOUR: Pale straw.
NOSE: Fruity, with delicate grassy character.
PALATE: Medium/full-bodied, with delicate fruit and some complexity
SWEETNESS: 1.   Good value for money.

WINE: **AMBRA FRASCATI (DOC)**
SUPPLIER: Fabiano
COUNTRY: Italy 1986
PRICE: £2.69 (70cl)
COLOUR: Pale straw with green tinges.
NOSE: Vinous with some stalky fruit.
PALATE: Medium/full-bodied, with good depth of fruit flavour.
SWEETNESS: 2.   Good value for money.

WINE: **GALLO SAUVIGNON BLANC**
COUNTRY: California 1985
PRICE: £2.99 (75cl)
COLOUR: Straw.
NOSE: Excellent bouquet with intense, grassy Sauvignon Blanc character.
PALATE: Medium-bodied, with grassy Sauvignon Blanc fruit balanced with crisp acidity. Well-made wine.
SWEETNESS: 2.   Excellent value for money.

WINE: **CH D'AIGUEVILLE BLANC Côtes du Rhône (AC)**
COUNTRY: France 1986
PRICE: £2.99 (75cl)

COLOUR:	Straw.
NOSE:	Stalky, with an oily fruity character.
PALATE:	Full-bodied, with grassy fruit and high acidity. Some complexity of flavour.
SWEETNESS:	2. Value for money.

WINE: ORLANDO JACOB'S CREEK

COUNTRY:	Australia 1986
PRICE:	£2.99 (75cl)
COLOUR:	Deep straw with green tinges.
NOSE:	Yeasty, floral and fruity.
PALATE:	Full-bodied, soft and fruity, with good balance of acidity and balance.
SWEETNESS:	2. Good value for money.

WINE: TRIER RÖMERLAY KABINETT

SUPPLIER:	R. Müller
COUNTRY:	Germany 1983
PRICE:	£2.69 (70cl)
COLOUR:	Mid/deep straw with green tinges.
NOSE:	Light, delicate fruity bouquet.
PALATE:	Medium-bodied, sweet, honeyed and fruity, with good acidity.
SWEETNESS:	4. Value for money.

WINE: ST JOHANNER ABTEI AUSLESE

SUPPLIER:	R Müller
COUNTRY:	Germany 1983
PRICE:	£3.39 (70cl)
COLOUR:	Deep straw.
NOSE:	Attractive, intense fruit with some noble rot.

PALATE: Full-bodied, rich and sweet with strong honeyed character on finish.

SWEETNESS: 7.   Excellent value for money.

RED WINES

WINE: **VIN DE TABLE ROUGE Carcassonne**
COUNTRY: France
PRICE: £1.79 (70cl)
COLOUR: Red with purple tinges.
NOSE: Attractive fruity bouquet.
PALATE: Medium-bodied, with good depth of fruit fla-
vour and a pleasant finish.
TASTE: A.   Good value for money.

WINE: **HUNGARIAN MERLOT**
SUPPLIER: Hungarovin
COUNTRY: Hungary
PRICE: £1.89 (70cl)
COLOUR: Deep red/ruby.
NOSE: Ripe, raisined Merlot fruit with slightly stalky
character.
PALATE: Medium/full-bodied, with rich, raisined fruit
flavour and good tannin. Easy drinking style.
TASTE: D.   Good value for money.

WINE: **BULGARIAN CABERNET SAUVIGNON**
COUNTRY: Bulgaria 1983
PRICE: £1.99 (70cl)
COLOUR: Brown/red.
NOSE: Bouquet of ripe raisined fruit.

PALATE: Medium/full-bodied, soft and fruity, with some bottle-aged development.

TASTE: C.   Good value for money.

WINE: **MINERVOIS (AC)**
COUNTRY: France 1985
PRICE: £1.99 (70cl)
COLOUR: Deep red/ruby.
NOSE: Intense, attractive, fruity bouquet with slight vinegar character.
PALATE: Medium-bodied, soft, crisp and fruity. Some complexity.
TASTE: C.   Good value for money.

WINE: **CORBIÈRES (AC)**
COUNTRY: France 1986
PRICE: £1.99 (70cl)
COLOUR: Deep red with purple tinges.
NOSE: Raisined, stalky fruity bouquet.
PALATE: Soft and fruity, with pleasant tannin and oak flavour.
TASTE: C.   Good value for money.

WINE: **BAIRRADA**
SUPPLIER: Borges & Irmão
COUNTRY: Portugal 1983
PRICE: £2.49 (75cl)
COLOUR: Brown.
NOSE: Vanillan oak aroma with underlying fruit and some vinegar character.

PALATE:	Full-bodied, rich and rounded with intense vanillan oak flavours.
TASTE:	D.

WINE:	**CHIANTI AMBRA (DOCG)**
SUPPLIER:	R.D.M. Castellina
COUNTRY:	Italy 1985
PRICE:	£2.49 (70cl)
COLOUR:	Red/brown.
NOSE:	Earthy/fruity bouquet with slight vinegar character.
PALATE:	Medium/full-bodied, with pleasant fruit and acidity. Some complexity.
TASTE:	D. Value for money.

WINE:	**MONTEPULCIANO D'ABRUZZO (DOC)**
SUPPLIER:	Bianchi
COUNTRY:	Italy 1985
PRICE:	£2.99 (70cl)
COLOUR:	Ruby red.
NOSE:	Complex, with attractive fruity bouquet.
PALATE:	Full-bodied, rich and fruity with good acidity. Slight vinegar character adds to complexity. Has cellaring potential of 12-18+ months.
TASTE:	D. Excellent value for money.

WINE:	**COOKS DRY RED**
COUNTRY:	New Zealand
PRICE:	£2.89 (75cl)
COLOUR:	Brown.
NOSE:	Attractive with good fruit and oak, also some bottle-age development.

PALATE:	Balanced oak and acidity, with matured Pinot Noir and Cabernet Sauvignon fruit flavours.
TASTE:	B. Value for money.

WINE:	**CH D'AIGUEVILLE (AC)**
SUPPLIER:	Caves St Pierre
COUNTRY:	France 1986
PRICE:	£2.99 (75cl)
COLOUR:	Red.
NOSE:	Intense fruity bouquet, with oak and slight stalkiness.
PALATE:	Soft, with good balance of fruit/oak/acidity. Pleasant lingering finish.
TASTE:	C. Good value for money.

SPARKLING WINE

WINE:	**RIVIERA SPUMANTE**
PRICE:	£2.69 (70cl)
COLOUR:	Straw with green tinges.
NOSE:	Delicate fruity bouquet.
PALATE:	Medium/full-bodied, very sweet, with good depth of fruity/grapey Muscat flavour.
SWEETNESS:	7. Value for money.

WILLIAM LOW

WHITE WINES

WINE: **LIEBFRAUMILCH Qualitätswein Rheinpfalz**
COUNTRY: Germany 1987
PRICE: £1.85 (70cl)
COLOUR: Pale straw.
NOSE: Very aromatic, floral and fruity.
PALATE: Light/medium-bodied, soft and with lovely fresh fruitiness.
SWEETNESS: 5.   Good value for money.

WINE: **LAMBRUSCO BIANCO**
COUNTRY: Italy
PRICE: £1.89 (70cl)
COLOUR: Very pale straw.
NOSE: Spicy with a hint of cinnamon.
PALATE: Light/medium-bodied, soft and smooth with some sweetness.
SWEETNESS: 6.   Value for money.

WINE: **SOAVE (DOC)**
COUNTRY: Italy 1987
PRICE: £1.95 (70cl)
COLOUR: Pale/mid straw.
NOSE: Vinous with underlying fruit.

PALATE: Light/medium-bodied. Fruit flavours are very delicate and the finish is crisp.

SWEETNESS: 2.   Very good value for money.

WINE: **BLANC DE BLANCS Vin de Table**
COUNTRY: France
PRICE: £1.99 (70cl)
COLOUR: Pale/mid straw.
NOSE: Very light fruit and vinous character.
PALATE: Light/medium-bodied, slightly sweet and with smooth texture.
SWEETNESS: 3.

WINE: **BEREICH NIERSTEIN Qualitätswein Rheinhessen**
COUNTRY: Germany 1986
PRICE: £2.05 (70cl)
COLOUR: Straw.
NOSE: Lovely floral, fruity fragrance.
PALATE: Medium-bodied, very grapey and has a soft finish.
SWEETNESS: 3.   Very good value for money.

WINE: **BEREICH BERNKASTEL Qualitätswein Mosel**
COUNTRY: Germany 1986
PRICE: £2.05 (70cl)
COLOUR: Pale straw with green tints.
NOSE: Light and fruity with a faint chalky, earthy character.

PALATE:	Light/medium-bodied. Fruit is delicate, grapey and slightly sweet. Crisp acid finish.
SWEETNESS:	3. Good value for money.

WINE:	**PIESPORTER MICHELSBERG** **Qualitätswein Mosel**
COUNTRY:	Germany 1987
PRICE:	£2.25 (70cl)
COLOUR:	Pale straw with green tints.
NOSE:	Light fragrant bouquet.
PALATE:	Light/medium-bodied, with delicate grapey fruit and very crisp acidity.
SWEETNESS:	3. Good value for money.

WINE:	**OPPENHEIMER KRÖTENBRUNNEN** **KABINETT (QMP) Rheinhessen**
COUNTRY:	Germany 1986
PRICE:	£2.49 (70cl)
COLOUR:	Pale straw with green tints.
NOSE:	Very intense floral, fruity bouquet.
PALATE:	Medium/full-bodied, with excellent intensity of grape flavours. Lingering grapey finish.
SWEETNESS:	4. Excellent value for money.

WINE:	**MUSCADET DE SÈVRE ET MAINE (AC)**
SUPPLIER:	Bonhomme
COUNTRY:	France 1986
PRICE:	£2.85 (70cl)
COLOUR:	Pale straw.
NOSE:	Vinous/chalky bouquet.

PALATE: Medium-bodied, fruity and more rounded than many Muscadets.

SWEETNESS: 1.

WINE: **TORRES VIÑA ESMERALDA**
COUNTRY: Spain 1987
PRICE: £3.75 (75cl)
COLOUR: Pale/mid straw.
NOSE: Very intense floral grapey nose.
PALATE: Medium/full-bodied, soft and flavoursome. A fruity wine with smooth texture. A wine for most palates.

SWEETNESS: 3.

RED WINES

WINE: **LAMBRUSCO DELL'EMILIA**
COUNTRY: Italy
PRICE: £1.89 (70cl)
COLOUR: Light/mid-red.
NOSE: Light with spicy fruit.
PALATE: Light/medium-bodied; spicy fruit has a hint of cinnamon.
TASTE: A.   Value for money.

WINE: **VALPOLICELLA (DOC)**
COUNTRY: Italy 1987
PRICE: £1.95 (70cl)
COLOUR: Light red.
NOSE: Light, spicy fruit with some stalkiness.
PALATE: Medium-bodied, soft with reasonable depth of fruit.
TASTE: B.   Value for money.

WINE:	**ROUGE DE FRANCE Vin de Table**
COUNTRY:	France
PRICE:	£1.99 (70cl)
COLOUR:	Red.
NOSE:	Shows ripe, raisined fruit.
PALATE:	Medium-bodied, with soft, light peppery fruit. Crisp finish.
TASTE:	A. Value for money.

WINE:	**BORDEAUX SUPÉRIEUR (AC)**
COUNTRY:	France
PRICE:	£2.55 (70cl)
COLOUR:	Red.
NOSE:	Attractive cassis/stalky bouquet.
PALATE:	Medium/full-bodied, with lovely fruit and soft tannin. Oak flavour lingers in the mouth.
TASTE:	C. Good value for money.

WINE:	**MONTEPULCIANO D'ABRUZZO (DOC)**
SUPPLIER:	Bianchi
COUNTRY:	Italy 1985
PRICE:	£2.59 (70cl)
COLOUR:	Dark red with purple tints.
NOSE:	Complex tarry, liquorice bouquet.
PALATE:	Medium/full-bodied, rich and rounded, with tarry/liquorice flavours evident on the nose. Well integrated oak/tannin/acid. Good for short term (6-12 months) cellaring.
TASTE:	C. Excellent value for money.

WINE:	**CH DE POUZOLS (AC) Minervois**
COUNTRY:	France 1986
PRICE:	£2.59 (70cl)
COLOUR:	Red.
NOSE:	Reasonable depth of grassy/stalky fruit.
PALATE:	Full-bodied, with peppery fruit and good tannin/acid and oak. Crisp finish.
TASTE:	C.

WINE:	**FITOU (AC)**
SUPPLIER:	Parmentier
COUNTRY:	France
PRICE:	£2.85 (70cl)
COLOUR:	Red/dark red.
NOSE:	Pleasantly fruity.
PALATE:	Full, soft, smooth and mouth-filling, with some complexity.
TASTE:	D. Good value for money.

WINE:	**CLARET (AC)**
SUPPLIER:	Simon
COUNTRY:	France
PRICE:	£2.95 (70cl)
COLOUR:	Dark red with purple tints.
NOSE:	Attractive cassis, stalky Cabernet fruit.
PALATE:	Full-bodied, with good fruit and tannin. Balance is good. Some astringency on finish.
TASTE:	C. Excellent value for money.

WINE:	**CHIANTI CLASSICO (DOCG)**
SUPPLIER:	Rocca Delle Macie
COUNTRY:	Italy 1986

PRICE:	£3.35 (75cl)
COLOUR:	Red.
NOSE:	Rich, ripe, tarry fruit.
PALATE:	Full-bodied, rich and rounded, with tarry, liquorice fruit and pleasing tannic astringency. Oak comes through on finish. Worth cellaring 12-18 months.
TASTE:	D. Excellent value for money.

WINE:	**TORRES CORONAS**
COUNTRY:	Spain 1984
PRICE:	£3.55 (75cl)
COLOUR:	Deep red/ruby.
NOSE:	Intense, buttery oak dominates fruit.
PALATE:	Full-bodied, velvety smooth texture. Complex buttery oak and fruit flavours are enhanced by slight astringency. A red for most palates.
TASTE:	C. Excellent value for money.

WINE:	**LA VALLIÈRE (AC) Médoc**
COUNTRY:	France
PRICE:	£3.69 (70cl)
COLOUR:	Mid/dark red
NOSE:	Lifted fruity bouquet.
PALATE:	Full, very smooth and rounded with soft tannin, pleasant oak flavour and a lingering finish.
TASTE:	C. Good value for money.

WINE:	**RIOJA (DO) Marqués de Caceres**
COUNTRY:	Spain 1983
PRICE:	£3.95 (75cl)

COLOUR:	Dark red/ruby.
NOSE:	Oak dominates the fruit aromas.
PALATE:	Full-bodied with good depth of tarry fruit and oak flavours. High tannin and acidity will help it keep. Needs 12 months to show its potential.
TASTE:	C. Value for money.

WINE:	**BEAUJOLAIS-VILLAGES (AC)**
SUPPLIER:	Ch du Ringuet, Favrot
COUNTRY:	France 1986
PRICE:	£4.19 (75cl)
COLOUR:	Red with purple tints.
NOSE:	Lovely fragrant fruity bouquet.
PALATE:	Medium/full-bodied with good balance of soft fruit/tannin/acidity.
TASTE:	B. Value for money.

WINE:	**MILDARA SHIRAZ Coonawarra**
COUNTRY:	Australia 1984
PRICE:	£4.25 (75cl)
COLOUR:	Dark red.
NOSE:	Excellent spicy, peppery fruit.
PALATE:	Medium/full-bodied and velvety smooth. Rich, spicy, peppery fruit is in harmony with oak flavours. Delicious!
TASTE:	E. Excellent value for money.

MAJESTIC WINE WAREHOUSES

WHITE WINES

WINE: **VALMADURO VINO BLANCO (DO)**
COUNTRY: Spain
PRICE: £1.79 (70cl)
COLOUR: Straw.
NOSE: Pleasant fruit aroma and slight vanilla character.
PALATE: Medium-bodied, rounded with good depth of flavour. Finish is lingering and flavoursome.
SWEETNESS: 2.   Very good value for money.

WINE: **VIN DE PAYS CHARANTAIS BLANC DE BLANCS**
SUPPLIER: Sylvain
COUNTRY: France
PRICE: £1.99 (70cl)
COLOUR: Straw.
NOSE: Light fruity/floral bouquet.
PALATE: Light/medium-bodied, soft and fruity with balanced acidity.
SWEETNESS: 2.   Value for money.

WINE: **BORDEAUX BLANC DE BLANCS (AC)**
SUPPLIER: Sichel
COUNTRY: France
PRICE: £1.99 (75cl)
COLOUR: Pale/mid straw.
NOSE: Attractive with apple and fruity characters.

PALATE: Light/medium-bodied, with delicate appley/fruity flavour.

SWEETNESS: 1. Value for money.

WINE: **WEHLENER SONNENUHR RIESLING Qualitätswein**
SUPPLIER: St Augustus
COUNTRY: Germany 1987
PRICE: £2.75 (75cl)
COLOUR: Pale straw.
NOSE: Pleasant aroma of the Riesling grape and some floral character.
PALATE: Light/medium-bodied, with fruity Riesling flavour. Finish is crisp with a hint of apple flavour.

SWEETNESS: 3. Value for money.

WINE: **SAUVIGNON DE TOURAINE (AC)**
SUPPLIER: Saget
COUNTRY: France 1987
PRICE: £2.89 (75cl)
COLOUR: Pale/mid straw.
NOSE: Light grassy Sauvignon Blanc aroma.
PALATE: Light/medium-bodied, with delicate Sauvignon Blanc flavour. Good acidity on a flavoursome finish.

SWEETNESS: 1. Value for money.

WINE: **CANTERBURY SAUVIGNON BLANC**
SUPPLIER: Stratford
COUNTRY: California 1986
PRICE: £2.99 (75cl)

COLOUR: Straw.
NOSE: Delicate grassy/gooseberry aromas.
PALATE: Medium-bodied, with good depth of grassy Sauvignon Blanc flavour and some bottle development.
SWEETNESS: 2.   Value for money.

WINE: **VIN DE PAYS DU JARDIN DE LA FRANCE, SAUVIGNON SEC**
SUPPLIER: De Guerois
COUNTRY: France 1987
PRICE: £2.99 (75cl)
COLOUR: Pale/mid straw.
NOSE: Attractive grassy/yeasty bouquet.
PALATE: Medium-bodied with delicate flavour of the Sauvignon Blanc grape. Well-balanced wine with a clean finish.
SWEETNESS: 1.   Value for money.

WINE: **AYLER KUPP RIESLING Qualitätswein.**
SUPPLIER: St Augustus
COUNTRY: Germany 1987
PRICE: £3.25 (75cl)
COLOUR: Pale straw.
NOSE: Attractive bouquet with strong Riesling fruit character.
PALATE: Medium/full bodied, with very floral, fruity flavour. Finish is crisp and fruity.
SWEETNESS: 3.   Very good value for money.

WINE: **VILLA ANTINORI (VDT)**
SUPPLIER: Antinori
COUNTRY: Italy 1986

105

PRICE: £3.49 (75cl)
COLOUR: Straw.
NOSE: Strong boiled-sweet character.
PALATE: Medium-bodied, with good depth of vinous flavour. Light caramel flavour on the finish.
SWEETNESS: 2.   Value for money.

WINE: **CH LA JAUBERTIE (AC)**
SUPPLIER: Ryman
COUNTRY: France 1987
PRICE: £3.95 (75cl)
COLOUR: Very pale straw.
NOSE: Excellent intensity of grassy Sauvignon Blanc aroma and some yeast character.
PALATE: Medium/full-bodied, with very grassy fruit flavour and some yeast character on a crisp, balanced finish.
SWEETNESS: 1.   Excellent value for money.

WINE: **CH LA TOUCHE, MUSCADET DE SÈVRE ET MAINE**
SUPPLIER: Vinet
COUNTRY: France 1986
PRICE: £3.49 (75cl)
COLOUR: Pale/mid straw with green tints.
NOSE: Attractive aroma of Muscadet fruit with some chalky character.
PALATE: Medium-bodied, with good depth of Muscadet flavour. Finish is flavoursome with slight apple character.
SWEETNESS: 1.   Value for money.

WINE: **OAK CASK CHARDONNAY**
SUPPLIER: Wyndham Estate
COUNTRY: Australia 1986
PRICE: £3.99 (75cl)
COLOUR: Dark straw/golden.
NOSE: Strong bouquet of oak and fruit.
PALATE: Full-bodied, very oaky with good depth of fruit flavour.
SWEETNESS: 2.   Very good value for money.

WINE: **TULLOCH CHARDONNAY**
COUNTRY: Australia 1986
PRICE: £4.75 (75cl)
COLOUR: Straw.
NOSE: Excellent bouquet of Chardonnay fruit and oak.
PALATE: Full-bodied, with excellent depth of fruit flavour enhanced by oak maturation. Very flavoursome finish.
SWEETNESS: 2.   Excellent value for money.

WINE: **RIOJA RESERVA TONDONIA**
SUPPLIER: Heredia
COUNTRY: Spain 1981
PRICE: £4.99 (75cl)
COLOUR: Straw/golden.
NOSE: Complex bouquet of vanillan oak with underlying fruit.
PALATE: Full-bodied, with excellent depth of fruit and oak flavour. Complex wine showing good bottle-age development.
SWEETNESS: 2.   Very good value for money.

RED WINES

WINE:	**VIN DE PAYS DE LA VALLÉE DU PARADIS (VDT)**
SUPPLIER:	Bouffet
COUNTRY:	France 1986
PRICE:	£1.85 (70cl)
COLOUR:	Red with purple tints.
NOSE:	Lively, fruity bouquet.
PALATE:	Medium-bodied, crisp and fruity, with firm tannin and good balance.
TASTE:	B. Good value for money.

WINE:	**VIN DE PAYS DU GARD**
COUNTRY:	France 1986
PRICE:	£1.99 (70cl)
COLOUR:	Light/mid red.
NOSE:	Spicy/fruity bouquet.
PALATE:	Light/medium-bodied, soft and spicy with light tannin. Easy drinking style.
TASTE:	B. Value for money.

WINE:	**CÔTES DU ROUSSILLON VILLAGES (AC)**
SUPPLIER:	Co-op St Vincent
COUNTRY:	France 1986
PRICE:	£2.15 (70cl)
COLOUR:	Red with purple tints.
NOSE:	Attractive, fruity bouquet.
PALATE:	Medium-bodied, with pleasant fruity flavour and slight tannic astringency.
TASTE:	B. Value for money.

WINE:	**GRENACHE MERLOT (VDT), DOM DE LENTHÉRIC**
COUNTRY:	France 1985
PRICE:	£2.35 (70cl)
COLOUR:	Red with blue tints.
NOSE:	Stalky, slightly burnt/fruity character.
PALATE:	Medium-bodied, with light fruit and some raspberry flavour on the finish.
TASTE:	B.

WINE:	**CH VAUGELAS, CORBIÈRES (AC)**
SUPPLIER:	Bouffet
COUNTRY:	France 1985
PRICE:	£2.39 (75cl)
COLOUR:	Dark red with blue tints.
NOSE:	Very attractive with rich, ripe, honeyed/fruity bouquet.
PALATE:	Medium/full-bodied, with slightly spicy/raisined fruit. Slight tannic astringency on the finish.
TASTE:	C. Good value for money.

WINE:	**SYRAH (VDT)**
SUPPLIER:	Chantovent
COUNTRY:	France 1985
PRICE:	£2.49 (75cl)
COLOUR:	Dark red with purple tints.
NOSE:	Spicy/peppery bouquet.
PALATE:	Full-bodied, with good depth of spicy/peppery flavour and firm tannin.
TASTE:	D. Very good value for money.

WINE:	**HOUSE CLARET (AC)**
SUPPLIER:	Sichel
COUNTRY:	France
PRICE:	£2.55 (75cl)
COLOUR:	Red with blue tints.
NOSE:	Attractive with strong aroma of Cabernet fruit and slightly stalky character.
PALATE:	Full-bodied, smooth and flavoursome, with good balance of tannin and acidity.
TASTE:	C. Very good value for money.

WINE:	**SPANNA (VDT)**
SUPPLIER:	Vallana
COUNTRY:	Italy 1983
PRICE:	£2.99 (75cl)
COLOUR:	Dark red.
NOSE:	Excellent aroma of the Nebbiolo grape with strong tarry character.
PALATE:	Full-bodied, with rich, ripe, robust flavour and pleasant oak and tannin on a slightly astringent finish.
TASTE:	D. Excellent value for money.

WINE:	**CÔTES DU VENTOUX (AC)**
SUPPLIER:	Jaboulet Aîné
COUNTRY:	France 1986
PRICE:	£2.99 (75cl)
COLOUR:	Red.
NOSE:	Fruity bouquet with boiled-sweet character.
PALATE:	Full-bodied, with good depth of flavour and a fruity, slightly tannic finish.
TASTE:	D. Good value for money.

WINE:	**PENFOLDS EDEN VALLEY SHIRAZ**
COUNTRY:	Australia 1984
PRICE:	£3.25 (75cl)
COLOUR:	Dark red with brown tints.
NOSE:	Excellent bouquet of vanilla/buttery oak and underlying fruit.
PALATE:	Full-bodied, with good depth of ripe Shiraz fruit flavour enhanced by oak maturation. Good balance of tannin/oak/acidity. Lingering, flavoursome finish.
TASTE:	E. Excellent value for money.

WINE:	**CH MONT-REDON, CÔTES DU RHÔNE (AC)**
SUPPLIER:	D'Exploit
COUNTRY:	France 1985
PRICE:	£3.49 (75cl)
COLOUR:	Red with brown tints.
NOSE:	Lively, spicy/fruity bouquet.
PALATE:	Full-bodied, soft and smooth, with good depth of flavour and balanced tannin and oak. Persistent finish.
TASTE:	C. Very good value for money.

WINE:	**LA CLOTIÈRE, SAUMUR CHAMPIGNY (AC)**
COUNTRY:	France 1981
PRICE:	£3.89 (75cl)
COLOUR:	Red/brown.
NOSE:	Excellent combination of complex fruit aromas and bottle-age development.

PALATE: Full-bodied, with excellent complexity of flavour. Good balance of fruit/oak/acidity/tannin. Ready for drinking.

TASTE: B.   Excellent value for money

WINE: **CH MEAUME (AC)**
SUPPLIER: Johnson-Hill
COUNTRY: France 1985
PRICE: £3.95 (75cl)
COLOUR: Dark red with purple tints.
NOSE: Strong claret bouquet with slightly vinegar character.
PALATE: Full-bodied, smooth and very fruity, with firm tannin on an astringent finish.
TASTE: C.   Good value for money.

WINE: **SYRAH**
SUPPLIER: Phelps
COUNTRY: California 1980
PRICE: £4.25 (75cl)
COLOUR: Red/brown in colour.
NOSE: Attractive bouquet of fruit, oak and bottle-age development.
PALATE: Full-bodied, very smooth and flavoursome, with excellent depth of flavour.
TASTE: D.   Very good value for money.

WINE: **ST EMILION GRAND CRU (AC)**
SUPPLIER: L'Union des Producteurs
COUNTRY: France 1983
PRICE: £4.75 (75cl)

COLOUR: Red/brown.

NOSE: Excellent rich, ripe, fruity bouquet with attractive oak and some stalky character.

PALATE: Full-bodied, very soft, smooth and rounded, with excellent fruit flavour. Good balance of tannin/fruit/oak/acid. Finish is warm and persistent.

TASTE: D.   Excellent value for money.

WINE: **STRATFORD CABERNET SAUVIGNON**

COUNTRY: California 1984

PRICE: £4.99 (75cl)

COLOUR: Dark red.

NOSE: Attractive aroma of the Cabernet Sauvignon grape with slight grapey/jammy character.

PALATE: Full-bodied, rich, ripe and robust, with firm tannin on a pleasantly oaky finish.

TASTE: D.   Excellent value for money.

WINE: **BOURGOGNE (AC)**

SUPPLIER: Dom Clairdau

COUNTRY: France 1980

PRICE: £4.99 (75cl)

COLOUR: Brown/red.

NOSE: Excellent bouquet of developed earthy/Pinot Noir grapes and oak.

PALATE: Medium-bodied, with very attractive earthy Burgundy regional character. Finish has lovely oak and bottle-age development.

TASTE: B.   Excellent value for money.

ROSÉ WINE

WINE:	**CH LA JAUBERTIE (AC)**
SUPPLIER:	Ryman
COUNTRY:	France 1987
PRICE:	£3.29 (75cl)
COLOUR:	Cherry pink.
NOSE:	Lively, fruity bouquet with some stalky character.
PALATE:	Medium/full-bodied, very fruity and flavoursome. Finish is fruity and persistent. More body than most rosé wines.
SWEETNESS: 3.	Excellent value for money.

SPARKLING WINE

WINE:	**MARCEL NEAU MÉTHODE CHAMPENOISE (AC)**
COUNTRY:	France 1985
PRICE:	£4.99 (75cl)
COLOUR:	Straw with green tints.
NOSE:	Very attractive bouquet of fruit and yeast.
PALATE:	Full-bodied, very soft and creamy, with good depth of flavour and crisp acidity.
SWEETNESS: 2.	Excellent value for money.

MARKS & SPENCER

WHITE WINES

WINE:	**CÔTES DE GASCOGNE VDP**
COUNTRY:	France 1987
PRICE:	£2.35 (75cl)
COLOUR:	Very pale straw.
NOSE:	Reasonable depth of fruit and some yeast character (from the yeasts which convert the grape sugars to alcohol during fermentation).
PALATE:	Light/medium-bodied, slightly sweet with rounded fruity flavours.
SWEETNESS:	2.

WINE:	**BEREICH NIERSTEIN Qualitätswein**
COUNTRY:	Germany 1986
PRICE:	£2.65 (75cl)
COLOUR:	Pale straw.
NOSE:	Attractive, with lifted, grapey bouquet.
PALATE:	Light/medium-bodied, medium sweet with smooth grapey fruit flavour.
SWEETNESS:	3.

WINE:	**SOAVE CLASSICO (DOC)**
COUNTRY:	Italy 1986
PRICE:	£2.75 (75cl)
COLOUR:	Very pale straw.
NOSE:	Reasonable fruit and some vinous/stalky odours.

PALATE: Light/medium-bodied, with light, chalky fruit flavour. Crisp finish.

SWEETNESS: 2.

WINE:	**MOSCATEL DE VALENCIA (DOC)**
COUNTRY:	Spain
PRICE:	£2.75 (75cl)
COLOUR:	Straw with green tints.
NOSE:	Very intense, grapey, fruity bouquet.
PALATE:	Full, sweet, with luscious, fruity flavour. Inexpensive dessert-wine style.

SWEETNESS: 8.   Value for money.

WINE:	**PIESPORTER MICHELSBERG** **Qualitätswein**
COUNTRY:	Germany 1987
PRICE:	£2.99 (75cl)
COLOUR:	Pale straw with green tints.
NOSE:	Light, grassy fruit.
PALATE:	Light/medium-bodied, with light sweet fruit and a crisp finish.

SWEETNESS: 3.

WINE:	**RIOJA VINO BLANCO (DO)**
COUNTRY:	Spain 1985
PRICE:	£2.99 (75cl)
COLOUR:	Pale/mid straw.
NOSE:	Attractive vanillan oak and light fruit.
PALATE:	Medium/full-bodied, soft and smooth, with strong oak flavours and light fruit.

SWEETNESS: 2.   Value for money.

WINE:	**FRASCATI (DOC)**
COUNTRY:	Italy 1986
PRICE:	£2.99. (75cl)
COLOUR:	Pale straw.
NOSE:	Light delicate fruit.
PALATE:	Medium-bodied, soft and rounded.
SWEETNESS:	2.

WINE:	**CHARDONNAY VENEZIA-GIULIA**
COUNTRY:	Italy 1987
PRICE:	£2.99 (75cl)
COLOUR:	Pale straw with green tints.
NOSE:	Light fruity bouquet.
PALATE:	Medium-bodied, with light fruit and a crisp finish.
SWEETNESS:	2.

WINE:	**SAUVIGNON**
COUNTRY:	France
PRICE:	£2.99 (75cl)
COLOUR:	Pale/mid straw.
NOSE:	An attractive grassy bouquet, a characteristic of the Sauvignon Blanc grape.
PALATE:	Light/medium-bodied, with grassy fruit flavours and a crisp finish.
SWEETNESS:	1. Value for money.

WINE:	**CH BONNET Entre-Deux-Mers (AC)**
COUNTRY:	France 1986
PRICE:	£3.25 (75cl)
COLOUR:	Straw with green tints.
NOSE:	Reasonably fruity bouquet.

PALATE: Medium-bodied with a soft texture. Light grassy fruit on finish.
SWEETNESS: 1.

WINE: **CHARDONNAY**
COUNTRY: France
PRICE: £3.25 (75cl)
COLOUR: Straw with green tints.
NOSE: Light, with some fruit salad aromas.
PALATE: Medium/full-bodied, with fruit salad flavours and crisp acidity.
SWEETNESS: 2.   Value for money.

WINE: **VOUVRAY (AC) Domaine de la Racanderie**
COUNTRY: France 1987
PRICE: £3.50 (75cl)
COLOUR: Pale/mid straw with green tints.
NOSE: Aromatic fruit with some earthiness.
PALATE: Medium-bodied, soft and slightly sweet, with pleasant fruit flavours and a lingering fruity finish.
SWEETNESS: 4.   Value for money.

WINE: **JEUNES VIGNES (VDT)**
COUNTRY: France
PRICE: £4.50 (75cl)
COLOUR: Straw with green tints.
NOSE: Pleasant fruity bouquet.

PALATE:	Medium/full-bodied, soft and rounded, with good depth of fruit flavour. Good balance and persistent finish.
SWEETNESS:	2. Value for money.

RED WINES

WINE:	**GAMAY**
COUNTRY:	France
PRICE:	£2.50 (75cl)
COLOUR:	Pinkish red.
NOSE:	Light, fragrant bouquet.
PALATE:	Light/medium-bodied with light, lifted fruit. Hints of cinnamon spiciness in this pleasant, easy drinking style.
TASTE:	A.

WINE:	**CHIANTI (DOCG)**
COUNTRY:	Italy 1986
PRICE:	£2.99 (100cl)
COLOUR:	Vibrant red.
NOSE:	Attractive, spicy, fruity bouquet.
PALATE:	Medium-bodied, spicy, tangy with smooth texture and a crisp finish.
TASTE:	D. Value for money.

WINE:	**CLARET (AC)**
COUNTRY:	France 1985
PRICE:	£2.99 (70cl)
COLOUR:	Red.
NOSE:	Attractive fruitiness, with the characteristic aroma of the Cabernet Sauvignon grape.

119

PALATE: Medium-bodied, pleasantly fruity with some tannin. Good, fruity finish.

TASTE: C.   Value for money.

WINE: **CH SABLES PEYTRAUD (AC)**
COUNTRY: France 1986
PRICE: £2.99 (75cl)
COLOUR: Red/ruby.
NOSE: Light jammy, fruity bouquet.
PALATE: Medium-bodied with good tannin and light fruit.
TASTE: C.

WINE: **CÔTES DU RHÔNE (AC)**
COUNTRY: France
PRICE: £3.50 (100cl)
COLOUR: Red.
NOSE: Light, peppery, fruity bouquet.
PALATE: Medium/full-bodied, with peppery fruit and slight astringency. Finish is crisp and shows pleasant oak flavour and tannin.
TASTE: C.

WINE: **MÉDOC (AC)**
COUNTRY: France 1985
PRICE: £3.75 (75cl)
COLOUR: Dark red.
NOSE: Characteristic aroma of the Cabernet Sauvignon grape variety.

PALATE:	Medium/full-bodied. Fruit and acidity are in harmony. Needs some cellaring to show its best.
TASTE:	D.

WINE:	**BAROLO (DOCG)**
COUNTRY:	Italy 1983
PRICE:	£3.99 (75cl)
COLOUR:	Red/brown.
NOSE:	Loads of oak and tarry, liquorice fruit.
PALATE:	Full, smooth and rounded, with tarry fruit and strong oak flavours. Finish is crisp with pleasant astringency. I have seen better Barolos but at this price must be considered good value.
TASTE:	E. Good value for money.

WINE:	**CH HAUT GAILLARDET (AC)**
COUNTRY:	France 1985
PRICE:	£3.99 (75cl)
COLOUR:	Red/deep red with purple hue.
NOSE:	Reasonably fruity bouquet.
PALATE:	Medium/full-bodied, fruity with good tannin and oak flavours on the finish.
TASTE:	C.

WINE:	**RIOJA RESERVA (DO) Marqués del Romeral**
COUNTRY:	Spain 1981
PRICE:	£3.99 (75cl)
COLOUR:	Red/brown.
NOSE:	Lovely, vanillan oak and fruit.

PALATE: Medium/full-bodied, smooth, rounded and very oaky with a crisp finish.

TASTE: C.   Good value for money.

WINE: **BURGUNDY (AC)**
COUNTRY: France 1985
PRICE: £3.99 (75cl)
COLOUR: Red.
NOSE: Very appealing strawberry/raspberry/earthy Pinot Noir fruit.
PALATE: Medium-bodied, very flavoursome with excellent balance of fruit/oak/acidity.
TASTE: B.   Very good value for money.

ROSÉ WINE

WINE: **BLUSH (VDP)**
COUNTRY: France
PRICE: £2.49 (70cl)
COLOUR: Pale pink.
NOSE: Attractive, delicate fruit bouquet.
PALATE: Light/medium-bodied, with adequate fruit flavour and a soft finish.
SWEETNESS: 3.

SPARKLING WINES

WINE: **FRIZZANTE DRY**
COUNTRY: Italy
PRICE: £2.75 (75cl)
COLOUR: Very pale straw.
NOSE: Vinuous with some fruitiness.

PALATE: Light/medium-bodied, semi-sparkling with faint appleish flavour.
SWEETNESS: 3.

WINE: **SPARKLING MEDIUM DRY.**
COUNTRY: France
PRICE: £3.75 (75cl)
COLOUR: Very pale straw.
NOSE: Vinous with some stalkiness.
PALATE: Medium-bodied, slightly sweet with crisp acidity.
SWEETNESS: 4.

WINE: **SPARKLING DRY ROSÉ.**
COUNTRY: France
PRICE: £3.75 (75cl)
COLOUR: Pale pink.
NOSE: Light, fruity bouquet.
PALATE: Light/medium-bodied, with light fruit and crisp acidity.
SWEETNESS: 4.

WINE: **ASTI SPUMANTE (DOC)**
COUNTRY: Italy
PRICE: £3.99 (75cl)
COLOUR: Very pale straw.
NOSE: Very grapey bouquet.
PALATE: Medium-bodied, with intense grape flavours and a soft, rounded finish.
SWEETNESS: 7.

ODDBINS

WHITE WINES

WINE: **CASTILLO DE ALHAMBRA**
COUNTRY: Spain 1986
PRICE: £1.99 (75cl)
NOSE: Intense fruity bouquet.
PALATE: Yeasty with underlying fruit and a clean, crisp finish.
SWEETNESS: 3.   Good value for money.

WINE: **McWILLIAMS COLOMBARD/ CHARDONNAY**
COUNTRY: Australia 1987
PRICE: £5.99 (2 litres) £2.25 (75cl)
COLOUR: Straw.
NOSE: Good fruit, with the Colombard overshadowing the Chardonnay fruit.
PALATE: Full-bodied, with excellent fruit and clean, lingering finish. The quality of this wine should change opinions about wine boxes.
SWEETNESS: 2.   Excellent value for money.

WINE: **DÃO, Branco Granado**
SUPPLIER: Sogrape
COUNTRY: Portugal 1986
PRICE: £2.49 (75cl)
COLOUR: Pale straw.
NOSE: Dominated by yeast character, with attractive underlying fruit; lovely nose.

PALATE: Medium-bodied, very yeasty and with pleasing astringency. Good finish on an attractive style of wine.

SWEETNESS: 2.   Value for money.

WINE: **PINOT BLANC**
SUPPLIER: Scherer
COUNTRY: France 1986
PRICE: £2.69 (70cl)
COLOUR: Attractive straw.
NOSE: Good Pinot Blanc fruit.
PALATE: Medium/full-bodied with good fruit and a very clean finish without the coarseness often found in Pinot Blanc wines.

SWEETNESS: 3.   Value for money.

WINE: **TOLLEY'S CHENIN/COLOMBARD**
COUNTRY: Australia 1987
PRICE: £2.99 (75cl)
COLOUR: Straw with green tinges.
NOSE: Very yeasty with good fruit and oak.
PALATE: Medium-bodied, very oaky, with good fruit and acidity.

SWEETNESS: 2.   Good value for money.

WINE: **CHARDONNAY Domaine des Hautes de Sanziers**
COUNTRY: France 1987
PRICE: £3.49 (75cl)
COLOUR: Light golden.
NOSE: Intense fruit-salad Chardonnay aroma

| PALATE: | Medium/full-bodied, with good fruit and balanced acidity. Well-made wine with good style. |
| SWEETNESS: | 2. Value for money. |

WINE:	**JOÃO PIRES CATARINA**
COUNTRY:	Portugal 1986
PRICE:	£3.69 (75cl)
COLOUR:	Straw/golden.
NOSE:	Very attractive with vanillan oak odours dominating.
PALATE:	Dominated by oak, which has been skilfully balanced with fruit and acid. The finish is crisp and lingering.
SWEETNESS:	2.

WINE:	**CHÂTEAU COUCHEROY Graves**
COUNTRY:	France 1986
PRICE:	£3.79 (75cl)
COLOUR:	Straw with green tinges.
NOSE:	Grassy fruit and some yeast character.
PALATE:	Medium-bodied with good fruit and crisp acidity. Touch coarse on finish.
SWEETNESS:	1.

WINE:	**ARROYO SECO PINOT BLANC**
SUPPLIER:	Jekel
COUNTRY:	California 1985
PRICE:	£3.99 (75cl)
COLOUR:	Pale straw with green tinges.
NOSE:	Lifted, honeyed fruit and some oak.

PALATE: Medium-bodied, with clean oak dominating a lengthy finish.

SWEETNESS: 2.

WINE: **JEKEL JOHANNISBERG RIESLING**

COUNTRY: California 1986

PRICE: £3.99 (75cl)

COLOUR: Straw.

NOSE: Very attractive with excellent fruit and some noble rot.

PALATE: Full, soft and fruity, with a clean, crisp finish.

SWEETNESS: 4.   Good value for money.

WINE: **FREINSHEIMER GOLDBERG RIESLING SPÄTLESE**

COUNTRY: Germany 1985

PRICE: £4.99 (70cl)

COLOUR: Pale golden.

NOSE: Excellent intense fruity bouquet.

PALATE: Rich, balanced and very fruity. Very good wine.

SWEETNESS: 6.   Very good value for money.

WINE: **SANCERRE (AC) Rothureau**

COUNTRY: France 1986

PRICE: £4.99 (75cl)

COLOUR: Pale straw with green tinges.

NOSE: Very pleasant, with intense 'gooseberry', grassy Sauvignon Blanc fruit.

PALATE:	Medium-bodied, with very good Sauvignon. Blanc fruit and crisp finish. Good style.
SWEETNESS:	1. Good value for money.

WINE:	**SAXONVALE SEMILLON/ CHARDONNAY**
COUNTRY:	Australia 1987
PRICE:	£4.99 (75cl)
COLOUR:	Pale/mid straw.
NOSE:	Dominated by very attractive yeast character with good underlying fruit.
PALATE:	Full, soft and rounded, with pleasant yeasty flavours and persistent finish.
SWEETNESS:	2. Value for money.

RED WINES

WINE:	**CASTILLO DE ALHAMBRA Tinto**
COUNTRY:	Spain 1986
PRICE:	£1.99 (75cl)
COLOUR:	Vibrant ruby red.
NOSE:	Strawberry fruit aroma.
PALATE:	Light, fruity, clean and balanced. Good light style.
TASTE:	A. Value for money.

WINE:	**ODDBINS RED VDP des Côtes Catalanes**
COUNTRY:	France 1986
PRICE:	£2.49 (75cl)
COLOUR:	Red with purple tints.
NOSE:	Intense jammy fruit with some spiciness.

PALATE:	Light/medium-bodied, with spicy fruit and crisp acidity on a pleasantly astringent finish.
TASTE:	B. Value for money.

WINE:	**CHAMUSCA Tinto Velho**
COUNTRY:	Portugal 1980
PRICE:	£2.49 (75cl)
COLOUR:	Red/brown.
NOSE:	Complex mix of fruit and oak, intensified by slight vinegar character.
PALATE:	Full, soft, rounded, oaky, with good underlying fruit. The finish is clean and with slight astringency.
TASTE:	D. Excellent value for money.

WINE:	**PERIQUITA**
SUPPLIER:	Fonseca
COUNTRY:	Portugal 1982
PRICE:	£2.99 (75cl)
COLOUR:	Red/brown.
NOSE:	Intense raisined fruit and very oaky.
PALATE:	Sweetish, raisined fruit and intense oak flavour. Some bottle-age development is evident.
TASTE:	D. Good value for money.

WINE:	**QUINTA D'ABRIGADA**
COUNTRY:	Portugal 1984
PRICE:	£3.49 (75cl)
COLOUR:	Vibrant red.
NOSE:	Intense floral/crushed flowers fragrance.

PALATE:	Similar flowery flavours, with oak and crisp acidity present on a finish of good length.
TASTE:	D.

WINE:	**MADIRAN Domaine de Duisse**
COUNTRY:	France 1985
PRICE:	£3.99 (75cl)
COLOUR:	Dark red/ruby.
NOSE:	Very raisined, tarry fruit and a hint of vinegar.
PALATE:	Rich, full and fruity, with crisp acidity on a clean, tannic finish Some astringency.
TASTE:	D.

WINE:	**CHÂTEAU DE BRISSAC Anjou Villages**
COUNTRY:	France 1986
PRICE:	£3.99 (75cl)
COLOUR:	Red.
NOSE:	Rich, complex and very fruity.
PALATE:	Fruity, very dry and astringent.
TASTE:	B. Value for money.

WINE:	**TOLLANA SHIRAZ/CABERNET SAUVIGNON**
COUNTRY:	Australia 1982
PRICE:	£3.99 (75cl)
COLOUR:	Red with some brown tints.
NOSE:	Attractive bouquet of vanillan oak and jammy fruit.

PALATE: Medium-bodied, with jammy fruit and oaky finish. Bottle-age development showing.

TASTE: D.   Value for money.

WINE: **CAHORS Prieure de Cenac**
COUNTRY: France 1985
PRICE: £4.99 (75cl)
COLOUR: Dark red with purple tinges.
NOSE: Lifted, raisined fruity bouquet.
PALATE: Full-bodied with very rich fruit. Good tannin on a warming finish.
TASTE: C.

WINE: **BANYULS DOUTRES**
COUNTRY: France 1985
PRICE: £4.99 (75cl)
COLOUR: Red with purple tinges
NOSE: Very intense bouquet of raisined fruit and Brandy spirit.
PALATE: Full, rich, luscious, with good tannin and a lingering sweet finish.
TASTE: E.   Value for money.

WINE: **SAXONVALE SHIRAZ**
COUNTRY: Australia 1985
PRICE: £4.99 (75cl)
COLOUR: Deep red/ruby.
NOSE: Peppery Shiraz fruit aroma, with buttery, vanillan oak.

PALATE: Full, soft and rich, with sweet oak and peppery fruit. Some chocolate flavours beginning to develop on a crisp, lengthy finish.

TASTE: E.   Value for money.

ROSÉ WINE

WINE: **DON HERMANO ROSADO**
COUNTRY: Portugal 1986
PRICE: £3.19 (75cl)
COLOUR: Pink/amber.
NOSE: Stalky with underlying fruit.
PALATE: Crisp, clean and fruity. Good style.
SWEETNESS: 4.

SPARKLING WINE

WINE: **SEGURA VIUDAS BRUT NV CAVA**
COUNTRY: Spain
PRICE: £4.65 (75cl)
COLOUR: Straw.
NOSE: A combination of yeast and apple odours
PALATE: Soft and yeasty. Interesting style.
SWEETNESS: 2.

SAINSBURY

WHITE WINES

WINE: **VIN DE PAYS DES CHARANTES**
COUNTRY: France
PRICE: £1.99 (75cl)
COLOUR: Pale straw with green tints.
NOSE: Vinous with light fruity fragrance.
PALATE: Medium-bodied, rounded, with grassy fruit and a crisp finish. Well-made quaffing wine.
SWEETNESS: 1. Value for money.

WINE: **SAUVIGNON DE TOURAINE (AC)**
COUNTRY: France
PRICE: £2.25 (75cl)
COLOUR: Pale straw with green tints.
NOSE: Excellent Sauvignon Blanc fruit (very grassy character) and slight stalkiness which adds complexity.
PALATE: Light/medium-bodied, soft and rounded, with grassy fruit flavour and fairly high acidity. Crisp fruity finish. Good wine for those who enjoy Sauvignon Blanc but do not wish to pay for the more expensive Sancerre wines.
SWEETNESS: 1. Very good value for money.

WINE: **ORVIETO CLASSICO (DOC)**
COUNTRY: Italy 1987
PRICE: £2.59 (75cl)
COLOUR: Very pale straw/watery.

NOSE: Vinous.

PALATE: Light/medium-bodied, vinous and with a light nutty flavour which lingers pleasantly. A style of wine which will compliment food.

SWEETNESS: 2. Good value for money.

WINE: **VERDICCHIO DEI CASTELLI DI JESI CLASSICO (DOC)**

COUNTRY: Italy

PRICE: £2.79 (75cl)

COLOUR: Pale/mid straw.

NOSE: Very honeyed and fruity.

PALATE: Light/medium-bodied, with very delicate, honeyed fruit and a soft finish.

SWEETNESS: 1. Good value for money.

WINE: **ALSACE (AC)**

COUNTRY: France

PRICE: £2.85 (75cl)

COLOUR: Straw with green tints.

NOSE: Very aromatic, and demonstrates the unique regional characteristics of Alsace.

PALATE: Medium/full-bodied, with good complexity of flavour resulting from the blending of different grape varieties.

SWEETNESS: 2. Excellent value for money.

WINE: **EITELSBACHER MARIENHOLZ RIESLING (QBA)**

COUNTRY: Germany 1986

PRICE: £2.95 (75cl)

COLOUR: Pale/mid straw.

NOSE:	Very floral, grapey, fruity, with honeyed overtones.
PALATE:	Medium-bodied and slightly sweet, with intense Riesling fruit flavour. A well-balanced wine with outstanding fruity flavour.
SWEETNESS:	4. Excellent value for money.

CHARDONNAY ALTO-ADIGE (DOC)

WINE:	**CHARDONNAY ALTO-ADIGE (DOC)**
COUNTRY:	Italy 1987
PRICE:	£3.39 (75cl)
COLOUR:	Pale straw and slightly sparkling.
NOSE:	Similar peach/fruit salad aromas often found in Australian and Californian Chardonnays. More aromatic than most Chardonnays from this region.
PALATE:	Full-bodied, mouth-filling and fruity with a persistent flavoursome finish.
SWEETNESS:	2. Very good value for money.

WINE:	**VERNACCIA DI SAN GIMIGNANO (DOC)**
COUNTRY:	Italy 1986
PRICE:	£3.45 (75cl)
COLOUR:	Deep straw with green tints, very slight fizziness.
NOSE:	Unique, with a bouquet which may remind some of lemon marmalade.

PALATE: Full-bodied and very fruity. Slight sweetness compliments this differently styled wine. A wine which can be enjoyed on its own.

SWEETNESS: 2.   Value for money.

WINE: **ALSACE GEWÜRTZTRAMINER (AC)**
COUNTRY: France 1986
PRICE: £3.59 (75cl)
COLOUR: Deep straw/golden.
NOSE: Very powerful bouquet of spicy Gewürztraminer fruit.
PALATE: Medium/full-bodied, with strong spicy fruit flavour and a soft, fruity finish.
SWEETNESS: 3.   Good value for money.

WINE: **QUINCY (AC)**
SUPPLIER: Duc de Berri
COUNTRY: France 1986
PRICE: £3.95 (75cl)
COLOUR: Straw with green tints.
NOSE: Has some grassy/lime characters and some may find similarity to blackcurrant leaves.
PALATE: Full-bodied, rounded and very fruity with a crisp finish.
SWEETNESS: 1.   Good value for money.

WINE: **WHITE BURGUNDY CHARDONNAY (AC)**
COUNTRY: France
PRICE: £3.98 (75cl)
COLOUR: Straw with green tints.

NOSE: Subtle and vinous, with light fruit and some grassy character.

PALATE: Medium/full-bodied, pleasantly rounded with delicate fruit flavours and a persistent, clean finish.

SWEETNESS: 2.   Value for money.

WINE: **COOKS SAUVIGNON BLANC**
COUNTRY: New Zealand 1987
PRICE: £4.50 (75cl)
COLOUR: Straw with green tints.
NOSE: Very intense Sauvignon Blanc aroma.
PALATE: Medium/full-bodied, with very grassy/gooseberry flavours and a crisp, fruity finish. Typical of the variety.
SWEETNESS: 1.   Value for money.

WINE: **BERRI ESTATES CHARDONNAY**
COUNTRY: Australia 1987
PRICE: £4.55 (75cl)
COLOUR: Deep straw.
NOSE: Excellent bouquet of buttery oak and fruit salad Chardonnay character.
PALATE: Full-bodied, very fruity and flavoursome with pleasant combination of fruit and oak flavours on the finish.
SWEETNESS: 2.   Excellent value for money.

RED WINES

WINE: **ARRUDA**
COUNTRY: Portugal
PRICE: £1.98 (75cl)

137

COLOUR: Deep red.

NOSE: Lots of raisined, fruity odours.

PALATE: Medium/full-bodied, with sweetish fruit and good tannin and acidity. Strong flavour of old oak dominates a lingering aftertaste. A bargain!

TASTE: D.　　　　　　Excellent value for money.

WINE: **CLARET, Bordeaux Supérieur (AC)**

COUNTRY: France

PRICE: £2.45 (75cl)

COLOUR: Dark red with purple tints.

NOSE: Very aromatic, with good Cabernet fruit enhanced by ageing in oak barrels which imparts a woody flavour and adds to the wine's complexity.

PALATE: Medium/full-bodied with good fruit flavour, firm tannin and balanced oak. Slightly astringent finish.

TASTE: C.　　　　　　Excellent value for money.

WINE: **RIOJA, VIÑA ALBERDI (DO)**

COUNTRY: Spain 1984

PRICE: £2.95 (75cl)

COLOUR: Red/brown.

NOSE: Lovely combination of vanillan oak and sweet fruit.

PALATE: Full-bodied and very oaky, with rich, ripe fruit. Needs approximately 2 years cellaring to show its full potential.

TASTE: C.   Very good value for money.

WINE: **CALIFORNIAN ZINFANDEL**
PRICE: £2.98 (75cl)
COLOUR: Red.
NOSE: Strong liquorice/fruity aromas.
PALATE: Full-bodied, with very mouth-filling fruit and also a touch of oak flavour on the finish. Zinfandel is a variety of increasing popularity.
TASTE: C.   Very good value for money.

WINE: **ROMEIRA GARRAFEIRA**
SUPPLIER: Caves Velhas
COUNTRY: Portugal 1978
PRICE: £3.45 (75cl)
COLOUR: Dark red.
NOSE: Attractive bouquet of oak and ripe, raisined fruit.
PALATE: Full-bodied, with tarry fruit, strong oak flavour, and soft tannin on a crisp finish.
TASTE: D.   Very good value for money.

WINE: **WYNDHAMS BIN 937 Cabernet Sauvignon**
COUNTRY: Australia 1983
PRICE: £3.65 (75cl)
COLOUR: Ruby red/purple.
NOSE: Very intense Ribena bouquet.

PALATE:	Full, very soft and rounded with sweetish Ribena fruitiness. A red with velvety texture.
TASTE:	D. Excellent value for money

WINE:	**DOMAINE ST APOLLINAIRE (AC) Côtes du Rhône**
COUNTRY:	France 1985
PRICE:	£3.75 (75cl) organic wine
COLOUR:	Interesting wine visually as has a combination of deep red and brown colour with purple tints.
NOSE:	Intense raisined fruit and some cold tea character.
PALATE:	Full-bodied, with very floral, fruity flavours. Strong tannin and some astringency on finish.
TASTE:	C.

WINE:	**ST EMILION (AC)**
COUNTRY:	France
PRICE:	£3.89 (75cl)
COLOUR:	Very deep red with purple tints.
NOSE:	Excellent, rich, earthy, fruity nose which should develop more complexity if cellared.
PALATE:	Full-bodied, with high tannin and acidity. Rich, rounded fruit and oak flavours. An excellent mouth-filling wine. A bargain for the cellar!
TASTE:	C. Excellent value for money.

WINE:	**RED BURGUNDY (AC) PINOT NOIR**
COUNTRY:	France
PRICE:	£3.95 (75cl)
COLOUR:	Red/brown (often termed brick-red).

NOSE: Excellent depth of Pinot Noir fruit and good earthy Burgundy character.

PALATE: Medium/full-bodied, with good Pinot Noir fruit and balance of fruit/oak/acidity. An inexpensive wine useful as a benchmark for its grape. Worth cellaring for 12-24 months, and should be velvety soft by that time.

TASTE: B.   Excellent value for money.

WINE: **VILLA ANTINORI CHIANTI CLASSICO RISERVA (DOCG)**

COUNTRY: Italy 1982

PRICE: £4.65 (75cl)

COLOUR: Dark red with brown tints.

NOSE: Attractive tarry fruit character which is intensified by slight vinegar.

PALATE: Full-bodied and tannic, with tarry fruit and high astringency. Finish is crisp and persistent. Short-term cellaring potential (6-12 months).

TASTE: D.   Value for money.

WINE: **TORRES GRAN CORONAS Reserva**

COUNTRY: Spain 1982

PRICE: £4.75 (75cl)

COLOUR: Dark red with brown tints.

NOSE: Very strong buttery oak and fruit.

PALATE: Full-bodied, with velvety smooth texture and lovely balance of fruit/oak/acidity. Flavoursome lingering finish.

TASTE: D.   Excellent value for money.

ROSÉ WINE

WINE: **CÔTES DE PROVENCE ROSÉ (AC)**
COUNTRY: France
PRICE: £2.59 (75cl)
COLOUR: Pink amber.
NOSE: A delicate fruity fragrance.
PALATE: Light/medium-bodied, with soft delicate fruit flavour. Easy drinking style.
SWEETNESS: 2.   Very good value for money.

SPARKLING WINE

WINE: **PROSECCO**
COUNTRY: Italy
PRICE: £3.69 (75cl)
NOSE: Combination of vinous/fruity/stalky odours.
COLOUR: Pale straw.
PALATE: Medium-bodied, with slightly sweet fruity flavour. Soft creamy texture in the mouth. Good sparkling style for those who find Champagne too tart.
SWEETNESS: 5.   Value for money.

TESCO

WHITE WINES

WINE: **VINHO VERDE (RD)**
COUNTRY: Portugal.
PRICE: £2.19 (75cl)
COLOUR: Straw with green tints.
NOSE: Light, vinous bouquet.
PALATE: Light/medium-bodied with reasonable depth of fruit. Well balanced, with some spiciness and crisp acidity on the finish.
SWEETNESS: 2.   Value for money.

WINE: **DOMAINE D'ESCOUBES (VDP)**
SUPPLIER: Grassa
COUNTRY: France 1987
PRICE: £2.29 (75cl)
COLOUR: Pale straw.
NOSE: Excellent for a wine at this price; pleasant yeast characters and intense grassy fruit.
PALATE: Medium/full-bodied, yeasty and with very rounded fruit. Clean finish on a well-made wine.
SWEETNESS: 2.   Excellent value for money.

WINE: **ZELLAR SCHWARZEKATZ**
       Qualitätswein Mosel
COUNTRY: Germany 1987
PRICE: £2.39 (75cl)
COLOUR: Very pale straw.

NOSE: Floral and fruity.
PALATE: Light/medium-bodied, with good appleish fruit, crisp acidity and good length.
SWEETNESS: 4. Value for money.

WINE: **BIANCO DI CUSTOZA (DOC)**
COUNTRY: Italy
PRICE: £2.49 (75cl)
COLOUR: Pale straw.
NOSE: Very aromatic, with pleasant combination of fruit and vinosity.
PALATE: Light/medium-bodied and rounded, with floral flavour and a crisp finish.
SWEETNESS: 2. Value for money.

WINE: **SILVANER Qualitätswein Rheinpfalz**
COUNTRY: Germany
PRICE: £2.49 (70cl)
COLOUR: Pale straw with green tinges.
NOSE: Intense Sylvaner fruit.
PALATE: Medium-bodied, with good depth of fruit and a clean finish. Well made.
SWEETNESS: 4.

WINE: **SOAVE CLASSICO (DOC)**
COUNTRY: Italy 1986
PRICE: £2.69 (70cl)
COLOUR: Pale straw with green tinges.
NOSE: Vinous with underlying fruit.

PALATE: Medium-bodied, rounded and fruity with faint almond flavour. Very clean finish.

SWEETNESS: 2.   Value for money.

WINE: **VERDICCHIO CLASSICO (DOC)**
COUNTRY: Italy
PRICE: £2.75 (75cl)
COLOUR: Straw with green tinges.
NOSE: Very attractive, lifted fruit and some stalkiness.
PALATE: Light/medium-bodied, with good balance of fruit and acidity. Finish is clean and persistent.
SWEETNESS: 2.   Value for money.

WINE: **RHINE RIESLING Padthaway**
COUNTRY: Australia
PRICE: £2.99 (75cl)
COLOUR: Straw with green tints.
NOSE: Good intensity of the aroma of the Riesling grape, which is very fruity.
PALATE: Medium/full-bodied, with very flavoursome fruit and tangy acid on the finish.
SWEETNESS: 4.   Very good value for money.

WINE: **WILTINGER SCHARZBERG Kabinett (QMP) Mosel**
COUNTRY: Germany 1983
PRICE: £2.99 (75cl)
COLOUR: Pale straw.
NOSE: Very aromatic with intense fruity Riesling bouquet.

PALATE: Medium-bodied, with intense Riesling fruit and bottle-age development.

SWEETNESS: 4.   Excellent value for money.

WINE: **PINOT GRIGIO (DOC)**
SUPPLIER: Tiefenbrunner
COUNTRY: Italy 1986
PRICE: £3.25 (70cl)
COLOUR: Pale straw.
NOSE: Delicate vinous/fruit bouquet.
PALATE: Medium-bodied, soft, rounded and fruity. Good finish.
SWEETNESS: 2.   Value for money.

WINE: **COOKS CHARDONNAY**
COUNTRY: New Zealand 1987
PRICE: £3.49 (75cl)
COLOUR: Deep straw with green tints.
NOSE: Complex peach, fruit salad aroma enhanced by oak.
PALATE: Full-bodied, with excellent peach fruit flavour and well-integrated oak. Crisp finish.
SWEETNESS: 2.   Excellent value for money.

WINE: **CHARDONNAY Padthaway**
COUNTRY: Australia
PRICE: £3.69 (75cl)
COLOUR: Deep straw with green tints.
NOSE: Very attractive combination of fruit and oak aromas.

PALATE: Full-bodied, with mouth-filling fruity flavour. Soft texture and tasty oak flavours result in a pleasant aftertaste.

SWEETNESS: 2.   Very good value for money.

WINE: **LUGANA (DOC)**
SUPPLIER: Figli
COUNTRY: Italy 1986
PRICE: £3.99 (75cl)
COLOUR: Straw.
NOSE: Very grapey. More aromatic than many Italian white-wine styles.
PALATE: Full-bodied, with delicate but mouth-filling fruit and a crisp finish.

SWEETNESS: 2.   Good value for money.

WINE: **BINGER SCHARLACHBERG RIESLING (QMP) Rheinhessen Kabinett Trocken**
COUNTRY: Germany 1986
PRICE: £4.39 (75cl)
COLOUR: Straw with green tints.
NOSE: Very attractive, with good intensity of fruit.
PALATE: Medium-bodied, with pleasant fruitiness and a crisp finish.

SWEETNESS: 4.

RED WINES

WINE: **SICILIAN RED WINE.**
COUNTRY: Italy
PRICE: £1.99 (75cl)
COLOUR: Red with purple tints.

NOSE:	Unusual, but quite attractive. Has a faint butterscotch/boiled-sweet bouquet.
PALATE:	Light/medium-bodied, with soft, sweet, fruity flavour. Good easy drinking party wine.
TASTE:	A. Value for money.

WINE:	**CORBIÈRES (AC)**
COUNTRY:	France
PRICE:	£2.19 (70cl)
COLOUR:	Deep red/ruby.
NOSE:	Light fruit with some stalkiness.
PALATE:	Medium/full-bodied, with reasonable fruit and high acidity and tannin.
TASTE:	C. Value for money.

WINE:	**CÔTES DU RHÔNE (AC)**
COUNTRY:	France
PRICE:	£2.39 (70cl)
COLOUR:	Red/brown.
NOSE:	Good depth of slightly raisined fruit and some vinegar character which lifts the fruit.
PALATE:	Full-bodied, well rounded with pleasing fruitiness.
TASTE:	C. Good value for money.

WINE:	**BAIRRADA**
COUNTRY:	Portugal 1982
PRICE:	£2.39 (70cl)
COLOUR:	Red/brown.
NOSE:	Attractive bouquet with floral fruitiness and strong oak.

PALATE: Full-bodied, with strong oak and tarry fruit flavours uplifted by slight vinegar flavour. Finish is persistent and tannic.

TASTE: D.   Very good value for money.

WINE: **DOMAINE DES BAUMELLES Luberon**
COUNTRY: France 1987
PRICE: £2.69 (75cl)
COLOUR: Ruby red.
NOSE: Intense floral/crushed flower bouquet.
PALATE: Medium/full-bodied, again with floral, fruity flavours. Unusual, interesting style of wine which should promote the odd debate around the dining table.

TASTE: B.   Value for money.

WINE: **CHIANTI CLASSICO (DOCG)**
COUNTRY: Italy 1986
PRICE: £2.89 (70cl)
NOSE: Strong smell of violets.
PALATE: Medium/full-bodied, with good fruit and strong oak flavours. Lingering aftertaste. Lighter than many Classicos but represents excellent value.

TASTE: D.   Excellent value for money.

WINE: **KAPELLENER KLOSTER LIEBFRAUENBERG DORNFELDER ROTWEIN (QBA) Trocken**
COUNTRY: Germany 1986
PRICE: £3.19 (75cl)
COLOUR: Red with purple tints.

NOSE: Light fragrant, fruity bouquet.

PALATE: Medium-bodied and very fruity with a hint of chalk coming through. Serve from a decanter and wait for the excuses from your friends when they try to guess its origins.

TASTE: A.   Value for money.

WINE: **CABERNET SAUVIGNON Padthaway**

COUNTRY: Australia

PRICE: £3.29 (75cl)

COLOUR: Red.

NOSE: Attractive bouquet of blackcurrant fruit and buttery oak.

PALATE: Full-bodied, soft and oaky with lovely fruit flavour and soft tannin. Agreeable finish.

TASTE: D.   Excellent value for money.

WINE: **TINTO VELHO**

SUPPLIER: Casa Agricola

COUNTRY: Portugal 1980

PRICE: £3.65 (75cl)

COLOUR: Deep red.

NOSE: Heavily raisined fruit aroma and appealing vanillan oak.

PALATE: Full-bodied, with raisined fruit flavour, strong tannin and slight astringency. Hints of crushed flowers come through on the finish. Good example of raisined fruit character.

TASTE: D.   Excellent value for money.

WINE:	**ROSSO CONERO (DOC)**
SUPPLIER:	Mario Marchetti
COUNTRY:	Italy 1982
PRICE:	£3.69 (75cl)
COLOUR:	Deep red/ruby.
NOSE:	Complex fruit and oak bouquet.
PALATE:	Full-bodied, smooth and richly flavoured with high tannic astringency. Oak flavour lingers on the finish. Good example of astringency in a wine.
TASTE:	D. Good value for money.

WINE:	**CH LÉON (AC) Premières Côtes de Bordeaux**
COUNTRY:	France 1985
PRICE:	£3.79 (75cl)
COLOUR:	Ruby/red.
NOSE:	Excellent, smelling strongly of the Cabernet Sauvignon grape and oak.
PALATE:	Full-bodied, showing the quality of the vintage. Balance of fruit/oak/acid is very good.
TASTE:	C. Excellent value for money.

WINE:	**BARBARESCO (DOC)**
COUNTRY:	Italy 1980
PRICE:	£4.59 (75cl)
COLOUR:	Dark red with brown tints.
NOSE:	Agreeable complexity of tarry, liquorice fruit and strong old oak.

| PALATE: | Full-bodied, rich and rounded. Forceful fruitiness is matched by high acidity and oak extract. Wine of character. |
| TASTE: | E. Excellent value for money. |

ROSÉ WINES

WINE:	**SPANISH ROSÉ (DO)**
COUNTRY:	Spain
PRICE:	£1.85 (75cl)
COLOUR:	Pink/amber.
NOSE:	Reasonable fruit and slight stalkiness.
PALATE:	Light/medium-bodied, with good depth of fruit.
SWEETNESS:	3. Very good value for money.

WINE:	**ROSÉ FRIZZANTE**
COUNTRY:	Italy
PRICE:	£2.15 (70cl)
COLOUR:	Pink/amber. Sparkling.
NOSE:	Very spicy, herbal fruit.
PALATE:	Light/medium-bodied with spicy fruit and a clean finish. Well made.
SWEETNESS:	7. Good value for money.

SPARKLING WINES

WINE:	**MOSCATO SPUMANTE**
COUNTRY:	Italy
PRICE:	£2.79 (70cl)
COLOUR:	Pale straw.

NOSE: Concentrated Muscat grapes. Muscat wines smell very grapey.

PALATE: Medium-bodied, soft and sweet, with strong grape flavour. Finish is crisp and flavoursome.

SWEETNESS: 6.   Good value for money.

WINE: **SPARKLING LIEBFRAUMILCH**
COUNTRY: Germany
PRICE: £3.09 (75cl)
COLOUR: Pale straw with green tints.
NOSE: Light, lifted fruit.
PALATE: Light/medium-bodied, with soft, fruity flavour and a crisp, clean finish. Well-made sparkling wine.
SWEETNESS: 5.

WINE: **CRÉMANT DE LOIRE (AC) Villeneuve**
COUNTRY: France
PRICE: £4.99 (75cl)
COLOUR: Rose/pink/amber.
NOSE: Pleasantly vinous, and with some stalkiness.
PALATE: Medium-bodied, vinous and stalky with good acidity and clean finish.
SWEETNESS: 3.

THRESHER

WHITE WINES

WINE:	**CAMPAGNARD BLANC DE BLANCS (VDP)**
SUPPLIER:	L'Estagnon
COUNTRY:	France
PRICE:	£1.99 (70cl)
COLOUR:	Straw.
NOSE:	Vinous with underlying stalky fruit.
PALATE:	Medium-bodied, fruity and mouthfilling with good balance. Pleasant finish.
SWEETNESS:	2.

WINE:	**CHARDONNAY DEL COLLE (VDT)**
COUNTRY:	Italy
PRICE:	£2.59 (75cl)
COLOUR:	Pale/mid straw.
NOSE:	Pleasant Chardonnay fruit aromas.
PALATE:	Medium/full-bodied, very soft and pleasantly fruity with a soft finish.
SWEETNESS:	2. Good value for money.

WINE:	**CORBIÈRES BLANC DE BLANCS (AC)**
SUPPLIER:	L'Estagnon
COUNTRY:	France 1987
PRICE:	£2.59 (70cl)
COLOUR:	Pale straw
NOSE:	Very strong stalky character.

PALATE: Medium-bodied with light, delicate fruit and some grassy/stalky flavours on the finish.

SWEETNESS: 2.   Value for money.

WINE: **CHARDONNAY KHAN KRUM RESERVE**

COUNTRY: Bulgaria 1985
PRICE: £2.69 (70cl)
COLOUR: Straw.
NOSE: Exhibits excellent oak and fruit aromas for a wine at this price.
PALATE: Full-bodied, very soft, with peach fruit and oak flavour of some complexity. Crisp oaky finish.
SWEETNESS: 2.   Excellent value for money.

WINE: **DOMAINE DU TARIQUET**

SUPPLIER: Grassa
COUNTRY: France 1987
PRICE: £2.85 (70cl)
COLOUR: Pale/mid straw.
NOSE: Attractive tropical fruits character.
PALATE: Medium-bodied with very pleasant mouth-filling fruity flavour. Crisp, fresh finish.
SWEETNESS: 2.   Very good value for money.

WINE: **CH DU FONGRAVES (AC)**

SUPPLIER: Gornac
COUNTRY: France
PRICE: £3.65 (75cl)
COLOUR: Pale/mid straw.
NOSE: Light vinous bouquet with some grassy character.

PALATE: Medium-bodied, vinous with underlying fruit flavour and a crisp finish.

SWEETNESS: 1.

WINE: **RAIMAT CHARDONNAY**
COUNTRY: Spain 1987
PRICE: £3.99 (75cl)
COLOUR: Straw.
NOSE: Complex fruity bouquet with vanillan overtones.
PALATE: Full-bodied, with pleasant mouth-filling fruity flavour. Good Chardonnay fruit flavour on the finish.
SWEETNESS: 2.   Very good value for money.

WINE: **PENFOLDS SEMILLON/CHARDONNAY**
COUNTRY: Australia 1985
PRICE: £4.29 (75cl)
COLOUR: Straw with green tints.
NOSE: Intense, complex fruity bouquet. Both varieties well matched in terms of intensity of aroma.
PALATE: Full-bodied, very fruity and flavoursome with a crisp finish of some complexity. Good style.
SWEETNESS: 2.   Good value for money.

WINE: **TOCAI ZENATO (DOC)**
COUNTRY: Italy 1987
PRICE: £4.29 (75cl)
COLOUR: Pale/mid straw.
NOSE: Attractive bouquet, honeyed fruit.

PALATE: Full-bodied, very rounded with slightly honeyed fruit flavour and a crisp finish.

SWEETNESS: 2.

RED WINES

WINE: **CAMPAGNARD ROUGE (VDP)**
SUPPLIER: L'Estagnon
PRICE: £1.99 (70cl)
COLOUR: Red with blue tints.
NOSE: Fruity bouquet with strong stalky character.
PALATE: Medium-bodied, light, fruity and crisp with
good tannin.
TASTE: A.   Value for money.

WINE: **BULGARIAN CABERNET SAUVIGNON**
SUPPLIER: Vinimpex
COUNTRY: Bulgaria 1984
PRICE: £2.29 (75cl)
COLOUR: Red with brown tints.
NOSE: Intense ripe, raisined fruit and oak.
PALATE: Full-bodied, with rich, raisined fruit and soft
tannins. Finish is oaky and lingering.
TASTE: C.   Excellent value for money.

WINE: **CÔTES DU RHÔNE (AC)**
COUNTRY: France
PRICE: £2.59 (70cl)
COLOUR: Red.
NOSE: Light, delicately spicy bouquet.

PALATE:	Full-bodied, with firm tannin and spicy/peppery fruit flavour. Persistent finish.
TASTE:	C. Good value for money.

WINE:	**FAUGÈRES (AC)**
SUPPLIER:	L'Estagnon
COUNTRY:	France 1986
PRICE:	£2.59 (70cl)
COLOUR:	Red.
NOSE:	Attractive stalky fruit.
PALATE:	Full-bodied, robust with firm tannin and high acidity.
TASTE:	C. Good value for money.

WINE:	**ORIAHOVITZA CABERNET SAUVIGNON**
SUPPLIER:	Vinimpex
COUNTRY:	Bulgaria 1980
PRICE:	£2.69 (70cl)
COLOUR:	Red/brown.
NOSE:	Complex bouquet of buttery oak and ripe Cabernet Sauvignon fruit aromas.
PALATE:	Full-bodied, soft and rounded with ripe fruit and strong oak flavour. Very lingering, full finish.
TASTE:	C. Excellent value for money.

WINE:	**DOM ST EULALIE MINERVOIS (AC)**
COUNTRY:	France 1986
PRICE:	£2.99 (70cl)
COLOUR:	Ruby red.
NOSE:	Bouquet of rich, ripe, raisined fruit.

PALATE: Full-bodied, very soft, smooth and rounded. Flavoursome peppery finish.

TASTE: C.   Very good value for money.

WINE: **BAIRRADA (RD)**
SUPPLIER: Mealhada
COUNTRY: Portugal 1984
PRICE: £2.99 (75cl)
COLOUR: Red with brown tints.
NOSE: Very intense spicy, raisined fruit.
PALATE: Full-bodied, with strong oak and ripe fruit flavour. High acidity on an astringent finish.
TASTE: D.   Very good value for money.

WINE: **CH LA GORDONNE (AC)**
SUPPLIER: Pierrefeu
COUNTRY: France 1987
PRICE: £2.99 (75cl)
COLOUR: Dark red.
NOSE: Attractive fruity aromas and some stalkiness.
PALATE: Full-bodied and robust, with rounded fruit flavour and soft tannin. Full, flavoursome finish with slight astringency.
TASTE: D.   Excellent value for money.

WINE: **CH MONICHOT (AC)**
SUPPLIER: Grillet
COUNTRY: France 1983
PRICE: £3.95 (75cl)
COLOUR: Red.
NOSE: Intense, attractive fruity bouquet, reflecting the quality of the vintage.

PALATE:	Full-bodied, with rich, ripe Cabernet flavour and balanced oak. Lingering pleasant finish.
TASTE:	C. Very good value for money.

WINE: BEAUJOLAIS-VILLAGES

SUPPLIER:	Duboeuf
COUNTRY:	France 1987
PRICE:	£3.99 (75cl)
COLOUR:	Light red with blue tints.
NOSE:	Exhibits well the lively aromas of the Gamay grape.
PALATE:	Light/medium-bodied, with delicate, fruity flavour and excellent balance.
TASTE:	B. Very good value for money.

WINE: TRES TORRES SANGREDETORO

COUNTRY:	Spain 1984
PRICE:	£3.99 (70cl)
COLOUR:	Red/ruby.
NOSE:	Intense ripe, fruity bouquet.
PALATE:	Full-bodied, velvety smooth with soft tannins and a very crisp astringent finish.
TASTE:	D. Good value for money.

WINE: WYNNS SHIRAZ

COUNTRY:	Australia 1985
PRICE:	£4.09 (75cl)
COLOUR:	Red/ruby.
NOSE:	Complex peppery fruit/oak bouquet.
PALATE:	Full-bodied, soft with mouth-filling jammy/berry flavours. Finish is oaky and flavoursome

with firm tannin. Worth cellaring for 12-24+ months.

TASTE:	E.	Very good value for money.

WINE: **PENFOLDS KOONUNGA HILL**
COUNTRY: Australia 1985
PRICE: £4.29 (75cl)
COLOUR: Red.
NOSE: Complex, with a bouquet of buttery oak and rich fruit aromas.
PALATE: Full-bodied, velvety smooth with rich fruit flavours enhanced by lovely oak. A robust wine with a crisp, flavoursome, slightly astringent finish.
TASTE: E.   Excellent value for money.

WINE: **MONDAVI CABERNET SAUVIGNON**
COUNTRY: California 1985
PRICE: £4.55 (75cl)
COLOUR: Red/ruby.
NOSE: Excellent intensity of the stalky/berry aromas found in well-made Cabernet Sauvignon wines.
PALATE: Full-bodied, with intense, spicy blackcurrant fruit which has been aged in oak. Finish is crisp and astringent. Cellaring potential 12–24+ months.
TASTE: D.   Excellent value for money.

WINE: **BOURGOGNE PINOT NOIR (AC)**
COUNTRY: France 1985
PRICE: £4.75 (75cl)
COLOUR: Light/mid red with brown tints.

NOSE:	Strong aroma of the Pinot Noir grape and oak.
PALATE:	Medium/full-bodied, with strong oak flavour and subtle strawberry/raspberry fruit flavour in good balance. Good tannin and some astringency on the finish. Cellaring potential 12-24 months.
TASTE:	B. Value for money.

WINE:	**CALVET RESERVE (AC)**
SUPPLIER:	Calvet
COUNTRY:	France 1983
PRICE:	£4.85 (75cl)
COLOUR:	Red/brown.
NOSE:	Attractive, with rich, ripe fruit aromas. Some bottle-aged development is evident, adding to complexity.
PALATE:	Medium/full-bodied, soft and rounded with pleasant fruit and oak flavour. Soft tannin on the finish.
TASTE:	C. Good value for money.

ROSÉ WINE

WINE:	**LAMBRUSCO BLUSH**
COUNTRY:	Italy
PRICE:	£1.99 (70cl)
COLOUR:	Pale pink/pastel.
NOSE:	Strong appleish bouquet.
PALATE:	Light/medium-bodied, with crisp appleish flavour.
SWEETNESS:	6. Value for money.

UNWINS

WHITE WINES

WINE: **BLANC DE BLANCS Vin de Table**
SUPPLIER: P. Montmorin
COUNTRY: France
PRICE: £1.99 (70cl)
COLOUR: Pale straw.
NOSE: Vinous with underlying fruit.
PALATE: Light, soft, with delicate fruit and a touch of sweetness.
SWEETNESS: 2.

WINE: **TAFELWEIN Furstenberg**
PRICE: £1.99 (70cl)
COLOUR: Straw.
NOSE: Attractive, light, fruity bouquet.
PALATE: Light and clean with reasonable depth of fruit.
SWEETNESS: 5.

WINE: **BULGARIAN RIESLING**
SUPPLIER: Vinimpex Sofia
COUNTRY: Bulgaria
PRICE: £2.39 (70cl)
COLOUR: Mid/dark straw.
NOSE: Attractive Riesling grape aroma and some stalkiness.

PALATE: Medium-bodied, fruity, with good acidity. Reasonable quaffing wine.

SWEETNESS: 4.

WINE: **LIEBFRAUMILCH Rheinhessen Qualitätswein**

COUNTRY: Germany 1986

PRICE: £2.39 (75cl)

COLOUR: Pale straw.

NOSE: Very attractive fruity bouquet.

PALATE: Light, medium sweet, with clean fruit and balanced acidity. Very pleasant quaffing wine.

SWEETNESS: 5.   Good value for money.

WINE: **ANJOU BLANC (AC)**

SUPPLIER: Les Vins du Val De Loire

COUNTRY: France 1986

PRICE: £2.49 (70cl)

COLOUR: Straw.

NOSE: Vinous, with some underlying fruit.

PALATE: Medium/full-bodied, with delicate fruit and crisp acidity. Finish is fruity and lingering.

SWEETNESS: 3.

WINE: **CHÂTEAU CARLASSE (AC) Bordeaux**

SUPPLIER: Y. Mau

COUNTRY: France 1986

PRICE: £2.79 (75cl)

COLOUR: Pale straw with slight pétillance.

NOSE: Light, grassy, fruity bouquet.

PALATE: Pleasantly rounded with good balance of fruit and acidity and a clean finish. An inexpensive white most will enjoy.

SWEETNESS: 1. Good value for money.

WINE: **MUSCADET DE SÈVRE ET MAINE SUR LIE Domaine du Cleray**
COUNTRY: France 1986
PRICE: £3.49 (75cl)
COLOUR: Deep straw.
NOSE: Good depth of fruit and some yeast character from time spent *sur lie* (on yeast lees).
PALATE: Full-bodied, fruity and crisp, with good length and a fruity finish. Well-made wine.
SWEETNESS: 1. Good value for money.

WINE: **JOÃO PIRES MOSCATO**
COUNTRY: Portugal 1987
PRICE: £3.95 (75cl)
COLOUR: Straw.
NOSE: Very intense bouquet of Muscat fruit.
PALATE: Medium-bodied, with strong Muscat fruit flavour, crisp acidity and lingering finish.
SWEETNESS: 4.

WINE: **MÂCON SUPÉRIEUR (AC)**
SUPPLIER: E. Loren
COUNTRY: France 1986
PRICE: £4.45 (75cl)
COLOUR: Straw/golden.
NOSE: Pleasant bouquet of fruit and oak.

PALATE: Medium/full-bodied, oaky, with balanced acidity and reasonable depth of finish.

SWEETNESS: 2.

WINE: **VOUVRAY, CHÂTEAU MONTCONTOUR CB**
COUNTRY: France 1985
PRICE: £4.49 (75cl)
COLOUR: Straw
NOSE: Good depth of delicate Chenin Blanc fruit aromas.
PALATE: Medium/full-bodied, with very attractive Chenin Blanc fruit flavour and well-balanced acidity. Well-made wine.

SWEETNESS: 5.   Value for money.

RED WINES

WINE: **ROUGE DE FRANCE Vin de Table**
SUPPLIER: P. Montmorin
COUNTRY: France
PRICE: £1.99 (70cl)
COLOUR: Red.
NOSE: Earthy/jammy fruity bouquet with a touch of spice.
PALATE: Light/medium-bodied, with spicy fruit flavour and a fruity, lingering finish. Very pleasant, easy drinking style.

TASTE: A.   Value for money.

WINE: **CORBIÈRES (AC)**
SUPPLIER: Trois Couronnes
COUNTRY: France 1986

PRICE:	£2.35 (75cl)
COLOUR:	Deep red with purple tinges.
NOSE:	Attractive, jammy/fruit bouquet.
PALATE:	Medium-bodied, soft and rounded, with good depth of fruit. Long, lingering finish for an inexpensive wine.
TASTE:	C. Excellent value for money.

WINE:	**CÔTES DU ROUSSILLON (AC)**
SUPPLIER:	Felix Laquebrou
COUNTRY:	France 1986
PRICE:	£2.59 (70cl)
COLOUR:	Deep red with purple tinges.
NOSE:	Lively, earthy/fruity bouquet.
PALATE:	Medium-bodied, with good fruit flavour and acidity.
TASTE:	B. Good value for money.

WINE:	**CÔTES-DU-RHÔNE (AC)**
SUPPLIER:	Louis Mousset
COUNTRY:	France 1986
PRICE:	£2.65 (70cl)
COLOUR:	Red.
NOSE:	Pleasant bouquet of spicy fruit.
PALATE:	Light/medium-bodied, with attractive fruit flavour and balanced acidity. Finish is clean and persistent.
TASTE:	C. Good value for money.

WINE:	**CHÂTEAU DE MONJAN (AC) Coteaux du Languedoc**
COUNTRY:	France 1986

PRICE: £2.89 (70cl)
NOSE: Jammy fruit with a hint of stalkiness.
PALATE: Medium-bodied, with good balance of fruit, acid, tannin and oak.
TASTE: B.   Good value for money.

WINE: **CLARET (AC) Bordeaux Supérieur**
SUPPLIER: Y. Mau
COUNTRY: France 1986
PRICE: £2.99 (75cl)
NOSE: Light fruit and some stalkiness
PALATE: Medium/full-bodied, with adequate fruit and tannin. Good quaffing wine at this price.
TASTE: C.   Value for money

WINE: **CAHORS (AC) Les Côtes d'Olt**
COUNTRY: France 1983
PRICE: £3.15 (70cl)
COLOUR: Dark red.
NOSE: Dominated by intense, spicy/cinnamon fruitiness.
PALATE: Medium-bodied, with balanced fruit and acidity; finish has pleasant tannic astringency. Less tannic than many Cahors wines, resulting in a more elegant style. Good now, but a further 12-24 months would be well rewarded.
TASTE: C.   Good value for money.

WINE: **CHIANTI CLASSICO (DOCG)**
SUPPLIER: Fattoria Santedame
COUNTRY: Italy 1985
PRICE: £3.49 (70cl)

COLOUR: Dark red.

NOSE: Fruity/earthy bouquet with slight vinegar character.

PALATE: Medium/full-bodied, well balanced with crisp acidity and tannic astringency. Reasonable length of finish. Cellaring for up to 2 years would be beneficial.

TASTE: D.　　　　　　　　Good value for money.

WINE: **CHÂTEAU LA CHATAIGNÈRE**
Bordeaux Supérieur

COUNTRY: France 1985

PRICE: £3.79 (75cl)

COLOUR: Dark red with purple tinges.

NOSE: Fruity with well-integrated oak aroma.

PALATE: Full-bodied, very fruity with good depth of fruit/vegetable flavours. A tannic wine with a persistent finish. Inexpensive wine which may surprise after 18-24 months cellaring.

TASTE: C.　　　　　　　　Good value for money.

WINE: **DOMAINE DE SEGONZAC Premières**
Côtes De Blaye (AC)

COUNTRY: France 1985

PRICE: £3.99 (75cl)

COLOUR: Dark red with purple tinges.

NOSE: Very attractive, with good depth of fruity aromas.

PALATE:	Medium-bodied, with good balance of rich fruit and tannin. Overall, a well-structured wine ready for drinking.
TASTE:	C. Value for money.

WINE:	**CROZES-HERMITAGE (AC)**
SUPPLIER:	Louis Mousset
COUNTRY:	France 1986
PRICE:	£4.19 (75cl)
COLOUR:	Dark red.
NOSE:	Strong bouquet of agreeably spicy fruit.
PALATE:	Medium/full-bodied with adequate spicy, Syrah fruit. Good price for Crozes-Hermitage.
TASTE:	D. Good value for money.

WINE:	**BOURGOGNE (AC) Tastevin**
SUPPLIER:	A. Bichot & Cie
COUNTRY:	France 1984
PRICE:	£4.65 (75cl)
COLOUR:	Light red.
NOSE:	Excellent depth of attractive Pinot Noir fruit aroma and a pleasant earthy character.
PALATE:	Medium-bodied, with balanced fruit flavour, acid and oak. Finish is fruity and persistent. It proves that good Burgundy can be bought for under £5 and that the better producers can make quality wine in poorer vintages.
TASTE:	B. Excellent value for money.

WINE:	**CHÂTEAU LES DEUX MOULINS (AC) Médoc**
COUNTRY:	France 1985

PRICE:	£4.65 (75cl)
COLOUR:	Dark red.
NOSE:	Good depth of attractive Cabernet fruit and oak aromas.
PALATE:	Full-bodied with good, fruity flavour and pleasant tannic astringency.
TASTE:	D. Excellent value for money.

WINE:	**CHÂTEAU LA ROSÉ ST SAUVER (AC) Haut-Médoc**
COUNTRY:	France 1983
PRICE:	£4.79 (75cl)
COLOUR:	Dark red.
NOSE:	Excellent bouquet of complex Cabernet fruit and oak, with a touch of stalkiness which adds complexity.
PALATE:	Full-bodied, rich and very complex for a claret at this price. Well-made wine from a good year. Some crystals are present in it; decant to remove them.
TASTE:	D. Excellent value for money.

WINE:	**GIGONDAS (AC)**
SUPPLIER:	Louis Mousset
COUNTRY:	France 1986
PRICE:	£4.99 (75cl)
COLOUR:	Deep red.
NOSE:	Complex, with lifted, rich, spicy fruit and some stalkiness.

PALATE: Full-bodied, with strong, peppery fruit. A well-balanced wine with a long, fruity finish. Would improve with 18-24 months cellaring.

TASTE: D.   Excellent value for money.

ROSÉ WINES

WINE: **ROSÉ DE FRANCE Vin de Table**
SUPPLIER: P. Montmorin.
COUNTRY: France.
PRICE: £1.99 (70cl)
COLOUR: Pink/amber
NOSE: Vinous
PALATE: Light, dry vinous with a touch of spicy fruit flavour.
SWEETNESS: 4.   Value for money.

WINE: **ROSÉ D'ANJOU**
SUPPLIER: P. Montmorin
COUNTRY: France 1986
PRICE: £2.49 (70cl)
COLOUR: Pink/amber.
NOSE: Vinous and stalky.
PALATE: Light/medium-bodied, with delicate fruit and a touch of sweetness.

VICTORIA WINE

WHITE WINE

WINE: **GEWÜRZTRAMINER FRUSKA GORA**
COUNTRY: Yugoslavia
PRICE: £2.19 (70cl)
COLOUR: Straw.
NOSE: Attractive bouquet of spicy Gewürztraminer fruit.
PALATE: Light in body, with strong spicy fruit flavour. Easy drinking style.
SWEETNESS: 4.   Good value for money.

WINE: **VINHO VERDE GATÃO (DO)**
SUPPLIER: B & I
COUNTRY: Portugal
PRICE: £2.59 (70cl)
COLOUR: Straw. Very slightly sparkling.
NOSE: Vinous with underlying fruit/stalky character.
PALATE: Light/medium-bodied, with delicate fruit flavour. Lingering finish.
SWEETNESS: 4.   Value for money.

WINE: **BECHTHEIMER PILGERPFAD KERNER KABINETT (QMP)**
SUPPLIER: Egberts
COUNTRY: Germany 1987
PRICE: £2.89 (70cl)
COLOUR: Straw.
NOSE: Excellent floral, fruity bouquet.

PALATE: Medium-bodied, soft and very fruity with well balanced acidity. Good wine style.

SWEETNESS: 4.   Very good value for money.

WINE: **WHITE BURGUNDY (AC)**
COUNTRY: France 1986
PRICE: £3.79 (70cl)
COLOUR: Straw.
NOSE: Very attractive honeyed fruit bouquet.
PALATE: Medium/full-bodied, with good depth of fruit flavour and strong honeyed character. Well-made wine.

SWEETNESS: 2.   Very good value for money.

WINE: **CHARDONNAY TRENTINO (DOC)**
SUPPLIER: Cavit
COUNTRY: Italy 1987
PRICE: £3.79 (75cl)
COLOUR: Pale straw.
NOSE: Very stalky with underlying fruit aromas.
PALATE: Medium/full-bodied, rounded, with very attractive Chardonnay fruit flavour. Hint of oak on the finish.

SWEETNESS: 2.   Good value for money.

WINE: **MILDARA CHARDONNAY**
SUPPLIER: Church Hill
COUNTRY: Australia 1987
PRICE: £3.99 (75cl)
COLOUR: Mid/deep straw with green tints.
NOSE: Very woody, with peach, fruit salad bouquet.

PALATE: Medium/full-bodied, with strong oak and fruit salad flavours. High acidity.

SWEETNESS: 2.   Value for money.

WINE: **CRANMORE, ISLE OF WIGHT WINE**
COUNTRY: England 1984
PRICE: £3.49 (70cl)
COLOUR: Pale/mid straw.
NOSE: Attractive floral/fruity bouquet.
PALATE: Medium-bodied, crisp, with pleasant fruit flavour and high acidity.
SWEETNESS: 2.

WINE: **MUSCADET DE SÈVRE ET MAINE**
SUPPLIER: Poiron
COUNTRY: France 1987
PRICE: £3.85 (75cl)
COLOUR: Pale straw with green tints.
NOSE: Strong bouquet of chalky/Muscadet fruit.
PALATE: Medium-bodied, with good depth of flavour of the Muscadet grape. Very crisp finish.
SWEETNESS: 1.

WINE: **CARR TAYLOR, DRY ENGLISH WINE**
COUNTRY: England 1986
PRICE: £4.49 (70cl)
COLOUR: Pale straw with green tints.
NOSE: Fruity/floral bouquet.
PALATE: Medium-bodied, fresh and very fruity. Easy drinking style with a very crisp finish.
SWEETNESS: 2.

WINE:	**MONDAVI SAUVIGNON BLANC**
COUNTRY:	California 1986
PRICE:	£4.25 (75cl)
COLOUR:	Straw.
NOSE:	Attractive grassy/Sauvignon Blanc bouquet with subtle oak character.
PALATE:	Full-bodied, with excellent depth of fruity flavour enhanced by a hint of oak. Well-balanced wine.
SWEETNESS: 2.	Good value for money.

RED WINES

WINE:	**VALPOLICELLA (DOC)**
COUNTRY:	Italy
PRICE:	£1.99 (70cl)
COLOUR:	Light red.
NOSE:	Spicy, fruity bouquet.
PALATE:	Light in body, with good fruit flavour and a crisp finish.
TASTE: B.	Good value for money.

WINE:	**YUGOSLAV CABERNET SAUVIGNON**
COUNTRY:	Yugoslavia
PRICE:	£2.19 (70cl)
COLOUR:	Dark red with blue tints.
NOSE:	Very rich, ripe/raisined fruit bouquet.
PALATE:	Medium-bodied, with ripe/raisined fruit flavour and a hint of oak on the finish.
TASTE: D.	Good value for money.

WINE:	**LE PAS DU MEUNIER CÔTES DU RHÔNE (AC)**
SUPPLIER:	Coulon
COUNTRY:	France 1985
PRICE:	£3.49 (75cl)
COLOUR:	Dark red with blue tints.
NOSE:	Very spicy/fruity bouquet.
PALATE:	Full-bodied, with spicy flavours and a slightly astringent finish.
TASTE:	C. Value for money.

WINE:	**CHIANTI CLASSICO SANTA CRISTINA (DOCG)**
SUPPLIER:	Antinori
COUNTRY:	Italy 1986
PRICE:	£3.59 (75cl)
COLOUR:	Dark red with blue tints.
NOSE:	Excellent spicy/tarry fruit and oak aromas.
PALATE:	Full-bodied, rich and robust, very flavoursome with firm tannin and a slightly astringent finish.
TASTE:	D. Excellent value for money.

WINE:	**RED BURGUNDY (AC)**
COUNTRY:	France 1985
PRICE:	£3.79 (70cl)
COLOUR:	Red.
NOSE:	Ripe, fruity bouquet.
PALATE:	Medium-bodied, with attractive fruit and some oak flavours. Very crisp finish.
TASTE:	B.

WINE:	**MARQUES DE RISCAL RIOJA RESERVA (DO)**
COUNTRY:	Spain 1983
PRICE:	£4.29 (75cl)
COLOUR:	Dark red with brown tints.
NOSE:	Very oaky with a strong aroma of crushed flowers.
PALATE:	Full-bodied, with warm, fruity flavour. Firm tannin and an astringent finish.
TASTE:	D.

WINE:	**ORIAHOVITZA CABERNET SAUVIGNON**
SUPPLIER:	Vinimpex
COUNTRY:	Bulgaria 1981
PRICE:	£2.69 (70cl)
COLOUR:	Red/brown.
NOSE:	Has excellent bouquet of vanillan oak and strong Ribena-blackcurrant Cabernet Sauvignon character.
PALATE:	Full-bodied, very oaky, with ripe fruity flavour and good balance.
TASTE:	C. Excellent value for money.

WINE:	**TINTO DA ANFORA**
SUPPLIER:	Pires
COUNTRY:	Portugal 1982
PRICE:	£4.49 (75cl)
COLOUR:	Dark red with brown tints.
NOSE:	Very earthy, with tarry fruit and strong oak character.

178

PALATE:	Full-bodied, with rich, ripe, earthy/fruity flavours and strong oak. Finish is oaky, with firm tannin and raisined fruit flavour.
TASTE:	D.

WINE:	**WYNNS OVENS VALLEY SHIRAZ**
COUNTRY:	Australia 1984
PRICE:	£4.49 (75cl)
COLOUR:	Dark red.
NOSE:	Strong bouquet of ripe, raisined fruit and oak.
PALATE:	Full-bodied, smooth with good depth of pleasant fruit and oak flavour.
TASTE:	E.

WINE:	**TORRES GRAN SANGREDETORO RESERVA.**
COUNTRY:	Spain 1984
PRICE:	£4.79 (75cl)
COLOUR:	Dark red.
NOSE:	Excellent, complex bouquet of buttery/vanillan oak character with strong underlying fruit.
PALATE:	Full-bodied, very smooth, with excellent depth of fruit flavour. Good balance of fruit/oak/tannin. Warm, persistent finish.
TASTE:	D. Excellent value for money.

WINE:	**MONTANA CABERNET SAUVIGNON**
COUNTRY:	New Zealand 1986
PRICE:	£4.89 (75cl)
COLOUR:	Dark red.

NOSE:	Excellent intensity of complex chillies/green pepper aromas.
PALATE:	Full-bodied, with excellent depth of fruity flavour enhanced by oak maturation.
TASTE:	D. Very good value for money.

SPARKLING WINES

WINE:	**DE NEUVILLE SPARKLING SAUMUR (AC)**
COUNTRY:	France
PRICE:	£4.59 (75cl)
COLOUR:	Straw.
NOSE:	Attractive appleish/fruity bouquet.
PALATE:	Medium-bodied, with lovely soft, smooth texture. Slight appleish flavour and some attractive bottle-age development.
SWEETNESS:	2. Good value for money.

WINE:	**BLANC FOUSSY BRUT DE TOURAINE (AC)**
SUPPLIER:	St Roch
COUNTRY:	France 1984
PRICE:	£4.99 (75cl)
COLOUR:	Straw with green tints.
NOSE:	Attractive bouquet of honeyed fruit.
PALATE:	Medium-bodied, soft and creamy, with good depth of flavour. Well-balanced wine with a fruity finish.
TASTE:	A. Very good value for money.

WAITROSE

WHITE WINES

WINE: **DOMAINE DE PLANTERIEU VDP Gascogne**
COUNTRY: France 1987
PRICE: £2.35 (70cl)
COLOUR: Pale straw.
NOSE: Excellent, intense yeasty nose and has good depth of floral fruit
PALATE: Medium-bodied, very fruity, with a strong yeast character and a hint of sweetness on the finish.
SWEETNESS: 3.   Excellent value for money.

WINE: **RHEINHESSEN KABINETT**
COUNTRY: Germany 1985
PRICE: £2.69 (70cl)
COLOUR: Straw.
NOSE: Attractive floral, fruity bouquet.
PALATE: Medium/full-bodied, very fruity, rich and sweet.
SWEETNESS: 4.   Value for money.

WINE: **RHEINGAU KABINETT**
COUNTRY: Germay 1983
PRICE: £2.99 (70cl)
COLOUR: Straw.
NOSE: Intense fruity bouquet.

PALATE: Light and delicate, with good depth of flavour. Good German style.

SWEETNESS: 4.   Good value for money.

WINE: **HAUT POITOU SAUVIGNON (VDQS)**
COUNTRY: France 1987
PRICE: £2.99 (75cl)
COLOUR: Pale straw.
NOSE: Delicate grassy/Sauvignon Blanc fruit aroma.
PALATE: Light, with grassy fruit flavour and a crisp finish.

SWEETNESS: 1.   Value for money.

WINE: **SOAVE CLASSICO (DOC)**
SUPPLIER: Zenato
COUNTRY: Italy 1987
PRICE: £3.19 (75cl)
COLOUR: Straw.
NOSE: Very fruity bouquet.

PALATE: Medium-bodied and very fruity, with crisp acidity and a persistent finish.

SWEETNESS: 2.   Value for money.

WINE: **WINES OF ENGLAND, Moorlynch Somerset**
COUNTRY: England 1985
PRICE: £3.79 (75cl)
COLOUR: Pale straw.
NOSE: Very fruity/perfumed bouquet.
PALATE: Medium-bodied, sweet with light fruit and good acidity.

SWEETNESS: 4.

WINE:	**DOMAINE DU TARIQUET VDP Côtes de Gascogne**
COUNTRY:	France 1986
PRICE:	£3.99 (75cl)
COLOUR:	Straw.
NOSE:	Lovely, lively fruit bouquet.
PALATE:	Full-bodied, rounded and balanced. Lingering fruity finish.
SWEETNESS: 2.	Value for money.

WINE:	**MOUNTAIN VIEW CHARDONNAY**
COUNTRY:	California 1986
PRICE:	£3.99 (75cl)
COLOUR:	Straw.
NOSE:	Fruit salad/Chardonnay aroma and buttery oak character.
PALATE:	Medium/full-bodied, soft and rounded, with very good depth of Chardonnay fruit flavour.
SWEETNESS: 2.	Excellent value for money.

WINE:	**CHÂTEAU LOUPIAC (AC)**
SUPPLIER:	Gaudiet
COUNTRY:	France 1983
PRICE:	£4.55 (75cl)
COLOUR:	Dark straw/golden.
NOSE:	Very fruity.
PALATE:	Full-bodied, sweet, rich, with a lengthy, fruity finish.
SWEETNESS: 8.	Good value for money.

WINE:	**SANCERRE (AC) Domaine du Fort**
COUNTRY:	France 1986

PRICE:	£4.95 (75cl)
COLOUR:	Straw/dark straw.
NOSE:	Attractive bouquet of grassy/Sauvignon Blanc fruit.
PALATE:	Medium-bodied, soft and fruity, with some honeyed flavours on a crisp, clean, lengthy finish.
SWEETNESS: 1.	Good value for money.

RED WINES

WINE:	**CARAFE RED TABLE WINE Sardegna**
COUNTRY:	Italy
PRICE:	£2.59 (100cl)
COLOUR:	Red/brown.
NOSE:	Light fruity bouquet.
PALATE:	Medium-bodied, with good depth of fruit flavour and balanced acidity. Well made.
TASTE:	A. Value for money.

WINE:	**CASTILLO DE LIRIA (DO) Valencia**
COUNTRY:	Spain
PRICE:	£1.75 (70cl)
COLOUR:	Red with purple tinges.
NOSE:	Fruity with strong liquorice character.
PALATE:	Medium-bodied, with attractive liquorice flavours.
TASTE:	B. Value for money.

WINE:	**MILION MERLOT**
SUPPLIER:	Vranje
COUNTRY:	Yugoslavia 1984

PRICE:	£2.19 (70cl)
COLOUR:	Red.
NOSE:	Excellent bouquet, with strong Merlot fruit aroma.
PALATE:	Medium-bodied, soft and fruity. Finish is short.
TASTE:	B. Value for money.

WINE:	**SAINT-CHINIAN (AC)**
COUNTRY:	France
PRICE:	£2.25. (70cl)
COLOUR:	Deep red with blue tints.
NOSE:	Delicate fruit and some earthy character.
PALATE:	Medium-bodied, with pleasant fruit flavour and crisp acidity. Some astringency. Good quaffing wine.
TASTE:	B.

WINE:	**CHIVITE GRAN FEUDO (DO) Navarra**
COUNTRY:	Spain 1984
PRICE:	£2.29 (75cl)
COLOUR:	Dark red.
NOSE:	Good combination of rich fruit and oak.
PALATE:	Medium-bodied, soft with sweet/buttery character from the oak. Pleasant lingering finish.
TASTE:	B. Good value for money.

WINE:	**SEIGNEURET (AC) Côtes de Duras**
COUNTRY:	France 1985
PRICE:	£2.29 (70cl)
COLOUR:	Red with blue tinges.

NOSE:	Fruity bouquet with a slightly vinegar character.
PALATE:	Astringent, with pleasant fruity finish.
TASTE:	B. Value for money.

WINE:	**CH MARSEAU CÔTES DU MARMANDAIS (VDQS)**
COUNTRY:	France 1986
PRICE:	£2.39 (75cl)
COLOUR:	Red with blue tinges.
NOSE:	Intense, lively fruity bouquet.
PALATE:	Medium-bodied, oaky and with good depth of flavour and balanced acidity. Slight astringency on the finish.
TASTE:	B. Good value for money.

WINE:	**GAIERHOF, TEROLDEGO ROTALIANO (DOC)**
COUNTRY:	Italy 1986
PRICE:	£2.89 (75cl)
COLOUR:	Red with purple tinges.
NOSE:	Attractive fruity bouquet.
PALATE:	Full-bodied, rich with soft texture and good depth of fruit flavour and balanced acidity.
TASTE:	D. Good value for money.

WINE:	**TINTO DA ANFORA, JOÃO PIRES**
COUNTRY:	Portugal 1983
PRICE:	£3.19 (75cl)
COLOUR:	Dark red.
NOSE:	Stalky, with strong oak character.

PALATE: Full-bodied, oaky with rich fruit flavours and a persistent finish.

TASTE: D.   Value for money.

WINE: **CHÂTEAU SENAILHAC, BORDEAUX (AC)**

COUNTRY: France 1985
PRICE: £3.25 (75cl)
COLOUR: Dark red.
NOSE: Good depth of Cabernet fruit aromas.
PALATE: Light/medium bodied, with lovely fruit and balanced oak.
TASTE: C.

WINE: **DOMAINE DE LERET-MONPEZAT Cahors (AC)**

COUNTRY: France 1983
PRICE: £3.29 (75cl)
COLOUR: Red/brown.
NOSE: Fruity, liquorice bouquet with some stalkiness.
PALATE: Medium/full-bodied, soft and with good fruit flavour and oak. Finishes with a touch of astringency.
TASTE: C.

WINE: **FETZER ZINFANDEL**
COUNTRY: California 1984
PRICE: £3.59 (75cl)
COLOUR: Dark red.
NOSE: Excellent intensity of fruit.
PALATE: Sweet fruit and a very pleasant finish.
TASTE: B.   Value for money.

WINE:	**BERRI ESTATES CABERNET/SHIRAZ**
COUNTRY:	Australia 1985
PRICE:	£3.79 (75cl)
COLOUR:	Dark red with purple tints.
NOSE:	Rich fruit and attractive, buttery oak.
PALATE:	Full-bodied with good fruit and oak.
TASTE:	D. Good value for money.

WINE:	**GRAN CONDAL Rioja Reserva (DO)**
COUNTRY:	Spain 1981
PRICE:	£3.99 (75cl)
COLOUR:	Red with some brown tints.
NOSE:	Very oaky, vanillan, with good underlying fruit
PALATE:	Medium/full-bodied, oaky, with rich fruit and strong vanillan/oak character.
TASTE:	D. Value for money.

WINE:	**BOURGOGNE PINOT NOIR (AC) Buxy**
COUNTRY:	France 1985
PRICE:	£3.99 (75cl)
COLOUR:	Light/mid red.
NOSE:	Very oaky with delicate fruit.
PALATE:	Light/medium-bodied, with strong oak and light fruit flavour. One for oak lovers.
TASTE:	B.

WINE:	**CROZES-HERMITAGE (AC) Cave de Clairmonts**
COUNTRY:	France 1985
PRICE:	£3.99 (75cl)
COLOUR:	Dark red/purple.
NOSE:	Excellent, spicy, peppery bouquet.

188

PALATE:	Full-bodied, soft and flavoursome with balanced fruit/oak/acidity.
TASTE:	D. Good value for money.

WINE: **MOUNTAIN VIEW PINOT NOIR**

COUNTRY:	California
PRICE:	£3.99 (75cl)
COLOUR:	Dark amber.
NOSE:	Soft, attractive Pinot Noir bouquet.
PALATE:	Light, with pleasant Pinot Noir fruit flavour.
TASTE:	B. Value for money.

WINE: **COOKS CABERNET SAUVIGNON**

COUNTRY:	New Zealand 1985
PRICE:	£4.25 (75cl)
COLOUR:	Dark red.
NOSE:	Very intense Cabernet Sauvignon fruit aroma.
PALATE:	Medium/full-bodied, rich and fruity with sweet oak flavour. Finish is pleasant and persistent.
TASTE:	D.

WINE: **CHÂTEAU MUSAR**

SUPPLIER:	Gaston Hochar
COUNTRY:	Lebanon 1980
PRICE:	£4.65 (75cl)
COLOUR:	Red/brown.
NOSE:	Very attractive tarry fruit and oak.
PALATE:	Full-bodied, rich with mouth-filling flavour and balanced oak.
TASTE:	D.

WINE:	**CHÂTEAU HAUT PORTETS Graves (AC)**

COUNTRY: France 1985
PRICE: £4.65 (75cl)
COLOUR: Dark red.
NOSE: Good depth of fruit, but needs time to develop a more complex bouquet.
PALATE: Full-bodied, rich, robust and fruity, with soft tannic astringency on the finish. Pleasant now but will improve with 2-3 years cellaring.
TASTE: C.

WINE: **VENEGAZZU Vino da Tavola**
COUNTRY: Italy 1983
PRICE: £4.95 (75cl)
COLOUR: Red/brown.
NOSE: Some complexity, with lively fruity bouquet, good oak and some medicinal odours.
PALATE: Full-bodied, with rich, sweet fruit, pleasant astringency and good acidity. This wine is just beginning to soften and should cellar well.
TASTE: D.

ROSÉ WINE

WINE: **CANTE CIGALE GRENACHE VDP de l'Hérault**
COUNTRY: France 1986
COLOUR: Pale pink.
NOSE: Intense aroma of Grenache fruit.

PALATE: Light/medium-bodied, very fruity and flavoursome with a crisp finish.

SWEETNESS: 4.   Value for money.

SPARKLING WINE

WINE: **CASTELLBLANCH CRISTAL BRUT CAVA**

COUNTRY: Spain

PRICE: £3.99 (75cl)

COLOUR: Straw.

NOSE: Vinous with some yeast character.

PALATE: Light/medium-bodied, with a crisp, clean finish. Good sparkling wine.

SWEETNESS: 2.   Very good value for money.

WINE: **DELACOTE SAUMUR (AC) Brut**

COUNTRY: France

PRICE: £4.85 (75cl)

COLOUR: Pale straw

NOSE: Strong yeast character, with good depth of underlying fruit.

PALATE: Full-bodied, soft and rich with crisp acidity. Excellent sparkling wine.

SWEETNESS: 2.   Very good value for money

WIZZARD WINE WAREHOUSES

WHITE WINES

WINE: **DOMAINE DE MONTMARIN (VDP)**
SUPPLIER: de Bertier
COUNTRY: France 1987
PRICE: £2.39 (75cl)
COLOUR: Pale straw.
NOSE: Vinous with underlying fruit and some stalky character.
PALATE: Medium/full-bodied, rounded with tangy fruit and crisp acidity.
SWEETNESS: 2.

WINE: **VERDICCHIO DEI CASTELLI DI JESI CLASSICO (DOC)**
COUNTRY: Italy
PRICE: £2.79 (75cl)
COLOUR: Straw with green tints.
NOSE: Attractive, perfumed character.
PALATE: Medium/full-bodied, very soft and rounded. Easy drinking style of wine.
SWEETNESS: 2.   Value for money.

WINE: **VOUVRAY (AC)**
SUPPLIER: Saget
COUNTRY: France 1987
PRICE: £2.99 (75cl)
COLOUR: Straw.

NOSE:	Exhibits well the floral fragrances of the Chenin Blanc grape.
PALATE:	Medium/full-bodied, with floral/honeyed fruit and a crisp finish.
SWEETNESS:	3. Good value for money.

WINE:	**CHARDONNAY, DOMAINE LA SOURCE (VDP)**
SUPPLIER:	Besinet
COUNTRY:	France 1987
PRICE:	£2.99 (75cl)
COLOUR:	Straw/deep straw with green tints.
NOSE:	Excellent bouquet of peach and fruit salad.
PALATE:	Full-bodied, with strong fruit flavour and some grassy character. Pleasant fruity finish.
SWEETNESS:	2. Good value for money.

WINE:	**MUSCADET SUR LIE, LE SOLEIL NANTAIS (AC)**
SUPPLIER:	Guilbaud
COUNTRY:	France 1987
PRICE:	£3.29 (75cl)
COLOUR:	Pale/mid straw.
NOSE:	Intense aroma of the Muscadet grape and some grassy character.
PALATE:	Medium/full-bodied, with good depth of Muscadet fruit and some lemony flavours.
SWEETNESS:	1. Very good value for money.

WINE:	**APREMONT, VIN DE SAVOIE (AC)**
SUPPLIER:	Cavaille
COUNTRY:	France
PRICE:	£3.49 (75cl)

COLOUR:	Straw with green tints.
NOSE:	Combination of fruit and yeast odours with some earthiness.
PALATE:	Full-bodied, with grassy fruit flavours and a crisp finish. Good style of some complexity.
SWEETNESS:	2. Very good value for money.

WINE:	**FORSTER SCHNEPFENFLUG SPÄTLESE (QMP)**
COUNTRY:	Germany 1985
PRICE:	£3.49 (75cl)
COLOUR:	Golden.
NOSE:	Excellent intensity of the spicy aromas of the Gewürztraminer grape.
PALATE:	Medium/full-bodied, velvety soft and mouth-filling with strong Gewürztraminer fruit and a smooth, fruity finish.
SWEETNESS:	6. Excellent value for money.

WINE:	**HARDY'S EARLY BIRD DRY WHITE**
COUNTRY:	Australia 1988
PRICE:	£3.69 (75cl
COLOUR:	Deep straw with green tints.
NOSE:	Very oaky, with grassy fruit and some yeast character.
PALATE:	Medium/full-bodied, with good balance of fruit/oak/ acidity. Finish is fruity and persistent.
SWEETNESS:	2. Very good value for money.

| WINE: | **CHABLIS (AC)** |
| SUPPLIER: | Regnier |

COUNTRY:	France 1986
PRICE:	£4.99 (70cl)
COLOUR:	Deep straw.
NOSE:	Complex bouquet of Chardonnay fruit with honeyed overtones.
PALATE:	Full-bodied, with strong honeyed/fruit flavours and a crisp, lingering finish.
SWEETNESS: 1.	Excellent value for money.

RED WINES

WINE:	**VIN DE TABLE ROUGE**
SUPPLIER:	Duboeuf
COUNTRY:	France
PRICE:	£2.49 (75cl)
COLOUR:	Red.
NOSE:	Light, delicate bouquet.
PALATE:	Medium-bodied, soft and fruity. Easy drinking style.
TASTE:	A.

WINE:	**FETZER PREMIUM RED**
COUNTRY:	U.S.A.
PRICE:	£2.69 (75cl)
COLOUR:	Red/dark red.
NOSE:	Excellent, with complex bouquet of buttery oak and fruit.
PALATE:	Full-bodied, very soft and rounded with pleasant fruit and oak flavour. Finish is lingering with soft tannin.
TASTE:	C. Excellent value for money.

WINE:	**GRAVE DEL FRIULI, CABERNET**
SUPPLIER:	La Delizia
COUNTRY:	Italy 1986
PRICE:	£2.89 (75cl)
COLOUR:	Red/dark red with blue tints.
NOSE:	Good intensity of slightly raisined Cabernet fruit.
PALATE:	Full-bodied, soft in texture with mouthfilling ripe fruit flavours. Good overall balance.
TASTE:	D. Excellent value for money.

WINE:	**ANJOU-VILLAGES (AC)**
SUPPLIER:	Besombes
COUNTRY:	France 1985
PRICE:	£2.99 (75cl)
COLOUR:	Ruby/red.
NOSE:	Attractive, stalky Cabernet Franc character.
PALATE:	Medium-bodied, with pleasant floral, fruit flavour and some stalkiness and astringency.
TASTE:	B. Very good value for money.

WINE:	**CAHORS (AC)**
SUPPLIER:	Vigouroux
COUNTRY:	France 1985
PRICE:	£2.99 (75cl)
COLOUR:	Dark red with blue tints.
NOSE:	Strong bouquet of very ripe, raisined fruit.
PALATE:	Full-bodied, with rich, ripe, raisined fruit. Finish is fruity with some astringency from the tannins.
TASTE:	C. Good value for money.

WINE:	**BEAUJOLAIS RÉGNIÉ, DOM DU POTET (AC)**
SUPPLIER:	Duboeuf
COUNTRY:	France 1987
PRICE:	£3.89 (75cl)
COLOUR:	Red with blue tints.
NOSE:	Intense aroma of the Gamay grape used to produce Beaujolais wines.
PALATE:	Medium-bodied, velvety smooth and very fruity. Delightful light, fruity quaffing wine.
TASTE:	B. Value for money.

WINE:	**PINOT NOIR BOURGOGNE (AC)**
SUPPLIER:	Lebreton
COUNTRY:	France 1983
PRICE:	£3.99 (75cl)
COLOUR:	Red with brown tints.
NOSE:	Very attractive bouquet of earthy Pinot Noir fruit.
PALATE:	Medium-bodied, with earthy/raspberry/strawberry fruit and balanced tannin and acidity. A bargain.
TASTE:	B. Excellent value for money.

WINE:	**CH LAROCHE BEL AIR (AC)**
SUPPLIER:	Palau
COUNTRY:	France 1985
PRICE:	£3.99 (75cl)
COLOUR:	Dark red.
NOSE:	Excellent intensity of complex fruit aromas enhanced by oak maturation.

| PALATE: | Full-bodied, very soft and smooth, with lovely fruit flavours and good tannin. A bargain. |
| TASTE: | C. Excellent value for money. |

ROSÉ WINE

WINE:	**CH THIEULEY, CLAIRET**
SUPPLIER:	Courselle
COUNTRY:	France 1987
PRICE:	£3.19 (75cl)
COLOUR:	Pink/amber.
NOSE:	Good intensity of aroma of the Cabernet Franc grape.
PALATE:	Medium-bodied, soft with mouth-filling fruit and a crisp, lingering finish.
SWEETNESS:	4. Excellent value for money.

SPARKLING WINE

WINE:	**CRÉMANT TOURAINE ROSÉ (AC)**
COUNTRY:	France
PRICE:	£4.89 (75cl)
COLOUR:	Pink/amber. Sparkling wine.
NOSE:	Very fruity with some stalkiness.
PALATE:	Medium/full-bodied, very creamy and fruity with a crisp, fruity finish.
SWEETNESS:	2. Good value for money.

A

ABBOCCATO Italian term for sweet or semi-sweet, used particularly for ORVIETO wines.

ABFÜLLER German term for a bottler. **Abfüllung** indicates that a wine has been bottled at the estate where it was made. Similar to CHÂTEAU-BOTTLED of French wines. *See also* ERZEUGERABFÜLLUNG.

ABOCADO Spanish term for medium-sweet table wine.

ABRUZZI mountainous region of eastern central Italy, whose most famous wine is the satisfying red DOC Montepulciano d'Abruzzo grown from the Montepulciano grape. Other DOC wines include the rosé, Cerasuolo, and Trebbiano d'Abruzzo, a dry white.

AC abbreviation for APPELLATION D'ORIGINE CONTRÔLÉE, the highest French wine classification. It indicates that the wine meets strict requirements concerning area of production, grape types, strength, quantity and other factors, but is not necessarily a guarantee of quality. *See also* VDQS.

ACACIA WINERY winery in the NAPA VALLEY district of California's North Coast region, specializing in high quality CHARDONNAY and PINOT NOIR wines.

ACESCENT term meaning slightly sour or turning sour, indicating an excess of ACETIC ACID in a wine.

ACETIC a tasting term indicating smelling and tasting of a mixture of acetic acid and ethyl acetate, reminiscent of vinegar. VOLATILE and PRICKED are similar terms.

ACETIC ACID a volatile acid present in all wines. Produced during fermentation by acetobacteria, it may turn wine into vinegar if not controlled. Many winemakers believe small but detectable quantities of it are important in the make-up of wine, but others consider it a negative factor.

ACHAIA-CLAUS one of the largest wine firms in Greece.

ACIDS natural constituents of grapes and wine, influencing their character. Various acids occur naturally in grapes, influenced by the species, soil conditions and micro-organisms. Others result from fermentation, and more can develop during winemaking. Most acids are important in minute quantities as they contribute to the quality of wine. The main acids in wine are tartaric and malic. Lack of acid makes a wine flat or flabby, too much makes it too tart. A balance of acid and fruit gives a pleasing combination of flavour and freshness. The presence of acids in a wine is important when considering its potential for cellaring. Wines with low acidity are generally unsuitable for keeping.

ACIDITY tasting term indicating the quality of tartness or sharpness to a wine; the presence of agreeable fruit acids.

ACONCAGUA VALLEY wine region in central Chile producing commendable red wines from CABERNET SAUVIGNON grapes.

ADAMADO Spanish term for soft and elegant.

ADEGA Portuguese equivalent of a Spanish BODEGA, a wine cellar or shop, or a wine producer.

ADELAIDE capital of South Australia's largest wine-producing state and a winemaking area. Vineyards were first established in 1837 and plantings expanded for many years. Several of the country's largest wine companies were established in the city and it remains the hub of the Australian wine industry. Few of the vineyards have escaped the growth of suburbia, but a notable exception is the Penfold's Magill vineyard, the original source of grapes for the world-famous GRANGE HERMITAGE. Public outcry in the early 1980s saved it from housing development.

ADGESTONE English estate at Brading on the Isle of Wight, producing light, dry wines from early-ripening MULLER-THURGAU, Reichensteiner and Seyval Blanc grapes.

AFAMES dry red wine from Cyprus, one of the best made from the MAVRON grape.

AFTERTASTE the brief 'memory' of a wine that it leaves in the mouth and nose after it has been swallowed. Equivalent to FINISH.

AGASSAC, CHÂTEAU D' CRU GRAND BOURGEOIS EXCEPTIONNEL wine from the HAUT-MÉDOC district of BORDEAUX.

AGE a crucial factor in the suitability of wine for drinking. As a rule, inexpensive, ordinary wines are made to be drunk right away and may deteriorate rather than improve with age. Most dry white wines will benefit from a year or two in the bottle, and sweet whites longer. Light reds and rosés should generally be drunk young. Full-bodied reds may take several years to reach their peak. Non-vintage champagne will often be better after a year or two of storage while vintage champagne should improve for many years. The same goes for vintage PORT, SHERRY and MADEIRA.

AGGRESSIVE term used when a wine 'attacks' the taste buds, either with excessive ACIDITY or TANNIN.

AGLIANICO grape variety of Greek origin grown in the southern Italian provinces of Campania and Basilicata for the production of red wine. In Basilicata it is used for the region's DOC wine, **Aglianico del Vulture**, a quality red considered by some to be the best red wine from southern Italy.

AGRARIA Italian term for an estate winery. Equivalent to AZIENDA AGRICOLA.

AGULHA DO demarcated Portuguese VINHO VERDE, dry and slightly petillant and sold in stone bottles.

AHR region of northwest Germany, one of 11 wine regions defined by German law (*see* GERMANY). Ahr wines are both red and white but are rarely seen outside Germany. The extreme northerly situation makes it difficult for red grapes to ripen properly. The best known is SPÄTBURGUNDER.

AIGLE important wine-growing town in the Chablais district of Vaud, Switzerland, producing dry white DORIN wines.

AIREN white-wine grape grown in the region of LA MANCHA in central Spain.

AIX-EN-PROVENCE ancient capital of PROVENCE.

AJACCIO the main city of CORSICA.

ALAMBRADO Spanish term meaning 'wrapped in a fine wire netting'. Bottles of Spanish quality wines are often presented in this way.

ALAMEDA COUNTY wine region of California encompassing the LIVERMORE VALLEY, known for its fine white wines.

ALAVESA area of RIOJA in northern Spain producing quality wines. Alavesa is heavier than most Rioja wines.

ALBA major wine centre of PIEMONTE, northwest Italy, the home of BARBARESCO, BARBERA and BAROLO wines.

ALBA FLORA white wine of the island of Majorca.

ALBA IULIA a semi-dry white wine produced in Romania.

ALBANA grape variety grown in the Emilia-Romagna region of northern Italy, used to produce fairly strong, dry and semi-sweet white wines. **Albana di Romagna** is a dry or semi-sweet DOC wine from the Po Valley.

ALBARIÑO grape variety of Galicia in northwest Spain used in making fresh, floral, crisp, slightly sparkling whites. **Albariño del Palacio** is such a wine.

ALBARIZA chalky soil of the Spanish Sherry country around Jerez de la Frontera in southwest Spain, from which the finest sherries are produced.

ALCAMO full dry white and red DOC wines from region of western Sicily, centred on the town of Alcamo.

ALCOBAÇA wine-growing region on the western coast of Portugal just north of Lisbon, producing red and white wines.

ALCOHOL in wine, the ethyl alcohol produced as a result of fermentation of the grape MUST by the action of yeasts which convert the sugar to alcohol, with CARBON DIOXIDE gas being given off.

ALCOHOL CONTENT the percentage of ALCOHOL contained in a wine, expressed as a percentage of the total volume. The figure is usually given on the bottle label or packaging. Table wines normally contain between 8 and 14 percent, with fortified wines generally having between 17 and 22 percent. A high percentage of alcohol does not necessarily make for better wine.

ALDEHYDES organic compounds present in grapes and also produced by the oxidation of alcohol during fermentation. They contribute to the characteristic bouquet of a wine and are especially important in both the production and resultant odours of SHERRY.

ALEATICO grape variety of the MUSCAT family grown in Italy for the production of sweet red wines. These include two DOC wines, **Aleatico di Gradoli** from Viterbo near Rome, and **Aleatico di Puglia** from Puglia in southern Italy. It is also used on Elba for **Aleatico di Portoferraio** (Portoferraio is the capital of Elba).

ALELLA mostly white DO wines from the Alella district of Catalonia in Spain, north of Barcelona. The semi-sweet white is preferred to the dry. **Alella Vinicola** is a wine cooperative of the area which produces red and white wines. Allella whites have a SWEETNESS RATING of 2.

ALENTIGO very large undemarcated area of the Minho in northwestern Portugal, producing red wines, including BORBA.

ALEZIO strong full-bodied DOC red (and also rose) wines from PUGLIA on the Adriatic coast of southern Italy.

ALGARVE recently demarcated DO region of the south coast of Portugal. The area of vineyards is the Lagoa, producing white champagne-type wines and reasonable red and white table wines.

ALGERIA country of North Africa which, during the years of French colonization, was a vast wine producer. The industry is now in decline but Algeria is still the most important wine-producing country of North Africa and source of a number of very agreeable reds and reasonable whites, including RED INFURIATOR. The principal wine-growing regions are Oran and Alger. *See also* APPELLATION D'ORIGINE GARANTIE.

ALICANTE demarcated DO region on Spain's Costa Blanca. It produces full-bodied red wines and some white wines.

ALIGOTÉ white-wine grape variety of BURGUNDY. It produces reasonable wines in better years and is also used for making sparkling wines.

ALLEGRINI producer of quality Veronese wines, including VALPOLICELLA.

ALLESVERLOREN wine estate in the MALMESBURY region of South Africa producing mostly red wines.

ALLIACEOUS tasting and smelling of garlic, a condition that sometimes occurs when sulphur dioxide combines with alcohol in wine.

ALMACENISTA old, dry, very high quality SHERRY which is not blended.

ALMADEN VINEYARDS producer of very large quantities of wine in Santa Clara County, California, near San Jose, where the first European vines were planted commercially in 1852. The company makes many styles of wine, with some likeable varietals, including CHARDONNAY and CABERNET SAUVIGNON. Its higher-priced wines bear the Charles le Franc label.

ALMANSA demarcated DO area in the Albacete district of eastern Spain producing full-bodied red wines.

ALMEIRIM Portuguese red, rosé and white wines produced by Adega Cooperative.

ALOQUE light, strong rosé wine made from black and white grapes in the Valdepeñas region of central Spain.

ALOXE-CORTON commune lying at the northern end of the Côte de Beaune in Burgundy whose red and white wines are of good to excellent quality. Wines sold as Aloxe-Corton are the communal wines. Of higher quality are those whose labels add the individual vineyards. Corton-Charlemagne is regarded by many as one of the world's finest white wines. Very high quality are those which do not bear the name Aloxe at all but CORTON alone or Corton followed by another designation.

ALPHEN old-established winery and vineyard in Cape Province, South Africa.

ALSACE formerly German, now French demarcated region bordering the Rhine, mainly producing a wide range of white, dry wines of consistent quality. Unlike other French wines, the AC names of the region consist of the grape variety (which are similar to those used in the German Rhine areas), often in conjunction with the name of a town, and the maker or shipper's name, although a very few CRUS exist. In character, the wines range from very dry to almost sweet. These delicate wines are typically very floral with subtle, deep-lingering fruit flavours. The best wines are made from Gewürztraminer and Riesling grapes. Increasing popularity with the general wine-buying public has led a number of retailers to bring in own-brand wines of good quality and at reasonable prices. At the other end of the scale some excellent wines exist and represent value for money.

ALSHEIM wine-growing town of GROSSLAGE Krotenbrünnen in RHEINHESSEN, Germany.

ALTO South African estate at STELLENBOSCH in the Cape, well-known for its full-bodied red wines.

ALTO ADIGE northern, DOC wine-growing area of the TRENTINO-ALTO ADIGE region of Italy, the Italian Tyrol, best known for its fresh, ripe white wines named from the grapes from which they are made. Some rosé and red wines are also produced. CHARDONNAY wines from the area are rapidly increasing in quality.

ALVARINHO Portuguese grape variety grown to make white VINHO VERDE wines. **Alvarinho de Moncao** (DO) is one of the best Vinhos Verdes of Portugal, with more flavour and strength than most others.

ALVEAR SHERRY firm in southern Spain. Their best-known product is Fino CB Sherry.

AMABILE Italian term for slightly sweeter than semi-sweet (*abboccato*) but not as sweet as sweet (*dolce*).

AMADOR COUNTY wine-producing area of California, located in the foothills of the Sierra Nevada mountains. It produces quality wines, especially from ZINFANDEL grapes.

AMARANTE area within the VINHO VERDE region of Portugal which produces a fresh white wine of the same name.

AMARO Italian term for bitter.

AMARONE strong, bitter red wine from the VENETO region of Italy, made with half-dried grapes. Regarded as the best wine of Verona. *See also* RECIOTO DELLA VALPOLICELLA.

AMBOISE town in the LOIRE Valley, France, not far from the region of Vouvray, producing red, white and rosé wines.

AMBONNAY village in CHAMPAGNE, France, where the best still, red wine of the region, BOUZY ROUGE, is produced. *See also* COTEAUX CHAMPENOIS.

AMELIORATION process of adding to grape juice or new wine, or treating it, to improve quality.

AMIGNE grape variety grown in the Valais region of Switzerland, giving an agreeably perfumed wine which is dry and full-bodied.

AMMERSCHWIHR important commune of Alsace producing mostly white wines and some red from ancient vineyards.

AMONTILLADO Spanish term for a type of SHERRY with amber colour and medium body. This medium-dry wine may appeal to those who find FINO Sherry too intense in flavour. Good accompaniment for most soups. SWEETNESS RATINGS are Dry Amontillado 3, Full Amontillado 4.

AMOROSO full-bodied, dark and sweet SHERRY. Not as dark in colour or as full-bodied as OLOROSO but sweeter than AMONTILLADO. It is sweetened for the British trade and unknown in Spain.

207

AMPLE term used to indicate that a wine is full-tasting and well-rounded in aroma, bouquet and flavour. Equivalent to weight or BODY.

AMPURDÁN COSTA BRAVA vineyard area in the province of Gerona in northeast Spain, recently DO demarcated, producing pleasant white and rosé wines.

AMSELFELDER sweet red produced in Yugoslavia from PINOT NOIR grapes.

AMTLICHE PRÜFUNG German term for the official test on QUALITATSWEIN wines. Chemical and sensory analyses are carried out and an **Amtliche Prüfungsnummer (AP)** allocated to the wine and printed on the label.

ANARES red wine from the RIOJA region of Spain produced by Bodegas Olarra.

ANBAUGEBIET German term for a designated wine-growing region. There are 11 of these *bestimmte* (designated) Anbaugebiete (*see* GERMANY). The QbA (*Qualitätswein bestimmter Anbaugebiete*) on a label names the Anbaugebiet from which the wine comes.

ANDALUSIA region in southwest Spain where SHERRY is produced in the area around JEREZ de la Frontera. Málaga (a sweet dessert wine) and the wines of MONTILLA-MORILES are also produced in other areas of the region.

ANDEAN brand name used by PEÑAFLOR, the Argentinian wine producer.

ANDRON-BLANQUET, CHÂTEAU CRU GRAND BOURGEOIS EXCEPTIONNEL wine from the SAINT-ESTEPHE commune in BORDEAUX.

AÑEJADO POR Spanish label term meaning 'aged by'.

ANGAS BRUT ROSÉ Australian sparkling wine produced by Hill Smith.

ANGÉLUS, CHÂTEAU L' GRAND CRU red wine from the SAINT-EMILION district of BORDEAUX.

ANGLUDET, CHÂTEAU CRU BOURGEOIS SUPÉRIER EXCEPTIONNEL wine from the MARGAUX commune in BORDEAUX.

ANJOU major wine-producing region in the LOIRE Valley, France, best known for its popular rosé wines, including Rosé d'Anjou and the superior Cabernet d'Anjou. It also produces fine white wines from the PINEAU DE LA LOIRE (CHENIN BLANC) grape, and red and sparkling wines. Anjou includes the districts of **Anjou-Coteaux de la Loire** which produces semi-sweet AC white wines of good quality, BONNEZEAUX, COTEAUX DE L'AUBANCE, COTEAUX DU LAYON, SAUMUR and COTEAUX DE SAUMUR. All Anjou white and rosé wines have a SWEETNESS RATING of 4.

ANNABERG famous vineyard in the Rheinpfalz wine region of Germany, producing full-bodied RIESLING and SCHEUREBE wines. Its labels bear its name alone, which is unusual on German wines.

AÑO Spanish term for the age in years of a wine at the time of bottling. This practice is not allowed by the EEC which Spain joined in 1986, so this information will be found only on older labels.

ANREICHERUNG German term for 'enrichment', the addition of sugar to wine MUST to ensure that the wine will have adequate alcohol and body. The sugar may be in the form of either concentrated grape juice or cane sugar.

ANTINORI Florentine wine family in Italy, producing fine DOC wines such as CHIANTI and ORVIETO wines and also good vini da tàvola.

AOC abbreviation for APPELLATION D'ORIGINE CONTRÔLÉE, used less frequently than AC.

AP abbreviation for AMTLICHE PRÜFUNGSNUMMER, the number allocated to a German Qualitätswein when it has passed a series of tests. It is then printed on the label.

APETLON village on the Neusiedlersee in Burgenland, Austria, producing sweet white SANDWEIN.

APERITIF French term for an appetiser, a drink taken before meals to stimulate the palate, e.g. dry Sherry or Vermouth.

APHRODITE well-known dry white wine of Cyprus.

APPELLATION French term for the 'name' of a wine, that which it may bear according to the control laws. France has a system of four appellations: AC, VDQS, VIN DE PAYS and VIN DE CONSOMMATION COURANTE. Many other countries now have an appellation system. In Italy it consists of DOC and DOCG regulations, in Spain and Portugal DO systems, in Germany QmP, QbA and TAFELWEIN levels, and in South Africa WINE OF ORIGIN rules. Chile classifies its wines by age. The US and Australia have no official controls although the NAPA VALLEY in the US and the Victoria and Mudgee in Australia are introducing systems. In these countries more information is given on labels and quality resides in the winery and grape variety. The positive side of non-appellation is that producers are not bound by rules and can experiment with new methods, grapes and regions.

APPELLATION D'ORIGINE CONTRÔLLÉE French term for the 'controlled-origin name' of a French wine, abbreviated as AC or AOC. The Institut National des Appellations d'Origine imposes a number of stringent requirements on producers that must be satisfied if their wines are to qualify for the desired appellation. These include area of production, permissible grape vines, minimum alcohol content, viticultural practices, maximum permissible harvest, and wine-making procedures.

A grower in the designated Bordeaux region will, for instance, be permitted to use the 'Bordeaux' appellation on meeting certain requirements, but if he wishes to use the appellation of the Bordeaux district in which his vineyard lies, say Haut-Médoc, he must meet more demanding standards. And more exacting standards yet can be applied. In Beaujolais, for example, nine villages each has its own appellation or CRU.

APPELLATION D'ORIGINE GARANTIE French term for 'guaranteed-origin name' of an Algerian wine. A limited number of Algerian wines may bear this official appellation.

APREMONT white wine produced in the SAVOIE district of France.

APULIA English name for PUGLIA.

ARAGON region of northeast Spain producing table wines of high alcoholic strength.

ARBIN lively red wine of SAVOIE, France.

ARBOIS famous vineyard region of the JURA in eastern France, producing mainly pleasant dry white AC wines, the best known being VIN JAUNE.

ARCINS, CHÂTEAU D' CRU BOURGEOIS wine from the HAUT-MÉDOC district of BORDEAUX.

ARGENTINA wine-producing country of South America, fifth in the world in terms of production. It produces mostly table wines from largely Italian grapes although French varieties like CHARDONNAY and CABERNET SAUVIGNON are now being used. Some excellent wines are being produced and exported by Peñaflor, the country's largest wine producer, which uses the Andean brand name.

ARKANSAS American state producing generally fairly sweet table wines. Most of the wine is produced around the town of Altus by the Mount Bethel, Post, Sax and Wiederkehr wineries.

ARLAY, CHÂTEAU D' château at Arlay in the JURA

Mountains district of France producing red, white and rosé wines and VIN JAUNE.

ARNEIS DEI ROERI soft, full, dry white table wine produced in PIEMONTE, northern Italy.

AROMA tasting term used to describe the smell of a wine. If no particular aroma is present, the wine is described as vinous. Aroma and BOUQUET are sometimes used synonymously. Some tasters apply the term aroma to the smell of the grape and bouquet to the ageing. If a grape produces a strongly scented smell, e.g. Muscat, Gewürztraminer, this is described as **aromatic**.

ARROSÉE, CHÂTEAU L' GRAND CRU red wine from the SAINT-EMILION district of BORDEAUX.

ARSINOE brand name of a dry white wine from Cyprus.

ASCIUTTO Italian term for dry, used particularly in Sicily.

ASENOVGRAD demarcated wine region of BULGARIA producing Cabernet Sauvignon, Merlot and Mavrud wines.

ASPIRAN commune in the department of HÉRAULT in southern France, producing the white CLAIRETTE DU LANGUEDOC wines.

ASSISI town in Umbria in central Italy from which come the attractive table wines Rosso di Assisi and Bianco di Assisi.

ASSMANNHAUSEN village on the River Rhine in the RHEINGAU region of West Germany whose sweet red wines are considered by many to be the best in Germany.

ASTI town in PIEMONTE in northwest Italy whose name has become famous for ASTI SPUMANTE, although that wine is also made elsewhere. Moscato d'Asti, a sparkling MUSCAT wine, is made here.

ASTI SPUMANTE sparkling, bubbly, usually sweet white wine made by the CHAMPAGNE METHOD. It takes its name from the town of ASTI but is also made elsewhere. It has a SWEETNESS RATING of 7.

ASTRINGENCY tasting term used to describe sharpness in a wine. It is detected by a puckering sensation in the mouth and caused by a high TANNIN content, absorbed from the skins and seeds. In red wines it sometimes indicates that they will be long-lived. HARSH, ROUGH and TANNIC are related terms.

ASZTALI BOR Hungarian term for ordinary wine.

ASZU Hungarian term for grapes affected by NOBLE ROT which are used to make the sweet TOKAJI wines.

ATTICA wine district south of Athens in Greece, producing red, white and rosé wines. It is particularly known for the production of RETSINA wines.

AUBANCE tributary of the river Loire in France, on whose slopes are produced COTEAUX DE L'AUBANCE wines.

AUBE wine-growing department of France adjoining the Marne, producing mainly ordinary white wines and sometimes better sparkling wines.

AUBUIS French term for soil formation found in parts of Touraine particularly favourable to the growth of CHENIN BLANC vines and responsible for VOUVRAY amongst other wines. It is coarse limestone with chalky clay on top.

AUDE important (in quantity) VIN DE PAYS wine-growing department of southwest France producing mostly quaffing red wines and some white and sparkling wines.

AUSBRUCH Austrian category of sweet, rich wine.

AUSEIGENEM LESEGUT German term meaning EST-ATE-BOTTLED.

AUSLESE German word for 'selection' and a category of quality wine made from selected, very ripe grapes which may be affected by NOBLE ROT, resulting in sweet wines. The wine must be made from grapes of a sweetness potential of 83 degrees OECHSLE. The best Auslese wines are made from the RIESLING grape.

AUSONE, CHÂTEAU excellent red PREMIER GRAND CRU wine from the SAINT-EMILION district of BORDEAUX, commanding high prices.

AUSTERE tasting term for a wine with a strong, firm style without being generous in flavour.

AUSSTICH term used in Austria for selected high quality wines kept back after the harvest.

AUSTRALIA wine-making country since the early days of colonization by Britain and now a producer of a proliferation of wines, many of excellent quality. The principal wine-growing states in order of quantity are SOUTH AUSTRALIA, NEW SOUTH WALES, VICTORIA, WEST AUSTRALIA, QUEENSLAND and TASMANIA. Production has increased rapidly in the past 25 years but the lack of a central APPELLATION system tends to confuse the newcomer. The state of Victoria and the area of MUDGEE are introducing systems, and much information on a wine is given on the label. Notable wine-growing districts are: in New South Wales, the HUNTER VALLEY, famous for its fine red and white wines (especially CHARDONNAY and SEMILLON), and Mudgee; in Victoria, the northeast, source of fortified and dessert wines, and the central region, whence come some good red and white varietals as well as the fine wines of the GREAT WESTERN region; in South Australia, the BAROSSA VALLEY, the area surrounding ADELAIDE, COONAWARRA, CLARE and the MURRAY VALLEY, all producing quality wines; and in Western Australia, the SWAN VALLEY, where table and fortified wines are produced, and the MARGARET RIVER region, an area of great recent success.

AUSTRIA country producing mostly light wines, from crisp to fruity, and generally drier than German wines. Labelling broadly follows the German pattern, the sequence being village, vineyard, grape variety, grade of quality, and vintage. The principal wine-growing areas are Burgenland, which produces excellent sweet dessert wines; Nieder-Österreich (Lower Austria) which contains eight wine districts, notable among them Wachau for RHEINRIESLINGS, Voslau for soft red wines and Gumpoldskirchen for full-bodied white wines. The suburbs of Vienna (Wien), the capital, produce wine of quality and also HEURIGEN, unforgettable new wines which are sold in bars also called Heurigen.

In the wake of the 1986 glycol additions scandal, prices in the UK plummeted. The offenders have all been dealt with and the wines are now perfectly safe. The stigma remains, however, and has kept prices low, resulting in good bargains in most Austrian wines.

AUXERRE the main city of the department of Yonne in the CHABLIS region of France, producing good quality whites.

AUXERROIS alternative name for the PINOT GRIS grape, and a pleasant white wine from Luxembourg.

AY town in the CHAMPAGNE area of France, the ancient capital of the region. It houses some of the major names in the champagne industry, including Bollinger.

AZIENDA Italian term for a business. **Azienda Agricola**, literally 'large farm', on a label means that a particular estate makes and bottles its own wine (*see also* AGRARIA), while **Azienda Vinicola** ('wine-producing business') indicates that the producer does not grow the grapes but does make the wine. **Azienda Vitivinicola** indicates that the estate grows vines but also buys in from others.

B

BABEASCA NICORESTI red wine produced in the Focsani wine-growing region of Romania in the town of Nicoresti.

BABICH vineyard of good repute in Auckland, New Zealand, producing white and red wines from Pinot Noir, Cabernet,Sauvignon, Chenin Blanc and Müller-Thurgau grapes.

BABY DUCK sweet sparkling red wine from Canada.

BACHARACH district in the MITTELRHEIN in Germany, producing white wines mainly consumed locally.

BAD DÜRKHEIM town in the RHEINPFALZ region of Germany, producing a wide range of quality white wines and some of the best known red wine of the region.

BAD KREUZNACH city in the NAHE region of Germany, its name being given to the whole lower Nahe region. Its wines are regarded as the best in the region.

BADACSONY one of the best wine districts of Hungary on northern shore of Lake Balaton. Its wines are usually labelled Badacsony, followed by the name of the grape, e.g. Badacsony Keknyelu.

BADEN southernmost vineyard area in Germany, located in the southwest, producing white and red wines, some of the best being made from MULLER-THURGAU and SPÄTBURGUNDER grapes. The main producer is the ZBW cooperative, but there are individual growers experimenting in the production of full-bodied wines to accompany food.

BAG-IN-BOX WINES *see* WINE BOX.

BAILEY'S WINERY winery in northeast Victoria, Australia, producing good full-bodied red wines and white dessert wines. Best known for superlative liqueur Muscats.

BAIRRADA large, recently DO demarcated wine-growing area in Portugal, producing mostly red table wines from Baga grapes and sparkling white wines. Some of the red reserve wines (GARRAFEIRA) are of good to excellent quality and generally represent great value for money. Their TASTE RATING is D.

BALANCE tasting term indicating a harmonious balance of a wine's constituents, with no one characteristic predominant.

BALATON wine district in Hungary near the BADACSONY district on the northern shore of Lake Balaton, producing good red and white wines.

BALBACH ERBEN wine grower at NIERSTEIN in the Bereich of Nierstein in the RHEINHESSEN region of Germany, producing some of the best RIESLINGS of the region.

BALGOWNIE WINERY producer based in the town Bendigo in Victoria, southern Australia, producing quality VARIETAL wines in this cool-climate region.

BALTHAZAR or BALTHASAR large bottle which holds the equivalent of 16 bottles of, usually, champagne (12.8 litres/2.75 gallons).

BANAT vineyard in Romania, mainly producing white table wines. It also produces the well-known red wine Kardarka de Banat.

BANDA AZUL brand name of popular red wine produced in the Rioja Alta region of northern Spain by Bodegas Paternina. **Banda Dorado** is the white version.

BANDOL AC area in PROVENCE, producing wines labelled Bandol or Vin de Bandol, mainly red and rosé but some whites, mostly consumed locally. The reds are the best in quality and have a TASTE RATING of D.

BANYULS AC area of GRAND ROUSSILLON in southern

France producing the sweet red fortified wine *vin de liqueur* made from Grenache grapes.

BARANCOURT CHAMPAGNE producer in Bouzy in the Champagne region of France, producing BLANC DE NOIRS, rosé and Bouzy Champagne.

BARBACARLO red wine produced in the FRECCIAROSSA district of southern LOMBARDY in Italy.

BARBADILLO SHERRY firm of Sanlúcar de Barrameda in Spain, producing a variety of good to very good quality Sherries representing great value.

BARBARESCO DOCG red wine, one of Italy's finest. Made from the renowned NEBBIOLO grape, Barbarescos show robust character, depth and complexity and are generally more approachable at a younger age than the nearby and more famous BAROLO wines. Produced in Barbaresco and the neighbouring villages of Treiso and Neive in the PIEMONTE region, they have a TASTE RATING of D.

BARBAROUX grape variety grown around CASSIS, near Marseilles in PROVENCE to make red and rosé wines.

BARBERA versatile red-wine grape variety extensively planted in northern Italy where it produces high quality wines. The style of wine varies according to the grape's location. Cool-climate grapes produce fruity wines, whilst grapes from warmer climates make softer, more rounded wines, ready for drinking at a much earlier age. In north-west Italy **Barbera Amabile**, a sweet, red sparkling wine, is made from the grape.

BARBERANI major wine producer of Umbria in Italy, making quality ORVIETO and Orvieto Classico wines.

BARBIER, RENÉ estate in the Catalonia region of Spain, producing white and good reds.

BARCA VELHA superior Portuguese table wine made by the Port producer, Ferreira.

BARCELO firm in MÁLAGA, southern Spain, producing a variety of fortified wines, some under the brand name Bacarles.

BARDOLINO light, dry red DOC wine of the Verona area of northeast Italy. The wine is well regarded outside Italy and is untypically fresh by Italian standards with a TASTE RATING of A. Best drunk young.

BAROLO this noble red DOCG wine is the most famous of all Italian wines. It starts out hard and tannic, but after 5-8 years begins to soften and develop into a complex full-bodied wine. Reserves from good vintages will last for decades. Regarded by many as being the Italian 'first growth'. It has a TASTE RATING of E.

BAROSSA VALLEY major vine-growing area of South Australia, 35 miles northeast of Adelaide, producing sound varietal and blended wines. Settled in the early 1840s by German immigrants, it still shows German influence. A wide range of excellent wines is made by several producers including Orlando, Seppelt, Tollana and Hill Smith, and recently pioneered high-altitude vineyards are producing first-class wines

BARREL wooden cask used for the initial ageing of wine. In the first year wines are kept in lightly bunged barrels and topped up regularly to reduce oxidation. Wines are often fermented in oak barrels to add pleasant woody flavours.

BARRICA Spanish term for BARRIQUE.

BARRIQUE type of French barrel, of which the *barrique bordelaise* is an example. Its capacity is 255 litres.

BARROCÃO firm in Sangalhos, Portugal, producing sparkling DAO wines under the brand Diamante Azul, VINHO VERDE wines under the name Diamante Verde and other red and white wines.

BARSAC one of the five AC communes of the SAUTERNES region of southern BORDEAUX. Barsac wines are of high quality, the best rivalling the top Sauternes. NOBLE ROT results in sweet, luscious dessert wines rarely equalled outside France. The SWEETNESS RATING is 8, but relatively small quantities are sold in the UK.

BARSONYOS-CSASZAR wine-growing district of northern Hungary of which MOR is the best-known centre.

BARTON MANOR vineyard on the Isle of Wight off the south coast of England producing medium-dry and dry white wines, usually blended.

BASILICATA region of southern Italy notable for its only DOC wine, the sturdy red AGLIANICO del Vulture, grown in vineyards on the slopes of Monte Vulture, an extinct volcano. Other good VINI DA TÀVOLA are also produced.

BASSERMAN-JORDAN historic wine estate founded in the 13th century in DEIDESHEIM in the RHEINPFALZ province of southern Germany.

BASTARDO one of the leading red wine grape varieties used in Portugal for the production of PORT.

BASTO official subregion of the VINHO VERDE district of northwest Portugal, producing mainly red wines and also some whites.

BASTOR LA MONTAGNE, CHÂTEAU producer of sweet white wines in the SAUTERNES region of BORDEAUX which are good value for money.

BATAILLEY, CHÂTEAU cinquième GRAND CRU wine from the PAUILLAC commune of BORDEAUX.

BÂTARD-MONTRACHET dry, rich white wine of the CÔTE DE BEAUNE of Burgundy. The wine is a GRAND CRU produced in the CHASSAGNE-MONTRACHET and PULIGNY-MONTRACHET vineyards and ranks second only to CHEVALIER-MONTRACHET.

BÉARN province of France consisting of most of the Basses-Pyrénées. It produces sweet white wine and some dry whites and rosés.

BEAUCASTEL, CHÂTEAU DE large estate and château of CHÂTEAUNEUF-DU-PAPE in the Rhône Valley, France.

BEAUJOLAIS world-famous wine region of southern BURGUNDY. The Gamay grape excels here, producing refreshingly fruity light-bodied reds with distinct strawberry flavour. The TASTE RATING is A. The basic appellation 'Beaujolais' applies to wines produced in the southern districts of the region. These are fairly straightforward easy-drinking wines. Many of them now go under the **Beaujolais Nouveau** label, when the year's harvest of very young wine is shipped around the world during the last week of November each year in the wine industry's greatest marketing extravaganza. Nouveau wines can range from very acceptable light, fruity wine in good years to hard, thin acidic wines in poor years. Public interest in Nouveau wines tends to diminish after a month or so of release, and as these wines are often at their best six or eight months later, bargains can be found.

Beaujolais Superieur on a label indicates an ordinary Beaujolais wine with a greater than 10 percent alcohol content. It has a TASTE RATING of B.

In the northern part of Beaujolais are 40 villages entitled to the appellation **Beaujolais-Villages**. Wines from these communes have more body and depth and a TASTE RATING of B. By law these wines may not be released before 15 December each year, and they keep for 12 to 24+ months.

The best Beaujolais come from the **Beaujolais Crus**, nine villages (*crus*) whose wines have their own individual characteristics and are heavier than ordinary Beaujolais wines, with a TASTE RATING of B. Some crus benefit from keeping, particularly if produced in better years, e.g. 1985. The nine villages are: BROUILLY, CHÉNAS, CHIROUBLES, CÔTE DE BROUILLY, FLEURIE, JULIÉNAS, MORGON, MOULIN-À-VENT, and ST AMOUR. A tenth village, RÉGNIÉ, is seeking to become a cru. Because of its currently lower status its wines represent good value. White wines from Beaujolais, **Beaujolais Blanc**, are made from Chardonnay grapes and are fairly rare.

BEAULIEU (1) vineyard in Hampshire, England, producing light white wines from the Müller-Thurgau grape; (2) well-regarded vineyard in NAPA VALLEY, California, producing some of the best wines of the US.

BEAULIEU ROSÉ, CHÂTEAU DE producer of value-for-money wines in the Coteaux d'Aix en Provence area of PROVENCE.

BEAULIEU-SUR-LAYON commune in the Coteaux du Layon district of ANJOU in the Loire Valley, which has the right to an AC classification. It produces sweet and some dry white wines.

BEAUMES DE VENISE area in the department of VAUCLUSE in southern France producing sweet fortified wine from the MUSCAT grape. Excellent dessert wine.

BEAUMONT-SUR-VESLE village in the Canton de Verzy in CHAMPAGNE. Champagnes produced here are classified 100 percent in the CIVC rating.

BEAUNE walled city of the CÔTE DE BEAUNE district of BURGUNDY and the centre of the Burgundy wine trade. The nearby vineyards produce good to excellent red and white wines. The red wines have a TASTE RATING of C. Famous for the annual sale of wines for the Hospices de Beaune.

BEAUROY vineyards of the Painchy commune in the CHABLIS area of France producing PREMIERS CRUS white wines.

BEAUSITE, CHÂTEAU CRU GRAND BOURGEOIS EXCEP-TIONNEL wine from the SAINT-ESTEPHE commune in BOR-DEAUX producing value-for-money red wines.

BECHTHEIM vineyard of the Gottesshilfe GROSSLAGE where the Geysberg, Rosengarten and Stein vineyards are situated. Produces wine from the RIESLING, SYLVANER and PORTUGIESER grapes.

BEERENAUSLESE the third sweetest German category of QmP white wines. The wines are made from selected individual overripe grapes, normally affected by *Edalfaule* (NOBLE ROT) with a potential sweetness of 110 degrees OECHSLE. The result is wines of intense sweetness with a honeyed character and a SWEETNESS RATING of 8. They age well and will improve for many years.

BEESWING filmy sediment which occurs in old bottled PORTS.

BELAIR, CHÂTEAU red PREMIER GRAND CRU wine from the SAINT-EMILION district of BORDEAUX, neighbouring the famous Château AUSONE but producing value-for-money red wines.

BELGRAVE, CHÂTEAU cinquième GRAND CRU wine from the HAUT-MÉDOC district of BORDEAUX.

BELI BURGUNDEC Yugoslavian name for the PINOT BLANC grape.

BELINGARD, CHÂTEAU estate producing dry white and red wines in the BERGERAC district of France.

BELL'AGIO brand name of a sweet white MOSCATO wine of Italy.

BELLAPAIS a sweet sparkling wine of Cyprus.

BELL CANYON CELLARS *see* BURGESS CELLARS.

BELLEGARDE commune on the plain of LANGUEDOC in France which produces light, yellow Clairette de Belle-garde wine from the Clairette grape.

BELLE RIVE JACQUES LALANNE, CHÂTEAU DE producer of sweet white wines in the LOIRE district of France.

BELLET AC vineyard district of PROVENCE on the French Riviera. Produces red, white and rosé wines which are the best in the area, but little is sold outside the area.

BELLEVUE, CHÂTEAU GRAND CRU wine from the SAINT-EMILION district of BORDEAUX.

BELLEVUE LA FORÊT, CHÂTEAU producer of red and rosé wines in the Côtes du FRONTONNAIS district north of Toulouse.

BELLEVUE-MONDOTTE, CHÂTEAU producer in the SAINT-EMILION district of BORDEAUX of value-for-money red wines.

BELLINGHAM brand name of a wine produced by Union Wine of Paarl/Stellenbosch, South Africa.

BELLROSE VINEYARD winery in the SONOMA district of California, north of San Francisco, growing mostly Cabernet Sauvignon grapes.

BEL - ORME - TRONQUOY - DE - LALANDE, CHÂTEAU CRU GRAND BOURGEOIS wine from the HAUT-MÉDOC district of BORDEAUX producing value-for-money red wines.

BENDIGO town and vineyard area in VICTORIA.

BEN EAN historic vineyard in the Hunter Valley in New South Wales, producing some of the finest wines.

BENEDE-ORANJE demarcated WO wine-growing district around the Orange River in South Africa.

BENMARL highly regarded vineyard in the Finger Lakes district of the Hudson River Valley, New York State.

BENTONITE clay from Wyoming used for clarifying wines, preventing discolouration caused by suspended particles. This process is carried out at the FINING stage.

BERBERANA BODEGAS wine producers of the RIOJA ALTA region of northern Spain producing red and white wines. The reds include 3 AÑO CARTA DE PLATA and full-bodied 5 AÑO CARTA DE ORO. Whites include the fruity Berberana.

BEREICH German term for district. In the German classification system, roughly equivalent to the AC system of France, a Bereich is a subdivision of each of the 11 designated quality wine regions (BESTIMMTEN ANBAUGEBIETE), producing QbA wines. The most basic wines have just a Bereich name but there are further layers of quality. Each Bereich consists of one or more vineyard sections (GROSSLAGEN) which in turn are subdivided into individual vineyards (EINZELLAGEN), each of which is associated with a town (*Weinbauorte*).

BERGERAC city and wine-growing area of southwest France producing red, rosé and white vins de pays and AC wines from nine appellations. The best known are MONBAZILLAC, a sweet white and Bergerac red (TASTE RATING C) and dry white (SWEETNESS RATING 1), but red and medium-sweet white Côtes de Bergerac are also found.

BERGÈRES-LES-VERTUS CHAMPAGNE vineyard of the Marne Valley in France, classified 90 percent (red) and 93 percent (white) in the CIVC rating.

BERGHEIM village in ALSACE, France, producing some well-regarded wines.

BERGWEILER-PRÜM-ERBEN important wine firm of the MOSEL-SAAR-RUWER region, owning a number of good vineyards in the region.

BERINGER wine company in the NAPA VALLEY, California, producing varietal vintage wines such as Barenblut, and some Sherry and Port.

BERNKASTEL town and BEREICH vineyard area in the middle MOSEL-SAAR-RUWER area. The wines have a SWEETNESS RATING of 4 and vary from average to very good, Bereich Bernkastel Riesling being the top wine. Located at the village of Bernkastel-Kues is the famous vineyard Bernkasteler Doktor, so called because its wine is said to have cured an illness suffered by Prince-Bishop Boemund II of Trier in the 14th century. Wines from it and the neighbouring vineyard of Bernkasteler-Graben are labelled *Bernkasteler Doktor und Graben*.

BERONIA brand name of red and white wines produced by Bodegas Beronia in the RIOJA region of Spain.

BERRI ESTATES large cooperative producer of wine boxes (e.g. Fruity Gordo) at Riverland, South Australia, currently also producing varietal wines of ever-increasing quality.

BERTANI long-established producer in the VENETO region of Italy of the DOC wines SOAVE, BARDOLINO, and VALPOLICELLA.

BERTOLA SHERRY producers in the JEREZ region of southern Spain.

BERTOLI, FRANCESCO producer of DOC wines, CHIANTI and Chianti Classico, around Siena in TUSCANY.

BERTRAMS wine house in South Africa known for its quality red wines, especially Cabernet Sauvignon.

BESSERAT DE BELLFON CHAMPAGNE firm in the town of AY in the Champagne region of France, also producing CRÉMANT wines.

BEST'S winery in the Great Western region of Victoria, southern Australia, producing table and fortified wines including an unusual red wine labelled Bin 0, excellent Chardonnays, and a well-known sparkling wine made by the CHAMPAGNE METHOD.

BEYCHEVELLE, CHÂTEAU excellent quatrième GRAND CRU wine from the SAINT-JULIEN commune in BORDEAUX.

BEYER, LEÓN long-established producer of mostly Riesling and Gewürztraminer quality wines in EGUISHEIM in the ALSACE region of France.

BIANCHELLO DEL METAURO light, dry white DOC wine from the MARCHE region of east-central Italy.

BIANCO Italian term for white wine.

BIANCO D'ARQUATA excellent white wine of Umbria in central Italy.

BIANCO DI ALESSANO grape grown in the PUGLIA region of Italy.

BIANCO DI CUSTOZA white DOC wine from round Lake Garda in the VENETO region of northern Italy. This crisp light wine is gaining recognition and increasing sales in the UK. Made from blended grapes, including Trebbiano and Tocai.

BIANCO DI SCANDIANO sweetish white DOC wine, sometimes sparkling, made in EMILIA ROMAGNA, Italy.

BIANCO DI TOSCANA white wine from TUSCANY in northwestern Italy. Generally of only average quality and vinous, without distinctive fruit character. The main grape variety is Trebbiano.

BIANCOLELLA Italian white wine grape grown on the island of ISCHIA off southwest Italy and on CORSICA.

BIANCONE Italian grape variety grown on Corsica.

BIANCO VERGINE DELLA VALDICHIANA dry, fresh white DOC wine of TUSCANY in Italy.

BICHOT, ALBERT wine-grower and merchant in BURGUNDY with interests in a number of vineyards in BEAUNE and CHABLIS.

BIDDENDEN vineyard in Kent in southeast England

producing white and rosé wines from Müller-Thurgau, Ortega and Pinot Noir grapes.

BIENVUE-BÂTARD-MONTRACHET white wine from BURGUNDY classified as a GRAND CRU. The vineyard is situated in the CÔTE DE BEAUNE district and is part of the PULIGNY-MONTRACHET and CHASSAGNE-MONTRACHET communes.

BIG tasting term for a wine with a greater than usual amount of alcohol, body and flavour. Not necessarily used as an indication of quality.

BIGI, LUIGI & FIGLIO large, reliable producer of DOC wines from UMBRIA, including ORVIETO and Vino Nobile di Montepulciano, and EST! EST!! EST!!! from Latium.

BIJELO Yugoslavian term for white wine.

BIKAVER Hungarian term for 'Bull's Blood', from the EGER region of northeastern Hungary; a full-bodied, dark, long-living wine.

BILBAINAS firm in Bilbao in the RIOJA region of northern Spain producing red and white wines, sweet and dry, still and sparkling, and a dessert wine (Brillante).

BIN place where bottles of wine are stored, e.g. a cupboard or similar container where wines can be protected against movement or sudden temperature changes. Bin numbers are frequently used in Australia and occasionally elsewhere as a label for a wine.

BINGEN village and BEREICH in the RHEINHESSEN area of Germany which includes the GROSSLAGEN of Abtei, Adelberg, Kaiserpfalz, Kurfurstenstuck, Rheingrafenstein and Sankt Rochuskapelle. **Binger Rochusberg** is a very good quality wine from Bingen.

BIONDI-SANTI producer of the DOC wine BRUNELLO DI MONTALCINO at Siena in TUSCANY, a rich, dark-red wine of great distinction.

BISCHOFLICHES WEINGUT group of vineyards in the MOSEL-SAAR-RUWER region of Germany, made up of three original domaines: Hohe Domkirche, Bischöfliches Konvikt and Bischöfliches Priesterseminar, these three names still being used on the labels.

BISSEUIL CHAMPAGNE vineyard of the Canton D'Ay in the Rheims district of France, classified 93 percent in the CIVC rating.

BITTER tasting term for a wine whose AFTERTASTE has a lingering bitterness. Not to be confused with ACIDITY in red table wines.

BLADDER PACK *see* WINE BOX.

BLAGNY village in the CÔTE DE BEAUNE area of France, producing red and white wines which are incorporated in the communes of MEURSAULT and PULIGNY-MONTRACHET and overshadowed by them. Bargains are to be had in wines under the Blagny label.

BLANC French term for white wine.

BLANC DE BLANCS white wine made from only white grapes, particularly used of CHAMPAGNE made from CHARDONNAY fruit only.

BLANC DE NOIRS white wine made from red-wine grapes. Of CHAMPAGNE it means it has been made from PINOT NOIR or PINOT MEUNIER grapes.

BLANC FUMÉ alternative name for the SAUVIGNON BLANC grape.

BLANCHOTS GRAND CRU of CHABLIS in central France, produced in the commune of Fye. Chablis is regarded as part of BURGUNDY.

BLANCK, MARCEL producer of long-lived quality wines in ALSACE.

BLANCO Spanish white wine.

BLANDY important shippers of MADEIRA wine with aristocratic labels. Best known is Duke of Clarence MALMSEY.

BLANQUETTE DE LIMOUX sparkling wine produced in the communes surrounding LIMOUX in southwest France. CHAMPAGNE METHOD technique results in clean crisp wines which have style and are good value.

BLASS, WOLF producer of quality blended wines in the BAROSSA VALLEY, Australia.

BLATINA wine produced at Bosnia-Herzegovina in Yugoslavia, not far from Dubrovnik near the coast of Dalmatia.

BLAUBURGUNDER term used in Austria for the PINOT NOIR grapes used for producing red wines.

BLAUER PORTUGIESER grape used in Austria for producing light-style red wine.

BLAUER WILDBACHER red-wine grape grown in the province of STYRIA in Austria and used in the production of Schilcherwein.

BLAUFRÄNKISCHE red-wine grape similar to GAMAY grown in the Austrian lake district.

BLAYE town and AC region of BORDEAUX, producing reasonable quality whites and some reds. Two other ACs of the area are PREMIÈRES CÔTES DE BLAYE and CÔTES DE BLAYE.

BLAZQUEZ SHERRY firm in the BALBAINA district of JEREZ in northern Spain producing a variety of Sherries, including Carta Blanca, Carta Roja and Carta Oro.

BLEICHERT German term for rosé wine.

BLENDING winemaking practice which involves the selection and mixing of wines from different areas, grape varieties or years to produce a wine superior to the individual wines in its make-up. The blending of a lesser wine with a better one can improve the characteristics of the inferior wine, a practice which has resulted in some spurious Burgundys. All SHERRY and most CHAMPAGNE is blended. Wines which are made from the same grape variety and labelled as such are called VARIETAL wines, or, in France, CÉPAGE.

BLOOM thin opaque coating that forms on grapes and other fruits. It contains the yeasts which bring about fermentation.

BLUE DANUBE brand of Austrian wine made by the firm of Lenz Moser from Gewürztraminer and Wälschriesling grapes.

BLUE NUN best-selling brand of LIEBFRAUMILCH, a light and fruity German wine exported in great quantity by the firm of Sichel.

BLUE STRIPE brand of white wine made from Chenin Blanc and Verdelho grapes by the firm of Houghton in Western Australia. Now renamed Supreme Dry White.

BÔA BISTA well-known vineyard of the Alto-Douro in Portugal producing fine quality wines.

BOAL *see* BUAL.

BOARCAL Portuguese grape variety used in the making of red VINHO VERDE wines.

BOBADILLA large, quality producers making inexpensive Sherries, particularly FINO.

BOBERG designated wine-growing area of South Africa whose liqueur wines, e.g. Sherries and Ports, may bear the WO seal. Table wines are also produced.

BOCKSBEUTEL (BOXBEUTEL) flask-shaped wine bottle used in some areas of Austria and Germany.

BOCKSTEIN highly reputed vineyard in the MOSEL-SAAR-RUWER region of Germany.

BODEGA Spanish term for (1) a place for storing wine, e.g. a wine shop or cellar; (2) a winery or wine producer.

BODENHEIM village in the GROSSLAGE of Sankt Alban in the RHEINHESSEN area of Germany whose vineyards produce spicy whites and some reds.

BODENSEE BEREICH in the BADEN area of southwest Germany producing SEEWEINE (Lake Wines). The better wines come from around Meersburg, although it is mainly drunk locally.

BODY tasting term for the consistency, thickness, substance or depth of a wine. Closely related to ALCOHOL content but flavour and TANNIN also contribute. Usually associated with high quality red wines. *See also* TASTE RATING.

BOEKEL long-established merchant and wine-grower of Alsace, based in Mittelbergheim.

BOGDANUSA Yugoslavian grape used in the production of white wine. The resulting wines have floral characters.

BOISSET, JEAN CLAUDE merchant in Nuits St-Georges on the Côte d'Or district of Burgundy producing many fine wines.

BOLLA well-known wine house in Verona in northern Italy producing DOC wines, BARDOLINO, VALPOLICELLA and SAOVE.

BOLLINGER celebrated CHAMPAGNE firm in the town of AY in the Champagne region of France producing wines of consistently high quality and breeding, including vintage, nonvintage and rosé.

BOMMES commune in the SAUTERNES area of BORDEAUX. Produces the PREMIERS CRUS, Château La Tour-Blanche, CLOS HAUT-PEYRAGUEY, and Château RAYNE VIGNEAU.

BONARDA grape used for the production of dark red, sometimes sparkling wine, mostly around ASTI in northwest Italy, and also in Brazil.

BONNES MARES, LES GRAND CRU red BURGUNDY from the CHAMBOLLE-MUSIGNY commune in the CÔTE DE NUITS. Very full-bodied, rich wines.

BONNET, CHÂTEAU in the CHÉNAS area of BORDEAUX producing red and white wines.

BONNEZEAUX subregion of ANJOU in the LOIRE Valley of France; of AC status, it produces good sweet wines from Chenin Blanc grapes often affected by NOBLE ROT.

BOR Hungarian term for wine.

BORBA vine-growing area in the Alentejo region of Portugal producing strong quaffing red wines.

BORDEAUX renowned wine-growing region of France, producing much of the country's fine wines. The region is centred on the town of Bordeaux in western France, along the river Gironde and the two rivers that join to feed it, the Dordogne and the Garonne.

Bordeaux wines are blended: the red from the Cabernet Sauvignon, Cabernet Franc, and Merlot grapes; the white from Sauvignon Blanc, Semillon and Muscadelle. Red Bordeaux (known as CLARET from the original French CLAIRETTE) is generally drier and lighter than BURGUNDY, and the better wines take longer to mature, producing arguably the world's finest wines. There are still numerous clarets available at reasonable prices, and the quality of these wines seems to be consistently improving. The variable weather of this coastal region can dictate the quality of the wines from year to year, but advances in wine technology have reduced vintage variations. White Bordeaux ranges from the dry Premières Côtes de Bordeaux and Graves to the full sweetness of Sauternes and Barsac. Whites are a blend of Semillon, Sauvignon Blanc and Colombard.

There are four types of Bordeaux bottlings: **Bordeaux Rouge, Bordeaux Blanc,** regional bottlings and château bottlings. **Bordeaux Supérieur** is an AC which indicates a higher minimum alcohol content than simple Bordeaux.

The main subregional appellations include BLAYE; Côtes de Bourg, east of Haut-Médoc, across the River Gironde from Margaux, which produces good quality reds at affordable prices; and east of SAINT-EMILION, Côtes de Castillon, which produces fair to good quality red wine, and Côtes de Francs, lesser red and dry white wines.

Top subregional appellations are SAUTERNES, BARSAC, MÉDOC, HAUT-MÉDOC, SAINT-ESTÈPHE, PAUILLAC, SAINT-JULIEN, MARGAUX, LISTRAC, MOULIS, POMEROL, SAINT-EMILION, and GRAVES. Within these, some 200 individual châteaux (often just parcels of land) are classified according to the quality of their wines into PREMIERS CRUS, deuxièmes crus, troisièmes crus, quatrièmes crus, cinquièmes crus and, below this, CRUS BOURGEOISES. The GRAND CRU châteaux produce superlative wines that few can afford on a regular basis, but anyone interested in wines should try some, both for enjoyment and as a benchmark for evaluation of other wines.

BORGES E IRMÃO producer of VINHO VERDE wines in Portugal including Gatão, and also Daõ wines.

BORGOGNO, GIACOMO E FIGLI producer of BAROLO wines in PIEMONTE, Italy.

BORRAÇAL Portuguese grape variety used in the making of red VINHO VERDE wines.

BOSA town on the west coast of Sardinia where the red DOC wine, Malvasia di Bosa, is produced.

BOSCA major wine producer of Asti in the PIEMONTE region of Italy. DOC wines include ASTI SPUMANTE, Barbera d'Asti and BARBARESCO.

BOTRYTIS CINERIA *see* NOBLE ROT.

BOTTOCINO red DOC wine produced in LOMBARDY, made from a blend of grapes with BARBERA predominating.

BOTTLE AGEING the process and changes which take place in wine while it remains in the bottle, beneficial only to certain types of wine. Most wines are ready to drink as soon as they are bottled and are not meant to be kept. In white wines the colour becomes golden and the fresh grape flavour and aroma are replaced by a more mature and complex vinosity. Certain fine wines, including the better Bordeaux and Burgundies, the best sweet wines, such as Sauternes, and vintage Port, need bottle ageing to reach their peak. Fino Sherries do not benefit from bottle ageing. There is no way of judging with any certainty when a wine will be at its best, but as a general rule the larger the bottle the slower the contents will mature. The MAGNUM size has long been considered the best for maturing CHAMPAGNE. It is possible to obtain advice from specialist catalogues or magazines or from knowledgeable merchants. Alternatively, a wine can be tested every six or twelve months. As it begins to show its best according to your palate, reduce the period of assessment to every two or three months and drink your remaining stocks when you feel the wine will not gain from any further keeping.

BOTTLES when made of glass, the best storage method for wine, as glass, made of lime, soda and silica, neither adds to nor detracts from a wine. Apart from the narrow neck which cuts down on OXIDATION and the PUNT which collects sediment, different styles of bottle have evolved in different areas, e.g. Bordeaux, Burgundy and Champagne each has its own shape of bottle, and other areas have quite distinct shapes, e.g. the Chianti FIASCO and the Verdicchio amphora. Red wines tend to be bottled in dark or light green glass and white wines in clear glass, although German wines from Mosel-Saar-Ruwer are normally bottled in green and from other regions in brown, and in fact dark glass is preferred as it protects wine from light. Bottle sizes also vary, the standard Burgundy and Bordeaux bottles containing 75cl and the flute-shaped bottle of Alsace and Germany 70cl. As from the end of 1988 75cl is the standard size for bottles in EEC countries, although wines will appear in 70cl bottles until stocks are exhausted. Bordeaux and Champagne have a wide range of sizes, the former varying from half bottle to imperial, the latter from quarter bottle to Methuselah.

BOTTLE SICKNESS temporary condition sometimes suffered by wine for a period after bottling.

BOTTLE STINK (BOTTLE ODOUR) unpleasant odour sometimes present when a wine is first opened. It should disperse within half an hour or so of opening, but if the odour persists it is likely to be a faulty bottle.

BOUCHAINÉ, CHÂTEAU vineyards in the NAPA VALLEY, California, producing VARIETAL wines.

BOUCHARD AÎNÉ ET FILS producer in the CÔTE D'OR in BURGUNDY with vineyards in MERCUREY and BEAUNE.

BOUCHARD PÈRE ET FILS merchant and grower in BURGUNDY producing BEAUNE, le MONTRACHET, CORTON and VOLNAY wines.

BOUCHES DU RHÔNE VDP region of PROVENCE producing red and rosé wines.

BOUCHÉT *see* CABERNET FRANC, CABERNET SAUVIGNON.

BOUGROS GRAND CRU vineyard of the CHABLIS district of central France producing expensive wines.

BOUQUET term for the fragrance of a newly opened wine, originating from fermentation and ageing. It is due to the vapourization of ESTERS and ethers in the wine. It dissipates fairly quickly and is replaced by the AROMA.

BOURDIEU, CHÂTEAU LE CRU BOURGEOIS wine from the Côtes de BLAYE district of BORDEAUX producing value-for-money red wines.

BOURG AC area in the BORDEAUX region of France, producing full-bodied red and white wines.

BOURGEOIS French term for 'middle', used in BORDEAUX rankings.

BOURGOGNE general appellation for the basic wines of BURGUNDY, either red or white, and of fair to good quality. **Bourgogne Rouge** means red wine made from Pinot Noir grapes. **Bourgogne Blanc** is white wine made from CHARDONNAY or PINOT BLANC grapes. **Bourgogne Grande Ordinaire** is a lower general appellation for reds, whites and rosés made from approved grape varieties within the region. 'Bourgogne' can also be followed by the name of the grape from which the wine is made. **Bourgogne Aligoté**, for example, is a white wine made from the ALIGOTÉ grape, sometimes with some CHARDONNAY. **Bourgogne Passe-tout-grains** is a red wine made from a blend of one-third PINOT NOIR and two-thirds GAMAY grapes.

BOURGUEIL town and AC area in the Touraine region of the Loire valley in France. The name is given to light crisp fruity red wine made from Cabernet Franc grapes.

BOUTARI firm in Salonika, Greece, producing mostly red and some white wines. The best is Grande Reserve Boutari.

BOUVET-LADUBAY wine producer in the SAUMUR district of the Loire Valley in France, best known for sparkling Saumur and CRÉMANT wines.

BOUZERON village in the Côte Chalonnaise of BURGUNDY producing quality white wines.

BOUZY village in the REIMS district of France which produces red grapes for the production of PREMIER CRU CHAMPAGNE and expensive light, still red wine known as **Bouzy Rouge**. Bouzy champagne is classified 100 percent in the CIVC rating.

BOXBEUTEL *see* BOCKSBEUTEL.

BOYD-CANTENAC, CHÂTEAU troisième GRAND CRU wine from the MARGAUX commune in BORDEAUX.

BRACHETTO grape grown in Italy for the production of red wine which is usually sweet and sparkling, e.g. **Brachetto d'Acqui**, a DOC wine from PIEMONTE.

BRAGA official subregion of the VINHO VERDE region of Portugal.

BRAMATERA robust red DOC wine from the PIEMONTE region of northern Italy.

BRANAIRE-DUCRU, CHÂTEAU quatrième GRAND CRU wine from the SAINT-JULIEN commune in BORDEAUX.

BRANCO Portuguese term for white.

BRANDLUFT RIESLINGS quality white wines from Alsace produced by E. BOEKEL, Mittelberheim.

BRAND'S LAIRA small quality producer in South Australia, with vineyards on the famous Terra Rossa soils of Coonawarra, producing excellent red wines.

BRANE-CANTENAC, CHÂTEAU deuxième GRAND CRU wine from the MARGAUX commune of BORDEAUX.

BRAQUET vine used in the production of red and rosé wines in the PROVENCE region of France.

BRAUNEBERG quality vineyards in the GROSSLAGE

Kurfürstlay in the MOSEL region of Germany. Some of the better wines are labelled FILZEN.

BREAKING-UP term used for a wine which is deteriorating as a result of old age or poor quality production.

BREAKY BOTTOM English producer making dry white wines similar to the slightly sweet wines of Germany.

BREATHING the practice of allowing wine to come into contact with air after uncorking. This enables the wine to 'open up' and show its odours and flavours more fully. Wines are often left to breathe for a while after being uncorked in order to release the BOUQUET.

BRÉDIF, MARC important wine-grower in Rochecorbon in the VOUVRAY district of Touraine in France.

BREEDING term for the overall inbred qualities of a wine, taking into account soil, climate, quality of production, bouquet and taste.

BREGANZE red and white DOC wines produced around the town of Breganze in the VENETO region of northeast Italy.

BREISACH wine village in the GROSSLAGE Vulkanfelsen in the KAISERSTUHL region of Germany.

BREISGAU BEREICH in the BADEN region of Germany.

BRENTANO, BARON VON wine estate of WINKEL in the RHEINGAU region of Germany.

BRESSANDES, LES two highly regarded vineyards in BURGUNDY, one in the ALOXE-CORTON commune, the other in BEAUNE. Both produce PREMIER CRU red wines.

BRICCO BOSCHIS famous vineyard owned by Fratelli Cavallotto, producing DOC BAROLO wines in PIEMONTE, Italy.

BRICCO MANZONI red wine blended from NEBBIOLO and BARBERA grapes, produced in PIEMONTE, Italy. Wine with good flavour and depth.

BRIGHTNESS term for the absence of suspended matter in a wine, giving good clarity.

BRILLIANCE term for good strength of colour as well as clarity in a wine.

BRISTOL CREAM brand name for sweetened old OLO-ROSO Sherry bottled by Harvey's of Bristol.

BRISTOL MILK name for any light sweetened SHERRY, first used in the 18th century.

BRITISH WINE cheap wine made in the UK from imported raisins or concentrated grape juice. British wine now bears the same rate of tax as the better quality ENGLISH WINES.

BROKENWOOD winery in the HUNTER VALLEY region of New South Wales producing varietal wines.

BROLIO quality CHIANTI CLASSICO from TUSCANY, Italy, sold in a bottle rather than in a FIASCO.

BROOKSIDE VINEYARD winery in SONOMA COUNTY, California, which holds an annual vintage wine festival. Its best known label is Assumption Abbey.

BROUILLY largest BEAUJOLAIS CRU. A light, very fruity wine, generally lacking the body of the other crus so best drunk within a year or two of production. The best wines are produced under the CÔTES DE BROUILLY appellation.

BROWN BROTHERS family winery in VICTORIA, Australia, producing varietal wines widely available in the UK. It is currently enjoying great success with a dessert wine made from Orange Muscat and Flora grapes.

BROWN SHERRY sweet dark AMOROSO Sherry with a SWEETNESS RATING of 9.

BRUCE WINERY, DAVID winery in the Novitiate of Los Gatos, CALIFORNIA. It has a few vineyards producing VARIETAL wines.

BRUISYARD English winery producing medium-dry wines from MULLER-THURGAU grapes.

BRUNELLO DI MONTALCINO red DOC wine from TUSCANY, Italy. Made from the Brunello grape, a clone of SANGIOVESE, it is regarded as one of the best wines of Italy. Characterized by intense fruit flavours this complex and robust wine will stand keeping for many years, even decades.

BRUT French term for the driest of CHAMPAGNE and sparkling wine styles. Once brut wines were completely dry, but nowadays most usually contain small amounts of residual sugar.

BUAL (BOAL) grape variety used to produce a full, sweet MADEIRA dessert wine, **Bual Madeira**, with a SWEETNESS RATING of 7.

BUCELAS golden wine from the DO area of Bucelas near Lisbon in Portugal. The wine is dry and light and is made from the Arinto grape.

BUCK'S FIZZ drink made of orange juice and champagne or a good quality sparkling wine, in the proportion of half and half.

BUCCI, FRATELLI major producer in the MARCHES area of Italy producing the DOC wine VERDICCHIO DEI CASTELLI DI JESI in a standard bottle rather than the traditional amphora.

BUENA VISTA vineyard at SONOMA, California, founded in 1857 by Agoston Haraszthy, the father of Californian viticulture, who also organized the Buena Vista Vinicultural Society in 1863.

BUGEY VDQS wines from the SAVOIE district of the Jura Mountains in France. The white is Roussette de Bugey, and reds, whites and rosés are sold under the name Vin de Bugey. Non-VDQS Bugeys may be blends.

BÜHL, REICHSRAT VON large wine estate at DEIDE-SHEIM in REHINPFALZ, southern Germany.

BULGARIA old wine-producing country of central Europe, which has seen many civilizations make wine on its soil. After World War I the vineyard areas increased substantially until the onslaught of World War II which decimated the industry. Bulgaria now gears its state-controlled industry to exporting for foreign currency, and to this end more than 70 percent of its production is sold to over 70 countries, and postwar development is continuing with significant plantings. The state bodies involved in the development and selling of the country's wines are VINIMPEX and VINPROM. Although not known for 'fine wine', Bulgaria makes very quaffable reds and passable whites, and some of the reserve wines are improving rapidly while remaining affordable. Local grapes are used to make basic wines sold under the MEHANA brand or as own-label brands, but good red wines are also produced from the MAVRUD grape. Also of higher quality are varietal wines from western European grapes, e.g. Cabernet Sauvignon, Chardonnay, Merlot, etc, sold at prices which make other producing countries wince. A new appellation system, Controliran, has been introduced for the top wines made from a variety of grapes chosen for specific areas to produce wines with their own regional character. These areas are: Asenovgrad, Harsovo, Juzhnyabryag, Kralevo, Lozica, Novo Selo, Oryahoviza, Preslav, Rozova Dolina, Sakak, Sakar, Stambolovo, Svishtov, and Varna.

BULLAY wine village in the GROSSLAGE Grafschaft in the Zell/Mosel subregion of MOSEL-SAAR-RUWER in Germany.

BULL'S BLOOD (EGRI BIKAVAR) brand of full-bodied red wine produced in the EGER district of Hungary.

BULLY HILL vineyard in the FINGER LAKES area of New York state, founded in 1970 and producing mostly VARIETAL wines.

BUNDESWEINPRAMIERUNG award by the German Agricultural Society to the best regional wines.

BUNG stopper made from wood, glass, or recently plastic, used to seal wine casks.

BURDON *see* CABALLERO.

BURGENLAND wine-producing area of Austria including the Neusiedlersee in the easternmost area of the country on the border with Hungary. Produces sweet wines from grapes affected by NOBLE ROT.

BÜRGERSPITAL ZUM HEILIGEN GEIST charity hospital in WURZBURG in the FRANCONIA region of Germany which owns a number of important vineyards and makes reasonable wines.

BURGESS CELLARS winery in the NAPA VALLEY region of California producing varietal wines. Also sells under the Bell Canyon Cellars label.

BURGUNDAC BIJELI Yugoslavian name for the CHARDONNAY grape, grown mostly in Serbia.

BURGUNDER German term for the PINOT grape. Varieties include SPÄTBURGUNDER, FRUHBURGUNDER, GRAUERBURGUNDER and WEISSBURGUNDER.

BURGUNDY (BOURGOGNE) renowned region producing some of the world's finest red and white wines along with large quantities of fair to average wines. The major subregions are CHABLIS, CÔTE DE NUITS, CÔTE DE BEAUNE, CÔTE CHALONNAISE, MÁCONNAIS and BEAUJOLAIS. The major grape varieties are the white CHARDONNAY which makes outstanding long-living wines and the red PINOT NOIR which makes full-bodied, rich and rounded wines with complex raspberry/

strawberry/earthy flavours and velvety-smooth texture.

Good Burgundy is very expensive and is unlikely to represent good value, but both reds and whites if carefully chosen can offer a standard against which to measure other wines. Factors in the high cost are the small holdings of individual growers and strong demand, particularly from the US. As a result high prices can be paid for wines which do not now deserve their cost. The consistency and quality of the less expensive Burgundies seem, however, to be rapidly improving, and some represent excellent value. Burgundy reds have a TASTE RATING of B and the whites a SWEETNESS RATING of 2.

Merchants (negociants) in Burgundy play an important role in wine production. Traditionally they bought the bulk of the region's production from small grower-producers then matured and blended the wines in their own cellars, those with their own vineyards adding their wine. The best negociants still produce good quality wines, but some are living on past performance and charge high prices for ordinary wines. More growers are starting to bottle and market their better wines themselves rather than see them blended with other growers' wines.

The appellation system of Burgundy is complex, with five AC levels: the general appellation BOURGOGNE; the regional appellation usually covering a negociant's blend of wines from a particular subregion, e.g. CÔTE DE BEAUNE; village appellations, the majority of villages having their own appellations covering the best of the nearby vineyards, e.g. FIXIN, NUITS ST-GEORGES, MOREY-ST-DENIS; PREMIER CRU appellations which include the name of the village and of the vineyard, e.g. Chambolle-Musigny/Les Amoureuses; and the top appellation, GRAND CRU, covering the best 30 or so vineyards which have their appellations and do not refer to their village or commune. *See also* BOURGOGNE.

BURING winery in the Murray River irrigation area of New South Wales, Australia, producing sweet wines.

BÜRKLIN-WOLF, DR large estate of the RHEINPFALZ area of Germany making quality wines.

BUSCHENSCHANK Austrian inn which sells the keeper's own wine. Marked by a fir branch over the entrance.

BUTT cask of just over 100 gallons, used commonly in Sherry production.

BUZAU wine-producing district of the Wallachia area of Romania.

BUZBAG dark red table wine produced near Elazig in central Turkey.

BUZET (CÔTES DE BUZET) AC area of France adjoining BORDEAUX. It produces quality red wines with keeping potential, similar to Bordeaux.

C

CABALLERO Spanish SHERRY producers of Puerto de Santa Maria. Their wines are sold in the UK under the Burdon label.

CABERNET D'ANJOU fruity rosé wine made in the ANJOU district of the Loire Valley from the CABERNET FRANC grape.

CABERNET DEL TRENTINO dry, full red DOC wine from the Alto Adige area of TRENTINO-ALTO ADIGE region of Italy, made from CABERNET SAUVIGNON and CABERNET FRANC grapes.

CABERNET DE SAUMUR rose wine from the AC SAU-MUR district of ANJOU in the Loire Valley.

CABERNET DI PRAMAGGIORE medium/full-bodied, dry red DOC table wine from the Veneto region of Italy, made from CABERNET FRANC and MERLOT grapes. Labelled RISERVA when aged over three years.

CABERNET FRANC quality red-wine grape variety of BORDEAUX, where it is blended with the more illustrious CABERNET SAUVIGNON and also MALBEC. While similar to Cabernet Sauvignon in many of its characteristics, it is somewhat softer and as such is useful for blending. It has good colour, flavour, tannin and acidity but is generally at its best when combined with other varieties rather than as a varietal wine. It is also planted in the Loire Valley in France and more recently in the US and Australia. In Touraine it is known as Breton and is elsewhere known as Bouchet, Bouchy and Veron.

CABERNET SAUVIGNON grape variety that produces some of the finest red wines, although often when blended with others. Plantings exist in almost every wine-producing country, but it is most famous for its leading role in the production of claret in BORDEAUX, especially from the Haut-Médoc region. It adds a 'green-berry', herbaceous and minty character to the nose of a wine. Its colour as a young wine is purple, which lightens with ageing. Because of the considerable TANNIN content, wines made from it need keeping to show their best. If properly aged, the tannin softens and the fruit characters and great structure are highlighted. Its TASTE RATING is D, but Cabernet Sauvignon wines from BULGARIA have a TASTE RATING of C. Most wine-producing areas of AUSTRALIA blend it with SHIRAZ to make excellent wines.

CABRIÈRES commune in COTEAUX DU LANGUEDOC in southern France producing Cabrieres VDQS wines.

CADARCA *see* KADARKA.

CADILLAC town and AC area of BORDEAUX, producing a sweetish white wine which makes a good apéritif when chilled.

CAGLIARI winemaking centre of southern SARDINIA producing red and white Campidano wines.

CAHORS tannic red wine with good depth of flavour from the AC region of the same name southeast of BORDEAUX.

CAIRANNE town commune of the CÔTES DU RHÔNE in southern France producing strong red wines entitled to the appellation Côtes du Rhône-Villages.

CAKEBREAD CELLARS winery in the NAPA VALLEY, California, producing quality CHARDONNAY, SAUVIGNON BLANC and CABERNET SAUVIGNON varietal wines.

CALABRESE adjective meaning 'of Calabria'.

CALABRIA area of southern Italy producing red, rosé and white wines. The most famous wine of the region is a white DOC from Cirò, a town where each of the above wine styles is produced.

CALDARO (LAGO DI CALDARO) light red DOC wine from the Alto Adige area of TRENTINO-ALTO ADIGE which has a slight almond flavour. Also known locally as Kaltereseewein.

CALEDON wine-growing area in the STELLENBOSCH district of the Cape, South Africa.

CALERA WINERY winery of San Benito in California.

CALIFORNIA state of the US where viticulture was pioneered in 1769 and which now produces vast quantities of wine from seven main regions: Central Coast, Central Valley, South Central Coast, Mendocino County, Sonoma County, Sierra Foothills, and the famous Napa Valley.

Grapes used in red-wine production include Pinot Noir, Cabernet Sauvignon, Merlot, and also the remarkable Zinfandel. For white-wine production, Riesling, Gewürztraminer, Sauvignon Blanc (Fumé Blanc), and Chardonnay, wines from the last in the better regions rivalling the best in the world.

The old tendency to produce wines of 14-15 percent alcohol combined with over-zealous use of oak barrels for maturing has faded, and the current wines are better balanced. Many wines still have too much flavour for some palates. A recent introduction has been COOLERS, a mixture of wine and fruit juices.

CALISSANO producers of ASTI SPUMANTE sparkling wine in the PIEMONTE region of Italy.

CALLAWAY WINERY winery in the Riverside Valley area of southern California, producing full-bodied reds and stylish whites.

CALLIGAS firm in Athens marketing red (Monte Nero), rosé (Calligas's Rosé) and dry white (Robola Calliga) wines from the Greek island of CEPHALONIA.

CALON-SÉGUR, CHÂTEAU troisième GRAND CRU wine from the SAINT-ESTÈPHE commune in BORDEAUX. Good value-for-money red wines.

CALUSO sweet, white DOC wines made from grapes dried on straw mats in the PIEMONTE area of northwest Italy around the town of Caluso. **Caluso Passito Liquorose** is a DOC fortified wine.

CALVET firm of wine growers and makers in the BORDEAUX and BURGUNDY regions of France.

CAMARATE light red wine from FONSECA in Portugal, made from CABERNET SAUVIGNON, Periquita and MERLOT grapes.

CAMENSAC, CHÂTEAU DU cinquième GRAND CRU wine from the HAUT-MÉDOC district of BORDEAUX. Good value-for-money red wines.

CAMPANAS, LAS village and wine area near Pamploma, Spain, and headquarters of the Vinicola Navarra company. Some wines bear the Las Campanas name.

CAMPANIA area of southwest Italy producing red and white wines including CAPRI, FALERNO and LACRIMA CHRISTI. Most of the wine produced does not have DOC status, but two wines which are well regarded are Solopaca and Taurasi.

CAMPBELLS OF RUTHERGLEN old wine family of Rutherglen, VICTORIA, southern Australia, producing fine liqueur MUSCATS and TOKAYS. Owners of the Bobbie Burns and Silverburn wineries.

CAMPO VIEJO large BODEGA of the RIOJA region of northern Spain and the name of one of its good red wines.

CANADA wine-producing country whose wines are made mostly in the NIAGARA peninsula of southern Ontario and also in British Columbia, in the Okanagon Valley. It produces mostly sweet dessert wines and table wines, blended from grapes based on VITIS LABRUSCA which is native to North America and not used in Europe. Some European VITIS VINIFERA strains are used in Ontario, but the wines they make are expensive and rarely seen in Europe.

CANARD-DUCHÊNE CHAMPAGNE firm based at LUDES in the Champagne region of France, producing Charles VII nonvintage, brut and vintage champagne. Now owned by VEUVE CLIQUOT.

CANDIA wines from the Greek island of Crete.

CANNONAU red-wine grape variety found in the Italian island of Sardinia. The dry or semi-sweet DOC wine **Cannonau di Sardegna** is made from it. Rosé wines are also made under this label. Classifications include RISERVA and Superiore. It is also used for non-DOC wines.

CANON FRONSAC AC district near Pomerol in the southern part of FRONSAC in BORDEAUX. The best wines are of good to very good quality. *See also* CÔTES DE FRONSAC.

CANTEIRO type of MADEIRA wine, matured by the sun.

CANTEMERLE, CHÂTEAU cinquième GRAND CRU wine from the HAUT-MÉDOC district of BORDEAUX. Good value-for-money red wines.

CANTENAC commune in the Haut-Médoc district of BORDEAUX containing many GRAND CRU châteaux. Its wines may be sold under the name of the MARGAUX commune. Top Châteaux include PALMER, BRANE-CANTENAC, KIRWAN, d'ISSAN and **Cantenac-Brown**, a Margaux troisième GRAND CRU wine.

CANTINA Italian term for a cellar or winery. **Cantina Sociale** is the name for a cooperative of growers.

CAPBERN-GASQUETON, CHÂTEAU CRU GRAND BOURGEOIS EXCEPTIONNEL wine from the SAINT-ESTÈPHE commune of BORDEAUX.

CAP BON area of Tunisia producing MUSCAT wines, also reds and rosés.

CAP CORSE *see* CORSICA.

CAP DE MOURLIN, CHÂTEAU GRAND CRU wine from the SAINT-EMILION district of BORDEAUX.

CAPENA white DOC wine produced in the LATIUM region of Italy, just north of Rome.

CAPEZZANA, TENUTA DI important wine firm of Florence in the TUSCANY region of Italy producing the DOC wines CARMIGNAÑO and Chianti Montalbano.

CAPRI dry white wine from the island of Capri in the Mediterranean, all of which is generally drunk locally. A few red and rosé wines are also produced.

CAPSULE cap which covers the cork of a bottle to provide additional sealing. Normally made of foil or lead, but plastic has become more common lately.

CARAGNANE *see* CARIGNAN.

CARAMANY wine cooperative and recent appellation of Latour-de-France in the MIDI, producing red and rosé wines.

CARBON DIOXIDE gas produced by the decomposition of sugar during fermentation and by active yeasts. Carbon dioxide helps prevent the oxidation of wine and is also used to produce the fizz in some drinks. In CHAMPAGNE the effervescence (carbon dioxide) is produced by secondary fermentation in the bottle, while some sparkling wines are carbonated by injecting carbon dioxide and retaining it under pressure in the bottle. It is the same method as used for soft drinks and produces a fairly poor quality fizz.

CARBONIC MACERATION method of making red wine in which the grapes ferment intact in sealed tanks instead of being crushed, producing a softer, fruitier quality; termed *Maceration Carbonique* in France. Such wines will not mature and should be drunk young.

CARBONNIEUX, CHÂTEAU *see* EAU MINERALE DE CARBONNIEUX.

CARBOY large glass or earthenware bottle with a protective wicker or plastic frame.

CARCAVELOS sweet white dessert wine from just west of Lisbon in Portugal. It is one of the principal wines of the DENOMINACAO DE ORIGEM.

CARDONNE, CHÂTEAU LA CRU GRAND BOURGEOIS wine from the MÉDOC district of BORDEAUX. Good value-for-money red wines.

CAREMA red DOC wine from Carema in PIEMONTE, northwest Italy. Made from the famous NEBBIOLO grape,

Carema wines are slightly less full-bodied and tannic than other wines from the same grape, e.g. BAROLO.

CARIGNAN red grape variety used for table and dessert wine production. It is extensively planted in the MIDI region of France, California, Australia, Spain, Algeria, Israel, Mexico and Morocco. In the US it is called Caragnane. Wines made from it have reasonable colour and good tannin but lack varietal character. It is often blended with other varieties to produce quaffing wine.

CARIÑENA red and white DO wines from the ARAGON district of northeast Spain.

CARMEL short for (1) Carmel Zion, an Israeli winery; (2) the Carmel Wine Co. Inc., New York, the export representative for most of the Israeli wines exported to the US and Canada.

CARMIGNANO quality red DOC wine from the area of the same name in the TUSCANY region of northern Italy. It is a CHIANTI-style wine made with a small percentage of CABERNET SAUVIGNON grapes.

CARNEROS CREEK WINERY winery at Carneros in California, producing varietal wines including full-bodied ZINFANDEL.

CARRAS, CHÂTEAU quality French-style wine produced in northern Greece from Bordeaux grapes.

CARRASCAL sherry-producing area north of JEREZ in Spain.

CARSO red and white DOC table wines produced in the FRIULI-VENEZIA GIULIA region of Italy. The reds are made from the Terrano grape and the whites from MALVASIA.

CARTA DE ORO see BLAZQUEZ and BERBERANA.

CARTA DE PLATA see BERBERANA.

CARR-TAYLOR VINEYARDS vineyards near Hastings, England, producing dry and medium-dry white wines.

CARTE D'OR RIESLING white wine made at the YALUMBA winery in the BAROSSA VALLEY, Australia. A famous name in Australia because although the wine is of good quality the TV commercial for it features Manuel from *Fawlty Towers* and outshines the wine.

CARTHAGE, COTEAUX DE good wines produced by the state wine cooperative of Tunisia.

CARVALHO *see* FERREIRA.

CASA term meaning a company or firm in Italy, Portugal and Spain.

CASA DA SEARA demarcated DO white wine from the VINHO VERDE region of Portugal. The two varieties are *petillement* and *meio seco*, the latter being drier.

CASA DA VILACETINHO demarcated DO wine from the VINHO VERDE region of Portugal.

CASAL Portuguese term meaning a company or partnership.

CASALINHO demarcated light wine from the VINHO VERDE region of Portugal.

CASAL MENDES brand of DO white wine from the VINHO VERDE region of Portugal produced by Caves Alianca.

CASAL MIRANDA demarcated DO white wine from the VINHO VERDE region of Portugal.

CASAR Spanish term for a village.

CASAR DE VALDAIGO wine producers of LEON in Spain producing light red wines.

CASA VINÍCOLA Italian term for a wine firm which buys in grapes rather than growing them.

CASE wood or cardboard container for shipping wine, holding a dozen ordinary-sized bottles.

CASK wooden barrel bound with metal hoops which is used for maturing, storing and shipping wines. Casks of various capacities and types of wood are used, with oak being widely accepted as the best. Each type of oak imparts a different flavour and odour to wine.

CASSIS (1) town in the PROVENCE area of southern France, near Marseille, producing crisp white wines; (2) black-currant liqueur made principally in northern France.

CASTEL DENIELIS brand name for a good, dry wine from Greece.

CASTEL DEL MONTE red, white and rosé DOC wines from the Bari area of PUGLIA, southeast Italy. The red wine, made from Bombino Nero and MONTEPULCIAÑO grapes, is considered the best and may receive the RISERVA appellation after three years ageing with one year in oak.

CASTELLI DI JESI *see* VERDICCHIO DEI CASTELLI DI JESI.

CASTELLI ROMANI name given to the wines, mostly dry whites, from the *Colli Albani* (Alban Hills), south of Rome in the LATIUM region of Italy. The best, and probably the best known, is FRASCATI.

CASTELLO Italian word for a castle but, as with CHÂTEAU, on a wine label indicates that the grapes come from a particular estate or vineyard.

CASTELLO DI CACCHIANO estate at Siena in the TUSCANY region of northern Italy producing a DOC CHIANTI CLASSICO.

CASTELLO DI NIPOZZANO important non-Classico CHIANTI vineyard near Florence in TUSCANY, owned by FRESCOBALDI.

CASTELLO DI UZZANO vineyard south of Florence in TUSCANY, making a well-known DOC CHIANTI CLASSICO.

CASTELLO DI VOLPAIA vineyard near Siena in TUSCANY making a DOC CHIANTI CLASSICO.

CASTEL SAN MICHELE good red wine produced in TRENTINO-ALTO ADIGE, northern Italy, from a blend of CABERNET SAUVIGNON and MERLOT grapes.

CASTÉRA, CHÂTEAU DU CRU BOURGEOIS château in the lower MÉDOC district of BORDEAUX producing good value-for-money red wines.

CASTILLO DE YGAY red wine produced in the RIOJA region of Spain. Very long-lasting Gran Reserva.

CATALAN VINS DE PAYS area of ROUSSILLON in the MIDI of France producing good-value red and white wines.

CATALONIA northern province of Spain producing a wide variety of table wines as well as brandy and vermouth. The major wine regions are PENEDÈS, ALELLA, TARRAGONA and PRIORATA. Other DO areas include AMPURDÁN, COSTA BRAVA, CONCA DEL BARBERA, and GRANDESA TERRALTA. Catalonian winemakers are possibly the most progressive in Spain and recently have been widely planting varieties of VITIS VINIFERA. Barcelona, the provincial capital, is the region's major city.

CATARATTO grape grown in Sicily for the production of MARSALA and table wines.

CATAWBA American grape variety from the species VITIS LABRUSCA grown in the HUDSON RIVER VALLEY, New York State, and around LAKE ERIE.

CAVA term for sparkling wine made by the CHAMPAGNE METHOD in Spain. Quality is rapidly improving, with some very good examples now available.

CAVALLOTTO, FRATELLI wine producer in the BAROLO area of Italy making quality Barolo and BARBERA wines.

CAVE, CAVES French term for cellar or wine firm. **Cave Coopérative** is a term for a cooperative.

CAVIT major wine producers of Trento in TRENTINO-ALTO ADIGE, northern Italy, producing wines of good value, especially Chardonnay and Gran Spumante.

CAYMUS VINEYARDS winery in the NAPA VALLEY,

California, producing very good Cabernet Sauvignon wine.

CELLAR room for storing wine. Ideally a cellar should be cool, dry, dark and free from vibration.

CELLETICA town north of Brescia in LOMBARDY, northern Italy, which has given its name to a fragrant dry red DOC wine.

CENCIBEL red wine grape grown in the LA MANCHA area of central Spain.

CENICERO wine village in the RIOJA ALTA region of Spain. A wine festival is held here every September.

CENTRAL VALLEY major wine region of CALIFORNIA stretching from near Sacramento in the north to Bakersfield in the south. Also known as San Joaquin Valley. Subregions are Fresno, Kern, Merced, Sacramento, Stanislaus and Tulare. Vast quantities of both 'jug' and good quality wines are made in the region. The main district is known as Escalon-Modesto. The quality of the wines is improving with the planting of new grape varieties and the use of new winemaking techniques.

CEOA VELHA DO wine from Moncao in the VINHO VERDE region of Portugal.

CEPA Spanish term for grape variety or wine.

CÉPAGE French term for grape variety, e.g. Cabernet Sauvignon.

CEPHALONIA Greek island on which the dessert wine MAVRODAPHNE is produced.

CERASUOLO pleasant rosé DOC wine produced in the ABRUZZI region of east-central Italy. From the same region comes **Cerasuolo d'Abruzzo**, a light red or rosé, mostly drunk locally.

CERES wine-growing area northwest of Cape Town in Cape Province, South Africa.

CERETTO major producer of the PIEMONTE region of Italy making quality BAROLO and BARBARESCO wines.

CERETTO, CASTELLO DI estate in TUSCANY, Italy, producing DOC CHIANTI CLASSICO wines.

CÉRONS area in the BORDEAUX district of southwest France producing both dry and sweet white wines. Grapes used are the same as for Sauternes and Barsac: Sauvignon Blanc, Semillon and Muscadelle, but the wines do not have the same intensity or lusciousness. Some very good buys are currently available.

CERVETERI red and white DOC wines produced in LATIUM, west-central Italy. MONTEPULCIANO and SANGIOVESE grapes are used for the red wines and the whites are mainly from TREBBIANO, with some MALVASIA.

CESANESE Italian red-wine grape used in the LATIUM region to produce sound full-bodied wines. **Cesanese di Affile** are dry, semi-sweet and sweet DOC wines of high quality and very rare. **Cesanese del Piglio** are very good, strong, dry or semi-sweet DOC wines.

CESARE, PIO producer in the PIEMONTE region of Italy of fine wines including BAROLO and BARBARESCO.

CH abbreviation for CHÂTEAU.

CHABLAIS white wine from the Chablais district of the VAUD region of Switzerland.

CHABLIS town and wine-producing area of BURGUNDY in central France given its own AC in 1938. The CHARDONNAY grape is grown here and produces white wines which range from fair to superlative. Unfortunately, the fame has brought high prices which in many cases are not justified by the product. Excellent Chardonnay wines are now appearing from Australia and California which, if not capturing the style of Chablis, are more pleasing to the pocket and often the palate.

The greatest of the Chablis wines are the seven GRAND CRU from vineyards close to the town of Chablis whose status came with the AC in 1938: Blanchots, Bougros, Les Clos, Grenouilles, Les Preuses, Valmur and Vaudésir. The wines are dry, white, rich and very flavoursome and, although expensive, useful as a benchmark for tasting.

The second rank of Chablis wines is the PREMIER CRU. These are normally labelled with the name of one of the 23 premiers crus vineyards. They vary greatly in quality, but wines from FOURCHAUME are usually good value for money.

CHALONE VINEYARDS vineyards at high altitude in the Salinas Valley, California, producing good wines, mainly from the PINOT NOIR and CHARDONNAY grapes.

CHALONNAIS region in the centre of BURGUNDY in France, also known as the Côte Chalonnaise. It produces red and white wines and a large amount of sparkling wine. Communes with AC status are Givry, Mercurey, Montagny and Rully. These wines are improving in quality and represent better value than the very expensive CÔTE DE NUITS and CÔTE DE BEAUNE wines.

CHAMBERS ROSEWOOD WINERY winery in RUTHERGLEN in Victoria, southern Australia, best-known for its excellent liqueur MUSCAT.

CHAMBERTIN GRAND CRU vineyard of the GEVREY-CHAMBERTIN commune in the Côte de Nuits region of BURGUNDY. It produces superlative red wine with the simple appellation Chambertin on the label, together with the vintage year (see CHAMBERTIN-CLOS DE BEZE. Only Pinot Noir vines are planted.

CHAMBERTIN-CLOS DE BÈZE GRAND CRU vineyard adjoining Chambertin in the GEVREY-CHAMBERTIN commune in BURGUNDY, producing excellent red wine in great demand and consequently very expensive. Its wine is comparable to, and often considered superior to, CHAMBERTIN and is sold under that name as well as its own, this being allowed by law because of its equivalent quality.

CHAMBOLLE-MUSIGNY one of the best communes in the CÔTE DE NUITS district of BURGUNDY. It produces mostly red wines from Pinot Noir grapes, its best being the GRAND CRU BONNES MARES and MUSIGNY. Many notable PREMIER CRU wines include Les Amoureuses, Les Musigny, Les Bonnes Mares and Les Charmes. CHARDONNAY grapes are used to produce a white called **Musigny Blanc**.

CHAMBRER French term for bringing a red wine up to room temperature. This should be done gradually.

CHAMPAGNE white sparkling wine produced around Reims and Épernay in northern France by the CHAMPAGNE METHOD. Only wines from the demarcated areas are allowed to bear the name. The wine is made from the white CHARDONNAY grape to which the red varieties PINOT NOIR and PINOT MEUNIER are sometimes added. After fermentation, wines of different vintages are blended, bottled, and matured for a minimum of two years, so allowing a wine of consistent style and quality to be produced. This style of wine is known as **non-vintage** or **NV** and is considered by the majority of champagne houses as their most important style. Wine made from the grapes of only one harvest is known as **vintage**. It can only be made if growing conditions are favourable, although recently the popularity of this style has led a number of houses to produce single vintage wines which would have been more suitable for NV wines. Some good wines are available at inexpensive prices. As these cheaper wines are matured for the minimum period, another two years keeping allows them to develop a fuller, more flavoursome style. Other styles of champagne are: BLANC DE BLANCS, BLANC DE NOIRS, ROSE CHAMPAGNE, BRUT, DEMI-SEC, and RICHE. Most champagne is branded and is available in a range of bottle sizes: quarter bottle, half bottle, bottle, MAGNUM, JEROBOAM REHOBOAM and METHUSELAH. Even larger sizes are the SALMANAZAR, BALTHAZAR, and NEBUCHADNEZZAR. Champagne bottles should be opened carefully with the bottle facing away from people as the high pressure of the wine on the cork can cause injury.

CHAMPAGNE METHOD the method by which champagne is given its sparkling quality, developed in the late 17th-early 18th century by the Benedictine monk Dom Perignon and little changed since. Following very rapid pressing of the grapes the juice and the skins are in contact for as little time as possible, a normal fermentation is carried out in steel or wooden tanks, with sugar added to the MARC, if necessary, in a process called CHAPTALIZATION. After two to three weeks, the wine is RACKED to remove dead yeast cells and sediment and then blended with other wines from both past and current vintages in a process called *assemblage*. A mixture of wine, yeast and sugar is added to the wine to activate a second, or secondary, fermentation in the bottle (it is this which imparts the bubbles and flavours to champagne). The wine is then bottled in heavier than average champagne bottles to withstand the pressure of the fermentation, capped and stacked to develop. After three to five years the wine is cleared of any remaining sediment in processes called *remuage* and DÉGORGEMENT, and quickly topped up with the DOSAGE. The cork is then inserted, the wire cage affixed and the champagne is ready for labelling and despatch.

CHAMPILLON CHAMPAGNE vineyard of the Canton d'Ay

in the REIMS area of France. Champagnes produced here are classified 93 percent in the CIVC rating.

CHAMPS PIMONT highly reputed PREMIER CRU vineyard of the BEAUNE commune of BURGUNDY.

CHANTE-ALOUETTE highly regarded dry, white HERMITAGE wines from the RHÔNE VALLEY, produced by M. CHAPOUTIER. Wine is blended from the Alouette vineyard and from neighbouring ones.

CHANTOVENT wine company in the MINERVOIS district of the MIDI, supplying table wines produced by a number of local cooperatives.

CHAPELLE-CHAMBERTIN small GRAND CRU vineyard of the GEVREY-CHAMBERTIN commune in BURGUNDY which produces wines of lesser body than CHAMBERTIN.

CHAPELLE-MADELAINE, CHÂTEAU GRAND CRU wine from the SAINT-EMILION district of BORDEAUX.

CHAPOUTIER, M. important wine-grower and NÉGOCIANT of the RHÔNE VALLEY with vineyards in CÔTE ROTIE, ST JOSEPH, HERMITAGE, and CHÂTEAUNEUF-DU-PAPE.

CHAPPELLET VINEYARDS vineyard on Pritchard Hill in the NAPA VALLEY, California, producing full-bodied varietal wines.

CHAPTALIZATION the addition of cane sugar to the MUST in order to raise the alcohol content of wine, including CHAMPAGNE. Developed by a Frenchman, Jean Chaptal, the practice is often abused and is illegal in California and Australia.

CHARACTER tasting term meaning combination of vinosity, balance, and style.

CHARBONO red-wine grape grown principally in California's NAPA VALLEY. It produces deep-coloured full-bodied wines.

CHARDONNAY white grape variety which produces the currently most sought-after white wine in the UK because of the depth of fruity flavour it gives its wines. The major white variety from BURGUNDY, Chardonnay is also blended with PINOT NOIR and PINOT MEUNIER to produce CHAMPAGNE. This celebrated grape is versatile in adapting to different climates and produces excellent full-bodied wines in numerous regions including eastern Europe and South America. Recent examples from Australia and the US have rivalled all but the very best from Burgundy. Extremely fruity in their style, these Australian and US wines are often described as having 'fruit salad', buttery or apple flavours. Ageing in oak barrels adds depth of flavour and complexity. Also known as Arnoison, Aubaine, Beaunois, and Melon Blanc.

CHARLEMAGNE (1) vineyard of the ALOXE-CORTON and PERNAND VERGELESSES communes in the CÔTE DE BEAUNE district of France, once owned by the Emperor Charlemagne; (2) GRAND CRU white BURGUNDY wine which is normally sold under the CORTON-CHARLEMAGNE appellation, one of the world's finest white wines.

CHARLES LE FRANCE brand name of wines produced by the ALMADEN vineyards in California.

CHARMAT METHOD process devised in the early 20th century by Eugene Charmat for producing larger quantities of sparkling wine by second fermentation under pressure in specially designed tanks. After fermentation the wine is filtered and bottled with the same dosage mixture as used in the CHAMPAGNE METHOD. Wines made in this way are of consistent quality but below that of wines made by the Champagne method of which it is a cheaper copy. Termed *Cuve close* in France and Tank or Bulk process in some countries.

CHARMES-CHAMBERTIN GRAND CRU vineyard of the GEVREY-CHAMBERTIN commune in BURGUNDY. The vineyard is allied with the MAZOYÈRES-CHAMBERTIN vineyard and wines produced by both are sold under the name Charmes-Chambertin.

CHARNU French term meaning fleshy when used of a wine.

CHARTA organization of leading RHEINGAU producers in Germany set up to develop dry wines for drinking with food. Bottles containing wines from Charta producers feature an arched-window symbol.

CHASSAGNE-MONTRACHET outstanding commune of the CÔTE DE BEAUNE area of Burgundy, producing red and white wines, of which the whites are the best known. The commune adjoins another excellent commune to the north, PULIGNY-MONTRACHET and shares the vineyards of Les Montrachet and Bâtard Montrachet.

CHASSELAS white grape used in the production of light table wines, widely planted throughout Europe and the rest of the world.

CHASSE-SPLEEN, CHÂTEAU excellent CRU GRAND BOURGEOIS wine from the MOULIS district of BORDEAUX. Often regarded as unfortunate not to have been given a numbered CRU status.

CHÂTEAU (CH) French term for a castle and its associated wine estate, although some châteaux are no more than villas.

CHÂTEAU BOTTLED term meaning a wine bottled within a château and made with its own grapes rather than blended. Can indicate that the wine is of higher quality than other wines of its region. The French term *Mis en bouteilles au château...* often appears on the label.

CHÂTEAU-CHALON AC appellation of the dry and very yellow-coloured wines produced in the JURA region of France.

CHÂTEAUMEILLANT red and rosé VDQS wines produced near Bourges in the upper LOIRE Valley in western France from PINOT NOIR and GAMAY grapes.

CHÂTEAUNEUF-DU-PAPE famous red and small quantity of white AC wine from plantings of 7,400 acres in the Vaucluse department of the RHÔNE VALLEY near Avignon. A blended wine, it may have up to 13 different grape varieties in its make-up. GRENACHE is the major variety, and SYRAH and CINSAULT make up the bulk of the blend. The vines grow on ground covered with large smooth rounded stones which reflect heat during the day and retain it into the night as the air temperature falls. The style of the wine has changed over the years from one which needed many years keeping to reach its best to the current 3-5 years. The small amount of white wine made does not rival the reds in quality. The best wines are normally CHÂTEAU BOTTLED. The red has a TASTE RATING of D.

CHATILLON-EN-DIOIS red, white and rosé VDQS wines from the department of Drome in the RHÔNE VALLEY.

CHAUTAUQUA wine-growing area in New York State, US, extending from Lake Erie to Ohio. Produces mostly table wines.

CHAUVENET, F. important wine merchants in NUITS ST GEORGES in BURGUNDY, producing mostly table wines. Their best known red wine is Red Cap sparkling Burgundy.

CHAVE, GÉRARD important grower of quality red and white HERMITAGE wines in the Rhône Valley, France.

CHAVES BODEGA in the GALICIA district of northern Spain producing sparkling wine from the Albariño grape.

CHAVIGNOL commune in the Loire Valley near SAN-CERRE in eastern France. Produces Sancerre-labelled white wines from SAUVIGNON BLANC.

CHEILLY-LES-MARANGES AC area in the CÔTE DE BEAUNE district of BURGUNDY producing red and white wines. The better wines bear the appellation Côte de Beaune in addition to the commune name.

CHELOIS hybrid grape used for table-wine production in New York State. This red grape has the 'foxy' characteristic common to many native American varieties.

CHÉNAS one of the nine CRUS of the BEAUJOLAIS area of BURGUNDY. Chénas is the smallest and is located within MOULIN-À-VENT but has its own appellation. Its wines are fuller bodied with similar depth of flavour to MORGON with keeping potential of 5-6 years.

CHENIN BLANC principal grape variety for the white wines of the LOIRE Valley where it may sometimes be affected by NOBLE ROT and used for making dessert-style wines. It is also grown in Argentina, California, Mexico and South Africa. It may be fermented dry or may have some sweetness depending on style. Its wines are light, fruity and floral with a SWEETNESS RATING of 4 and are generally most enjoyable when young. Also known as *Pineau de la Loire* and *Blanc d'Anjou*.

CHEVAL BLANC, CHÂTEAU rich, red PREMIER GRAND CRU wine from the SAINT-EMILION district of BORDEAUX. Considered to be the greatest of the Saint-Emilion wines.

CHEVALIER MONTRACHET GRAND CRU white wine vineyard located within the commune of PULIGNY-MONTRACHET in the CÔTE DE BEAUNE district of BURGUNDY in eastern France.

CHEVERNY white VDQS wine produced in the LOIRE Valley region of western France.

CHIANTI world-famous red wines from the Chianti area of TUSCANY in Italy, promoted from DOC to DOCG in 1984. Made from a blend of SANGIOVESE and other grapes, with the white TREBBIANO and MALVASIA being used less as more CABERNET SAUVIGNON and MERLOT are introduced, they have a TASTE RATING of D. They are made in two styles, one a light-bodied wine for early drinking, the other a RISERVA matured for a minimum of three years in casks to make a fuller, more complex wine. The wine is made in seven areas: Classico, the central area around Siena; Rufina and *Colli Fiorentini* (the Florentine Hills), north of Florence; Montalbano, Senesi, Aretini, and *Colli Pisane* (the Pisan Hills). **Chianti Classico** is the finest wine, with a higher alcohol content, greater body and complexity than ordinary Chianti. They age well, with the riservas capable of lasting ten or more years. Their high quality and relatively low price result in excellent-value wines. The name Chianti can appear on other wines so the authentic wines carry a seal: a black cockerel for Chianti Classico, and a white cherub (*putto*) for wines from the other areas.

CHIARETTO quality rosé wine made from mostly the Gropello grape variety in the Lake Garda area of LOMBARDY in Italy.

CHIAVENNASCA local name for NEBBIOLO grapes in the Valtellina area of LOMBARDY in Italy.

CHIGNIN white table wines produced at Chignin in the SAVOIE district of eastern France.

CHIGNY-LES-ROSES CHAMPAGNE of the Canton de Verzy in the Champagne region of France. Classified 94 percent in the CIVC rating.

CHILE second largest wine-producing country of South America after ARGENTINA. There are vineyards as far north as Coquimbo and as far south as Valdivia producing quality red and white wines from VITIS VINIFERA vines. The CABERNET SAUVIGNON and CHARDONNAY are currently of a very good standard. High altitudes (17,000 feet) mean cool and rainy growing conditions resulting in higher concentration of flavour. Modern techniques including cold fermentation and stainless steel instead of wood, largely introduced by Miguel Torres, the Spanish producer, have set high standards for the future in good value and style. Apart from Torres, other major producers are Cousiño Macul and Concha y Toro.

CHILFORD HUNDRED vineyard in Cambridgeshire, England, producing dry wines from MÜLLER-THURGAU, Huxelrebe, Schonburger and Ortega grapes.

CHILSDOWN vineyard in Sussex, England, making dry but full white wines from MÜLLER-THURGAU, Reichensteiner, and Seyval Blanc grapes.

CHINON town and subdistrict of TOURAINE in the LOIRE Valley of France, producing light fruity dry red from CABERNET FRANC grapes with a TASTE RATING of B. The best Chinon wines will stand keeping.

CHIROUBLES one of the nine CRUS of the BEAUJOLAIS district of BURGUNDY producing a light, very fruity wine best drunk young.

CHIVITE large wine company in northern Spain producing a dry white wine of the same name.

CHOREY-LÈS-BEAUNE minor red wine-producing commune near BEAUNE in BURGUNDY. The wine is sold either as Chorey or, when blended, as CÔTE DE BEAUNE-VILLAGES.

CHOUILLY CHAMPAGNE of the Canton d'Épernay in the Champagne region of France. Produces red and white wine, the red being classified 90 percent in the CIVC rating and the white 95 percent.

CHRISTIAN BROTHERS monastic order in California, owners of six wineries. Important and large producers of dessert wines and brandy, their best known wines are Château La Salle and PINEAU DE LA LOIRE.

CHUSCLAN village and commune in the RHÔNE VALLEY of France, producing red, white and rosé wines under the Côtes du Rhône appellation.

CINQUETERRE sweet white DOC wine made from raisined grapes near La Spezia in LIGURIA, Italy. *Cinqueterre* means 'five lands' and refers to the towns of Corniglia, Riomaggiore, Vernazza, Monterosso and Manarola set on the coast at the foot of very steep vineyards.

CINSAULT quality red variety which is a mainstay of CHÂTEAUNEUF-DU-PAPE. Used extensively in the CÔTES DU RHÔNE, but also the Midi, Algeria, Morocco, Tunisia, and South Africa. It has a good colour and scented fruit smell. Because of lack of TANNIN, it is often blended with other varieties such as GRENACHE or CARIGNAN. Also known as Picardan Noir, Espagne, and Málaga.

CINZANO large Italian wine company producing a variety of wines including vermouth, sparkling wines (including ASTI SPUMANTE) and table wines.

CIRÒ name given to red, white and rosé DOC wines from the towns of Cirò and Cirò Marina in CALABRIA, southern Italy. Reds and rosés are made from the Gaglioppo grape and the whites from Greco Bianco. **Cirò di Calabria** is one of the best known red wines of the region.

CISSAC village and vineyard area in the HAUT-MÉDOC area of BORDEAUX, north of PAUILLAC. There is also a château of the same name.

CITRAN, CHÂTEAU value-for-money red CRU GRAND BOURGEOIS EXCEPTIONNEL wine from the HAUT-MÉDOC district of BORDEAUX.

CITRIC ACID acid found in all grape varieties. Not as high in percentage terms as tartaric acid and malic acid. In hot areas it is often added to raise the total acidity of wine.

CIVC percentage system for rating CHAMPAGNE, administered by the Comité Interprofessionel du Vin de Champagne. Vineyards are given a rating between 80 and 100 per cent, depending on the average quality of the fruit when harvested.

CLAIR-DAÜ large wine domaine of the CÔTE D'OR district of BURGUNDY with interests in a number of the well-known communes of the region including Marsannay, Gevrey-Chambertin, Chambolle-Musigny, Morey Saint-Denis, and Vosne-Romanée.

CLAIRET French term describing young, light, fruity red wine once made from a blend of white and red grapes, now usually made from red grapes only. It is produced from mature grapes which are fermented for only a day or two and treated with sulphur to encourage MALOLACTIC FERMENTATION. The word CLARET is derived from it.

CLAIRET DE MOSELLE rose wine produced near the city of Metz in the LORRAINE district of northeast France.

CLAIRETTE grape variety grown in southern France, Algeria, Morocco and South Africa. It produces only average white wine, including **Clairette de Bellegarde**, a light white wine from the LANGUEDOC area of the MIDI; **Clairette de Die**, dry white and sparkling wines (made by the CHAMPAGNE METHOD) produced around the village of Die on the Drome River in the RHÔNE VALLEY; and **Clairette du Languedoc**, a light white quaffing AC wine made near Montpellier in the Midi. Those wines labelled Clairette de Languedoc, sometimes with a commune name, are strong and dry, and those labelled Rancio are stronger and made from overripe grapes.

CLAPE, LA VDQS area of the COTEAUX DU LANGUEDOC district of the MIDI in southern France, producing good red, white and rosé wines with good short-term keeping potential.

CLARET English name for red BORDEAUX wine, derived from the French word CLAIRET. While the modern *clairet* is young and light, claret now refers to the older red wine of the region. Other countries have used the name to describe their wines, but this practice is now disappearing.

CLARETE Spanish term for light red wines.

CLARE VALLEY vine-growing region of South Australia, 130 kms north of Adelaide, which produces very good quality wines from a range of VITIS VINIFERA varieties. The area has a hot climate and low rainfall, and the quality of the wines is largely due to the skills of the winemakers. Good wines are made by Enterprise, Grosset, Mitchell Cellars, Quelltaler and Stanley, amongst others.

CLARKE, CHÂTEAU CRU BOURGEOIS wine from the LISTRAC district of BORDEAUX. A château to watch as currently many improvements are being made.

CLASSICO Italian word meaning classic, used to describe wines from a controlled, normally central, part of a DOC area, e.g. CHIANTI Classico, ORVIETO Classico.

CLASSIFICATION OF 1855 classification rating BORDEAUX wines into five categories of quality, prepared for the Paris Exposition of 1855. The rankings have remained much the same, with few alterations. Some châteaux deserve better classifications and others are fortunate to be classified at all, but the system is still reasonably accurate. *See* BORDEAUX.

CLASTIDIUM very good quality dry, fruity white wine produced in LOMBARDY, northern Italy. The wine is aged in oak casks for many years and keeps extremely well.

CLASTIDO red, white and ROSATO DOC table wines produced in LOMBARDY, northern Italy.

CLEAN term for a wine free from any foreign (or 'off') odour or flavour. It does not necessarily indicate high quality. Often used to describe wine which is fresh and pleasant.

CLERC-MILON, CHÂTEAU cinquième GRAND CRU wine from the PAUILLAC commune of BORDEAUX. Good value for money.

CLEVNER (KLEVNER) term used in ALSACE for the PINOT BLANC grape. In Austria it is called Klevner or Burgunder and in Switzerland Klevner refers to the PINOT NOIR grape.

CLIMAT French Burgundian term for an individual vineyard. The BORDEAUX equivalent is CRU.

CLIMAT DU VAL *see* CLOS DU VAL.

CLIMENS, CHÂTEAU PREMIER GRAND CRU sweet white BARSAC wine from BORDEAUX.

CLOS French term for a vineyard enclosed by a wall. In BURGUNDY may also describe a castle. Clos and CHÂTEAU are names associated with higher quality vineyards as distinct from CÔTE (hillside) vineyards.

CLOS, LES GRAND CRU vineyard of the CHABLIS area of BURGUNDY.

CLOS DE BÈZE top GRAND CRU vineyard of the GEVREY-CHAMBERTIN commune in the CÔTE DE NUITS district of BURGUNDY, producing excellent full-bodied red wine. Some of its wine is labelled CHAMBERTIN or **Chambertin-Clos de Bèze** since the vineyard adjoins and is equal in quality to the Chambertin vineyard.

CLOS DE CHÊNE MARCHAND vineyard of SANCERRE in the upper LOIRE Valley, France.

CLOS DE LA PERRIERE good quality red vineyard in

the FIXIN commune in Burgundy's CÔTE DE NUITS. Part of this vineyard has PREMIER CRU status.

CLOS DE LA ROCHE GRAND CRU vineyard of the MOREY-SAINT-DENIS commune in the CÔTE DE NUITS district of BURGUNDY.

CLOS DE L'ÉGLISE vineyard of the POMEROL district of BORDEAUX. Quality wines are made using a combination of new and old techniques.

CLOS DE L'ORATOIRE rich, GRAND CRU wine from the SAINT-EMILION district of BORDEAUX.

CLOS DES JACOBINS GRAND CRU vineyard of the SAINT-EMILION district of BORDEAUX producing excellent full-bodied wines.

CLOS DES LAMBRAYS PREMIER CRU vineyard of the MOREY-SAINT-DENIS commune in the CÔTE DE NUITS district of BURGUNDY.

CLOS DES MOUCHES, LE PREMIER CRU vineyard of the CÔTE DE BEAUNE district of BURGUNDY.

CLOS DE TART GRAND CRU vineyard of the MOREY-SAINT-DENIS commune in the CÔTE DE NUITS district of BURGUNDY.

CLOS DE VOUGEOT GRAND CRU vineyard of the VOUGEOT commune in BURGUNDY.

CLOS DU BOIS winery in California's SONOMA COUNTY producing very good quality varietal wines, especially CHARDONNAY and CABERNET SAUVIGNON.

CLOS DU VAL (1) winery in California producing varietal wines in the style of Bordeaux and Burgundy; (2) (or **Climat du Val**) highly reputed PREMIER CRU vineyard of Auxey Duresses in the CÔTE DE BEAUNE district of BURGUNDY.

CLOS FOURTET PREMIER GRAND CRU vineyard of the

SAINT-EMILION district of BORDEAUX, producing full-bodied red wines.

CLOS RENÉ highly reputed vineyard of the POMEROL district of BORDEAUX producing rich, full-bodied wines.

CLOS SAINT-DENIS GRAND CRU vineyard of the MOREY-SAINT-DENIS commune in the CÔTE DE NUITS district of BURGUNDY.

CLOS ST JACQUES PREMIER CRU vineyard of the GEVREY-CHAMBERTIN commune in the CÔTE DE NUITS district of BURGUNDY.

CLOS ST JEAN PREMIER CRU vineyard of the CHASSAGNE-MONTRACHET commune in the CÔTE DE BEAUNE district of BURGUNDY.

CLOS ST MARTIN GRAND CRU vineyard of the SAINT-EMILION district of BORDEAUX.

CLOUDY term for a wine containing haze or suspended matter.

CLOYING term for an excessively sweet wine (possibly because of insufficient acidity).

COARSE term for an unpleasantly 'rough' wine lacking FINESSE. Often caused by oxidation and characterized by a bitter AFTERTASTE.

COCKBURN old-established reputable PORT shippers.

CODORNÍU Spanish wine firm in CATALONIA producing sparkling wine by the CHAMPAGNE METHOD.

COLACICCHI, BRUNO producer in LATIUM, Italy, making the good vino da tàvola, Torre Ercolana, from CABERNET FRANC, MERLOT and CESANESE grapes.

COLARES small town and DO area near Sintra on the Atlantic coast of Portugal near Lisbon, producing mostly red wines made from RAMISCO grapes grown in sand dunes and resistant to phylloxera. The wines may be aged for over 10 years and labelled GARRAFEIRA or RISERVA.

COLHEITA Portuguese term for harvest or vintage.

COLLAR term for the label on the neck of a bottle. In French, **collerette**.

COLLI Italian word for hills.

COLLI ALBANI white, sometimes still, sparkling or sweet DOC wines from LATIUM, west-central Italy, made from MALVASIA and TREBBIANO grape varieties.

COLLI BERICI red and white DOC wines produced in VENETO, northeast Italy.

COLLI BOLOGNESE red and white DOC table wines of Bologna in EMILIA-ROMAGNA, northeast Italy.

COLLI DEL TRASIMENO red and white DOC wines produced in UMBRIA, west-central Italy, in an area around Lake Trasimeno. Grape varieties used are TREBBIANO, MALVASIA and VERDICCHIO for the whites, GAMAY for the red.

COLLI EUGANEI average red and white DOC wines produced in VENETO, northeast Italy.

COLLI LANUVINI good quality dry white DOC wines produced in LATIUM, west-central Italy.

COLLINE DI CALDARO *see* CALDARO.

COLLIO (COLLIO GORIZIANO) dry, white and slightly sparkling DOC wines and also small quantity of reds made in the area of Collio in FRIULI-VENEZIA-GIULIA, northeast Italy. The wines are named after their grapes which are of VITIS VINIFERA species, such as CHARDONNAY, CABERNET SAUVIGNON and MULLER-THURGAU.

COLLI ORIENTALI DEL FRIULI red, white and dessert DOC wines produced in FRIULI-VENEZIA-GIULIA, north-east Italy.

COLLIOURE dry red table wine made in the BANYULS region of southern France, near Roussillon.

COLLI PERUGINI red, white and rosé DOC wines produced in UMBRIA, west-central Italy, from SANGIOVESE and TREBBIAÑO Toscana grapes.

COLLI TORTONESE red and white DOC wines produced in the southeast of PIEMONTE, northern Italy.

COLMAN'S OF NORWICH brand of less expensive wines including WINE BOXES.

COLMAR town in Alsace, northeast France, where an annual wine fair is held.

COLOMBARD white-wine grape variety grown in the west of France, where it is used for the production of Cognac, and in Bordeaux where it is blended. It is also grown in Australia, California, Israel, Mexico and South Africa. Its other names are Bon Blanc, Colombaud, Pied-Tendre, Blanquette and Saint-Pierre. In California it is called Sauvignon Vert.

COLOUR good indicator of quality and of age, especially in red wines. The range of acceptable colour for white wines is from pale straw to dark gold, with green tinges being common and desirable as they indicate good winemaking technique. White wines which are brownish in colour should be approached with caution as brown tints can indicate poor quality because of OXIDATION or age. Rosé wines should be pink or amber in colour. Red wines have the greatest range and depth of colour. They vary from intense deep red and purple in young wines, through a brick-red colour as the wine ages, and finally on to a brownish-red when the wine is fully mature. Aged red wine may have sediment. This is natural and does not detract from quality, and careful decanting should remove it. Brown colour alone in either reds, whites or rosés, is a sign to take caution.

COL SANDAGO winery in the VENETO region of Italy. Its DOC wine is PROSECCO DI CONEGLIANO. Varieties include MERLOT, PINOT GRIGIO, and CABERNET SAUVIGNON.

COLTASSALA wine produced by CASTELLO DI VOLPAIA in TUSCANY, Italy.

COLUMBIA wine producer in Washington State, US, making quality varietal white wines from Gewürztraminer, Chardonnay and Cabernet Sauvignon grapes.

COMMANDARIA rich, sweet dessert wine from Cyprus which dates back, under its present name, to the order of the Knights Templar in the 12th century. It has a reputation for being very long-lived.

COMMANDERIE French term for an order of knights, now used by groups with a common interest, such as the **Commanderie du Bontemps de Médoc et de Graves**, a wine society whose members are mostly growers and shippers.

COMMUNE French term for a parish, also used for a group of wine growers whose wines are grown in a particular area and sold under a communal APPELLATION.

COMPLETER strong red table wine produced in the region of Grisons in eastern Switzerland from the Completer grape.

CONCA DE BARBERA area in Catalonia, northeast Spain, where white, red and some rosé DO classified wines are produced.

CONCANNON VINEYARD reputable winery in the LIVERMORE VALLEY, California, producing red and white table wines and the vintage dessert wine, MUSCAT DE FRONTIGNAN, and a very good SAUVIGNON BLANC.

CONCHA Y TORO largest wine producer in CHILE, making quality wines from VITIS VINIFERA grapes including CABERNET SAUVIGNON.

CON CRIANZA Spanish term for the keeping of wine. A wine so marked has been aged in oak in accordance with local regulations. One marked *sin crianza* is a new wine.

CONDADO DE HUELVA *see* HUELVA.

CONDE DE SANTAR quality wine estate of the DAO region of Portugal. It is the only single estate allowed to make Dao; all others are cooperatives.

CONDITION term for the clarity of a wine, e.g. a cloudy wine is said to be in poor condition.

CONDRIEU excellent white dry and semi-sweet wines from the RHÔNE VALLEY in France, made from the Viognier grape. Château GRILLET is the leading producer.

CONFRÉRIE French term for a brotherhood, used by groups with a common interest, such as **Confrérie des Chevaliers du Tastevin de Bourgogne**, an old wine society of Burgundy whose members are mostly shippers and growers, and the TOURAINÉ wine producer, **Confrérie des Vignerons de Oisly-et-Thesée**.

CONGRESS SPRINGS WINERY vineyard in the SANTA CLARA region of California producing red and white vintage varietal wines including a quality SAUVIGNON BLANC.

CONN CREEK WINERY vineyard of the NAPA VALLEY, California, producing varietal wines. Their best is the CABERNET SAUVIGNON.

CONSORTIUM SEAL *see* CONSORZIO.

CONSORZIO Italian term for a voluntary consortium comprising local growers and shippers, formed with the purpose of controlling the use of DOC names. Such organizations have legal powers. A consortium will often label its wine with a seal, e.g. CHIANTI, to indicate that the wine has passed tests.

CONSTANTIA valley in the Cape area of South Africa producing highly reputed wines of WO standard.

CONSUMO Portuguese term for ordinary wine.

CONTERNO, ALDO firm in PIEMONTE, northern Italy, whose DOC wines include BARBERA, BAROLO, and DOLCETTO D'ALBA.

CONTINO very rare, high quality red RIOJA favoured by King Juan Carlos of Spain, which has boosted sales.

CONTRATTO firm in the PIEMONTE region of northern Italy. Its DOC wines include ASTI SPUMANTE, BARBARESCO, BARBERA and BAROLO.

CONTROLIRAN Bulgarian term for controlled appellation. *See* BULGARIA.

CONTROLLED FERMENTATION relatively new technique using refrigeration to regulate fermentation, resulting in the retention of high levels of fruit aromas and flavour. It is particularly useful in areas which are very hot at harvest times. A heatwave in BORDEAUX during the 1985 vintage has led many châteaux to use refrigeration in fermentation.

COOKED term describing the character in wine brought about by the effect of heat. May occur naturally, such as in MADEIRA production or by artificially heating a wine.

COOKS WINE COMPANY vineyards in Auckland, New Zealand, producing varietal wines, many of which are exported including excellent CHARDONNAY and SAUVIGNON BLANC.

COOLER mixture of wine and fruit juices, produced particularly in Australia and California. Coolers have fruity flavours and reduced alcohol content and have proved very popular.

COONAWARRA vine-growing district of southeast South Australia. One of Australia's premier winemaking regions, it produces excellent CHARDONNAY, CABERNET

SAUVIGNON, SHIRAZ and SAUVIGNON BLANC varietals, many of which are now available in the UK.

COOPERATIVES wineries owned by groups of wine producers, formed for the purposes of cooperative marketing and capital investment.

COPERTINO red and rosé full-bodied, smooth, flavoursome DOC wines from PUGLIA, southwest Italy, made from Negroamaro grapes. A RISERVA is also produced.

CORA firm in the PIEMONTE region of northern Italy producing DOC ASTI SPUMANTE and vermouth.

CORBANS vineyards in Auckland, New Zealand, producing mostly white VARIETALS, many of which are exported.

CORBIÈRES VDQS wines from the MIDI area of southern France. The three types are Corbières, Corbières Supérieur and Corbières du Roussillon.

CORBIN, CHÂTEAU GRAND CRU wine from the SAINT-EMILION district of BORDEAUX.

CORBIN-MICHOTTE, CHÂTEAU excellent GRAND CRU wine from the SAINT-EMILION district of BORDEAUX.

CORDIER owner of many excellent companies and châteaux including Château TALBOT, Château CANTE-MERLE, Château GRUAUD-LAROSE, and Laurent PERRIER.

CORDTZ BROTHERS CELLARS winery in the SONOMA district of California producing varietal wines including CHARDONNAY, GEWÜRZTRAMINER and ZINFANDEL.

CORI town producing red and white DOC wines in LATIUM, east-central Italy. The main grape varieties used are MONTEPULCIAÑO (red) and Castelli (white).

CORK the thick light porous outer bark of the Mediterranean cork oak, *Quercus suber*, which is used to stopper wine bottles. Cork is grown mainly in southern Europe and

North Africa, but some production comes from California and Brazil. Wines for keeping should have long corks of good quality. Champagne corks have the word 'Champagne' printed on them. Wines for drinking young need only have short corks. Metal or plastic caps are now effectively used as stoppers for cheaper wines. These have the advantage of not suffering from occasional bacterial infections which can spoil a wine.

CORKED tasting term for the unpleasant odour of a wine tainted by a defective cork. It very rarely occurs, and often a wine which appears to be corked simply needs time to 'breathe'.

CORNAS good-value quality full-bodied red wine from the RHÔNE VALLEY area of France, made from the Syrah grape.

CORONATA light, white wine from LIGURIA on the Italian Riviera.

CORSE French term for full-bodied wine.

CORSE French word for Corsica. The appellation **Vin de Corse** denotes Corsican wines in general, produced from native grape varieties.

CORSICA French Mediterranean island producing generally full-bodied wines lacking FINESSE. Of the better wines, the best known outside Corsica is the apéritif Cap Corse and the best is PATRIMONIO ROSE.

CORTAILLOD highly regarded red wine produced at NEUCHÂTEL in northwest Switzerland.

CORTESE white-wine grape grown in PIEMONTE, northwest Italy, producing DOC wines including the dry, still or sparkling **Cortese dell'Alto Monferrato** and **Cortese di Gavi**, a minor dry white wine.

CORTON, LE vineyard of the ALOXE-CORTON commune of the CÔTE DE BEAUNE district of BURGUNDY. It produces white and (mostly) red GRAND CRU wines. The name Corton is usually followed by the area or vineyard from which the wines come. Some bear the commune name: ALOXE-CORTON.

CORTON-CHARLEMAGNE GRAND CRU white Burgundy wine from the ALOXE-CORTON commune in the CÔTE DE BEAUNE district of BURGUNDY.

CORTON-GRANCEY winery in ALOXE-CORTON in the CÔTE DE BEAUNE district of BURGUNDY, owned by the leading wine growers Louis Latour.

CORVINA VERONESE vine grown in the VENETO, northwest Italy, and used in the production of the wines of VALPOLICELLA.

CORVO state-owned winery in Sicily and brand name of red and white Sicilian wines produced there. **Corvo di Casteldaccia** is a dessert-style wine.

COS D'ESTOURNEL, CHÂTEAU deuxième GRAND CRU wine from the SAINT-ESTEPHE commune in BORDEAUX. It produces a good second wine, Marbuzet.

COSECHA Spanish term for a harvest or vintage.

COS LABORY, CHÂTEAU cinquième GRAND CRU wine from the SAINT-ESTEPHE commune in BORDEAUX.

COSSART GORDON old-established shippers of Portuguese MADEIRA wine.

COSTIÈRES-DU-GARD red, white and rosé VDQS wines produced near Nimes in the HÉRAULT area of southern France. The reds are full-bodied, and like most reds that the region produces are steadily increasing in quality.

COT *see* MALBEC.

CÔTE French term for a slope or hillside containing a vineyard, as distinct from CLOS, a vineyard enclosed by walls, or at a CHÂTEAU, or one which is individually named. In a wine name it is generally an indication of lesser quality than a château but better than average. The plural is **Côtes** and a similar term is CÔTEAU.

CÔTEAU French term meaning hillside (plural **coteaux**).

COTEAUX CHAMPENOIS still white, rosé and red wines from approved champagne grape varieties in the CHAMPAGNE region of France. See also AMBONNAY.

COTEAUX D'AIX EN PROVENCE VDQS wines from the Aix area of PROVENCE in southern France. Reasonable quality reds, also rosés and whites of lesser but improving quality.

COTEAUX D'ANCENIS VDQS red, rosé and white wines from the lower LOIRE VALLEY in France.

COTEAUX DE LA LOIRE district of ANJOU in the LOIRE Valley, France, producing mostly sweet wines from Chenin Blanc grapes.

COTEAUX DE L'ARDÈCHE area of the northern RHÔNE VALLEY in France, producing VIN DE PAYS. It makes good SYRAH red wines, and the white CHARDONNAY wines are improving.

COTEAUX DE L'AUBANCE straightforward, easy-drinking AC dry to semi-sweet white wines produced in the LOIRE Valley, France.

COTEAUX DE MASCARA district of the Oran region of Algeria, producing red, white and rosé wines of reasonable quality.

COTEAUX DE PIERREVERT light white and rosé VDQS wines from the CÔTES DU RHÔNE district of the southern Rhône in France.

COTEAUX DE SAUMUR AC white, red and sparkling wines produced in the upper Loire Valley, France. Best known are good quality sparkling wines made from CHENIN BLANC grapes by the CHAMPAGNE METHOD.

COTEAUX DES BAUX-DE-PROVENCE VDQS area producing red, white and rosé wines of reasonable standards. It shares the same appellation as COTEAUX D'AIX EN PROVENCE.

COTEAUX DE TLEMCEN district of the Oran region of Algeria, producing red, white and rosé wines.

COTEAUX DE TOURAINÉ local red, white and rosé wines produced around Touraine in France.

COTEAUX DU GIENNOIS red and white wine-producing VDQS area near SANCERRE in the upper LOIRE Valley, France.

COTEAUX DU LANGUEDOC VDQS appellation covering many areas of the MIDI region of France, producing firm, full-bodied red wines of better-than-average quality.

COTEAUX DU LAYON white, mainly sweet AC wine produced in the upper LOIRE Valley, France, from Chenin Blanc grapes. One of the best wines is BONNEZEAUX.

COTEAUX DU LOIR good to very good quality AC red, white and rosé wines produced in the LOIRE Valley, France.

COTEAUX DU TRICASTIN appellation of wines produced along the east bank of the southern Rhône in France. Medium/full-bodied red wines of soft texture, usually very good value for money.

COTEAUX DU VENDOMOIS red, white and rosé VDQS wines produced in the upper LOIRE Valley, France.

CÔTE CHALONNAISE region south of BEAUNE in BURGUNDY, named after Chalon-sur-Saône. Its best wines compare favourably with those of the CÔTE DE BEAUNE in price if not in overall quality. Wines from RULLY, GIVRY and

MERCUREY are of good to excellent quality while still being affordable.

CÔTE DE BEAUNE area of the CÔTE D'OR district of BURGUNDY. It produces mostly red wines and some dry white wines in 19 communes, including ALOXE-CORTON, CHASSAGNE-MONTRACHET and PULIGNY-MONTRACHET. Those wines labelled with an individual vineyard name, such as CORTON, are of the highest quality. **Côte de Beaune-Villages** are AC wines blended from those of 16 vineyards in the area. It is normally an appellation used by negociants who are able to produce a sound wine of commercial quantity by blending the lesser wines of the villages.

CÔTE DE BROUILLY small BEAUJOLAIS cru in BURGUNDY, producing relatively full-bodied red wines with good flavour and depth. They have a similar body to CHÉNAS or MORGON, with ageing potential of up to five years. *See also* BROUILLY.

CÔTE DE LECHET PREMIER CRU vineyard of the CHABLIS area of BURGUNDY.

CÔTE DE NUITS area of the CÔTE D'OR district of BURGUNDY, stretching from Fixin in the north to Premeaux in the south. It produces mostly red wines and some dry white wines, graded GRANDS CRUS, PREMIERS CRUS, and those from the individual communes, the quality of which varies from excellent to average. **Côte de Nuits-Villages** are lesser AC wines. Mainly red wines, they come from the villages of Brochon, Comblanchien, Corgoloin, Fixin, and Premeaux.

CÔTE DES BLANCS area of the CHAMPAGNE district of France.

CÔTE D'OR main area of BURGUNDY, producing red and white wines. Comprises the CÔTE DE NUITS and the CÔTE

DE BEAUNE. The finest white and red Burgundies come from the Côte d'Or vineyards.

CÔTE ROTIE (1) AC area near Vienne at the northern tip of the RHÔNE VALLEY in France, producing rich red wines, arguably the Rhône Valley's finest wine, from SYRAH grapes; (2) PREMIER CRU vineyard of the MOREY-SAINT-DENIS commune in the CÔTE DE NUITS area of BURGUNDY.

CÔTES plural of CÔTE.

CÔTES D'AGLY VDN area of the ROUSSILLON district of southern France producing mainly sweet white fortified wines.

CÔTES D'AUVERGNE VDQS wines from the LOIRE Valley in central France.

CÔTES DE BERGERAC red and white wine-producing area of the BERGERAC region of southwest France. Its best wine is the white MONBAZILLAC.

CÔTES DE BLAYE red and white wine-producing area of BORDEAUX. They are better than BLAYE wines but not as good as PREMIÈRES CÔTES DE BLAYE.

CÔTES DE BORDEAUX lesser sweet white wines from BORDEAUX. *See also* PREMIÈRES CÔTES DE BORDEAUX.

CÔTES DE BORDEAUX SAINTE MACAIRE white wine-producing district of BORDEAUX.

CÔTES DE BOURG *see* BOURG.

CÔTES DE CANON FRANSAC small area of BORDEAUX producing heavy red wines. It lies within the FRONSAC commune and produces the best of the wines of the area.

CÔTES DE CASTILLON area near SAINT-EMILION in BORDEAUX producing good red wines of improving quality.

CÔTES DE DURAS area near BERGERAC, to the southeast of BORDEAUX, producing red and white wines.

CÔTES DE FRONSAC *see* FRONSAC.

CÔTES DE GASCOGNE area of southwest France producing quaffing VDP wines, the whites superior to the reds.

CÔTES DE MELITON branded range of wines from Greece, made by CARRAS from imported grapes.

CÔTES DE MONTRAVEL area of the BERGERAC district of southwest France producing dry and semi-sweet wines.

CÔTES DE PROVENCE appellation for much of the southern area of PROVENCE, producing better rosé and red wines than white. The red wines are beginning to be made from grapes from outside the area, like MOURVÈDRE and SYRAH and have a TASTE RATING of B.

CÔTES DE ROUSSILLON AC wines of good quality from the MIDI region of France, especially the full-bodied, firm red wines which have a TASTE RATING of B. **Côtes de Roussillon-Villages** wines have greater alcohol and more finesse. *See also* GRAND ROUSSILLON.

CÔTES DE TOUL VDQS area of the LORRAINE district of northeast France producing mostly light rosé wines.

CÔTES DU FOREZ VDQS area around the Monts du Forez southwest of Lyon in France.

CÔTES DU FRONTON, LES cooperative producing red, rosé and white table wines in the Côtes du FRONTONNAIS in the JURANÇON district of southwest France. Largest of the area.

CÔTES DU FRONTONNAIS *see* FRONTONNAIS.

CÔTES DU HAUT-ROUSSILLON district near the Pyrenées in southwest France producing sweet fortified wines.

CÔTES DU JURA appellation of the Jura mountain district of eastern France producing red, white and rosé wines.

CÔTES DU LUBERON red and white VDQS wines from the RHÔNE VALLEY region of France.

CÔTES DU MARMANDAIS area southeast of Bordeaux in eastern France producing light red and white VDQS wines.

CÔTES DU RHÔNE AC wine-producing area by the River Rhône in southeast France producing red, white and rosé wines. A more controlled appellation is **Côtes du Rhône-Villages**, a group of communes which combine to make quality wines, generally good value for money. *See also* RHÔNE.

CÔTES DU VENTOUX large wine-producing district of the southern RHÔNE VALLEY area of France making red and some white wines and recently granted AC status.

CÔTES DU VIVRAIS VDQS wine-producing region of the southern RHÔNE VALLEY in France.

CÔTES ROANNAISES red VDQS wines from the LOIRE VALLEY in France, made from the GAMAY grape.

CÔTESTI white and red wines from the Focsani vineyard of Moldavia in Romania.

COTNARI vineyard in northeast Romania producing a white dessert wine under the name Cotnari. One of the best and most famous wines from Romania.

COUFRAN, CHÂTEAU GRAND BOURGEOIS CRU of the HAUT-MÉDOC district of BORDEAUX. Good value-for-money red wine.

COUHINS, CHÂTEAU GRAND CRU white wine from the GRAVES district of BORDEAUX.

COULANT term for wines with a low TANNIN and ALCOHOL content.

COULÉE DE SARRANT vineyard near Savennières in the COTEAUX DE LA LOIRE area of Anjou in northwest France. Produces good, naturally sweet wines.

COUPAGE, VIN DE French term for a blend of low and high alcohol wine.

COURTAKIS firm in Athens, Greece, and the name of their dark red wine.

COUSIÑO MACUL one of the major wine producers of CHILE, making the best red wines including CABERNET SAUVIGNON and good white wines.

COUTET, CHÂTEAU (1) GRAND CRU wine from the SAINT-EMILION district of BORDEAUX; (2) premier GRAND CRU sweet white BARSAC wine from BORDEAUX.

COUVENT-DES-JACOBINS, CHÂTEAU GRAND CRU wine from the SAINT-EMILION district in BORDEAUX.

CRADLE basket for holding a wine bottle for serving.

CRAIGMOOR winery in the MUDGEE district of New South Wales in Australia, producing quality VARIETAL wines.

CRAMANT village in the CHAMPAGNE region of France. *See also* CRÉMANT.

CRAS, AUX PREMIER CRU vineyard of the CÔTE DE BEAUNE district of BURGUNDY.

CRAS PREMIER CRU vineyard of the NUITS-ST GEORGES commune of the CÔTE DE NUITS district of BURGUNDY.

CREAM SHERRY Sherry style created for the UK market by adding extra sweetness to OLOROSO. It has a SWEETNESS RATING of 8.

CRÉMANT slightly sparkling, or 'creaming', white wine made in France from red and white grapes and produced in Burgundy (**Crémant de Bourgogne**, made with ALIGOTÉ and GAMAY grapes), the Loire (**Crémant de Loire**), and

Alsace (**Crémant d'Alsace**). Some CHAMPAGNES are cremant, e.g. **Crémant de Cramant**, made at CRAMANT.

CRÉPY light dry white AC wines produced in the Haut-Savoie area of eastern France.

CRESTA BLANCA WINERY winery near Ukiah in the MENDOCINO area of California, producing VARIETAL wines.

CRETE Greek island producing strong table wines. The reds are the best, but an excellent sweet white wine is made from MALVASIA grapes.

CRIADO Y EMBOTELLADO POR... Spanish term, literally 'grown and bottled by...'

CRIANZA Spanish word for 'keeping'. *See* CON CRIANZA.

CRIANZA DE CASTILLA LA VIEJA, BODEGAS DE firm in northern Spain producing good white and red wines, the latter from near Toledo and made from CABERNET SAUVIGNON grapes.

CRIOLLA grape variety for white and rosé wines. It originated in Europe but is also grown in Argentina, Mexico and California. Also known as Mission. Possibly best used for fortified wines.

CRIOTS-BÂTARD-MONTRACHET excellent GRAND CRU dry white wine from the CHASSAGNE-MONTRACHET commune in the CÔTE DE BEAUNE area of BURGUNDY.

CRNO Yugolslavian term (literally 'black') for red wine.

CROATTINA grape grown in LOMBARDY, northern Italy, and used in the production of red and rosé wines, particularly in OLTREPO PAVESE where it is widely planted.

CROFT old-established PORT firm of Portugal, producing quality VINTAGE and LATE BOTTLED vintage Ports.

CROQUE-MICHOTTE, CHÂTEAU full-bodied GRAND CRU wine from the SAINT-EMILION district of BORDEAUX.

CROWN OF CROWNS brand name of a LIEBFRAUMILCH sold by LANGENBACH of Worms in Germany.

CROZES-HERMITAGE red and white wines from the RHÔNE VALLEY area of France. The reds have an intense spicy-peppery SYRAH flavour and are usually good value.

CRU French word for growth. Refers to a high quality vineyard with an official classification (*cru classé*), such as GRAND CRU, PREMIER CRU, etc. *See also* CHAMPAGNE, CLASSIFICATION OF 1855.

CRU BOURGEOIS lower CRU classification of BORDEAUX wines. *See also* CLASSIFICATION OF 1855.

CRU BOURGEOIS SUPÉRIEUR ranking above CRU BOURGEOIS of BORDEAUX wines.

CRU GRAND BOURGEOIS EXCEPTIONNEL ranking for BORDEAUX wine which must be from the communes of the HAUT MÉDOC and also CHÂTEAU BOTTLED.

CRUSH process of crushing grapes to extract their juice.

CRUSHER mechanical device used in winemaking to extract juice from grapes before fermentation. Often incorporated is a de-stemming mechanism to remove stalks.

CRUST (1) deposit which forms round old port bottles; (2) term for sediment adhering to the inside surface of bottles of old wine, usually red.

CRUSTED PORT full-bodied but nonvintage type of PORT made from blended wines of different years, aged in oak. Usually will have sediment.

CRYSTALS potassium bitartrate crystals which can form on the cork and in the bottle. This is a natural precipitate which should not be taken to indicate poor quality.

CSOPAK vineyards in the BALATON district of Hungary producing reasonable white table wines.

CUIS vineyards in the Cuis area of the Côte des Blancs in CHAMPAGNE in northeast France, producing red and white wines. The red is classified 90 percent in the CIVC rating and the white 95 percent.

CUMBRERO dry white and red value-for-money wines produced in the RIOJA region of northern Spain by Bodegas Montecillo.

CUMIÈRES champagne-producing town and vineyards of the Canton d'Ay in the Reims area of CHAMPAGNE in northeast France. The wines, made from red grapes, are classified 90 percent in the CIVC rating.

CURÉ-LA-MADELAINE, CHÂTEAU GRAND CRU wine from the SAINT-EMILION district of BORDEAUX.

CUVAISON VINEYARD winery in the NAPA VALLEY area of California producing varietal and vintage wines, especially good CHARDONNAY and ZINFANDEL wines.

CUVE French term for a wine vat.

CUVE CLOSE French term for the method of making sparkling wine by fermentation in a sealed vat. *See* CARBON DIOXIDE, CHARMAT METHOD.

CUVÉE French term for (1) the contents of a vat; (2) a blend; (3) the final blend of CHAMPAGNE wines before bottling; (4) in BURGUNDY alternative term for CRU.

CVICEK rosé wine of the SLOVENIA district of Yugoslavia

CVNE abbreviation for Compañia Vinicola del Nort de España, a firm in the RIOJA region of northern Spain. Their best-known white wine is MONOPOLE but they also produce an excellent Imperial Rioja Reserva.

CYPRUS island in the eastern Mediterranean producing full, tannic red wines (TASTE RATING E), full-bodied dry white wines and Sherry-type wines. Also produces the famous dessert wine COMMANDARIA.

CZECHOSLOVAKIA eastern European wine-producing country. The main production areas are Bohemia, Moravia and Slovakia. Most of the wines produced are consumed within the country. Quality is said to vary, with some good wines being produced.

D

DACKENHEIM village of GROSSLAGE Kobnert in the Mittelhaardt BEREICH of the RHEINPFALZ region of Germany.

DALMATIA wine-producing area in western Yugoslavia producing heavy red and white wines and some rosés. It also produces cherry liqueurs, or Maraschino.

DALSHEIM wine-producing village in the RHEINHESSEN area of Germany.

DALWOOD vineyard in HUNTER VALLEY, New South Wales, Australia.

D'AMBRA firm in the CAMPANIA region of western Italy. Its DOC wine is ISCHIA.

DAME-JEANNE the original French term from which DEMIJOHN comes. It holds 5.45 litres.

DAMPIERRE commune of the COTEAUX DE SAUMUR district of ANJOU in northwest France producing white and rosé wines.

DÃO red and white DO wines from the north-central region of Portugal, 50 miles southeast of Oporto. The area produces mostly strong, smooth, red wines with a TASTE RATING of D.

DAUMAS GASSAC, MAS DE estate of the MIDI district of southern France producing good red wines from vines grown in rich volcanic soil.

DEALUL-MARE vineyard in the Carpathian mountains in Romania producing rich smooth red wines and white table wines.

DE BORTOLI family winery located at Griffith, New South Wales, Australia, producing mainly WINE BOX wines but also a superb 'botrytis-affected' Semillon.

DEBRO wine-growing area of MATRAALYA in Hungary. Its best known wine is the sweet HARSLEVELU.

DECANT to pour wine from a bottle to some other container, such as a decanter, in order to separate it from its sediment or deposit.

DE CHAUNAC grape variety grown in the Niagara area of Canada and New York State.

DÉGORGEMENT French term for the removal of the deposit from sparkling wines.

DEGRÉ ALCOOLIQUE French term for the percentage degree of alcohol by volume in a wine.

DEHLINGER WINERY winery in SONOMA, California, producing good CHARDONNAY, CABERNET SAUVIGNON and PINOT NOIR wines.

DEIDESHEIM important village of GROSSLAGE Hollenpfad in the BEREICH of RHEINPFALZ in Germany producing red and some white wines. Its best vineyards include **Deidesheimer Grainhubel, Deidesheimer Herrgotsacker**, and **Deidesheimer Leinhohle**.

DEINHARD large German firm of merchants based in Koblenz with vineyards in the MOSEL-SAAR-RUWER and RHEINPFALZ. It produces good wines under the Green Label brand. Also part owner of the BERNKASTLER DOKTOR vineyard.

DELAFORCE firm in Vila Nova de Gaia in Portugal producing some fine Port wines.

DELAS FRÈRES firm in Tournon in the northern RHÔNE VALLEY area of France producing red and white wines from vineyards in CORNAS, CÔTE ROTIE, CONDRIEU, and HERMITAGE.

DELAWARE white-wine grape grown in Ohio and New York State, US, in Brazil and in Japan.

DELICATE tasting term for a light wine which has subtle, appealing flavour.

DELOACH VINEYARDS vineyards and winery in the SONOMA region of California producing full-bodied red and white wines including a quality CHARDONNAY.

DELORME, ANDRÉ wine-growing merchants of the CÔTES CHALONNAISE based in Rully.

DELUZE, A. ET FILS wine shippers of BORDEAUX and owners of the châteaux CANTENAC-BROWN and Pareil de Luze.

DEMARCATED an area officially recognized by a regional or national authority. For a wine to be labelled with the name of the area it will usually have to meet miminum standards of quality. Most wines from France (AC), Italy (DOC), Portugal and Spain (DO) and Germany come from demarcated areas, and a similar system has been started in Bulgaria.

DEMESTICA leading brand of red and white Greek table wines sold by ACHAIA-CLAUS.

DEMIJOHN glass wicker-covered bottle containing one or more gallons of wine.

DEMI-SEC tasting term for medium-sweet wine, from the French for 'half dry'. Commonly used for CHAMPAGNE.

DENOMINACÃO DE ORIGEN see DO.

DENOMINACIÓN DE ORIGEN see DO.

DENOMINAZIONE DI ORIGINE CONTROLLATA see DOC.

DENOMINAZIONE DI ORIGINE CONTROLLATA E GARANTITA see DOCG

DENSIMETER see MUSTIMETER.

DEPAGNEUX, JACQUES wine merchants of BEAUJOLAIS.

DEPOSIT sediment which forms in a wine bottle. The deposit in red wines is bitter and should be separated from the wine by decanting.

DEPTH tasting term for a wine seeming to have several levels, or dimensions, of taste.

DESSERT WINE FORTIFIED sweet wine for drinking with desserts.

DEUTSCHER SEKT German term for sparkling wine made from German wines. Until 1986 the wine could come from other countries and be carbonated in Germany. Now such wine is labelled simply SEKT.

DEUTSCHER TAFELWEIN (DTW) German term for German table wine.

DEUTSCHES WEINSIEGEL German term (literally 'wine seal') for a red seal awarded to any German wines which exceed the standards of their class by specified points. Yellow seals are awarded for dry wines, and green for medium-dry wines. *See also* AMTLICHE PRÜFUNGSNUMMER.

DEUTZ & GELDERMAN champagne firm in AY in the CHAMPAGNE region of France.

DEUXIÈME CRU quality classification of CHAMPAGNE vineyard below GRAND CRU and PREMIER CRU.

DEXHEIM village of GROSSLAGE Gutes Domtal in the BEREICH of RHEINHESSEN in Germany.

DÉZALEY village and white wine of the Lavaux region of Switzerland.

DEZIZE-LES-MARANGES appellation in the CÔTE DE BEAUNE area of BURGUNDY producing light red and white wines. The best wines are labelled Dezize-les-Maranges-Côte de Beaune.

DHRON village of GROSSLAGE Michelsberg in the BEREICH of MOSEL-SAAR-RUWER in Germany.

DIABETIKERWEIN category of very dry German wine containing minimal unfermented sugar.

DIAMANTE *see* BARROCAO.

DIAMOND hybrid grape used for white wines in the US.

DIAMOND CREEK VINEYARDS vineyard in the NAPA VALLEY region of California producing CABERNET SAUVIGNON wines.

DIANA hybrid grape used for white wines in Ohio and New York State, US.

DIENHEIM village of GROSSLAGE Guldenmorgen in the BEREICH of RHEINHESSEN in Germany.

DIEZ-MERITO important firm in the JEREZ region of southern Spain producing a variety of sherries.

DIKMEN popular red table wine produced in Turkey.

DIMIAT (DIMYAT) native Bulgarian white-wine grape.

DO (1) abbreviation for *Denominacão de Origen*, the wine-control system of Portugal which guarantees that a wine comes from a DEMARCATED area (*região demarcada*) and has been produced according to agreed standards of soil conditions, grape variety, yield, production, age, degree of alcohol, etc. Demarcated areas include BAIRRADA, DAO, Moscato de Setúbal, Bucelas, COLARES, CARCAVELOS, and Minho for VINHO VERDE. MADEIRA and DOURO for PORT also come under this system of control; (2) abbreviation for *Denominación de Origen* ('designation of origin'), the control system of Spain which is based on the French AC system and certifies the origin of a wine and standards of production including permitted grape varieties, methods of manufacture, etc. Local *consejos reguladores* control each DO area, of which there are 26, covering over 60 per cent of the country's vineyards. SHERRY has its own control system.

DOC abbreviation for *Denominazione di Origine Controllata*, the wine control system of Italy which is based on the French AC system and was started in 1963. It regulates the grape varieties used, the vineyard, and winemaking practice. It is based on Italian grape varieties and covers about 200 wines, some 10 percent of the country's vineyards. Wines made from foreign grape varieties, including noble French varieties, cannot qualify for DOC status so such a wine, however good, must be classed as a VINO DA TÀVOLA. The DOC name on the label of a wine can appear in two forms: a geographical name alone, either an area name or the name of a village; or a geographical name with a grape name or a descriptive name.

DOCE Portuguese term for sweet wine.

DOCG abbreviation for *Denominazione di Origine Controllata e Garantita*, a recently introduced higher level of DOC, which guaranteees that wines not only come from demarcated areas and have met other DOC standards but have also been tasted and tested by an official government panel in Rome. They carry a paper seal of guarantee on top of the cork to ensure no tampering with the contents can occur. There are five DOCGs: BAROLO, BARBARESCO, BRUNELLO DI MONTALCINO, VINO NOBILE DI MONTEPULCIAÑO and the recently promoted CHIANTI.

DOISY-DAËNE, CHÂTEAU deuxième GRAND CRU BARSAC wine from BORDEAUX, an excellent dessert wine.

DOISY-DUBROCA, CHÂTEAU deuxième GRAND CRU BARSAC wine from BORDEAUX.

DOISY-VÉDRINES, CHÂTEAU deuxième GRAND CRU BARSAC wine from BORDEAUX.

DOLCEAQUA *see* ROSSESE DI DOLCEAQUA.

DOLCETTO red-wine grape grown in Italy, which produces full-bodied, flavoursome wines in the PIEMONTE region of northern Italy, including the DOC wines **Dolcetto d'Acqui**, a soft, light wine; **Dolcetto d'Alba**, a very rich full-flavoured wine; **Dolcetto di Diano d'Alba**, similar to Dolcetto d'Alba but even stronger; **Dolcetto di Dogliano**, and **Dolcetto di Ovada**.

DÔLE (1) grape used for making red wine (also known in France as GAMAY; (2) red wine made from the PINOT NOIR and/or Gamay grape in the VALAIS area of Switzerland. **Dôle de Sion** is probably the best, and Dôle Selection d'Or is made by Domaine Château Lichten.

DOM (1) abbreviation for DOMAINE; (2) German word for 'cathedral'. The word appears on the labels of wines from vineyards owned by TRIER Cathedral (*Hohe Domkircher*) in the MOSEL-SAAR-RUWER region.

DOM PÉRIGNON 17th-century Benedictine monk who invented the CHAMPAGNE METHOD and is recognized as the father of modern champagne. His name is used as a famous brand name by the champagne house MOET ET CHANDON.

DOMAINE French term for a wine estate (German *Domäne*). It may consist of a group of vineyards not adjoining each other.

DOMAINE BONNEAU DU MARTREY producer of ALOXE-CORTON in BURGUNDY making fine wines, including Corton Grand Cru and Cuvée Francoise de Salins.

DOMAINE CHANDON winery in the NAPA VALLEY area of California producing sparkling Champagne-type wines. Owned by the French group Moët-Hennessey.

DOMAINE CHÂTEAU LICHTEN large estate in the VALAIS region of Switzerland. Their best wine is Dôle Selection Or.

DOMAINE DE BELAIR brand name of a light red BORDEAUX wine.

DOMAINE DE CHEVALIER CRU classé wine estate of the GRAVES district of BORDEAUX producing fine red and white wines.

DOMAINE DELAGRANGE-BACHELET estate of CHASSAGNE-MONTRACHET in BURGUNDY with vineyard acreages in BÂTARD-MONTRACHET, Criots-Bâtard-Montrachet and the PREMIER CRU Caillerets.

DOMAINE DE L'EGLANTIÈRE estate in the CHABLIS district of France owned by Jean DURUP.

DOMAINE DE L'ÉGLISE estate of POMEROL in BORDEAUX.

DOMAINE DE MONT D'OR excellent vineyard in the VALAIS region of Switzerland. Produces good wines from CHASSELAS and SYLVANER. Its best wine comes from the Johannisberg RIESLING, the Arvine and the DÔLE.

DOMAINE DE MONT-REDON largest vineyard of CHÂTEAUNEUF-DU-PAPE in the RHÔNE VALLEY, France, producing excellent reds. Also the largest producer of white Châteauneuf-du-Pape.

DOMAINE DES COMTES LAFON producer of MEURSAULT in BURGUNDY, owning part of Le MONTRACHET and several other distinguished vineyards.

DOMAINE DE TOUTIGEAC estate of ENTRE-DEUX-MERS in BORDEAUX producing mainly red and a small quantity of white wines.

DOMAINE DU CHASSELOIR estate in the Loire Valley, France, producing MUSCADET de Sèvre-et-Maine Sur Lie.

DOMAINE DUJAC grower of MOREY-SAINT-DENIS in BURGUNDY with interests in several important vineyards. Produces high quality Burgundies including Clos de la Roche, Bonnes Mares, and Clos St-Denis.

DOMAINE DU VIEUX TÉLÉGRAPHIE estate of CHÂ-TEAUNEUF-DU-PAPE in the RHÔNE VALLEY region of France, producing a dark, well-fermented wine.

DOMAINE OTT estate of PROVENCE, southern France, exporting wines under the labels Clos Mireille, Château Romasson, and Château de Salle.

DOMAINE THÉNARD major grower of GIVRY. Also has large holding of Le MONTRACHET and other vineyards. Produces several GRAND CRU wines.

DOMECQ Spanish SHERRY firm, the oldest and largest in Spain.

DOMINIQUE, CHÂTEAU LA rich GRAND CRU wine from the SAINT-EMILION district of BORDEAUX.

DOMMA MARIA WINERY winery in the SONOMA region of California producing varietal wines including CABERNET SAUVIGNON and PINOT NOIR.

DON MIGUEL brand name of a white wine made in Chile from RIESLING and GEWÜRZTRAMINER grapes by Torres.

DONNAZ soft red DOC wine from the VALLE D'AOSTA region of northern Italy.

DONNICI light and fruity young red DOC wines from CALABRIA, southern Italy.

DOPFF ET IRION old-established firm in the Alsace district of France producing white wines.

DORIN name used in the VAUD district of Switzerland for the CHASSELAS grape.

DOSAGE French term for the process of adding sugar syrup to CHAMPAGNE and sparkling wines to sweeten them.

DOUDET-NAUDIN firm in Savigny in BURGUNDY producing dark, rich wines. They have interests in several well-known vineyards.

DOURO river in Portugal around which lies a demarcated region producing red VINHO MADURO wines (much of which is used for the production of PORT) and some whites and rosés. BARCA VELHA is produced here in good years.

DOURTHE FRÈRES wine merchants of Bordeaux.

DOUX French word for 'sweet'. When used of CHAMPAGNE it indicates a sweet variety not much consumed in the UK.

DOW'S PORT brand name of a dry PORT marketed by Silva & Cosens in Vila Nova de Gaia, Portugal.

DRAGASANI vineyard area in Romania producing white wines including Muskat Ottonel.

DRATHEN large-scale producer of low-cost German and EEC wines.

DRAYTON'S BELLEVUE firm in the HUNTER VALLEY region of New South Wales in Australia.

DROMERSHEIM village of GROSSLAGE Sankt Rochuskapelle in the BEREICH of RHEINHESSEN in Germany producing red and white wines.

DROUHIN, J. wine-growers of the CHABLIS region of France producing fine wines. They also have properties in BEAUNE producing red and white wines.

DRY tasting term for wines with an absence of sugar. Possibly the most misused term in wine tasting. When a wine is 'dry', it is just that, dry. When people wince and comment that a wine is 'very dry' they are mistaking a highly acidic wine for a dry one.

DRY CREEK VINEYARD vineyard in the SONOMA region of California producing white wines. Excellent CHARDONNAY, CABERNET SAUVIGNON and CHENIN BLANC.

DRY SACK brand name of a medium SHERRY.

DUBOEUF, GEORGES well-known wine merchants of BEAUJOLAIS.

DUCA DI SALAPARUTA wine producers of Sicily.

DUCKHORN VINEYARDS winery in the NAPA VALLEY, California, producing VARIETAL wines.

DUCLOT firm in BORDEAUX marketing fine wines.

DUCRU-BEAUCAILLOU, CHÂTEAU deuxième GRAND CRU wine from the SAINT-JULIEN commune of BORDEAUX.

DUFF GORDON SHERRY firm in El Puerto de Santa Maria, Spain, producing sherries for export only.

DUFOULEUR FRÈRES firm in NUITS-SAINT-GEORGES in BURGUNDY with interests in MERCUREY and CÔTE CHALONNAISE.

DUHART-MILON-ROTHSCHILD, CHÂTEAU quatrième PREMIER CRU wine from the PAUILLAC commune of BORDEAUX.

DUKE OF WELLINGTON brand name of SHERRY sold by Bodegas Internacionales in Spain.

DULCE Spanish word for 'sweet'.

DULL tasting term for a wine which is hazy because of suspended particles.

DUMB tasting term used for any quality wine which retains its strong TANNIN content for many years, tasting hard until it matures and becomes FIRM.

DUR French term for hardness of wine because of strong TANNIN content.

DURAS *see* CÔTES DU DURAS.

DURBACH village of GROSSLAGE Fursteneck in the BEREICH of Ortenau in Germany, producing highly reputable red and white wines.

DURBANVILLE one of the best wine-producing areas of South Africa, noted for its red wines.

DURIFF red-wine grape grown in California. Also known as Petite-Sirah.

DÜRKHEIM *see* BAD DÜRKHEIM.

DURNEY VINEYARDS winery in MONTEREY, California, producing varietal wines including quality CABERNET SAUVIGNON and RIESLING.

DÜRNSTEIN wine-producing town in the WACHAU district of Lower Austria producing white wines.

DURUP, JEAN important grower of the CHABLIS region of France with large vineyard areas. Brand names include Durup and DOMAINE DE L'ÉGLANTIÈRE.

DUTCHESS hybrid grape developed in the US and used for light, dry, white wines.

DUTRUCH-GRAND-POUJEAUX, CHÂTEAU CRU GRAND BOURGEOIS EXCEPTIONNEL wine from the MOULIS district of BORDEAUX.

DUVAL-LEROY producer of reasonably priced CHAMPAGNE under their own label and for UK outlets.

DYNASTY white wine made in China and imported into Europe by Remy Martin.

E

EARTHY tasting term for a wine with an odour and taste of the soil. *See also* GOÛT DE TERROIR.

EAST-SIDE WINERY large cooperative winery in the Sacramento valley area of California producing table and dessert wines often sold under other brand names.

EAU MINÉRALE DE CARBONNIEUX wine from the Château Carbonnieux in the GRAVES district of France. The name comes from the story of some monks of Bordeaux who sold their wine to Turkey by labelling it as mineral water to overcome the Islamic interdiction on wine.

ECHÉZEAUX GRAND CRU vineyard of the Flagey-Echézeaux commune in the CÔTE DE NUITS area of BURGUNDY.

EDELFÄULE German term for NOBLE ROT.

EDELKEUR sweet white wines produced by the South African firm of Nederburg, based in PAARL.

EDENKOBEN important village of GROSSLAGE Schloss Ludwigshohe in the BEREICH of Sudliche Weinstrasse in the region of Rheinpfalz in Germany.

EDMEADES VINEYARDS small winery in MENDOCINO, California, producing varietals such as GEWÜRZTRAMINER and ZINFANDEL. Sometimes uses unusual names for wine, e.g. Whale Wine.

EDNA VALLEY VINEYARDS winery of the SAN LUIS OBISPO district of California producing good CHARDONNAY.

EGER official wine district of the Northern Massif region of Hungary producing red and white table wines and some sweet wine styles. Its wines include the famous red Egri Bikaver (BULL'S BLOOD).

ÉGLISE-CLINET, CHÂTEAU L' excellent vineyard in the POMEROL district of BORDEAUX.

EGON MÜLLER-SCHARZHOF top wine estate in the MOSEL-SAAR-RUWER region of Germany producing some of the best quality, highest priced and most sought-after wines of the region.

EGRI wines from the district of EGER in Hungary. They include the red **Egri Bikaver** (*see* BULL'S BLOOD), the white **Egri Leanyka**, a white wine made from the Leanyka grape, and **Egri Kadarka**, a red wine made from the KADARKA grape, one of Hungary's better wines.

EGUISHEIM famous old wine village in the ALSACE region of northeast France.

EGYPT ancient wine-producing country whose soil and climate near the edge of the desert are capable of supporting vines for good quality wines. In the 20th century some good wines are produced in the Mariout vineyard to the west of the Nile delta.

EHRENFELSER hybrid white-wine grape from RIESLING and SYLVANER, grown in Germany.

EINZELLAGE German term for 'single vineyard'. Individual vineyards are centered on a GEMEINDE, a wine-growing village or commune, within a GROSSLAGE, a selection of vineyards, which in turn is within a BEREICH, a subregion, and an ANBAUGEBIET, a main region.

EISENSTADT town and wine-growing district of BURGENLAND in Austria where SANDWEIN is made.

EISWEIN German wine of the highest QmP classification, made from grapes frozen on the vine. Of great depth and power with a SWEETNESS RATING of 8, it is regarded as the best of German wines. Rare, prestigious and very expensive.

EITELSBACH wine-producing area near TRIER in the MOSEL-SAAR-RUWER region of Germany where the KARTHÄUSERHOFBERG vineyard is situated, which produces one of the top wines of the Ruwer valley.

ELABORADO POR Spanish term for 'made and aged by'.

ELBA full-bodied, fruity red and white sparkling DOC wines from the Italian island off the coast of TUSCANY.

ELBLING grape grown in France (Lorraine), Germany (upper Mosel) and Luxembourg, producing light, fruity wines. Also known as Kleinberger.

EL COTO fruity red and white wines marketed by Bodegas El Coto in the RIOJA region of northern Spain.

ELEGANT tasting term for wines which have FINESSE and BREEDING but are not overpowering.

ELK-COVE VINEYARDS small winery in the Williamette Valley, Oregon, US, producing varietal wines such as CHARDONNAY, PINOT NOIR and MERLOT.

ELTVILLE village in GROSSLAGE Heiligenstock in the BEREICH of Johannisberg in the RHEINGAU region of Germany. The Hessen State wine cellars are located here.

ELVIRA hybrid white-wine grape grown in the US and Canada.

EMBOTELLADO DE ORIGEN Spanish term for 'bottled by'.

EMERALD RIESLING hybrid grape grown in California and Israel.

EMILIA ROMAGNA wine-producing area of central Italy making red and white wines including LAMBRUSCO, ALBANA, GUTTURNIO DEI COLLI PIACENTINI and TREBBIANO DI ROMAGNA. The larger number of Lambrusco producers has meant a low percentage of wines (6 percent) are DOC.

EMVA CREAM sweet Sherry produced in Cyprus.

ENCLOS, CHÂTEAU L' good vineyard and quality wine from the POMEROL district of BORDEAUX.

ENFER D'ARVIER red DOC wine from the Arvier commune in the VALLE D'AOSTA region of northern Italy.

ENGARRAFADO NA ORIGEM Portuguese term for ESTATE-BOTTLED.

ENGLISH WINE produced on a relatively small scale by over 50 vineyards run by some of the keenest *vignerons* on earth. Their reputation and the wines themselves are steadily improving despite insufficient sunshine and too much rainfall. Most vineyards have planted vines successful in northern Germany where the climate is similar, grape varieties including ORTEGA, MULLER-THURGAU,

RIESLING, SYLVANER, Schonberger, SEYVAL BLANC and Huxelrube. As a result, most English wines are Germanic in style, being dry white wines with a SWEETNESS RATING of 2 or medium-dry with a SWEETNESS RATING of 3 or 4. Established producers with good distribution include Lamberhurst, Three Choirs, Spots Farm, Carr-Taylor, Bruisyard, and Wootton. The **English Vineyards Association** runs a voluntary Certification Trade Mark system which tests wines from a vintage.

ENKIRCH village of GROSSLAGE Schwarzlay in the BEREICH of Bernkastel in the MOSEL-SAAR-RUWER region of Germany, producing very good RIESLING wines.

ENTRE-DEUX-MERS light dry white wine from BORDEAUX. The name means 'between two seas' but refers to two rivers: the Garonne and the Dordogne. The appellation now is for dry white wines with a SWEETNESS RATING of 1, but at one time most of the wine was ordinary sweet white wine which lacked any noticeable winemaking skill. New technology has improved them enormously, producing wines with strong varietal flavour and crisp acidity at reasonable prices.

ÉPERNAY town and wine-producing area of Champagne in northeast France. Many top CHAMPAGNE houses have cellars and offices here.

EPESSES town and vineyard of the LAVAUX region of Switzerland.

ERBACH village of GROSSLAGE Deutelsberg in the BEREICH of Johannisberg in RHEINGAU, Germany, including the well-known **Erbacher Marcobrunn** which produces a full-bodied perfumed wine.

ERBALUCE DI CALUSO light, dry white DOC wine from Erbaluce grapes produced near Turin in PIEMONTE, northwest Italy.

ERDEN village of GROSSLAGE Schwarzlay in the BEREICH of Bernkastel in the MOSEL-SAAR-RUWER region of Germany producing good fruity wines including **Erdener Treppchen**, a well-known dry wine. The top EINZELLAGE, Prälat, is located here.

ERMITAGE dry white wine from the VALAIS district of Switzerland.

ERZEUGERABFÜLLUNG German term for ESTATE-BOTTLED or 'bottled by the producer'.

ESCHENDORF village of GROSSLAGE Kirchberg in the BEREICH of Maindreieck in the HESSISCHE BERGSTRASSE region of Germany.

ESPALIER method of trailing vines, involving a trellis supporting a trunk, one or two arms and several canes within the same plane.

ESPUMANTE Portuguese word for 'sparkling'.

ESPUMOSO Spanish word for 'sparkling'.

ESTATE-BOTTLED wine bottled at the estate where it was produced. Used as an indication of authenticity and, generally, of quality. *See also* AGRARIA, AUSEIGENEM LESEGUT, AZIENDA AGRICOLA, ENGARRAFADO NA ORIGEM, ERZEUGERABFÜLLUNG, MISE EN BOUTEILLES,

ESTERY tasting term for a fruity-tasting wine, caused by esters, compounds formed by the reaction between alcohol and acids, which are largely responsible for the different odours present in wines.

EST! EST!! EST!!! famous dry and semi-sweet white DOC wines made from MALVASIA and TREBBIANO grapes in Montefiascone in the LATIUM region of Italy.

ESTRELLA RIVER WINERY winery with extensive vineyards in the SAN LUIS OBISPO district of California producing varietal wines including good CHARDONNAY and ZINFANDEL.

ESTREMADURA area of west-central Portugal north of Lisbon producing red and white wines.

ESTAMPÉ French word meaning 'branded'.

ESTUFAS heating chambers used in MADEIRA, in which wine is heated and then allowed to cool; a process which takes place for a period of six months. It is intended to simulate a voyage round the world and hastens the maturing process.

ETHYL ALCOHOL main product of the fermentation of grape sugar and the only alcohol which is not poisonous to the human system.

ÉTIQUETTE French word meaning 'label'.

ETNA red, white and rosé DOC wines produced on the slopes of Mount Etna in Sicily.

ÉTOILE, L' good white AC wine from the JURA region of France.

EUXINOGRAD a cellar located in a former royal palace in the Black Sea area of Bulgaria, producing good quality white wine.

EVANGILE, CHÂTEAU L' quality full-bodied wine from the district of POMEROL in BORDEAUX.

EVEL red wine from the DOURO region of Portugal.

EXTRA SEC French term meaning extra dry. When used of CHAMPAGNE, the term indicates relative dryness, the driest champagnes being labelled BRUT.

EXTREMADURA area of Spain bordering Portugal, producing red and white wines.

EYRIE VINEYARDS vineyards in Willamette Valley, Oregon, US, producing varietal wines including good PINOT NOIR.

EZERJO grape variety used at Mor in Hungary to produce a full-bodied white wine of the same name. The grape is also used in Yugoslavia.

F

FACTORY HOUSE headquarters of the British PORT trade in Oporto, Portugal.

FAISCA sparkling rosé wine of Portugal, made by FONSECA

FAIVELEY, J. wine-growers of NUITS SAINT-GEORGES in BURGUNDY, owners of the biggest domaine, with interests in a number of important vineyards, the largest of which is MERCUREY. Among many, other vineyards are in Rully, Gevrey-Chambertin, and Chambolle-Musigny.

FALANGHINA see FALERNO.

FALERIO DEI COLLI ASCOLANI dry white DOC wine from the MARCHE region of east-central Italy, made from predominantly TREBBIANO Toscano grapes.

FALERNO semi-dry white wines and some red wines produced in the CAMPANIA area of southwest Italy, the reds from AGLIANICO grapes, the whites from Falanghina.

FALKENBERG vineyard of PIESPORT in the BEREICH of BERNKASTEL in the MOSEL-SAAR-RUWER region of Germany.

FALKENSTEIN vineyard of KONZ in the GROSSLAGE Scharzberg of the BEREICH of Saar-Ruwer in the MOSEL-SAAR-RUWER region of Germany, producing excellent RIESLINGS.

FALKENSTEIN-MATZEN eastern part of the WEIN-VIERTEL area of Austria producing light white wines.

FALLER, THEO top estate in the ALSACE region of France. Their labels include Domaine Weinbach and Cuvée Théo.

FAR NIENTE WINERY winery in the NAPA VALLEY region of California producing good varietal wines.

FARA red DOC wine of a full-bodied style from the PIEMONTE area of northwest Italy. Grapes used include BONARDA, NEBBIOLO, and VESPOLINA.

FARO red DOC table wine of Sicily made from predominantly Nerello grapes.

FAROS smooth red wine from the Yugoslavian island of Hvar.

FAT tasting term for a wine with big and soft qualities but without BODY.

FATTORIA Italian term for a wine farm.

FAUGÈRES AC wines from the COTEAUX DU LANGUEDOC in southern France. Smooth, full-bodied reds, whites and rosés.

FAURIE-DE-SOUCHARD, CHÂTEAU GRAND CRU wine from the SAINT-EMILION district of BORDEAUX.

FAUSTINO MARTINEZ, BODEGAS wine-growers and producers in the Alavesa district of RIOJA, northern Spain. Their best wine is the *gran reserva* Faustino.

FAVONIO wine estate near Foggia in PUGLIA, southeast Italy, producing full-bodied red and white wines.

FAZI-BATTAGLIA, TITULUS wine-growers of the MARCHE region of east-central Italy. Their DOC wines include ROSSO CONERO, ROSSO PICENO and VERDICCHIO DEI CASTELLI DI JESI.

FEDERWEISSER German term for new still sweet wine not fully fermented or filtered.

FEFIÑANES PALACIO light, dry, white table wine from GALICIA in northwest Spain, made from the Albariño grape.

FEHER BOR Hungarian term for white table wine.

FELSTAR estate in Essex in England producing dry and medium white, light red and some sparkling champagne-type wines.

FELTON-EMPIRE VINEYARDS winery of SANTA CRUZ in California producing VARIETAL wines. They have recently experimented, fairly successfully, with the computer analysis of the chemical consitutents of good French wines and the production of higher quality varietals based on the results of this.

FENDANT white wines of the VALAIS area of Switzerland.

FER vine grown in BERGERAC, southwest France, and used for the production of red wines.

FERMENTATION process of converting sugar into ethyl alcohol by yeasts. After crushing, the pulp of grape skins and juice, the MARC (to which small quantities of sulphur dioxide are normally added to inhibit biological activity and oxidation) is fermented, the process being started by the natural yeasts on the grape skins or by introducing a strain of yeast specially selected to impart pleasant aromas. During fermentation, the yeasts and their enzymes convert the grape sugars into ethanol (alcohol) with carbon dioxide being given off. The speed of fermentation depends very much on the temperature of the ferment and the type of yeast used. 'Cooler' fermentation produces more delicate, fruitier wines. If a dry wine is required, the fermentation will be allowed to continue until all the sugar has been converted to alcohol. For sweeter styles, the fermentation is stopped. *See also* CONTROLLED FERMENTATION.

FERRARI firm in the TRENTINO-ALTO ADIGE region of Italy producing excellent champagne-type wines.

FERREIRA large, historic firm in the DOURO region of Portugal, marketing bottled PORT and fine table wines.

FERRER, JOSE L. wine producers in the island of MAJORCA in the CATALONIA region of Spain producing red, and dry white wines.

FERRIÈRE, CHÂTEAU troisième GRAND CRU wine from the MARGAUX commune of BORDEAUX.

FETEASCA grape variety used in Romania for the production of aromatic white wines of the same name.

FETZER VINEYARDS winery in the MENDOCINO area of California, US, producing varietal wines widely available in the UK.

FÈVES, LES PREMIER CRU vineyard of the BEAUNE commune in the CÔTE DE BEAUNE district of BURGUNDY.

FÈVRE, WILLIAM large growers of GRANDS CRUS and PREMIERS CRUS wines in the CHABLIS region of France. New oak is used to produce full-bodied complex Chablis.

FEYTIT-CLINET, CHÂTEAU vineyard and wine from the POMEROL district of BORDEAUX.

FIANO DI AVELLINO light, white DOC wine produced in Avellino in the CAMPANIA area of southwest Italy. Made from the Fiano grape, it is a wine of light body with a smooth nutty flavour.

FIASCO Italian term for the straw or plastic-covered flask used for holding wine, especially CHIANTI. The plural is *fiaschi*.

FICKLIN VINEYARDS vineyard of Madera County in California producing Port-type wines.

FIELD STONE WINERY vineyard in SONOMA, California, producing good varietal wines from VITIS VINIFERA grapes.

FIEUZAL, CHÂTEAU DE GRAND CRU wine from the GRAVES district of BORDEAUX.

FIGEAC, CHÂTEAU premier GRAND CRU wine from the SAINT-EMILION district of BORDEAUX.

FILHOT, CHÂTEAU deuxième GRAND CRU sweet white SAUTERNES from BORDEAUX.

FILTRATION process of filtering suspended particles from wine prior to bottling.

FILZEN village of GROSSLAGE ROMERLAY in the BEREICH of SAAR-RUWER in the MOSEL-SAAR-RUWER region of Germany.

FINES-ROCHES, CHÂTEAU DES estate of CHÂTEAUNEUF-DU-PAPE in the RHÔNE VALLEY area of eastern France.

FINESSE tasting term for an elegant wine or wine of style and BREEDING.

FINGER LAKES important wine-growing area of New York State, US, where good dry sparkling wines are produced.

FINING method of clarifying young wine before bottling. Normally carried out using isinglass or a diatomaceous earth called Wyoming BENTONITE.

FINISH tasting term for the taste remaining after wine leaves the mouth. Equivalent to AFTERTASTE.

FINO very dry SHERRY with a SWEETNESS RATING of 2. Its particular character is attributable to FLOR yeasts.

FIORANO good red and white wines from near Rome in the LATIUM region of Italy. The reds are made from the classic Bordeaux blend of CABERNET SAUVIGNON and MERLOT, the whites are made from MALVASIA DI CANDIA.

FIRESTONE VINEYARD vineyard of SANTA BARBARA in California, producing good white varietals, particularly RIESLING, CHARDONNAY and CABERNET SAUVIGNON.

FIRM tasting term for a quality wine which has softened but is still in a HARD condition.

FISHER VINEYARDS vineyards in the SONOMA region of California producing varietal wines using CABERNET SAUVIGNON and CHARDONNAY.

FITOU AC area of the MIDI region of southern France, producing heavy red table wine from the CARIGNAN grape.

The style of these wines has changed from an overly tannic one to a more balanced elegant style with a TASTE RATING of D.

FIXIN red-wine commune of the CÔTE DE NUITS area of BURGUNDY. Situated at the north end of the Côte de Nuits, it neighbours the famous GEVREY CHAMBERTIN commune, but its wines represent reasonable value on the Burgundy scale of prices.

FLABBY tasting term for a wine lacking in acidity.

FLAGEY-ECHÉZEAUX commune in the CÔTE DE NUITS area of BURGUNDY and the home of the Echézeaux and Grands-Echézeaux vineyards, both producing wonderful wines.

FLAGON a large bottle for holding wine.

FLAT tasting term for (1) a sparkling wine which has lost its gas; (2) a still wine lacking acidity and therefore freshness.

FLEUR, CHÂTEAU LA GRAND CRU wine from the SAINT-EMILION district of BORDEAUX.

FLEUR DU CAP good red CABERNET SAUVIGNON produced by Bergkelder of STELLENBOSCH in South Africa.

FLEURIE one of the best and most popular of the nine BEAUJOLAIS CRUS and produced by the Fleurie commune. The best Fleurie wines are sold under the Fleurie name, others being labelled Beaujolais. The wine is light, fruity, and silky smooth and best drunk within a year or so of production. Strong demand has led to high prices so better value can be found from the other crus.

FLEUR-PETRUS, CHÂTEAU LA top quality wine from the district of POMEROL in BORDEAUX.

FLINTY term for some white-wine grapes which produce a 'gunflint' bouquet and flavour, due to the composition of the soil in which they grow.

FLOR special yeast which forms a white skin or crust on some types of SHERRY. The resulting wine is termed FINO. Fino sherries have a particular character which is attributable to flor yeasts.

FLORA Californian hybrid white grape devloped from GEWÜRZTRAMINER and SEMILLON.

FLORAL *see* FLOWERY.

FLORA SPRINGS WINERY winery in the NAPA VALLEY region of California producing varietal wines including CHARDONNAY, CABERNET SAUVIGNON and RIESLING.

FLORIO firm of MARSALA in Sicily marketing DOC Marsala wine.

FLOWERY (FLORAL) tasting term for the aroma (and sometimes the flavour), reminiscent of flowers or floral character, contributed to a wine by certain aromatic grape varieties.

FLUTE (1) tall thin glass often used for drinking champagne; (2) tall slender bottle used in ALSACE and Germany, and for some French wines, especially rosés.

FLYER term for any particle suspended in wine. *See also* BRIGHTNESS, CRYSTALS.

FOCSANI large wine region in Romania producing red and white table wines from the ODOBESTI, CÔTESTI, Panciu and NICORESTI subregions.

FOLLE BLANCHE white-wine grape used in the MUSCADET vineyards of Brittany in France and also in Armagnac and Cognac. Also known as Ripoul and GROS PLANT.

FOMBRAUGE, CHÂTEAU GRAND CRU wine from the SAINT-EMILION district of BORDEAUX.

FONBADET, CHÂTEAU CRU BOURGEOIS SUPÉRIEUR wine from the PAUILLAC commune of BORDEAUX.

FONPLÉGADE, CHÂTEAU sturdy GRAND CRU wine from the SAINT-EMILION district of BORDEAUX.

FONRÉAUD, CHÂTEAU CRU BOURGEOIS wine from the LISTRAC district of BORDEAUX.

FONROQUE, CHÂTEAU full-bodied GRAND CRU wine from the SAINT-EMILION district of BORDEAUX.

FONSECA firm producing fine vintage PORT and other quality wines. The more commercial Fonseca Bin 27 Port has good vintage character and is very reasonably priced.

FONTANA CANDIDA wine-growers of the LATIUM region of central Italy producing a DOC FRASCATI.

FONTANAFREDDA producers in the PIEMONTE region of northern Italy. Their DOC wines include ASTI SPUMANTE, BARBARESCO, BARBERA D'ALBA, DOLCETTO D'ALBA, and BAROLO.

FONTERUTOLI, CASTELLO DI wine-growers in the TUSCANY region of western Italy producing DOCG CHIANTI CLASSICO in the traditional style.

FOPPIANO WINERY winery in the SONOMA region of California producing varietal wines including CABERNET SAUVIGNON and CHENIN BLANC.

FORASTERA grape used on the Italian island of ISCHIA for the production of dry white wines of the same name.

FORST famous wine village of GROSSLAGEN Mariengarten and Schnepfenflug in the BEREICH of MITTELHAARDT in the RHEINPFALZ region of Germany. It contains the renowned JESUITENGARTEN vineyard.

FORTIA, CHÂTEAU estate of CHÂTEAUNEUF-DU-PAPE in the RHÔNE VALLEY area of eastern France.

FORTIFIED WINES wines with alcohol added during production, which results in a sweet, strong wine. The addition of alcohol also inhibits biological activity in wines, stabilizing them. Historically, this method of production enabled wines to be stored for long periods or to be shipped great distances without spoilage as the remaining residual sugar does not referment. Generally, fortified wines have a range of alcoholic strength of between 17 and 20 percent by volume, and styles include PORT, SHERRY and MADEIRA.

FORTS DE LATOUR, CHÂTEAU LES second label of the Château LATOUR estate in the PAUILLAC commune in BORDEAUX.

FORZATO Italian term for wine produced from overripe grapes.

FOURCAS-DUPRÉ, CHÂTEAU CRU GRAND BOURGEOIS EXCEPTIONNEL, making excellent wine from the LISTRAC district of BORDEAUX.

FOURCAS-HOSTEN, CHÂTEAU CRU GRAND BOURGEOIS EXCEPTIONNEL, making excellent wine from the LISTRAC district of BORDEAUX.

FOURCHAUME excellent PREMIER CRU vineyard of La Chappelle-Vaupelteigne canton in the CHABLIS area of BURGUNDY.

FOURNIER, CHARLES sparkling wines fermented in the bottle. Made by the GOLD SEAL winery in New York State, US, they are named after its former head.

FOURTET *see* CLOS FOURTET.

FOXY tasting term for the unpleasant odour and taste of wines made from VITIS LABRUSCA vines native to the US.

FRAIS French term for cool, fresh wine.

FRANC-DE-GOÛT French term for clean tasting.

FRANCE in 1987 the second largest wine-producing country after Italy, turning out 22.5 percent of the world's total wine production. In terms of quality France is by far the most important country. With few exceptions, ALSACE, BORDEAUX, BURGUNDY, CHAMPAGNE, RHÔNE and LOIRE wines are the finest examples of red, white and sparkling wines and provide the benchmarks by which other countries assess the quality of their own wines.

Recently France has met much competition from Australia, the US, Italy, Spain, Portugal, New Zealand and other countries as the quality of their wines has improved and they can provide comparable styles at better prices. France has reacted quickly by incoporating new winemaking technology to increase the quality of cheaper wines. France's position will remain strong, and as the competition continues to increase the consumer will fare well. *See also* AC, VDQS, VIN DE PAYS, and separate entries for individual regions.

FRANCIACORTA red and white wines from the province of Brescia in the LOMBARDY region of northern Italy. The best wines are the dry, red DOC **Franciacorta Rosso** and the sparkling white DOC **Franciacorta Pinot**.

FRANCISCAN VINEYARDS winery of the NAPA VALLEY area of California in the US, producing white wines.

FRANC-MAYNE, CHÂTEAU soft, GRAND CRU wine from the SAINT-EMILION district of BORDEAUX.

FRANCO-ESPAÑOLAS growers of the RIOJA region of northern Spain producing traditional red and white wines.

FRANCO FIORINA wine-producers in the PIEMONTE region of northern Italy. Their DOC wines include BARBARESCO, BARBERA D'ALBA, BAROLO, DOLCETTO D'ALBA and NEBBIOLO D'ALBA.

FRANCONIA English name for FRANKEN.

FRANKEN region of central Germany producing mostly white wines. It consists of three *Bereichen* (subregions): MAINVIERECK, MAINDREIECK and STEIGERWALD, and its best-known wine is the STEINWEIN produced in the BEREICH of Maindreieck.

FRANZIA winery in SAN JOAQUIN, California, producing mostly generic wine under a variety of labels.

FRAPPÉ French term for chilled or iced drink.

FRASCATI well-known dry, semi-sweet and sweet white wines from the *Colli Albani* (Alban Hills) area of the LATIUM region of Italy. The dry **Frascati Secco** has a SWEETNESS RATING of 2, and the sweet wine is known as *Canellino*.

FRECCIAROSSA vineyard of the LOMBARDY district of Italy whose production includes estate-bottled wines. The four types of wines produced are *Ambrato* (semi-sweet white), *Bianco* (dry white), *Rosso* (dry red) and *Saint George* (dry rosé).

FREEMARK ABBEY WINERY winery of the NAPA VALLEY area of California in the US producing varietal wines, especially PINOT NOIR and CHARDONNAY.

FREE-RUN wine that runs freely from the grapes after fermentation and before the skins are pressed to obtain the additional juice held within them. Highest quality wine is made from free-run juice.

FREIBURG village of GROSSLAGE Burg Zahringen in the BEREICH of BREISGAU in the BADEN region of Germany.

FREINSHEIM village of GROSSLAGE Kobnert in the BEREICH of MITTELHAARDT in the RHEINPFALZ region of Germany, producing red and white wines.

FREISA red-wine grape used in PIEMONTE, Italy, for the production of still wines, including **Freisa d'Alba** and **Freisa d'Asti** which is often sweet and slightly sparkling.

FREIXENET large wine producers of the CATALONIA region of southern Spain. Their popular labels include Brut Nature and Cordon Negro.

FRENCH COLOMBARD white-wine grape used for semi-dry wines in California, South Africa and New Zealand.

FRESCOBALDI outstanding growers of red and white wines in the TUSCANY region of western Italy. Their DOC wine is CHIANTI Rufina and a popular red is Castello di Nipozzano.

FRESH term used to describe the youthful, bright quality of young wines.

FRIEDRICH WILHELM GYMNASIUM secondary school in TRIER in the MOSEL-SAAR-RUWER region of Germany which owns a number of good vineyards, including the JESUITENGARTEN, named after the Society of Jesus.

FRIESSENHEIM village of GROSSLAGE Schutterlindenberg in the BEREICH of BREISGAU in the BADEN region of Germany.

FRIULI-VENEZIA-GIULIA region of northeast Italy bordering Austria and Yugoslavia. It has the DOC districts GRAVE DEL FRIULI, COLLI ORIENTALI DEL FRIULI, Collio Aquilea, LATISANA, and ISONZO. Wines are made mainly from single grape varieties and are labelled with the grape name. They include CABERNET SAUVIGNON, PINOT BLANC and MERLOT.

FRIZZANTE Italian term for semi-sparkling wine.

FROID French word for 'cold'.

FRONSAC AC area of BORDEAUX producing heavy red wines. It incorporates the smaller area of CÔTES DE CANON FRONSAC which produces the best of the area's wines.

FRONTIGNAN white dessert wine made from the grape of the same name in the BANDOL district of PROVENCE in southern France.

FRONTON good-value, easy-drinking red and rosé VDQS wines produced in southwest France.

FRÜHBURGUNDER German name for the PINOT NOIR grape. Also known as Spätburgunder.

FRUITY tasting term for the pleasant aromatic taste of a young wine with strong varietal character. The taste is derived from a combination of sugar, acid and grape flavour.

FRUSKA GORA vineyard area on the south bank of the Danube in Yugoslavia producing white and some red wines.

FUISSÉ village in the MÂCONNAIS. *See* POUILLY-FUISSÉ.

FUMÉ BLANC *see* SAUVIGNON BLANC.

FUMÉ DE POUILLY *see* POUILLY-FUMÉ.

FUMIGATION process of destroying bacteria and other foreign bodies in a wine barrel or vat by means of burning sulphur.

FUNCHAL town in MADEIRA where wine is aged and shipped.

FURMINT white grape used for the production of TOKAY wine in Hungary and also used in Austria, Bulgaria, Czechoslovakia and Romania.

FUT cask or barrel with a capacity of 400 litres.

G

GAFFELIÈRE, CHÂTEAU LA rich, red premier GRAND CRU wine from the SAINT-EMILION district of BORDEAUX.

GAGLIOPPO red-wine grape grown in CALABRIA in southern Italy and used in the production of the full-bodied red and rosé wines of Cirò.

GAGNARD-DELAGRANGE, JACQUES growers with DOMAINE based at MEURSAULT, with vineyards in CHASSAGNE-MONTRACHET and VOLNAY.

GAILLAC wine-producing district of southwest France

producing still wines (**Premiers Côtes de Gaillac**), sparkling white wines (**Gaillac Mousseux**), and red wines of increasing quality.

GAJA wine-growers of PIEMONTE in northern Italy, specializing in red ALBA wines.

GALICIA wine-producing area on the northwest coast of Spain producing wine under the VALDEORRAS, Valle de Monterray and RIBEIRO labels amongst many others. Climate, soil, grape varieties and winemaking practices are similar to those of the neighbouring VINHO VERDE region of Portugal.

GALILEE important wine-growing region of Israel.

GALLAIRE fruity BORDEAUX wine produced by SICHEL.

GALLO WINERY world's largest winery, in Modesto, California, producing mostly red and white table wines for the domestic market. Recently quality VARIETALS have been marketed.

GAMAY red-wine grape variety used widely in France and also in many other countries. Used in ANJOU as base for rosé wines and in BEAUJOLAIS to make delicious, light fruity wines of an attractive colour which are best consumed when young, although some of the more robust Beaujolais CRUS improve with keeping. Known in Yugoslavia as *Gamé*.

GAMBELLARA light, dry white DOC wines produced near SOAVE in the VENETO district of northwest Italy, produced mainly from the Garganega grape. *See also* RECIOTO DI GAMBELLARA.

GAMZA native grape variety of Bulgaria used for the production of red wines. Known in Hungary as KADARKA.

GANCIA producers of sparkling wine in the PIEMONTE region of northern Italy. Their DOC wines include ASTI SPUMANTE, OLTREPO PAVESE and Riesling della Rocca.

GANDESA, COOPERATIVE AGRICOLA DE cooperative and vineyard area of the Terra Alta DO region in CATALONIA in eastern Spain producing strong red and white wines.

GARD VDP department of southern France producing large quantities of vin ordinaire. It also produces the VDQS COSTIÈRES-DU-GARD and CLAIRETTE DE BELLEGARDE.

GARDA name used for various groups of wines produced around Lake Garda in the LOMBARDY area of Italy, such as RIVIERA DEL GARDA.

GARGANEGA vine grown in Italy and used in the production of white wines such as GAMBELLARA and SOAVE.

GARNACHA TINTA grape variety used extensively in RIOJA and other parts of Spain for the production of red wines.

GARRAFEIRA Portuguese term (literally 'private cellar') used on labels to indicate a RESERVA wine of a selected vintage that has been BOTTLE-AGED for several years.

GARVEY Sherry producers in the JEREZ region of southern Spain producing a range of good sherries.

GASEOSO Spanish term for sparkling wine made by the injection of CARBON DIOXIDE gas.

GATÃO demarcated VINHO VERDE wine from the Minho region of Portugal.

GATTINARA full-bodied dry, red wine produced in the PIEMONTE district of northwest Italy.

GAU-ALGESHEIM village of GROSSLAGE Abtei in the BEREICH of BINGEN in the RHEINHESSEN region of Germany.

GAU-BISCHÖFHEIM village of GROSSLAGE Sankt Alban in the BEREICH of NIERSTEIN in the RHEINHESSEN region of Germany.

GAVI *see* CORTESE.

GAY, CHÂTEAU LE quality wine from the POMEROL district of BORDEAUX.

GAY-LUSSAC chemical equation of fermentation of sugars to alcohol defined by Gay-Lussac, a French chemist, in 1910. He also devised a system of measuring alcohol in wine, expressed as percentage by volume.

GAZÉIFIÉ French term for sparkling wine produced by artificial carbonation.

GEBIET German term for wine region or district. *See also* ANBAUGEBIET.

GEELONG wine-growing area of VICTORIA, New South Wales, Australia, which has recently undergone a resurgence of plantings. Good CHARDONNAY and PINOT NOIR wines are now being produced.

GEISENHEIM village of the GROSSLAGE Erntebringer in the BEREICH of Johannisberg in the RHEINGAU region of Germany. Houses the Institut für Kellerwirtschaft del Forschungsanstalt, a research institute which sells some of its wines and the most important school of viticulture in Germany.

GEISWEILER ET FILS large growers in the CÔTE DE NUITS district of BURGUNDY producing red and white fine wines and table wines under various brand names.

GEMARKUNG former German term for a wine-town or village in Germany. The current official term is *Weinbauort*.

GEMEINDE German term for parish, village or wine commune within a GROSSLAGE or district.

GEMELLO WINERY winery in SANTA CLARA, California, producing red and white varietals. Their best known is their Zinfandel.

GENEROSO Spanish term for fortified or dessert wine.

GENEROUS tasting term for a wine with the qualities of strength, texture and depth of body.

GENEVA wine-growing area of Switzerland, most of its production being light, white wines for local consumption.

GENOVESELLA vine grown on the Mediterranean island of CORSICA.

GENTIL French term used in ALSACE in northeast France for the Riesling grape.

GERANIUM tasting term for an unpleasant smell, similar to that of crushed geraniums, occasionally found in red wine.

GERMANY central European country producing wines of ordinary to superb quality from 11 designated regions (ANBAUGEBIET): AHR, BADEN, FRANKEN, HESSICHE-BERG-STRASSE, MITTELRHEIN, MOSEL-SAAR-RUWER, NAHE, RHEINGAU, RHEINHESSEN, RHEINPFALZ and WÜRTTEMBERG. The styles produced vary greatly with the variation of climate and soil structure from region to region. Germany exports large quantities of LIEBFRAU-MILCH, NIERSTEIN and PIESPORTER MICHELSBERG, inexpensive wines of sound quality but very similar. For not much extra, more characterful wines are available with good depth of fruit flavour and value for money. Rheingau producers have formed the CHARTA organization to develop dryer fuller bodied wines. The appellation system is complex and strict and is based on sugar content and ripeness as well as area. There are three categories: DTW (DEUTSCHER TAFELWEIN) for ordinary table wines; QBA (*Qualitätswein bestimmter Anbaugebiete*), quality wines from demarcated areas; and QMP (*Qualitätswein mit Prädikat*), wines with special qualities. QmP wines have further sub-categories according to sweetness level/alcohol content: KABINETT, SPÄTLESE, AUSLESE, BEERENAUS-

LESE, TROCKENBEERENAUSLESE, and EISWEIN. Each region is divided into an area-district-village-vineyard (BEREICH-GROSSLAGE-GEMEINDE-EINZELLAGE) order, so the more names on the label the more individual the wine.

GEROPIGA sweet syrup made from grapes and used in Portugal for sweetening wines including PORT.

GEVREY-CHAMBERTIN important commune of the CÔTE DE NUITS district of BURGUNDY producing red wine. The best wines come from the CHAMBERTIN and CHAMBERTIN-CLOS DE BÈZE vineyards and from other GRAND CRU vineyards such as LATRICIÈRES, MAZOYÈRES and CHARMES, all of which carry the Chambertin appellation. Wines from the lesser PREMIER CRU vineyards of the commune usually bear the name GEVREY-CHAMBERTIN on the label, followed by the name of the vineyard, or GEVREY-CHAMBERTIN PREMIER CRU. The least of the wines simply bear the general appellation GEVREY-CHAMBERTIN.

GEWACHS German term meaning 'growth'.

GEWÜRZTRAMINER variety of TRAMINER vine and the classic white grape of the ALSACE region of France. It is also grown in Germany, Canada, US, Australia and New Zealand, amongst others. Wines made from it have an intense 'spicy' fruit effect on both the nose and palate. They have a SWEETNESS RATING of 4.

GEYSER PEAK WINERY winery in SONOMA, California, producing varietal wines and some sparkling wines.

GHEMME dry, slightly bitter red DOC wine produced in the PIEMONTE area of northwest Italy.

GHIAIE DELLA FURBA wine produced in the TUSCANY region of eastern Italy from CABERNET SAUVIGNON and CABERNET FRANC grapes.

GIACOBAZZI producers in the EMILIA-ROMAGNA region of northern Italy. Their DOC wines include LAMBRUSCO di Sorbara, Lambrusco Grasparossa di Castelvetro, and Lambrusco Salamino di Santa Croce.

GIACOSA, BRUNO producers in the PIEMONTE region of northern Italy. Their DOC wines include BARBARESCO, BARBERA D'ALBA, GRIGNOLINO D'ASTI and NEBBIOLO D'ASTI.

GIGONDAS AC commune of the CÔTES DU RHÔNE region of southeast France producing red, white and rosé wines. The reds are full-bodied and very flavoursome.

GILBEY firm importing Australian wine.

GIMMELDINGEN village of GROSSLAGE Meerspinne in the BEREICH of MITTELHAARDT in the RHEINPFALZ region of Germany.

GIPFEL GROSSLAGE of the BEREICH of OBERMOSEL in the MOSEL-SAAR-RUWER region of Germany. Its best-known wine-village is Nittel.

GIRÒ red-wine grown in the area of Cagliari in Sardinia. Produced from it are the sweet DOC wines **Girò di Cagliari** and **Girò di Sardegna**.

GIRONDE (1) largest department of France, whose borders coincide with BORDEAUX, except for the coastal strip to the west of the town of Bordeaux; (2) river estuary in Bordeaux region formed by the confluence of the Rivers Garonne and Dordogne.

GISBORNE wine-growing area of New Zealand on the east coast of North Island.

GISCOURS, CHÂTEAU troisième GRAND CRU wine from the MARGAUX commune of BORDEAUX.

GISSELBRECHT, LOUIS wine-producers of Dambach-la-Ville in ALSACE specializing in good RIESLING and GEWÜRZTRAMINER wines.

GIUMARRA VINEYARDS vineyards in SAN JOAQUIN valley in California producing vintage varietal red and white wines. Also produce large volume of dessert wines. Varieties include ZINFANDEL and Ruby Cabernet.

GIVRY small village and commune of the CÔTE CHALON-NAISE area of southern BURGUNDY producing red and some white wines.

GLASSES each of the major European wine-growing areas has developed its own glass, e.g. the *copita* from Spain for Sherry and from Alsace and Germany glasses with shallow bowls and sometimes coloured stems which reflect colour into white wines. As a general rule, for table wines glasses should be thin and clear, of a good size, and filled one-third to one-half full so the wine's bouquet has a chance to show itself. They should be stored with the bowl upwards so that unpleasant smells are not trapped. The standard tasting glass has a slightly curved-in top to trap the bouquet. Glasses for fortified wines can be smaller as their stronger bouquet does not need as much space.

GLEN ELGIN vineyard of New South Wales in Australia producing red and white table wines.

GLENLOTH vineyard of the REYNELLA district of the state of South Australia.

GLENORA WINE CELLARS winery in the FINGER LAKES district of New York State producing mainly white wines including some hybrid varietals.

GLENVALE wine producers of Hawkes Bay in New Zealand producing table and dessert wines. Grape varieties include PINOTAGE, MÜLLER-THURGAU, CHASSELAS, PALOMINO, Siebel, and CABERNET SAUVIGNON.

GLORIA, CHÂTEAU CRU BOURGEOIS wine from the SAINT-JULIEN commune of BORDEAUX.

GLYCERIN (GLYCEROL) chemical derived from sugar during the fermentation process, which contributes sweetness and smoothness to a wine.

GLUHWEIN a mixture of red wine, sugar, cinnamon and cloves, sometimes with a little brandy, heated but not boiled.

GOLDENER OKTOBER brand name of a wine sold by Sankt Ursula Wein Kellerei in Bingen in the RHEINHESSEN region of Germany.

GOLD SEAL WINERY winery in the FINGER LAKES district of New York State, US, producing sparkling wines and table wines from VITIS VINIFERA and VITIS LABRUSCA grapes. *See also* FOURNIER.

GOLDTRÖPFCHEN first-quality vineyard (EINZELLAGE) of PIESPORT in GROSSLAGE Michelsberg in the BEREICH of BERNKASTEL in the MOSEL-SAAR-RUWER region of Germany.

GOMBAUDE-GUILLOT, CHÂTEAU estate of POMEROL in BORDEAUX.

GONZALEZ BYASS important Sherry producers of the JEREZ region of southern Spain, best known for TIO PEPE, LA CONCHA and SAN DOMINGO. Its subsidiary, **Gonzalez y Dubosc**, produces a sparkling wine in CATALONIA.

GOSSET oldest CHAMPAGNE firm in Ay in the Champagne region of France, producing a range of non-vintage, Special Reserve, Brut Rosé and Grand Millésimé champagnes.

GOUGES, DOMAINÉ HENRI owner of the Clos des Porrets vineyard in BURGUNDY. Based in NUITS ST-GEORGES, Gouges also have vineyards in Les St-Georges, Les Pruliers and Les Vaucrains.

GOULBURN VALLEY table wine-growing area of VICTORIA, Australia.

GOULET, GEORGES CHAMPAGNE firm in REIMS in northern France producing a range of non-vintage, vintage and deluxe champagnes. Also produces a CRÉMANT style and dry red and white wines.

GOÛT French term for taste. **Gout americain** means a fairly sweet wine, **goût anglais** a dry wine, **goût francais** a very sweet wine. **Gout de rancio** is BOTTLE STINK, **goût de pierre à fusil** is GUNFLINT, and **goût de terroir** is the 'earthy' taste in some wines imparted by the soil in which the vines were grown.

GRAACH small village of GROSSLAGE Munzlay in the BEREICH of BERNKASTEL in the MOSEL-SAAR-RUWER region of Germany.

GRACCIANO wine producers in the TUSCANY region of northeastern Italy. Their DOC wines include VINO NOBILE DI MONTEPULCIANO and CHIANTI Colli Senesi.

GRAHAM, W. & J. PORT producers of Vila Nova de Gaia in Portugal, producing rich, sweet vintage Ports.

GRAMP'S ORLANDO winery in South Australia producing table, sparkling and fortified wines of excellent quality. Their CHARDONNAY and CABERNET SAUVIGNON wines represent good value for money.

GRAND-CORBIN, CHÂTEAU GRAND CRU wine from the SAINT-EMILION district of BORDEAUX.

GRAND-CORBIN-DESPAGNE, CHÂTEAU GRAND CRU wine from the SAINT-EMILION district of BORDEAUX.

GRAND CRU French term (literally 'great growth') for a great vineyard. In ALSACE, BORDEAUX, BURGUNDY and CHABLIS the term has official status. In Bordeaux *grand cru* vineyards are those which in the CLASSIFICATION OF 1855 rank next to the PREMIER CRU vineyards of Lafite, Latour, Margaux and Haut-Brion (with Mouton-Rothschild added later). Of about 2,000 vineyards, only 62 are *grands crus*. In Alsace, Burgundy and Chablis, a *grand cru* is a vineyard with its own AC, with no need to add a village name.

GRAND-MAYNE, CHÂTEAU GRAND CRU wine from the SAINT-EMILION district of BORDEAUX.

GRAND-PONTET, CHÂTEAU GRAND CRU wine from the SAINT-EMILION district of BORDEAUX.

GRAND-PUY-DUCASSE, CHÂTEAU cinquième cru wine from the PAUILLAC commune of BORDEAUX.

GRAND ROUSSILLON appellation of the MIDI region of southern France producing red, white and rosé wines. Incorporates BANYULS, CÔTES D'AGLY, CÔTES DU ROUSSILLON, MAURY and RIVESALTES.

GRANDS EPENOTS, LES PREMIER CRU vineyard of the POMMARD commune in the CÔTE DE BEAUNE district of BURGUNDY, producing excellent full-bodied red wines.

GRANDS-ECHÉZEAUX excellent red wines from the GRAND CRU vineyards of the FLAGEY-ECHÉZEAUX commune in the CÔTE DE NUITS district of BURGUNDY. These wines are amongst the greatest Burgundies, and when they do not meet the specified standards they are labelled simply with the general name VOSNE-ROMANÉE.

GRAND VIN French term meaning 'great wine' which can be applied to any wine from BORDEAUX from the level of Bordeaux Supérieur upwards.

GRANGE HERMITAGE red wine regarded as being Australia's finest, produced by Penfolds in South Australia.

GRANJO sweet white wine of Portugal produced from grapes on which NOBLE ROT is allowed to form.

GRAN RESERVA term for a wine from Spain showing that it is a quality wine which has been aged for a specified time, e.g. on a wine from RIOJA it will have been aged for five years.

GRAN SPUMANTE dry sparkling wine produced near ASTI in the PIEMONTE area of northwest Italy.

GRAN VAS Spanish term for sparkling wine made by the CHARMAT METHOD.

GRAN VINO term for a wine from CHILE which has been aged for six years. Produces particularly dry red wines.

GRÃO VASCO good brand of DÃO wine produced by SOGRAPE near the town of Viseu in Portugal.

GRAPES of the thousands of grape varieties and hybrids only about 50 feature prominently in commercial winemaking. Most of the world's quality wines are made from 'noble' varieties, those of the species VITIS VINIFERA, which produce wines of great flavour and finesse. Selection of a suitable variety or varieties for soil and climatic conditions which will also produce the desired VARIETAL or BLENDING style of the best quality is important as it takes five to seven years for vines to reach maturity. Some varieties travel well, e.g. the Burgundian CHARDONNAY which produces high quality wines in almost every region in the world suitable for viticulture. Another Burgundian grape, however, the red PINOT NOIR, is rarely sucessful away from 'home'. Pruning of the vines in January begins the growing cycle. By early April the new shoots appear and about two weeks later tendrils and leaves are noticeable. Flowering and pollination occur in late May/early June and the first berries appear in June. By August these have developed their colour of red or green, the start of the ripening process (in French *veraison*) which is complete by the middle of October to early November and the grapes are ready for harvesting. It takes roughly 100 days from flowering to harvest. In the Southern Hemisphere the whole process takes place six months earlier. *See also* CLONE, NOBLE ROT, VITIS LABRUSCA and individual names.

GRASEVINA a Yugoslavian RIESLING grape. Also known as Wälschriesling.

GRASSY tasting term for the 'green' herb-like aroma and occasionally flavour of a wine. Similar to ESTERY.

GRATIEN, ALFRED CHAMPAGNE firm of ÉPERNAY in the Champagne region of France producing excellent dry wines fermented in oak barrels.

GRATIEN & MEYER producers of sparkling SAUMUR wine, CRÉMANT DE LOIRE, rosé and dry red.

GRAUERBURGUNDER German name for the PINOT GRIS grape. Also known as Rulander. *See also* BURGUNDER.

GRAUVES CHAMPAGNE vineyard of the Canton d'Avize in the Arondissement d'Épernay in northeast France, classified 90 percent (red) and 95 percent (white) in the CIVC rating.

GRAVE DEL FRIULI DOC appellation covering 13 styles of wine from the Grave area of the FRIULI-VENEZIA-GIULIA district of northeast Italy. Grapes used include CHARDONNAY, PINOT BIANCO, PINOT GRIGIO, SAUVIGNON BLANC, MERLOT, CABERNET FRANCE and CABERNET SAUVIGNON.

GRAVES subregion of BORDEAUX adjoining the southern end of the MÉDOC. Its name is related to the very gravelly soil found throughout the region. It does not have the reputation of its illustrious neighbour, the HAUT-MÉDOC, but it produces outstanding wines, both red and white, the most famous wine being the remarkable Château HAUT-BRION, the only PREMIER CRU of Bordeaux from outside the Haut-Médoc. Other excellent wines are made at the châteaux Smith-Haut-Lafitte, Carbonnieux, Pape Clement, Haut-Bailly, Bouscaut, and La Mission-Haut-Brion. Château LAVILLE-HAUT-BRION, the region's only GRAND CRU for white wines, makes excellent whites as does DOMAINE DE CHEVALIER amongst many others. Although the region is best known for its white wines, the reds are of higher overall quality.

GRAVES DE VAYRES AC red and white wines produced near the village of Vayres in BORDEAUX.

GRAVES SUPÉRIEUR medium-dry strong white wine from GRAVES.

GRAVE-TRIGANT-DE-BOISSET, CHÂTEAU LA wine from the POMEROL district of BORDEAUX.

GRAVIÈRES, LES PREMIER CRU vineyard of SANTENAY in the CÔTE DE BEAUNE district of BURGUNDY.

GREY RIESLING white-wine grape related to the French *Chauche Gris* and grown in California. Also known as Gray Dutchess.

GREAT WESTERN wine-producing district of VICTORIA in southern Austalia producing sparkling wines and red and white table wines.

GREAT WESTERN WINERY winery in Hammondsport, New York State, producing champagne-type and hybrid varietal wines.

GRECO white-wine grape grown in Italy. In CALABRIA it produces **Greco di Gerace**, a dessert wine, and in CAMPANIA **Greco di Tufo**, a dry white wine.

GREECE the importance of Greece as a wine-producing country has diminished over the centuries, and although vast acreages are under vines, the wines are generally regarded as being inferior to those available elsewhere. There are exceptions such as the famous RETSINA and the sweet red dessert wine, MAVRODAPHNE. Other reasonable quality table wines are available, and the best of these can be very pleasant. A new appellation system has been introduced and in time should mean great improvement. Red Greek wines have a TASTE RATING of E.

GREEN tasting term for a young wine which is unbalanced because of excess ACIDITY (often caused by unripe grapes).

GREEN WINE term for wines from the VINHO VERDE (literally 'green wines') area of Portugal north of Oporto, which have a GREEN quality.

GRENACHE grape used for making strong, sweet wines. Widely planted throughout Europe, with vast acreages in Spain, it is also grown in Algeria, Australia, Israel, Mexico, Morocco, and California. It is a fruity grape with a very distinctive flavour but lacks colour. It makes excellent rosé wines but is generally blended for more full-bodied wines, e.g. in France where it is used in CHÂTEAUNEUF-DU-PAPE. Also known as Alicante, Carignane Rousse, Tinto, Alicantina and Garnacha.

GRENOUILLES one of the seven GRAND CRU vineyards of CHABLIS in central France.

GRÈVES, LES outstanding GRAND CRU vineyard of the ALOXE-CORTON village of CÔTE D'OR district of BURGUNDY.

GRGICH HILLS CELLARS winery in the NAPA VALLEY region of California producing varietal wines including excellent CHARDONNAY.

GRIGNOLINO grape used in the PIEMONTE area of Italy to make red wines of a pleasant character, particularly the slightly bitter **Grignolino d'Asti**.

GRIGNOLIO red-wine grape grown in Italy and in California.

GRILLET, CHÂTEAU AC white wine from the northern CÔTES DU RHÔNE area of eastern France.

GRILLO grape variety used in Marsala production.

GRINZING wine-producing village near Vienna in Austria. *See* HEURIGE.

GRIOTTE-CHAMBERTIN GRAND CRU vineyard of the GEVREY-CHAMBERTIN commune in the CÔTE DE NUITS district of BURGUNDY.

GRIP tasting term for the degree of firmness with which a wine 'grips' the mouth.

GRK dry white wine from DALMATIA in Yugoslavia.

GROLLEAU *see* GROSLOT.

GROMBALIA main wine-producing area of Tunisia.

GROSLOT French grape grown in the ANJOU district of western France and used in the production of rosé wines. Also known as Grolleau.

GROS MANSENG vine grown in the JURANÇON district of southwest France and used for white wines.

GROS NOIREN local term for the PINOT NOIR grape used in the Jura Mountains area of France.

GROS PLANT variety of grape grown in the MUSCADET area of the Loire Valley in France and used in the production of light, sharp local VDQS white wines including **Gros Plant du Pays Nantais**. Also known as Folle Blanche.

GROSSET wine producer in the CLARE VALLEY, Australia.

GROSSLAGE German term for a named group or district of vineyards, a subdivision of a BEREICH.

GRUAUD-LAROSÉ, CHÂTEAU deuxième GRAND CRU wine from the SAINT-JULIEN commune of BORDEAUX.

GRUMELLO red wine produced in the VALTELLINA valley in the LOMBARDY area of Italy.

GRUNBERGER STEEN white wine from STELLENBOSCH in South Africa.

GRÜNER VELTLINER white-wine grape variety grown in Austria, and also Germany and Hungary.

GUADET-SAINT-JULIEN, CHÂTEAU GRAND CRU wine from the SAINT-EMILION district in the BORDEAUX region of southwest France.

GUEBWILLER wine town in the ALSACE district of northeast France producing mainly RIESLING wines.

GUILD WINERIES AND DISTILLERIES large wine cooperative of the SAN JOAQUIN VALLEY area of California. Its best known brand is Vino da Tavola.

GUIRAUD, CHÂTEAU premier GRAND CRU SAUTERNES from BORDEAUX in southwest France.

GUMPOLDSKIRCHEN wine town near Vienna in Austria which produces the well-known white wine **Gumpoldskirchner**.

GUNDLACH-BUNDSCHU WINERY winery in SONOMA, California, producing varietal wines including good CHARDONNAY and CABERNET SAUVIGNON.

GUNFLINT tasting term for the flavour detectable in some dry white wines, such as Chablis, caused by chalk in the subsoil in which the vines are grown. The French term is *goût de pierre à fusil*.

GUNTERSBLUM village of GROSSLAGE Krotenbrünnen in the BEREICH of NIERSTEIN in the RHEINHESSEN region of Germany.

GUNTRUM, LOUIS wine estate of the RHEINHESSEN region of Germany producing Niersteiner and Oppenheimer wines.

GURPEGUI large wine producers in the RIOJA region of northern Spain. Their brand names include Dominio de la Plana, Berceo and Gonzalo de Berceo.

GUT German word for 'estate', hence WEINGUT, 'wine estate', equivalent to the French CLOS or CHÂTEAU.

GUTEDAL German name for the Chasselas grape, grown in Germany and California.

GUTTURNIO DEI COLLI PIACENTINI dry red wine from the EMILIA-ROMAGNA region of central Italy. ESPALIER method.

GYONGYOS-VISONTA region of Hungary producing red and white dry wines and some good sparkling white wines.

H

HAARDT village of GROSSLAGE Meerspinne in the BEREICH of MITTELHAARDT in the RHEINPFALZ region of Germany.

HACIENDA WINE CELLARS winery in the SONOMA district of California, producing VARIETAL wines.

HAGGIPAVLU oldest wine-shipping firm in Cyprus, based at Limassol.

HAHNHEIM village of GROSSLAGE Gutes Domtal in the BEREICH of NIERSTEIN in the RHEINHESSEN region of Germany.

HAJOS Hungarian village producing good red wines.

HALBROT Swiss term for rosé-style wine made from both black and white grapes.

HALBTROCKEN German word for 'half dry', meaning medium wines with a SWEETNESS RATING of 3.

HALF BOTTLE bottle with approximately half the capacity of a full wine bottle, i.e. 35 centilitres.

HALLGARTEN village of GROSSLAGE Mehrholzchen in the BEREICH of JOHANNISBERG in the RHEINGAU region of Germany. Its vineyards include Hendelberg, Jungfer, and the outstanding Schonhell, Deitelsburg and Wurzgarten.

HALLGARTEN, ARTHUR wine-exporters of London and Geisenheim in the RHEINGAU region of Germany exporting both estate and regional wines from all Germany.

HAMBLEDON wine estate in Hampshire, England, producing dry wines from CHARDONNAY, PINOT NOIR and SEYVAL BLANC grapes.

HANTEILLAN, CHÂTEAU CRU GRAND BOURGEOIS wine from the HAUT-MÉDOC district of BORDEAUX.

HANZELL VINEYARDS vineyard in the SONOMA region of California, producing full-bodied Burgundy-type wines using CHARDONNAY and PINOT NOIR vines.

HARASZTHY, J.J. winery in SONOMA, California, producing varietal wines from CHARDONNAY, GEWÜRZTRAMINER and ZINFANDEL grapes.

HARD tasting term for the hard quality of a wine, usually a young quality one, caused by an excess of TANNIN. With age, the wine will soften to FIRM which enhances the quality. *See also* HARSH.

HARDY, THOMAS large family wine company based in South Australia. Owners of Château REYNELLA and Houghton Wines and producers of excellent TAWNY Port.

HARGRAVE VINEYARDS winery in Long Island, New York State, US, producing VITIS VINIFERA wines.

HARO main centre of the RIOJA district of Spain. Many BODEGAS are situated here.

HARSH term for the excessively HARD quality of a wine caused by too much TANNIN. In reds results in a lack of harmony, in whites in a highly acidic wine lacking flavour.

HARSLEVELU grape variety used in Hungary for the production of TOKAY and other wines.

HARVEY'S British-owned SHERRY, PORT and wine shippers of JEREZ in southern Spain, best known for their Bristol Cream brand.

HARXHEIM village of GROSSLAGE Sankt Alban in the BEREICH of NIERSTEIN in the RHEINHESSEN region of Germany.

HATTENHEIM village of GROSSLAGE Deutelsberg in the BEREICH of JOHANNISBERG in the RHEINGAU region of Germany producing the great wines of the region. It is renowned for wines from the Mannberg, Nussbrunnen, and Wisselbrunnen vineyards.

HAUT (HAUTE) French word for 'high', referring to a higher geographical area. For example, HAUT-MÉDOC refers to the area upriver from MÉDOC.

HAUT-BAGES-LIBÉRAL, CHÂTEAU cinquième GRAND CRU wine from the PAUILLAC commune of BORDEAUX.

HAUT-BATAILLEY, CHÂTEAU cinquième GRAND CRU wine from the PAUILLAC commune of BORDEAUX.

HAUT-BENAUGE wine-producing region on the right bank of the River Garonne in the south of the ENTRE-DEUX-MERS district of southwest France. Its nine communes are d'Arbis, Cantois, Escoursons, Gornac, Ladaux, Mourens, Soulignac, Saint-Pierre-de-Bat, and Targon.

HAUT-BRION, CHÂTEAU premier GRAND CRU wine from the GRAVES district of BORDEAUX. One of the best Bordeaux wines.

HAUT-CORBIN, CHÂTEAU smooth GRAND CRU wine from the SAINT-EMILION district of BORDEAUX.

HAUT DAHRA region of Algeria producing red table wine.

HAUT-MARBUZET, CHÂTEAU CRU GRAND BOURGEOIS EXCEPTIONNEL wine from the SAINT-ESTÈPHE commune of BORDEAUX.

HAUT-MÉDOC area of the BORDEAUX region of southwest France producing some of its finest red wines including those of MARGAUX, PAUILLAC, SAINT-JULIEN and SAINT-ESTÈPHE.

HAUT-MONTRAVEL AC appellation in BERGERAC, southwest France.

HAUT-PEYRAGNEY, CHÂTEAU PREMIER CRU vineyard of the BOMMES commune in the SAUTERNES district of BORDEAUX. Produces sweet, white wine.

HAUT-POITOU VDQS red wine from near ANJOU in the Loire Valley, France.

HAUT PONTET, CHÂTEAU GRAND CRU of SAINT-EMILION in BORDEAUX.

HAUTVILLERS CHAMPAGNE village and vineyards of the Canton d'Ay in the Arrondissement de Reims in northeast France. Classified 90 percent in the CIVC rating. It was in the Abbey of the village that DOM PÉRIGNON invented the CHAMPAGNE METHOD.

HAWKE'S BAY important wine-growing area on the east coast of North Island, New Zealand.

HEAVY tasting term for a full-bodied but non-distinctive wine.

HEEMSKERK wine producers in Tasmania, Australia, producing good CHARDONNAY, CABERNET SAUVIGNON and PINOT NOIR wines.

HEIDSEICK, CHARLES important wine-producing firm based at Reims in the CHAMPAGNE region of France. The range of champagnes include NV, Vintage Brut, Vintage Rosé, Blanc de Blancs and La Royal.

HEIDSIECK MONOPOLE important wine-shipping firm based at Reims in the CHAMPAGNE region of France. Produces a good range of NV champagnes and the excellent Diamant Bleu.

HEILBRONN village of GROSSLAGE Staufenberg in the BEREICH of Württembergisch Unterland in the WÜRTTEMBERG region of Germany.

HEITZ WINE CELLARS wine producers in the NAPA VALLEY region of California producing varietals, Port, Sherry and sparkling wine. An excellent and famous wine is Martha's Vineyard Cabernet Sauvignon.

HENDERSON large wine-growing region near Auckland in New Zealand.

HENKELL producer of quality DEUTSCHER SEKT.

HENRIOT important CHAMPAGNE firm in REIMS in the Champagne region of France producing non-vintage, vintage and deluxe champagnes. Now owned by Charles HEIDSIECK.

HENRIQUES & HENRIQUES firm of MADEIRA wine shippers.

HÉRAULT important wine-producing department of southern France where 20 percent of France's wines originate.

HERMITAGE (1) famous district of the northern RHÔNE VALLEY area of France producing quality red and white wines from the SYRAH grape; (2) name sometimes used in Australia for wines made from the SHIRAZ grape. Excellent wines which represent good value for money.

HERRSCHAFT district of Switzterland on the Austrian border producing light red and sweet white wines.

HERXHEIM village of GROSSLAGE Herrlich in the BEREICH of SÜDLICHE WEINSTRASSE in the RHEINPFALZ region of Germany.

HESSISCHE BERGSTRASSE smallest German wine-growing ANBAUGEBIET, located just north of Heidelberg on the right bank of the River Rhine. Because of limited production, most of its wines are consumed within Germany.

HEURIGE German term meaning this year's wine (from *der heurige Wein*), also known as May wine. In Austria also the name for the inns at Grinzing near Vienna where the new wines of the area are sold.

HEYL ZU HERRNSHEIM wine estate in the NIERSTEIN area of RHEINHESSEN in Germany.

HIMMELREICH vineyard of GROSSLAGE Munzlay in the BEREICH of BERNKASTEL in the MOSEL-SAAR-RUWER region of Germany.

HOCHHEIM village of GROSSLAGE Daubhaus in the BEREICH of JOHANNISBERG in the RHEINGAU region of Germany. Origin of the term HOCK. Its Domdechaney vineyard produces a fruity wine.

HOCK English name for all wines from the RHEINGAU district of Germany and often used for all Rhine wines, derived from HOCHHEIM.

HOGSHEAD wine cask used mainly for bulk shipments and ageing of wines. Its capacity varies between 225 and 273 litres.

HOLLOW tasting term for a wine with no middle PALATE.

HOP KILN WINERY winery in the Russian River Valley near Healdsburg in SONOMA, California, producing VARIETAL wines.

HORAM MANOR winery in Sussex, England, owned by the Merrydown company, which sells a range of ENGLISH WINES.

HOSPICES DE BEAUNE charity hospital in the town of BEAUNE in BURGUNDY, founded in 1443. A number of vineyards are owned by the Hospices and in November each year an auction of its wines is held there. Ownership of these wines is much sought, and the prices raised set the value of the wines of the whole CÔTE D'OR district.

HOUGHTON largest winery and vineyards in Western Australia whose wines are now available in the UK. It is owned by Thomas HARDY.

HUDSON RIVER VALLEY important wine-producing area of New York State, US. Produces red, white and rosé wines from native vines.

HUELVA, CONDADO DE wine-producing DO province of EXTREMADURA, southern Spain, producing strong heavy wines.

344

HUET, GASTON highly reputed growers of VOUVRAY in the Touraine district of western France producing sweet and dry, still and sparkling wines.

HUGEL well-known growers and negociants of Riquewihr in ALSACE, northeast France. The Hugel style of white wine is fuller and very slightly sweeter than most Alsace producers'; a very commercial style.

HUMAGNE old vine of the VALAIS region of Switzerland, dating back to the early 14th century.

HUNGARY a wine-producing country for many centuries which is currently enjoying a resurgence of popularity in the UK because of quality and good value for money. The improved quality follows nationalization of the industry after World War II as the state-run export company, Monimpex, allows only wines of set quality standards to be exported. Wines of depth with unique style are becoming more widely available and are good value. Unlike Bulgaria, native rather than imported grapes are mainly used. Hungarian red wines (e.g. Bull's Blood) have a TASTE RATING of D, the whites a SWEETNESS RATING of 3 for dry wines and 4 for medium-dry wines. Its most famous wine is TOKAY ASZU.

HUNTER VALLEY wine-producing district of New South Wales in Australia producing mostly table wines. Unique SEMILLON wines are outstanding, and it also produces excellent CHARDONNAY and SHIRAZ wines.

HUNTINGDON ESTATE estate of MUDGEE in New South Wales, Australia, producing varietal wines especially CABERNET SAUVIGNON and CHARDONNAY.

HUSCH VINEYARDS vineyards in MENDOCINO, California, producing varietal wines. Grapes used include GEWÜRZTRAMINER, PINOT NOIR, SAUVIGNON BLANC, CHARDONNAY, and CABERNET SAUVIGNON.

HUXELREBE grape variety used for ENGLISH WINES.

HYBRID cross-bred grape, usually between an established stock such as VITIS VINIFERA and a native American variety. The purpose of hybridization is to produce a grape with a combination of characteristics suited to the environment in which it is to be grown. *See also* GRAPES.

HYDROGEN SULPHIDE gas with the smell of rotton eggs which can be given off by red wines. A fault usually found only in young red wines, it is caused by reduction of elemental sulphur.

HYDROMETER instrument for measuring the sugar content of unfermented wine (MUST). The hydrometer floats in a grape juice because sugar raises the specific gravity. The hydrometer is calibrated to give the amount of sugar in the solution.

HYMETTUS light dry red and white wines produced in Greece, near Mount Hymettus.

I

IHRINGEN village of GROSSLAGE Vulkanfelsen in the BEREICH of KAISERSTUHL in the BADEN region of Germany.

ILBESHEIM village of GROSSLAGE Herrlich in the BEREICH of SÜDLICHE WEINSTRASSE in the RHEINPFALZ region of Germany.

IMPERIAL (IMPERIALE) six-litre bottle for long storage of fine BORDEAUX wines.

IMPERIAL brand name of Spanish wines produced by CVNE.

INAO *see* INSTITUT NATIONAL DES APPELLATIONS D'ORIGINE.

INCRUSTATION formation of crust on PORT.

INDIA country with a small wine industry based on French methods with local grapes.

INFERNO red and white wine from VALTELLINA in the LOMBARDY region of northern Italy.

INGLEHEIM village of GROSSLAGE Kaiserpfalz in the BEREICH of BINGEN in the RHEINHESSEN region of Germany. Produces some of the best of the German red wines.

INGLENOOK VINEYARDS winery in the NAPA VALLEY, California, producing vintage VARIETAL wines.

INSTITUT NATIONAL DES APPELLATIONS D'ORIGINE administrative body, which administers the wine and spirit control laws of France. See AC.

IONA American hybrid grape used in New York State for the production of dry, sparkling white wines.

IPHOFEN village of GROSSLAGE Burgweg in the BEREICH of STEIGERWALD in the FRANKEN region of Germany.

IRANCY AC red and rosé wines from Yonne in northern BURGUNDY, often labelled Bourgogne Irancy.

IRON HORSE VINEYARDS vineyards in the SONOMA region of California producing the varietal wines CABERNET SAUVIGNON and CHARDONNAY.

IROULÉGUY red, white and rosé wines from the Pyrenées in southwest France. The reds are considered the best.

ISABELLA American grape with a slightly FOXY taste, used for blending in the production of sparkling wines. Also called Americano in Switzerland.

ISCHIA red and white DOC wines from the Italian island of Ischia; part of the CAMPANIA region of southwest Italy.

ISINGLASS substance used for the FINING of wines, derived from the bladders of freshwater fish.

ISKRA brand name of Bulgarian sparkling wines, red, rosé and white.

ISLE DE BEAUTÉ name of Corsica's VIN DE PAYS.

ISONZO red and white DOC wines produced in the FRIULI-VENEZIA-GIULIA region of northeast Italy.

ISRAEL wine-producing country with a wide variety of wine types. Mostly made near Tel-Aviv and Mount Carmel. Wines made from European varieties of grape, e.g. CABERNET SAUVIGNON, SEMILLON, and SAUVIGNON BLANC are beginning to be exported.

ISSAN, CHÂTEAU D' troisième GRAND CRU wine from the MARGAUX commune of BORDEAUX.

ISTRIA wine-producing area of Croatia in northern Yugoslavia. Its best-known wine is Malvazya, made from the Italian MALVASIA grape.

ITALY the world's leading producer of wine in terms of quantity. Italian wines are presently very popular in the UK, with good reason. The variety of styles at all prices ensures there is a wine for everyone. At one time Italy's consumption of wine was almost 100 litres per head per annum. This figure is now just under 82 litres, and the trend seems to be to drink less but of better quality. To improve quality for home and export markets, in 1963 an appellation system similar to the French was introduced. It ensures a guaranteed level of quality of wine and has three classifications: VINO DA TÀVOLA, DOC and DOCG.

The wine-producing regions are Valle d'Aosta, Piemonte, Lombardy, Veneto, Trentino-Alto Adige, Friuli-Venezia-Giulia, Liguria, Emilia-Romagna, Tuscany, Umbria, Marche, Latium, Abruzzi, Molise, Campania, Puglia, Basilicata, Calabria, Sicily and Sardinia.

IVES American grape variety producing wine with a FOXY taste.

J

JABOULET, PAUL wine grower and shipper of the HER-MITAGE district of the Rhône Valley in France.

JABOULET-VERCHERRE wine grower and shipper of BURGUNDY.

JACOB'S CREEK brand name of CABERNET SAUVIGNON wine from ORLANDO.

JACQUART cooperative in CHAMPAGNE producing quality, reasonably priced vintage, nonvintage and rosé wines.

JADOT, LOUIS wine shipper and joint owner of the CHAVELIER vineyard in the CÔTE DE BEAUNE area of BURGUNDY. Also joint owner of the CORTON-CHARLEMAGNE vineyard.

JAMES MUSCADINE grape variety grown in the south of the US. Characteristic, fruity aroma.

JAPAN country with a small winemaking industry now based on European and hybrid grapes following unsuccessful experiments with native American varieties. The market for local wines is not yet great, and there is more interest in imported wines, including highly expensive BORDEAUX château wines, possibly bought as a status symbol or an investment rather than for drinking.

JARDIN DE LA FRANCE area of the LOIRE valley in France producing VINS DE PAYS.

JASNIÈRES vineyard area of the COTEAUX DU LOIR in France producing semi-sweet white wines.

JEAN PERICO sparkling wine from the CATALONIA region of northeast Spain sold by GONZALEZ BYASS.

JEKEL VINEYARDS vineyards in the MONTEREY district of California producing varietal wines, the whites being particularly good.

JEREZ demarcated SHERRY-producing area of southwest Spain. The main town, **Jerez de la Frontera**, is the hub of the Sherry industry, the name itself coming from the town's former name of *Xeres*.

JEROBOAM large bottle (double magnum) equivalent to between four (champagne) and six (claret) bottles.

JESUITENGARTEN single vineyard (EINZELLAGE) of GROSSLAGE Mariengarten in the RHEINGAU region of Germany. Owned by the FRIEDRICH-WILHELM-GYMNASIUM it is one of the best in Germany.

JOHANNISBERG (1) BEREICH name given to the RHEINGAU region of Germany; (2) village of GROSSLAGE Erntebringer in the RHEINGAU with several vineyards producing excellent Rieslings. Wines from Schloss Johannisberg and Klaus Johannisberg vineyards are the best; (3) white wine from the VALAIS region of Switzerland, one of its best.

JOHANNISBERG RIESLING Californian name for the RIESLING grape and also known by this name in Mexico.

JOHANNISWEIN ceremonial wine ('St John's wine') produced at DEIDESHEIM in Germany and associated with good health, fertility and peace. Often drunk at weddings and other special occasions; particularly at Deidesheim on St John's day when the wine is blessed; a custom associated with the wine blessed by St John at the Last Supper.

JOHNSON'S ALEXANDER VALLEY WINE vineyards in the SONOMA region of California producing varietal wines. They include CHENIN BLANC, ZINFANDEL, CABERNET SAUVIGNON, and CHARDONNAY.

JORDAN VINEYARD vineyards in the Alexander Valley in the SONOMA region of California, specializing in claret-type wines. Grape varieties include CABERNET SAUVIGNON, MERLOT and CHARDONNAY.

JOSEPHSHÖF well-known EINZELLAGE of Graach in

GROSSLAGE Munzlay in the BEREICH of BERNKASTEL in the MOSEL-SAAR-RUWER region of Germany. The wines are, unusually, sold under the name of the vineyard itself.

JUFFER EINZELLAGE located at BRAUNEBERG in GROSSLAGE Kurfürstlay in the BEREICH of BERNKASTEL in the MOSEL-SAAR-RUWER region of Germany. It produces excellent RIESLING wines.

JULIÉNAS one of the nine BEAUJOLAIS CRU and one of the longest-lasting Beaujolais wines. It produces a fuller style of wine, one which is enjoyable as a young full-bodied wine or as a more elegant style after keeping.

JULIUS-ECHTER-BERG EINZELLAGE of IPHOFEN in GROSSLAGE Bergweg in the BEREICH of BACHARACH in the FRANKEN region of Germany.

JULIUSSPITAL wine-producing charity institution for the poor in WURZBURG in the FRANKEN region of central Germany, supported by the sale of its excellent wines

JUMILLA DO region of Valencia in southeast Spain producing stronger red wines with a TASTE RATING of E. Large plantings of vines have not been affected by PHYLLOXERA.

JUNGFER *see* HALLGARTEN.

JURA region of eastern France producing red, white and rosé wines. The region also produces sparkling wines, VIN JAUNE and VIN DE PAILLE. Its general AC areas are CÔTES DU JURA and Côtes du Jura Mousseaux, and the better wines come from ARBOIS, and L'ÉTOILE and the village of CHÂTEAU-CHALON.

JURANÇON area of southwest France producing rich, sweet white wines and some lesser quality dry white and rosé wines. Sweet Jurançon wines can be found at reasonable prices and are generally good value.

JUZHNYABRYAG Controliran wine area of BULGARIA making rosé wines.

K

KABINETT lowest and driest of the six categories of German QmP wines. Before fermentation the wine must have a minimum sweetness potential level of 70 degrees OECHSLE. The result is light wines made without added sugar with a SWEETNESS RATING of 4.

KABINETTWEIN German term for special reserve wine, selected from the best barrels of a vintage. The term applies mainly to Rhine wines.

KADARKA red-wine grape variety used extensively in Hungary and also in Yugoslavia, Austria, and Romania where it is known as Cadarca. Makes full-bodied wines.

KAEFFERKOPF vineyard in the village of AMMERSCHWIHR in the ALSACE region of northeast France.

KAHLENBERG town and vineyard of the KLOSTERNEUBERG area of the Danube region of Austria.

KAISER STUHL winery in the BAROSSA VALLEY region of New South Wales in Australia, owned by Penfolds.

KAISERSTUHL BEREICH of the BADEN region of Germany, the best wine-producing area of the region.

KALLIGAS *see* CALLIGAS.

KALLSTADT village of GROSSLAGE Kobnert in the BEREICH of MITTELHAARDT in the RHEINPFALZ region of Germany.

KALTERSEEWEIN *see* CALDARO.

KAMP tributary of the River Danube in Austria, the valley of which is a wine-growing area producing RIESLING and VELTLINER wines.

KANZEM village of GROSSLAGE Scharzberg in the BEREICH of SAAR-RUWER in the MOSEL-SAAR-RUWER region of rmany. Top vineyards include Altenberg, Horecker, chlossberg, and Sonnenberg.

KARLOVO town of central Bulgaria producing distinctive tasting wine from the MISKET grape.

KARTHÄUSERHOFBERG outstanding vineyard at Eitelsbach near Trier in the GROSSLAGE Römerlay of the MOSEL-SAAR-RUWER region of Germany.

KASEL important wine-village of GROSSLAGE Römerlay in the BEREICH of SAAR-RUWER in the MOSEL-SAAR-RUWER region of Germany.

KAYSERBERG famous wine-town and commune in Alsace, northeast France.

KECSKEMET important white wine-producing area of Hungary making Furmint Edes and Leanyka.

KEENAN WINERY vineyards in the NAPA VALLEY region of California producing varietal wines, including good CHARDONNAY, CABERNET SAUVIGNON, and PINOT NOIR.

KEKFRANKOS Hungarian name for the GAMAY grape.

KEKNYELU well-known flavoursome spicy white wine from the BADACSONY area of Hungary.

KELLER German term for wine cellar. **Kellerei** means 'wine producer'.

KELLERABFÜLLUNG German term for ESTATE-BOTTLED.

KENWOOD VINEYARDS vineyards in the SONOMA region of California producing varietal wines, including ZINFANDEL and CABERNET SAUVIGNON.

KEO firm in Cyprus blending wines from KHALOKHORIO for COMMANDARIA. Their well-known products include Aphrodite dry white wine.

KEPHALONIA *see* CEPHALONIA.

KEPHESIA winemaking region of Attica, the area around Athens, from where most RETSINA comes.

KEPPOCH-PADTHAWAY recently pioneered region to the south of Adelaide in South AUSTRALIA. First impressions are that the wines will be of good quality while not attaining the status of nearby COONAWARRA.

KERNER white-wine grape grown in Germany and South Africa, developed from the TROLLINGER and RIESLING.

KESSELSTADT estate of the MOSEL-SAAR-RUWER region of Germany with properties in many of the best wine-villages of the area, including GRAACH, PIESPORT, KASEL, and OBEREMMEL.

KESTEN village of GROSSLAGE Kurfürstlay in the BEREICH of BERNKASTEL in the MOSEL-SAAR-RUWER region of Germany. RIESLING is the widely planted grape.

KHALOKHORIO village in Cyprus producing COMMANDARIA liqueur wine from XYNISTERI grapes.

KIEDRICH village of GROSSLAGE Heiligenstock in the BEREICH of JOHANNISBERG in the RHEINGAU region of Germany.

KINHEIM village of GROSSLAGE Schwarzlay in the BEREICH of BERNKASTEL in the MOSEL-SAAR-RUWER region of Germany. RIESLING is the predominantly grown grape.

KIRCHENSTÜCK EINZELLAGE of FORST in GROSSLAGE Mariengarten in the BEREICH of MITTELHAARDT in the RHEINGAU region of Germany.

KIRWAN, CHÂTEAU troisième GRAND CRU wine from the MARGAUX commune of BORDEAUX.

KISBURGUNDI Hungarian name for the PINOT NOIR grape.

KISTLER CELLARS vineyards in the SONOMA region of California producing varietal wines, including CHARDONNAY, PINOT NOIR and CABERNET SAUVIGNON.

KLEIN KAROO *see* LITTLE KAROO.

KLEVNER (1) German name for the PINOT BLANC grape; (2) local name in ORTENAU in the BADEN region for the TRAMINER grape.

KLINGELBERGER name given to RIESLING produced in the BEREICH of ORTENAU in the region of BADEN in Germany.

KLÖCH district of STYRIA in Austria producing good quality wines, especially GEWÜRZTRAMINER wines.

KLOSTER EBERBACH monastery and vineyard near HATTENHEIM in the RHEINGAU region of Germany, home of the German Wine Academy. The great HOCK wine Steinberg is produced here.

KLOSTERNEUBERG monastery converted to a wine college and research institute on the River Danube near Vienna in Austria. Produces its own wines including Klosterdawn and Klostergarten.

KLÜSSERATH village of GROSSLAGE Sankt Michael in the BEREICH of Bernkastel in the MOSEL-SAAR-RUWER region of Germany.

KNIPPERLE white-wine grape used in ALSACE. Also known as Kipperle, Kleinergelber and Kleiner Rauschling.

KOKKINELI dry rosé wine produced on the island of Cyrpus.

KOLOSSI red and white table wines from Cyprus, produced by Sodap.

KÖNIGSBACH outstanding wine village of GROSSLAGE Meerspinne in the BEREICH of MITTELHAARDT in the RHEINPFALZ region of Germany. Top vineyards include Idig, Haag and Hinteriese.

KÖNIGSBERG (1) a GROSSLAGE of the BEREICH of OBERMOSEL in the MOSEL-SAAR-RUWER region of Germany; (2) vineyard of KLÜSSERATH in MOSEL-SAAR-RUWER.

KONOCTI WINERY winery in the LAKE COUNTY region of California producing mostly red varietal wines including ZINFANDEL and CABERNET SAUVIGNON.

KONSUMWEIN German term for ordinary everyday quaffing wine.

KONZ village of GROSSLAGE Scharzberg in the BEREICH of SAAR-RUWER in the MOSEL-SAAR-RUWER region of Germany.

KORBEL WINERY well-known sparkling wine producer in Sonoma, California.

KOSHER WINE Jewish ceremonial wine made to a high standard of purity. The name is also used in the US for Passover wine, which is sweeter and thicker.

KOSOVO (KOSMET) province of SERBIA in southwest Yugoslavia producing red and some white wines.

KOWERICH village of GROSSLAGE Sankt Michael in the BEREICH of BERNKASTEL in the MOSEL-SAAR-RUWER region of Germany.

KRAICHGAU vineyard area near Heidelberg in the BADEN region of Germany. It has three GROSSLAGEN: Hohenberg, Stiftsberg and Mannberg.

KRALEVO Controliran area of BULGARIA making RIESLING wines.

KRASKI TANNIC-tasting wine from ISTRIA in Yugoslavia.

KREMER, LOUIS producer of CHAMPAGNE making NV, vintage and rosé wines.

KREMS important town and wine region of the WACHAU district on the River Danube in Austria producing RIESLING wines.

KRESSMAN, E.S. reputable wine-shipping firm of BORDEAUX.

KREUZNACH BEREICH of the NAHE region of Germany. *See also* BAD KREUZNACH.

KRITER very good quality sparkling wine produced by Patriarche Père & Fils in BEAUNE in BURGUNDY.

KRÖV (CROV) wine-producing village in GROSSLAGE Nacktarsch in the BEREICH of BERNKASTEL in the MOSEL-SAAR-RUWER region of Germany.

KRUG CHAMPAGNE firm in REIMS in the Champagne region of France producing very high quality wines: vintage, Grand Cuvée NV, and recently Rosé NV. Regarded by many as the top champagne house.

KRUG WINERY, CHARLES old-established winery of the Napa Valley area of California producing VARIETAL wines. The best are labelled Charles Krug and others are labelled CK or Napa Vista.

KUCHELBERGER the best red wine from the Merano area of the Alto Adige region of TRENTINO-ALTO ADIGE in northern Italy.

KUEHN wine-grower and negociant at Ammerschwihr in ALSACE, owned by a cooperative. Wines include Charme d'Alsace.

KUENTZ-BAS wine-grower and negociant in the ALSACE region of France producing red and white, mostly dry wines, using RIESLING, GEWÜRZTRAMINER, PINOT BLANC, PINOT GRIS, PINOT NOIR and MUSCAT grapes.

KUPFERBERG large wine-producing firm based at Mainz, making DEUTSCHER SEKT.

KWV abbreviation for Kooperatieve Wijnbouwers Vereniging, the South African state wine cooperative which controls the South African wine industry. All growers contribute a substantial percentage of their crop to the cooperative.

KYKKO brand of table wine from Cyprus.

L

LABARDE one of the communes of HAUT-MÉDOC in BORDEAUX, northwest of Bordeaux. Its wines are sold under the name MARGAUX. Its most famous wine is Château GISCOURS.

LABASTIDA cooperative and vineyard area of the RIOJA ALAVESA region of northern Spain producing white and oak-aged red wines. The cooperative also has vineyards in the Samaniego area.

LABÉGORCE, CHÂTEAU CRU BOURGEOIS SUPÉRIEUR wine from the MARGAUX commune of BORDEAUX.

LABÉGORCE-ZÉDÉ, CHÂTEAU CRU BOURGEOIS SUPÉRIEUR wine from the MARGAUX commune of BORDEAUX.

LABRUSCA *see* VITIS LABRUSCA.

LA CHABLISIENNE, CAVE COOPERATIVE large cooperative producer and bottler in the CHABLIS area of Burgundy. Wine is labelled under the cooperative name or those of individual growers.

LA CÔTE vineyard area by Lake Geneva in the VAUD district of Switzerland producing white DORIN and SAVAGNIN.

LA CREMA VINERA vineyards in the SONOMA region of California, producing varietal wines including CHARDONNAY, CABERNET SAUVIGNON and PINOT NOIR.

LACRIMA DI CASTROVILLARI one of the best-known red table wines of CALABRIA in southern Italy. Made from Gaglioppo and Lacrima Nera grapes.

LACRIMA CHRISTI dry white and some red wine produced in the CAMPANIA region of southwest Italy. The name is literally 'tears of Christ', sometimes spelled *lagrima*.

LADOIX-SERRIGNY AC commune of the CÔTE DE BEAUNE district of BURGUNDY. Most often sold under the names CÔTE DE BEAUNE-VILLAGES or ALOXE-CORTON.

LAFAURIE-PEYRAGUEY, CHÂTEAU PREMIER GRAND CRU wine from SAUTERNES in BORDEAUX. Excellent Sauternes wine.

LAFITE-ROTHSCHILD, CHÂTEAU PREMIER GRAND CRU wine from the PAUILLAC commune in BORDEAUX. One of the best Bordeaux wines.

LAFLEUR GAZIN, CHÂTEAU distinguished estate of POMEROL in BORDEAUX.

LAFOES area south of the VINHO VERDE region of Portugal producing red and white wines. The best-known are Allegro, Evelita, Grandjo and Vila Real.

LAFON-ROCHET, CHÂTEAU quatrième GRAND CRU wine from the SAINT-ESTÈPHE commune in BORDEAUX.

LAGOA ordinary red and white wines produced in the ALGARVE district of Portugal.

LAGO DI CALDARO *see* CALDARO.

LAGOSTA well-known VINHO VERDE wine from Portugal.

LAGRANGE, CHÂTEAU (1) troisième GRAND CRU wine from the SAINT-JULIEN commune in BORDEAUX; (2) wine from the POMEROL district of BORDEAUX.

LAGREIN red-wine grape grown in the Alto Adige area of TRENTINO-ALTO ADIGE in northern Italy. It produces the DOC wines **Lagrein Rosato**, a rosé (German name *Kretzer*), and **Lagrein del Trentino**, a dry fruity red (German name *Dunkel*).

LAGRIMA sweet, fortified dessert wine from MÁLAGA in the ANDALUSIAN region of Spain.

LAGRIMA CHRISTI alternative spelling of LACRIMA CHRISTI.

LAGUARDIA centre of the RIOJA ALAVESA region of northern Spain, producing red table wines.

LAGUNE, CHÂTEAU LA troisième GRAND CRU wine from the HAUT-MÉDOC district of BORDEAUX.

LA INA Sherry made by Domecq. Excellent commercial FINO style.

LAKE COUNTY (1) wine-growing district of California; (2) brand name of wines from New York State, sold by the Taylor Wine Company.

LAKE ERIE wine-producing area of the eastern US producing red, white and sparkling wines. The wines are mostly produced around Sondusky.

LAKE'S FOLLY wine-producers of the HUNTER VALLEY in New South Wales, Australia, producing good varietal wines from CHARDONNAY and CABERNET SAUVIGNON vines.

LALANDE-BORIE, CHÂTEAU CRU BOURGEOIS SUPÉRIEUR wine from the SAINT-JULIEN commune of BORDEAUX.

LALANDE DE POMEROL commune of the POMEROL district of BORDEAUX. Some of its best wines come from Château Bel-Air.

LA MANCHA large wine-producing area of New Castile in central Spain producing mostly red wines and some dry whites with a SWEETNESS RATING of 2.

LAMARQUE, CHÂTEAU CRU GRAND BOURGEOIS wine from the HAUT-MÉDOC district of BORDEAUX.

LAMBERHURST PRIORY large estate in Kent, England, producing wines from a range of traditional grapes, including RIESLING, SEYVAL BLANC and REICHENSTEINER.

LAMBERT BRIDGE WINERY winery in the Dry Creek area of the northern SONOMA region of California pro-

ducing varietal wines including good CABERNET SAU-
VIGNON and CHARDONNAY.

LAMBERTI large-scale wine producers of the VENETO
region of northern Italy. Their DOC wines include BAR-
DOLINO, LUGANA, RIVIERA DEL GARDA, Bresciano, SOAVE
and Valpolicella-Recioto-Amarone.

LAMBRUSCO (1) red-wine grape grown in Italy; (2) foamy
sparkling red wines from the EMILIA-ROMAGNA area of
Italy including from Modena the crisp red DOC wines
Lambrusco Grasparossa di Castelvetro (made from
Lambrusco Grasparossa grapes), **Lambrusco Salamino
di Santa Croce** (made from Lambrusco Salamino grapes)
and **Lambrusco di Sorbara**; the DOC **Lambrusco
Reggiano** is a light red wine from Reggio-Emilia.

LAMONT WINERY winery in Kern in California producing generic and varietal wines under the La Mont and
Mountain Gold Labels.

LAMOTHE, CHÂTEAU deuxième GRAND CRU sweet
white SAUTERNES from BORDEAUX.

LAN label of Bodegas Lan, producers in the RIOJA region of
northern Spain. RESERVA wines are labelled Vina
Lanciano.

LANDGRÄFLICH HESSISCHES WEINGUT
holding of the Union of Rheingau Wine Growers in the
BEREICH of JOHANNISBURG in the RHEINGAU region of
Germany.

LANDMARK VINEYARDS vineyards in the SONOMA
region of California producing varietal wines including
CHENIN BLANC, GEWÜRZTRAMINER, PINOT NOIR and
CHARDONNAY.

LANDWEIN fairly dry category of German table wines
(literally 'country wine'). An everyday quaffing wine,
slightly stronger and of more character than TAFELWEIN.

LANESSAN, CHÂTEAU CRU BOURGEOIS SUPÉRIEUR wine from the HAUT-MÉDOC district of BORDEAUX.

LANGENBACH wine estate within the LIEBFRAUMILCH vineyards in the RHEINHESSEN region of Germany.

LANGENSTÜCK vineyard of ELTVILLE in the RHEINGAU region of Germany producing fairly full-bodied wines.

LANGLOIS-CHÂTEAU sparkling SAUMUR wine from the LOIRE Valley in France.

LANGOA-BARTON, CHÂTEAU troisième GRAND CRU wine from the SAINT-JULIEN commune of BORDEAUX.

LANGON centre of the GRAVES and SAUTERNES districts of BORDEAUX.

LANGUEDOC large area of southern France producing ordinary table wines, the best being CLAIRETTE DU LANGUEDOC and MINERVOIS.

LANIOTE, CHÂTEAU GRAND CRU wine from the SAINT-EMILION district of BORDEAUX.

LANSON CHAMPAGNE firm in Reims in the Champagne region of France producing NV and vintage wines of various styles under the Black Label brand.

LARCIS-DUCASSE, CHÂTEAU full-bodied GRAND CRU wine from the SAINT-EMILION district of BORDEAUX.

LARMANDE, CHÂTEAU GRAND CRU wine from the SAINT-EMILION district of BORDEAUX.

LA RIOJA wine-producing region of western Argentina.

LA RIVA SHERRY producers in the JEREZ region of southern Spain producing a very high quality range of Sherries. Tres Palmas is one of their best FINOS.

LAROQUE, CHÂTEAU GRAND CRU of SAINT-EMILION in BORDEAUX.

LAROSE-TRINTAUDAN, CHÂTEAU CRU GRAND BOURGEOIS wine from the HAUT-MÉDOC district of BORDEAUX.

LAROZE, CHÂTEAU GRAND CRU wine from the SAINT-EMILION district of BORDEAUX.

LARRIVET-HAUT-BRION, CHÂTEAU wine from the GRAVES district of BORDEAUX.

LASCOMBES, CHÂTEAU deuxième GRAND CRU wine from the MARGAUX commune in BORDEAUX.

LA SERRE, CHÂTEAU GRAND CRU of SAINT-EMILION in BORDEAUX.

LASKI RIESLING (RIZLING) Yugoslavian term for the Italian Riesling, with root stock from Italy. Wines made from it have a SWEETNESS RATING of 4.

LATE-BOTTLED category of PORT, describing a wine which comes from a single vintage and is then matured in wood for 4-6 years before bottling.

LATISANA red and white DOC wines produced in the FRIULI-VENEZIA-GIULIA region of northeast Italy.

LATIUM (LAZIO) region surrounding Rome on Italy's west coast. Produces a wide range of wine styles of which the DOC wines FRASCATI and EST! EST!! EST!!! are the most famous, although the VINO DA TÀVOLA Torre Ercolana is a quality wine. MERLOT and MONTEPULCIAÑO grapes are used to produce red wine of reasonable quality.

LATOUR, LOUIS reputable wine shipper in BURGUNDY and owner of part of the CHEVALIER, CORTON and CORTON CHARLEMAGNE vineyards.

LATOUR, CHÂTEAU PREMIER GRAND CRU wine from the PAUILLAC commune in BORDEAUX. One of the best wines of Bordeaux.

LATOUR-À-POMEROL, CHÂTEAU wine from the POMEROL district of BORDEAUX.

LATOUR DE FRANCE red and dry white AC wines of CÔTES DE ROUSSILLON-VILLAGES.

LATRICIÈRES-CHAMBERTIN GRAND CRU vineyard of the GEVREY-CHAMBERTIN commune in the CÔTE DE NUITS area of BURGUNDY. Produces red wines of great FINESSE.

LAUDUN highly regarded vineyard of the CÔTES DU RHÔNE district of southern France producing red, white and rosé wines.

LAUERBURG part owners of the BERNKASTELER DOKTOR vineyard in the MOSEL-SAAR-RUWER region of Germany.

LAUGEL, MICHEL large wine-producers in the ALSACE region of France.

LAURENT-PERRIER CHAMPAGNE firm of Tours-sur-Marne in the Champagne region of France.

LAURÉTAN, CHÂTEAU estate of PREMIÈRES CÔTES DE BORDEAUX in BORDEAUX, producing red and white wines.

LAURETS, CHÂTEAU DES leading estate of PUISSEGUIN-SAINT-EMILION in BORDEAUX.

LAVAUX vineyard area of the VAUD district of Switzerland producing white wine. Dézalay is widely regarded as its best vineyard.

LAVILLE-HAUT-BRION, CHÂTEAU estate in the GRAVES district of BORDEAUX in southwest France producing one of the best dry white wines of the region.

LAWRENCE WINERY large winery in the SAN LUIS OBISPO region of California, specializing in fruity varietals.

LAYON see COTEAUX DU LAYON.

LAZIO Italian name for LATIUM.

LEACOCK shippers of MADEIRA wine.

LEAKER term for a bottle with a faulty cork which allows air into the wine. See OXIDATION.

LEANYKA white-wine grape grown in Czechslovakia, Romania and Hungary.

LEBANON country of the Middle East producing mainly low quality table wines, most of which are grown in the Bekaa valley area. An exception is Château Musar, owned by Serge Hochar, which makes quality wines, the main grape varieties being CABERNET SAUVIGNON and CINSAULT.

LEES the sediment deposited by a wine during ageing, consisting of dead yeast and tartrate crystals.

LEEUWIN ESTATE wine-producers of Western Australia producing good varietal wines including an excellent CHARDONNAY.

LEIWEN village of GROSSLAGE Sankt Michael in the BEREICH of BERNKASTEL in the MOSEL-SAAR-RUWER region of Germany. Its best vineyard is Klostergarten, producing excellent fruity RIESLING wines.

LÉGERÈMENT DOUX Swiss term for wine having a significant residual sugar content.

LEGS term for the streaks of wine which trickle down the side of a glass after it has been swirled. They are caused by the viscosity of the alcohol and glycerine in the wine, so strong legs are usually a sign of high alcohol content, e.g. they are a characteristic of SAUTERNES.

LEISTADT village of GROSSLAGE Kobnert in the BEREICH of MITTELHAARDT in the RHEINPFALZ region of Germany.

LENZ-MOSER major Austrian wine producer and viticulturalist who introduced the Lenz-Moser method of trailing vines. Produces popular and fine wines, including the Blue Danube and Schluck brands.

LÉOGNAN commune of the GRAVES district of BORDEAUX which includes the châteaux Carbonnieux, Malartic-Lagraviere, Olivier, de Fieuzal and Haut-Bailly and Domaine de Chevalier.

LEÓN city in northwest Spain, centre of the winemaking province of Old Castile.

LEONE DE CASTRIS wine producers in the PUGLIA region of Italy. Their DOC wines include LOCORONTONDO, SALICE SALENTINO and Five Roses Rosato.

LÉOVILLE-BARTON, CHÂTEAU deuxième GRAND CRU wine from the SAINT-JULIEN commune of BORDEAUX.

LÉOVILLE-LAS CASES, CHÂTEAU deuxième GRAND CRU wine from the SAINT-JULIEN commune of BORDEAUX.

LÉOVILLE-POYFERRE, CHÂTEAU deuxième GRAND CRU wine from the SAINT-JULIEN commune of BORDEAUX.

LEROY wine-growers near Corton in the CÔTE DE BEAUNE district of BURGUNDY. Run by Mme Lalou Bize-Leroy, an outstanding grower and negociant.

LESSONA fine red NEBBIOLO DOC wine produced in the PIEMONTE region of northern Italy.

L'ÉTOILE *see* ÉTOILE.

LEVANTE wine-producing area of eastern Spain producing mostly sweetish red wines.

LIE French word for sediment or LEES. *See also* SUR LIE.

LIEBFRAUENSTIFT wine of the Liebfrauenkirche vineyards near WORMS in the RHEINHESSEN region of Germany. The name LIEBFRAUMILCH is said to have its origin here.

LIEBFRAUMILCH general name now legally applicable to any RHEINHESSEN QbA wines, although the better wines are labelled Rheinhessen. The name originally applied to the wines which are now termed LIEBFRAUENSTIFT. Liebfraumilch wines are a blend of RIESLING, SILVANER and MÜLLER-THURGAU grape varieties with a SWEETNESS RATING of 5.

LIESER village of GROSSLAGE Beerenlay in the BEREICH of

BERNKASTEL in the MOSEL-SAAR-RUWER region of Germany.

LIGHT tasting term for a wine which is low in ALCOHOL, BODY, flavour and TANNIN. Not a good characteristic of red wines but can be acceptable in whites, providing they have the other attributes of good fruit flavour and are in balance.

LIGURIA wine-producing region of the Italian Riviera producing ordinary wine which is dry and sweetish. CINQUETERRE is its best known wine.

LIKÖRWEIN German term for DESSERT WINE.

LIMASSOL major wine-shipping port in Cyprus.

LIMOUX AC city in southwest France where the still wine VIN DE BLANQUETTE and the sparkling BLANQUETTE DE LIMOUX are produced.

LIMPID tasting term for a wine which is crystal clear, transparent.

LINDEMAN pioneer wine-growing family which has been established in the HUNTER VALLEY, Australia, since 1842.

LINDOS well-known dry white wine from the Greek island of RHODES.

LIQUEUR DE TIRAGE French term for a mixture of sugar and wine added to sparkling wines such as champagne to induce secondary fermentation.

LIQUOREUX French term for rich, sweet wine.

LIQUOROSO Italian term for rich, sweet wine.

LIRAC district of the RHÔNE VALLEY in southeast France producing white, red and rosé wines.

LISTEL brand name of wines from SABLES DU GOLFE DU LION from the Bouches-du-Rhônes area of the Rhône delta in the MIDI region of France.

LISTRAC commune of the HAUT-MÉDOC district of BORDEAUX producing mostly full-bodied red wines. Includes the châteaux Fonreaud, Fourcas-Dupré and Fourcas-Hosten.

LITTLE KAROO (KLEIN KAROO) one of the two main wine-growing areas of South Africa. Produces mostly sweet and Sherry-type wines.

LITRE measure of volume consisting of 100cl (centilitres). Wine bottles currently contain 70 or 75cl (0.70 or 0.75 litres), but from 1988 must contain 75cl. Popular wines are often sold in litre bottles.

LIVELY tasting term for a wine with a natural, not excessive acidity which stimulates the palate.

LIVERMORE VALLEY area of Almeda County in California, producing very high quality full-bodied white wines and some good red wines. Its best wineries are the CONCANNON VINEYARD and WENTE BROTHERS VINERY.

LIVERSAN, CHÂTEAU CRU GRAND BOURGEOIS wine from the HAUT-MÉDOC district of BORDEAUX.

LIVRAN, CHÂTEAU CRU BOURGEOIS wine from the MÉDOC district of BORDEAUX.

LJUTOMER (LUTOMER) wine district of the Slovenia region of Yugoslavia producing well-known white wines from RIESLING grapes.

LLORDS & ELWOOD WINERY winery of the LIVERMORE VALLEY, California, producing mostly fortified wines.

LOCORONTONDO dry white DOC wine from the PUGLIA region of southwest Italy.

LOEL wine-producers in Cyprus producing Negro red and Palomino dry wines, KYKKO table wine, and COMMANDARIA fortified wines.

LOGROÑO city and centre of important wine-growing province of Spain which includes part of the RIOJA-ALTA. Produces excellent table wines.

LOIR tributary of the River LOIRE. *See* COTEAUX DU LOIR.

LOIRE river and major wine-producing area of central northwest France. The region is best known for dry to medium-dry white wines which are perfect for summer drinking. Good rosés and light fruity reds are also produced. SANCERRE, POUILLY FUMÉ, MUSCADET and VOUVRAY are the notable whites. ANJOU produces the best rosés and the better reds come from CHINON and BOURGUEIL.

LOMBARDY (LOMBARDIA) region of northern Italy producing red, white and rosé wines. Includes the district of VALTELLINA. Its best wine is the DOC LUGANA.

LOMELINO producer of MADEIRA wines, the oldest Portuguese firm to be so.

LONG FLAT brand name of red and white wines made by TYRRELL in HUNTER VALLEY, New South Wales.

LONG VINEYARDS vineyards in the NAPA VALLEY region of California producing varietal wines.

LÓPEZ DE HEREDIA, BODEGAS wine-producers in the RIOJA region of northern Spain producing oak-aged red and white wines.

LORCH village of GROSSLAGE Rüdesheim in the BEREICH of JOHANNISBERG in the RHEINGAU region of Germany.

LORON & FILS wine merchants in the BEAUJOLAIS district of BURGUNDY.

LORRAINE province of northeast France producing red, white and rosé wines, the reds being generally light and acidic. The two AC areas are CÔTES DE TOUL and Vin de la Moselle, the former producing light rose-type wines (VINS GRIS) and the latter both vins gris (including Clairet de Moselle) and some white wines.

LOS HERMANOS vineyard and winery owned by Nestle in the NAPA VALLEY, California.

LOUDENNE, CHÂTEAU CRU GRAND BOURGEOIS wine from the MÉDOC district of BORDEAUX.

LOUPIAC commune of BORDEAUX in southwest France producing sweet white wines.

LOUVIÈRE, CHÂTEAU LA wine from the GRAVES district of BORDEAUX.

LOUVOIS one of the best CRUS of the Canton d'Ay in the CHAMPAGNE region of France. Classified 100 percent in the CIVC rating.

LÖWENSTEIN, FURST old estate in FRANKEN making quality white wines.

LOWER LAKE WINERY winery in the LAKE COUNTY region of California, producing CABERNET SAUVIGNON and SAUVIGNON BLANC wines.

LUDES vineyard of Canton de Verzy in the CHAMPAGNE region of France. Classified 94 percent in the CIVC rating.

LUDON commune in the HAUT-MÉDOC area of BORDEAUX. Château La LAGUNE is the top château.

LUDWIGSHÖHE village of GROSSLAGE Krotenbrünnen in the BEREICH of Nierstein in the RHEINHESSEN region of Germany. Much of its output is blended and used in the production of LIEBFRAUMILCH.

LUGANA the leading white DOC wine produced in the LOMBARDY region of northern Italy.

LUGNY *see* MÂCON-LUGNY.

LUNGAROTTI wine producers in the UMBRIA region of Italy. Their DOCs include RUBESCO DI TORGIAÑO. Known also for their white Torre di Giano.

LUPE-CHOLET wine growers of NUITS-SAINT-GEORGES in BURGUNDY, producing PREMIER CRU Château Gris.

LUSSAC, CHÂTEAU DE estate of LUSSAC-SAINT-EMILION in BORDEAUX.

LUSSAC-SAINT-EMILION commune to the north of SAINT-EMILION in BORDEAUX, producing good red wines.

LUSTAU producers in the JEREZ region of southern Spain, producing a range of high quality Sherries.

LUTOMER *see* LJUTOMER.

LUXEMBOURG country producing light, fruity wines, mostly for local consumption. The best wines are white and made from Auxerrois, Elbling, Gewürztraminer, Pinot Gris, Riesling and Rivaner (Müller-Thurgau) grapes. They carry classifications of quality in ascending order: Marque National, Vin Classé, Premier Cru, and Grand Premier Cru. Labels also give information on grape variety, locality and vintage.

LYNCH-BAGES, CHÂTEAU cinquième GRAND CRU wine from the PAUILLAC commune of BORDEAUX.

LYNCH-MOUSSAS, CHÂTEAU cinquième GRAND CRU wine from the PAUILLAC commune of BORDEAUX.

LYTTON SPRINGS WINERY winery in the SONOMA region of California, well-known for their ZINFANDEL.

M

MA abbreviation for *Manipulant Acheteur*, which, on a CHAMPAGNE label, shows that the wine is the shop's own brand.

MACABEO white-wine grape variety used in Algeria, Morocco, Spain and southern France. It is often blended with other varieties to produce sweet fortified wines, but its dry wines have good balance of fruit and acidity.

MACAU commune in the HAUT-MÉDOC district of

BORDEAUX. Château Cantemerle is regarded as its best wine. Many châteaux with the status of CRU BOURGEOIS SUPÉRIEUR are located here.

MCDOWELL VALLEY VINEYARDS vineyard in Mendocino County of California.

MACERATION process of softening grapes for fermentation by steeping in liquid. *See also* CARBONIC MACERATION.

MACHARNUDO Sherry-producing area of JEREZ in Spain, northwest of Jerez de la Frontera.

MACHARD DE GRAMONT wine-growers of NUITS-SAINT-GEORGES in BURGUNDY, with holdings in several PREMIERS CRUS vineyards.

MÂCHÉ French term for a tired wine, affected by RACKING or travel. Literally 'mashed'.

MÂCON important wine city and AC area of BURGUNDY, producing red and white wines. Mâcon wines are usually good value and the quality is steadily improving. *See also* MÂCONNAIS.

MÂCON-BLANC-VILLAGES AC white wines from BURGUNDY, including those from the villages of Lugny, Clesse, Vinzelles and Prisse. These wines are beginning to represent value for money as the GRANDS CRUS continue their upward spiral. *See also* MÂCONNAIS.

MÂCON-CLESSE *see* MÂCON-BLANC-VILLAGES.

MÂCON-LUGNY village and AC area of the MÂCON district of BURGUNDY. Wines are of good quality. *See also* MÂCON-BLANC-VILLAGES.

MÂCONNAIS district of southern BURGUNDY, producing mostly white wines from CHARDONNAY grapes. The reds produced in the district are made from GAMAY. Most of the wines are sold as MÂCON, MÂCON SUPERIEUR, or under one of the four AC areas of the district: POUILLY-FUISSÉ (the best), POUILLY-LOCHE, POUILLY-VINZELLES and SAINT-VÉRAN. The lesser wines are labelled Mâcon-Rouge or Mâcon Blanc.

MÂCON-PRISSE *see* MÂCON-BLANC-VILLAGES.

MÂCON SUPÉRIEUR appellation for red and white wines produced around MÂCON in BURGUNDY. Similar to Mâcon but with more alcohol and body. *See also* MÂCONNAIS.

MÂCON VIRÉ village and location of a growers' cooperative in the MÂCON district of BURGUNDY. Wines are of good quality.

MACULAN sweet white and rosé wines from the Vicenza area of the VENETO region of Italy.

MCWILLIAMS estate and wine producer in the HUNTER VALLEY region of New South Wales, Australia. Producers of excellent un-oaked SEMILLON wines.

MADEIRA island off the coast of Morocco in the Atlantic Ocean which gives its name to wines produced within. Madeira is a wonderful, sweet dessert wine which is fortified by the addition of brandy and then aged in a SOLERA system, as for SHERRY. The wines are kept at high temperatures for long periods to gain the character once imparted by long sea journeys. This process also makes them very stable, so the wine once in the bottle will keep for many years. Four types of grape are used to make four styles of wine: Sercial, the driest; Verdelho (SWEETNESS RATING 5); Bual (SWEETNESS RATING 7); and Malmsey (SWEETNESS RATING 9).

MADIRIZATION character change in a wine resulting from oxidation of the alcohol to acetaldehyde which produces a slightly almond flavour. Caused by overlong storage in barrel, the process is accelerated by high temperatures. It may also occur in the bottle. Madirized wine loses its freshness and tastes musty but in MADEIRA it is a positive attribute and the taste is termed RANCIO.

MADIRAN full-bodied tannic red wine made from the Tannat grape in the Haut-Pyrénées district of southern France.

MADURO Portuguese term for mature wine.

MAFOUX, PROSPER important merchants in SANTENAY in BURGUNDY.

MAGDELAINE, CHÂTEAU PREMIER GRAND CRU wine from the SAINT-ÉMILION district of BORDEAUX. Wines of finesse and power.

MAGENCE, CHÂTEAU dry white wine from the GRAVES district of BORDEAUX.

MAGNUM double-sized bottle of 1.5 litres used for ageing certain wines, particularly some vintage Bordeaux and Burgundy, and for the secondary fermentation of Champagne. Champagne is often at its best from a magnum as the wine ages more slowly in larger bottles.

MAGRICO brand name of a good dry VINHO VERDE wine produced by Goncalves Monteiro of Valadares in Portugal.

MAIKAMMER well-regarded village of GROSSLAGE Mandelhohe in the BEREICH of SÜDLICHE WEINSTRASSE in the RHEINPFALZ region of Germany.

MAILBERG (1) village of the Danube region of Austria; (2) name of a wine from the WEINVIERTEL district.

MAILLY vineyard of the Canton de Verzy in the CHAMPAGNE region of France. Classified 100 percent in the CIVC rating for black grapes.

MAINDREIECK BEREICH of the central Franken region of Germany.

MAINVIERECK BEREICH of the western Franken region of Germany.

MAIPO VALLEY old and important wine-producing region of CHILE, making a number of well-regarded wines.

MAIRE, HENRI large, well-known producers in the JURA region of France producing a wide variety of wines.

MAISON French word for 'house', also used to mean 'a company'.

MAJORCA Balearic island in the Mediterranean producing heavy red wines around the area of Binisalem and less heavy wines around Felanitx.

MÁLAGA demarcated area of east ANDALUSIA in Spain renowned for DESSERT WINES. Málaga wine is unfortified and ranges from the very sweet *blanco dulce*, Lagrima and Lagrima Christi to fairly dry (*blanco seco*). Other grades are fairly sweet (*semi dulce*), amber coloured (Moscatel), luscious-sweet (Xeminez), strong (Roune and Tintillo de Málaga) and very strong (Pajarete).

MALARTIC-LAGRAVIÈRE, CHÂTEAU GRAND CRU wine from the GRAVES district of BORDEAUX, producing white wines.

MALBEC quality red-wine grape best known for its use in the clarets of BORDEAUX. Selected for its good colour and flavour, the softer Malbec is a perfect match for the more aggressive and robust CABERNET SAUVIGNON. It is also planted in Cahors, where it exhibits a deep red colour and a good depth of flavour, and grown in Argentina, Brazil, Italy, Madeira, Portugal, Spain, Switzerland, the US and Yugoslavia. Also known as Auxerrois, Cahors, Cot, Pied-Rouge.

MALESCOT SAINT-EXUPÉRY, CHÂTEAU troisième GRAND CRU wine from the MARGAUX commune of BORDEAUX.

MALIC ACID natural grape constituent which is converted to lactic acid by bacteria during MALOLACTIC

FERMENTATION. This is a secondary fermentation which occurs in most wines.

MALLE, CHÂTEAU DE deuxième GRAND CRU sweet white SAUTERNES from BORDEAUX.

MALMESBURY wine-producing area of the coastal belt region of South Africa.

MALMSEY English name for the MALVASIA vine and for wines produced from it, in particular the rich, dark, very sweet, full-bodied MADEIRA.

MALOLACTIC FERMENTATION secondary fermentation of wine in a barrel or bottle, caused by lactobacillus bacteria, which converts MALIC ACID to lactic acid. This reduction of the malic acid content softens a wine and makes it more drinkable. It also gives a wine its individual characteristics. Sometimes in the bottle it can result in a gaseous wine which is dull and unpleasant. This type of secondary fermentation is not the same as that used in the production of CHAMPAGNE METHOD, which is due to a sugar-yeast reaction.

MALTA Mediterranean island producing low quality red and white wines and some DESSERT WINES.

MALTROYE, CHÂTEAU DE LA estate of CHASSAGNE-MONTRACHET in the CÔTE D'OR district of BURGUNDY. Its white wines are often of outstanding quality.

MALVASIA Italian name of a white grape used in the production of sweet, heavy wines and fortified wines; particularly MALMSEY. It is also known as MONEMVASIA in Greece, MALVOISIE in France, Malvagia in Spain, and Malvazya in Yugoslavia, and is used in Argentina, Brazil, France, Italy, Madeira, Portugal, Sardinia, Spain, Switzerland, the US and Yugoslavia. In Italy it makes several DOC wines including, in the south, the amber-coloured dry, medium and semi-sweet wines **Malvasia di Bosa** and

Malvasia di Cagliari (with a bitter aftertaste) from Sardinia and **Malvasia delle Lipari**, a sweet, deep amber or dark straw-golden coloured wine made from dried grapes in the province of Messina in Sicily. From PIEMONTE come the red and rosato, sweet and semi-sweet sparkling light wines **Malvasia di Casorzo d'Asti** and the sweet red sparkling **Malvasia di Castelnuovo Don Bosco**

MALVOISIE *see* MALVASIA.

MAMERTINO strong, semi-sweet amber-coloured white table wine produced in Sicily.

MANCHA, LA *see* LA MANCHA.

MANCHUELA DO wines produced in the LA MANCHA-New Castille region of central Spain, normally drunk locally.

MANDEMENT district near Geneva in Switzerland producing dry, light wines from GAMAY and PERLAN grapes, mostly drunk locally.

MANDROLISAI red and rosé DOC wines produced on the island of Sardinia in Italy.

MANDURIA strong red DOC wines, often fortified, from the PUGLIA region of southern Italy.

MANIPULANT ACHETEUR *see* MA.

MANNBERG vineyard of STEINBERG in the RHEINGAU region of Germany.

MANTINIA a crisp white wine produced in the PELOPONNESE area of Greece.

MANTONICO grape grown in the CALABRIA region of Italy. Its best known wine is **Mantonico di Bianco**.

MANZANILLA light dry Sherry Fino-type wine with a slightly salty flavour and a SWEETNESS RATING of 1. Produced at SANLÚCAR DE BARRAMEDA in the JEREZ region of Spain, the wine may be fortified or unfortified and is sold as Manzanilla Pasada, Manzanilla Olorosa, Manzanilla Fina, Manzanilla and Amanzanillado.

MARASTINA white-wine grape used in the DALMATIA region of Yugoslavia.

MARATHEFTIKA red-wine grape used in Cyprus.

MARBUZET second wine from Château COS D'ESTOURNEL.

MARC residue of grape skins and seeds after the juice has been extracted.

MARCHANT, HENRI brand name of a sparkling wine produced by the Gold Seal vineyards in New York State.

MARCHE, LE area of east-central Italy producing red and white wines, mostly consumed locally, although the quality is improving. Its principal red wine is ROSSO PICENO. DOC wines include VERDICCHIO DEI CASTELLI DI JESI, VERDICCHIO DI MATELICA, ROSSO CONERO, BIANCHELLO DEL METAURO and VERNACCIA di Serrapetrona.

MARCHESE DI BAROLO long-established wine-producing firm of the PIEMONTE region of Italy, making ASTI SPUMANTE, BARBARESCO, BAROLO, CORTESE DI GAVI, and DOLCETTO D'ALBA among others.

MARCOBRUNN vineyard of ERBACH in the RHEINGAU region of Germany.

MARGAUX, CHÂTEAU world-famous premier GRAND CRU wine from the MARGAUX commune in BORDEAUX.

MARGARET RIVER wine-producing area of Western Australia, south of Perth. Produces quality CABERNET SAUVIGNON wines.

MARLBOROUGH town and wine-producing area at the north end of South Island, New Zealand. Its cool climate produces quality white wines at very reasonable prices, including CHARDONNAY and SAUVIGNON BLANC.

MARQUE French term for a brand or trade mark. *Grand marque* is used for some long-established brands of CHAMPAGNE of consistent quality.

MARQUE NATIONALE lowest classification of LUXEMBOURG wines.

MARQUIS D'ALESME BECKER, CHÂTEAU troisième GRAND CRU wine from the MARGAUX commune in BORDEAUX.

MARQUIS-DE-TERME, CHÂTEAU quatrième GRAND CRU wine from the MARGAUX commune in BORDEAUX.

MARTINA FRANCA light-coloured delicate DOC wine from the PUGLIA region of southwest Italy.

MARSALA dark sweet FORTIFIED WINE made in Marsala in Sicily, with a SWEETNESS RATING of 9. Also known as Samperi.

MARTINI, LOUIS M. well-known NAPA VALLEY winegrower at the turn of the century and founder of the family winery of the same name in California.

MARTINI & PRATI WINES large winery in the SONOMA area of California, producing generic wines.

MARTINI & ROSSI wine producers in the PIEMONTE region of northern Italy. Their DOC is ASTI SPUMANTE and other sparkling wines are also produced. Best known for their Martini vermouth.

MARTINSTHAL village of GROSSLAGE Steinmacher in the BEREICH of JOHANNISBERG in the RHEINGAU region of Germany.

MARZEMINO red-wine grape variety of TRENTINO-ALTO ADIGE and LOMBARDY in northern Italy. From the former comes **Marzemino del Trentino**, a dry, slightly bitter red DOC wine.

MAS term in southern France for a wine-producing farm.

MASCARA important wine-growing district of the Oran region of Algeria producing red, white and rosé wines.

MASCARÓ CAVES wine producers in CATALONIA, Spain, producing still and sparkling wines, and brandy.

MASI, CANTINA wine producers of the VENETO region of northern Italy. Their DOC wines include VALPOLICELLA, SOAVE and Campo Fiorin.

MASIA BACH sweet white and full-bodied red wines from CATALONIA in Spain. Now owned by Cordoniu.

MASSON, PAUL large well-known wine growers of the SANTA CLARA, SANTA CRUZ and MONTEREY districts of California, producing varietal, fortified and champagne-type wines.

MASTROBERADINO wine producers in the CAMPANIA region of Italy. Their DOC wines include FIANO DI AVELLINO, GRECO DI TUFO and Taurasi.

MATANZAS CREEK WINERY vineyards in the SONOMA region of California producing varietal wines including PINOT BLANC, CHARDONNAY, GEWÜRZTRAMINER, CABERNET SAUVIGNON and MERLOT.

MATARO red-wine grape grown in France, Australia and California. Also known as MOURVÈDRE.

MATEUS ROSÉ famous sweet rosé wine of Portugal, made by Sogrape.

MATINO red and rosé DOC wines from Lecce in the PUGLIA region of southeast Italy. The main grape variety used is Negroamaro.

MATRAALYA large wine-growing region of Hungary producing red and white wines. The best known is DEBRO Harselevu.

MATRAS, CHÂTEAU GRAND CRU wine from the SAINT-EMILION district of BORDEAUX.

MATUSCHKA-GREIFFENCLAU, GRAF owner of the SCHLOSS VOLLRADS estate in the RHEINGAU region of Germany.

MAUCAILLOU, CHÂTEAU CRU BOURGEOIS wine from the MOULIS district of BORDEAUX.

MAURY area of GRAND ROUSSILLON, France, producing sweet fortified wines. They have a slightly RANCIO character and some are labelled **Maury Rancio**.

MAUVEZIN, CHÂTEAU (1) GRAND CRU wine from the SAINT-EMILION district of BORDEAUX; (2) wine from the MOULIS district of BORDEAUX.

MAVRO Greek word for 'black'. **Mavro Naoussis** is a dry red wine from Macedonia in Greece.

MAVRODAPHNE OF PATRAS grape variety used in Greece and on the island of Cephalonia for the production of a well-known strong red dessert wine, sold under the Mavrodaphne name.

MAVRON red-wine grape used extensively in Cyprus.

MAVROUDI red-wine grape used in the ATTICA district of Greece.

MAVRUD (MAVROUD) red-wine grape used in southern Bulgaria to produce a wine of the same name.

MAXIMIN GRÜNHAUS outstanding estate of mainly RIESLING vines at MERTESDORF in GROSSLAGE Römerlay of the MOSEL-SAAR-RUWER region of Germany.

MAYACAMAS VINEYARDS winery of the NAPA VALLEY region of California, producing vintage varietal wines including CABERNET SAUVIGNON, CHARDONNAY, CHENIN BLANC and ZINFANDEL Rosé.

MAZIS-CHAMBERTIN   (MAZY-CHAMBERTIN) GRAND CRU vineyard of the GEVREY-CHAMBERTIN commune in the CÔTE DE NUITS area of BURGUNDY.

MAZOYÈRES-CHAMBERTIN GRAND CRU vineyard of the GEVREY-CHAMBERTIN commune in the CÔTE DE NUITS area of BURGUNDY. May also be sold as CHARMES, like the wines of the adjoining CHARMES-CHAMBERTIN vineyard.

MAZUELO red-wine grape variety used in the RIOJA region of northern Spain.

MECSEKALJA white-wine producing area of the Transdanubia region of Hungary. One of the 14 classified wine districts, producing good quality wines for export.

MEDEA red and white wines from the department of Alger in Algeria.

MÉDOC renowned wine region of BORDEAUX. A narrow strip of land on the left bank of the River Gironde, it is dotted with châteaux producing wines of topmost quality, with a TASTE RATING of D. It is subdivided into two main subregions: the Bas-Médoc and the Haut-Médoc, the latter having within its borders four of the five GRAND CRU châteaux. Médoc has six communes: Saint-Estèphe, Saint-Julien, Listrac, Margaux, Moulis and Pauillac. Grapes used are CABERNET SAUVIGNON, CABERNET FRANC, PETIT VERDOT and MERLOT, with CABERNET SAUVIGNON the principal variety.

MÉDOC NOIR alternative name for the MERLOT grape and used for some Hungarian red wines.

MEFFRE, GABRIEL DOMAINE based at Gigondas in the southern Rhône, France, which includes Château de Vaudieu and vineyards in Gigondas and Violes.

MEHANA brand name of Bulgarian table wines of reasonable quality and price.

MEHRING village of GROSSLAGE Sankt Michael in the BEREICH of BERNKASTEL in the MOSEL-SAAR-RUWER region of Germany, producing very floral RIESLING wines.

MEIRELES a sparkling VINHO VERDE wine from north-west Portugal.

MELETO good CHIANTI Classico wine from TUSCANY in central Italy, sold by Storiche Cantine.

MELINI wine-producers of TUSCANY in central Italy. Their DOC wines include CHIANTI, Chianti Classico, VERNACCIA di San Gimignano, VINO NOBILE DI MONTEPULCIANO and ORVIETO.

MELINOTS PREMIER CRU vineyard of the CHABLIS commune in BURGUNDY.

MELISSA light, dry, red and white DOC wines produced in CALABRIA, southern Italy. The reds are made from GAGLIOPPO grapes and the whites from Greco Bianco.

MELLOW tasting term for a wine which is soft, ripe, well matured.

MELON D'ARBOIS term for the CHARDONNAY grape used in ARBOIS in the JURA region of France.

MENDOCINO wine-producing district to the north of San Francisco in California. Its leading wineries include CRESTA BLANCA, FETZER and PARDUCCI.

MENDOZA largest wine-producing province of Argentina, bordering Chile. It produces over 75 percent of the country's output.

MÉNÉTOU-SALON red and white AC wines from the upper LOIRE in France. PINOT NOIR and SAUVIGNON BLANC are the grape varieties used.

MENISCUS the slightly curved surface of a liquid. When wine or MUST is being appraised, the reading is taken from the concave centre of the liquid.

MENNIG village of GROSSLAGE Scharzberg in the BEREICH of SAAR-RUWER in the MOSEL-SAAR-RUWER region of Germany.

MÉNTRIDA red DO wines from the LA MANCHA region of central Spain, made from mostly Garnacha Tinta grapes.

MERANESE DI COLLINA lesser light, red DOC wine from Merano in the Alto Adige area of TRENTINO-ALTO ADIGE in Italy.

MERCAPTAN tasting term for the unpleasant onion-like aroma of a wine caused by HYDROGEN SULPHIDE.

MERCIER CHAMPAGNE firm based at ÉPERNAY in the Champagne region of France. Owned by Moet Hennessey.

MERCUREY commune producing some of the best wines of the CHALONNAIS district of southern BURGUNDY. The wines are mostly reds from the PINOT NOIR grape. Some very good whites are also produced from CHARDONNAY grapes.

MERLOT red-wine grape grown in France, Argentina, Brazil, Chile, Hungary, Australia, Italy, Japan, Switzerland, the US and Yugoslavia. In France it is used particularly in the MÉDOC district of BORDEAUX. It is a very important ingredient in the composition of claret because of its softness and scented flavour. It is also the major variety in POMEROL and SAINT-EMILION, where it produces wine of the highest calibre. It has a pleasing colour and a unique varietal character on both the nose and palate. When blended, it does a first-rate job of filling, softening and balancing the final wine.

In Italy it is used in several regions to produce DOC wines, including from LATIUM **Merlot di Aprilia**, a smooth, lightish, dry red wine style; from VENETO **Merlot Colli Berici**, a flavoursome dry red wine, and **Merlot del Piave** and **Merlot di Pramaggiore**, full-bodied, dry red table wines; from FRIULI-VENEZIA-GIULIA the soft, smooth **Merlot Colli Orientali del Friuli**, the light, soft dry **Merlot Collio Goriziano**, and the light dry **Merlot Grave del**

Friuli and **Merlot Isonzo**. TRENTINO-ALTO ADIGE produces **Merlot del Trentino**, a dry red wine from the Alto Adige area.

MERTESDORF village of GROSSLAGE Römerlay in the BEREICH of SAAR-RUWER in the MOSEL-SAAR-RUWER region of Germany. Its outstanding estate is MAXIMIN GRUNHAUS.

MESNIL-SUR-OGER, LE CHAMPAGNE vineyard of the Canton d'Avize in the Champagne region of northeast France. Classified 99 percent in the CIVC rating. Champagne house Salon Le Mesnil produces excellent Blanc de Blancs Champagne.

METALLIC tasting term for a wine with the flavour of metal, usually caused by contact of grapes or wine with iron or copper during vinification.

MÉTAIREAU, LOUIS wine producer and small cooperative name in the MUSCADET district of the Loire in France, selling the best wines produced by nine contributing and associated growers in the area.

MÉTHODE CHAMPENOISE *see* CHAMPAGNE METHOD.

METHUSALAH large bottle used for champagne, with a capacity of eight ordinary bottles.

METTENHEIM village of GROSSLAGE Rheinblick in the BEREICH of NIERSTEIN in the RHEINHESSEN region of Germany producing reasonable quality red and white wines.

MEUNIER vines grown in the district of LORRAINE in northeast France, including PINOT MEUNIER, **Meunier Blanc** and **Meunier Gris**. They are used in the production of VIN GRIS.

MEURSAULT major white-wine district of the CÔTE DE BEAUNE in BURGUNDY. Its best wines include Les Perrières, Les Perrières-Dessus, Les Charmes-Dessus, Les

Genevriers-Dessus and La Gouttes d'Or. Meursault produces excellent full-flavoured CHARDONNAY whites with a distinct nutty aroma and flavour.

MEURSAULT, CHÂTEAU DE PREMIER CRU estate of POMMARD in BURGUNDY.

MEXICO country of central America with an old tradition of grape growing. Although large areas are under vines, the varieties planted are generally better suited to distillation than table wine production. The very dry, hot climate also does not lend itself to the production of quality wines.

MEYNEY, CHÂTEAU CRU GRAND BOURGEOIS EXCEPTIONNEL wine from the SAINT-ESTÈPHE commune in BORDEAUX.

MIDI large area of southern France producing a vast quantity of wines. It incorporates the regions of Corbières, Minervois, Côtes du Roussillon, Languedoc, Gard, Hérault and Aude. The standard of wines being produced in this part of France has been steadily rising.

MILANO WINERY winery in the MENDOCINO region of California producing varietal wines, including SAUVIGNON BLANC, GAMAY, ZINFANDEL and PETITE SYRAH.

MILL CREEK VINEYARDS vineyards in the SONOMA region of California producing varietal wines, including CHARDONNAY and CABERNET SAUVIGNON.

MILLÉSIMÉ French term for year of vintage, so a vintage wine is *Vin millésimé*.

MINERVOIS AC district of the Midi region in southern France producing red, white and rosé wines. Minervois reds are made from CARIGNAN, CINSAULT and GRENACHE grapes and are among the best-value reds available in the UK. They have a good body and fruit flavour and the TASTE RATING is C.

MINOS wine producers on the Greek island of Crete producing red (Castello and Castello Reserva), dry white (Minos Cava) and rosé (Minos) wines. It also makes red and white wines under the Candia label.

MIRAFLORES vineyard area of the JEREZ region of Spain where the finest dry MANZANILLA is produced.

MIRASSOU VINEYARDS family vineyard of the central coast MONTEREY area of California, producing VARIETAL wines.

MIS(E) EN BOUTEILLES French term for château or ESTATE-BOTTLED wines, the usual forms being *mis en bouteilles au château, mis en bouteilles au domaine* and *mis en bouteilles à la propriété.*

MISKET white-wine grape of the MUSCAT family, used in northern and central Bulgaria.

MISSION red-wine grape used in California: a VITIS VINIFERA variety exported from Europe in the 19th century.

MISSION-HAUT-BRION, CHÂTEAU LA GRAND CRU wine from the GRAVES district of BORDEAUX.

MITCHELTON wine producers in Victoria, Australia, producing good varietal wines, including good RIESLING and CABERNET SAUVIGNON wines.

MITTELHAARDT middle part of the RHEINPFALZ region of Germany, the full name of the BEREICH being Mittelhaardt-Deutsche Weinstrasse. Its best vineyards include those of KIRCHENSTÜCK and JESUITENGARTEN.

MITTELHEIM village of GROSSLAGE Erntebringer and Honigberg in the BEREICH of JOHANNISBERG in the RHEINGAU region of Germany, producing good RIESLINGS.

MITTELMOSEL part of the MOSEL-SAAR-RUWER region of Germany covering area of the BEREICH of BERNKASTEL.

MITTELRHEIN small region of the Rhine in Germany producing white wines mainly for local consumption. RIESLING is the predominant grape variety planted. Incorporates BACHARACH and RHEINBURGENGAU.

MOELLEUX French term for sweet fruity white wines.

MOËT ET CHANDON largest CHAMPAGNE firm based at ÉPERNAY in the Champagne region of northeast France. It is a large public company which owns the other houses of Mercier and Dom Ruinart, and it has joined forces with Hennessey Cognac to form Moët-Hennessey.

MOILLARD DOMAINE growers of NUITS SAINT-GEORGES in BURGUNDY, whose holdings include several PREMIERS CRUS vineyards in the CÔTE DE NUITS and the CÔTE DE BEAUNE.

MOMMESSIN growers of La Grange Saint-Pierre in the MÂCON area of BURGUNDY and owners of the GRAND CRU Clos de Tart. Producers of light fine wines and also VINS DE MARQUE and BEAUJOLAIS.

MONBAZILLAC sweet white dessert wine of BERGERAC in southwest France, the best wine of the region. It has a SWEETNESS RATING of 7.

MONBOUSQUET, CHÂTEAU GRAND CRU wine of SAINT-EMILION in BORDEAUX.

MONDAVI WINERY winery in the NAPA VALLEY region of California producing excellent red and white vintage and table wines including top quality CHARDONNAY and CABERNET SAUVIGNON varietals. Innovative winemakers at the forefront of wine technology.

MONDEUSE red-wine grape variety grown in southeast France, California, and Australia. It yields good colour and high tannin levels, but its plantings are slowly decreasing.

MONEMVASIA *see* MALVASIA.

MONFERRATO area of PIEMONTE in northwest Italy, producing large quantities of the region's red and white wines.

MONICA grape variety used in Sardinia for the production of dessert wines, including the red DOC wines **Monica di Cagliari**, a dry-medium or dry wine, and **Monica di Sardegna**, a medium-bodied dry wine.

MONIMPEX Hungarian State Export Agency based in Budapest. Authentic wines bottled and exported by Monimpex are labelled Magyar Allami Export Pincegazdasag.

MONOPOLE French term meaning exclusive (literally 'monopoly') found along with the shipper's brand name on a wine label. Wines so labelled are non-vintage blends but are usually consistent in quality. Also a term used in BURGUNDY to indicate the whole ownership of a vineyard by one owner.

MONOPOLE good oak-aged white wine produced by CVNE in the RIOJA ALTA region of northern Spain.

MONTAGNE-SAINT EMILION small AC commune of SAINT-EMILION in BORDEAUX and one of Saint-Emilion's four AC areas.

MONTAGNY AC village and commune of the CÔTE CHALONNAISE region of BURGUNDY, producing white wines from the CHARDONNAY grape.

MONTALCINO area of TUSCANY in central Italy. Produces the DOC red wine BRUNELLO DI MONTALCINO.

MONTANA WINES large wine-producers in Auckland, New Zealand, owned by the international company Seagram. They produce excellent varietal wines including SAUVIGNON BLANC and CHARDONNAY. Their best-known label is Marlborough.

MONTÁNCHEZ village in the EXTREMADURA district of central Spain producing a strong red wine with a FLOR.

MONTBRÉ CHAMPAGNE vineyard of the Canton de Verzy in the Champagne region of northeast France. Classified 94 percent in the CIVC rating for white grapes.

MONT DE MILIEU PREMIER CRU vineyard of the Fye and Fleys communes in the CHABLIS region of central France.

MONTECARLO red and dry white DOC wines from TUSCANY in central Italy. The white **Montecarlo Bianco** is better known than the red.

MONTECILLO wine producers in the RIOJA ALTA region of northern Spain, now owned by OSBORNE, producing dry red and white wines. Viña Monry is a good RESERVA.

MONTECOMPATRI COLONNA dry white wine from the LATIUM region of Italy.

MONTE CRISTO large firm and brand name of wines from the MONTILLA-MORILES district of southern Spain.

MONTÉE DE TONNERRE PREMIER CRU vineyard of the Fye commune in the CHABLIS region of central France.

MONTEFALCO sweet and dry red DOC wines from the UMBRIA region of central Italy.

MONTEFIASCONE town in the LATIUM region of Italy, producing the uniquely named EST! EST!! EST!!!.

MONTELENA, CHÂTEAU winery in the NAPA VALLEY region of California, producing quality varietal wines.

MONTEPALDI wine producers of Florence in the TUSCANY region of northwest Italy, producing the DOCG CHIANTI CLASSICO.

MONTEPULCIANO (1) quality red-wine grape grown in central Italy; (2) DOCG red wine from TUSCANY known as VINO NOBILE DI MONTEPULCIANO.

MONTEREY city and wine-growing district of California, producing varietal wines. The principal vineyards include CHALONE and MONTEREY VINEYARD.

MONTEREY PENINSULAR WINERY small winery in the MONTEREY region of California producing mostly red and some white varietal wines, including CHARDONNAY, CABERNET SAUVIGNON, and ZINFANDEL.

MONTEREY VINEYARD vineyard and winery in northern MONTEREY producing RIESLING, ZINFANDEL, GEWÜRZTRAMINER and SAUVIGNON BLANC varietal wines. It is owned by Coca-Cola.

MONTERREY cooperative wine producers in Orense in the Monterrey district of northern Spain producing red and white wines. The best are sold under the Castelo Monterrey label.

MONTEVINA WINES small vineyard and winery at Plymouth in Amador County, California, producing wines from BARBERA, SAUVIGNON BLANC, CHARDONNAY, and ZINFANDEL grapes.

MONTHELIE commune of the CÔTE DE BEAUNE district of BURGUNDY, producing red, white and sparkling wines. The wines are sold either as Monthelie or Monthelie-Côte de Beaune-Villages, the better ones usually featuring the name of the PREMIER CRU vineyard of origin.

MONTILLA-MORILES district of southern Spain producing apéritif and table wines, similar to SHERRY. Montilla dry wines have a SWEETNESS RATING of 2, medium-dry 3 and 4, and Montilla Cream 7.

MONTLOUIS white AC wines from the TOURAINE district of the LOIRE valley. Both still and sparkling whites are produced and the quality varies from good to average.

MONTMAINS PREMIER CRU vineyard of the CHABLIS region of central France.

MONTRACHET, LES GRAND CRU vineyard in the PULIGNY-MONTRACHET commune of the CÔTE DE BEAUNE area of BURGUNDY, producing distinguished dry white wines. The vineyard is shared by the communes of Puligny-Montrachet and CHASSAGNE-MONTRACHET.

MONTRAVEL dry and semi-sweet wines from BERGERAC in southwest France.

MONTROSE, CHÂTEAU deuxième GRAND CRU wine from the SAINT-ESTÈPHE commune in BORDEAUX.

MONTS DU TESSALAH red, white and rosé wines from the department of Oran in Algeria.

MOORILLA ESTATE wine producers in Tasmania producing varietal wines including PINOT NOIR and CABERNET SAUVIGNON.

MOR district of the Transdanubia region of northern Hungary producing mostly white wines including MORI EZERJO.

MORBISH wine village in BURGENLAND, Austria, producing sweet and dry, red and white wines.

MOREAU ET FILS, J. growers and negociants in the CHABLIS district of BURGUNDY. producing PREMIERS CRUS and GRANDS CRUS Chablis wines and white wines from outside the region.

MOREY-SAINT-DENIS village and commune of the CÔTE DE NUITS district of BURGUNDY producing red and some white wines. Its best wines are from the GRANDS CRUS vineyards of BONNES MARES, CLOS DE LA ROCHE, CLOS SAINT-DENIS and CLOS DE TART.

MORGON one of the nine BEAUJOLAIS CRUS of southern BURGUNDY. It produces a full-bodied style of wine with good keeping potential.

MORI EZERJO dry white wine made from the EZERJO grape in the MOR district of Hungary.

MORILES part of MONTILLA-MORILES in southern Spain.

MORIO-MUSKAT German white wine hybrid grape, developed from the SYLVANER and PINOT BLANC.

MOROCCO wine-producing country producing mostly reds and rosés. Morocco's industry was founded by the French. In general the wines are coarse and high in alcohol.

MORRIS producer of fine liqueur muscats and table wines in Rutherglen, Victoria, Australia.

MOSAIC brand name of sherries produced by KEO in Cyprus.

MOSCADELLO DI MONTALCINO semi-sparkling DOC white wine from the TUSCANY region of central Italy.

MOSCATEL DE SETÚBAL fortified sweet dessert wine from Setúbal near Lisbon in Portugal.

MOSCATO name used in Italy for the MUSCAT grape.

MOSCATO D'ASTI sparkling DOC MUSCAT wine produced at ASTI in PIEMONTE.

MOSCATO DEI COLLI EUGANEI DOC MUSCAT wine made in VENETO. It may be dry to sweet, still or sparkling.

MOSCATO DEL SALENTO red and white strong sweet dessert wines from PUGLIA.

MOSCATO DEL TRENTINO medium-sweet DOC wine produced in the Alto Adige area of TRENTINO-ALTO ADIGE.

MOSCATO DI CAGLIARI DOC dessert wine, usually fortified, from Sardinia.

MOSCATO DI CALABRIA sweet and semi-sweet wine from CALABRIA.

MOSCATO DI NOTO sweet, strong DOC dessert wine from Sicily.

MOSCATO DI PANTELLARIA DOC dessert wine from the island of Pantellaria in Italy. Three styles are made: dry, semi-sweet and sparkling.

MOSCATO DI SORSO-SENNORI sweet DOC dessert wine from Sardinia. Rich, luscious wine which is sometimes fortified.

MOSCATO DI TRANI very rich sweet white DOC wines produced in PUGLIA. Also the name of a LIQUOROSO wine produced in the same area.

MOSCATO SPUMANTE sparkling wine produced in California.

MOSELBLÜMCHEN German term (literally 'little flower of the Mosel') for sweet white wines produced in the MOSEL-SAAR-RUWER region.

MOSELLE French name for the Mosel river.

MOSEL-SAAR-RUWER major wine-producing region of western Germany, one of the 11 ANBAUGEBIETE. It runs from Koblenz to the Luxembourg border and includes the valleys of the Mosel, Saar and Ruwer rivers, producing mostly white wines. It consists of the BEREICHEN of OBER-MOSEL, SAAR-RUWER, BERNKASTEL and ZELL.

MOSS WOOD wine producers in the MARGARET RIVER district of Western Australia producing excellent varietal wines including CABERNET SAUVIGNON and CHARDONNAY.

MOSTAR dry white wine from Yugoslavia.

MOU French term for FLABBY.

MOUEIX, J.P. wine-shipper and owner of Châteaux La MAGDELAINE, Lafleur-Petrus, PETRUS and TROTANOY in BORDEAUX. Also administrator of Château LATOUR-À-POMEROL wine.

MOULDY tasting term for the 'off flavour' imparted to a wine by mouldy grapes or storage in a mouldy cask.

MOULIN-À-VENT well-known full-bodied red wine from one of the nine BEAUJOLAIS CRU in BURGUNDY. The fullest-bodied of all the crus, with the longest keeping potential (5-10 years) it is regarded as the most complex and 'serious'.

MOULIN-À-VENT, CHÂTEAU CRU GRAND BOURGEOIS wine from the MOULIS district of BORDEAUX.

MOULIN DU CADET, CHÂTEAU firm GRAND CRU wine from the SAINT-EMILION district in BORDEAUX.

MOULIS small commune of the HAUT-MÉDOC district of BORDEAUX. Châteaux Chasse-Spleen, Poujeaux-Theil and Maucaillou are situated there.

MOUNT EDEN VINEYARDS producers in the SANTA CLARA region of California producing varietal wines from grapes from their own and other vineyards including quality CHARDONNAY and PINOT NOIR wines.

MOUNT MARY vineyard in the Yarra Valley, Victoria, Australia, producing excellent CABERNET SAUVIGNON, CHARDONNAY and PINOT NOIR wines.

MOUNT PALOMAR WINERY winery in Riverside, California, producing varietal and branded wines including Rancho Temecula and Long Valley. Grape varieties planted include CHENIN BLANC, CABERNET SAUVIGNON, RIESLING and ZINFANDEL.

MOUNT VEEDER WINERY small winery in the NAPA VALLEY region of California producing varietal wines, especially CABERNET SAUVIGNON, CHENIN BLANC and ZINFANDEL.

MOURA BASTO a VINHO VERDE wine from northwest Portugal.

MOURISCO red-wine grape used in Portugal in the production of dry red and PORT wine.

MOURVAISON grape used in the Provence district of France for the production of red and rosé wines.

MOURVÈDRE red-wine grape grown in Algeria, the MIDI in France, and Spain. Also known as Beni Carlo, Catalan, Espar, Mataro, Negron and Tinto.

MOUSSEC brand of sparkling BRITISH WINE.

MOUSSEUX French term designating sparkling wine (other than champagne), used on French wine labels.

MOUSY tasting term for a wine with an undesirable flavour and taste as a result of bacterial spoilage.

MOUTON CADET brand name of BORDEAUX wines produced by La Baronnie, owned by the Rothschild family.

MOUTONNE, LA vineyard of the CHABLIS district of central France which has not been designated as a GRAND CRU but is regarded as of similar quality.

MOUTON-ROTHSCHILD, CHÂTEAU PREMIER CRU wine from the PAUILLAC commune of BORDEAUX. One of the best wines of Bordeaux.

MUDGEE wine-producing district of New South Wales in Australia.

MUFFA NOBILE Italian term for NOBLE ROT.

MUGA wine producers in the RIOJA region of northern Spain producing red and white and champagne-type wines (Conde de Haro).

MÜLHEIM village of GROSSLAGE Kurfürstlay in the BEREICH of BERNKASTEL in the MOSEL-SAAR-RUWER region of Germany, producing good quality RIESLING wines.

MULLED WINE diluted, spiced and sweetened wine which is heated and served hot.

MÜLLER-THURGAU white-wine grape variety widely used in Germany, crossbred from the RIESLING and SYLVANER varieties. Also used in Austria, California, England, Australia, Liechtenstein, Luxembourg, New Zealand and Switzerland. It makes a fruity wine which resembles the MUSCAT varieties in flavour.

MUMM large CHAMPAGNE firm in Reims in the Champagne region of France producing a range of vintage and non-vintage champagnes from a wide range of holdings.

MUNSTER SARMSHEIM village of GROSSLAGE Schlosskapelle in the BEREICH of Kreuznach in the NAHE region of Germany.

MURFATLAR vineyard near the Black Sea in Romania producing a white dessert wine.

MURRAY RIVER VALLEY area between New South Wales and Victoria in Australia producing table, fortified and Sherry-type wines.

MURRUMBIDGEE irrigation area of New South Wales in Australia producing table and fortified wines.

MUSAR, CHATEAU very good quality red wine produced by Caves Musar in the LEBANON.

MUSCADEL (MUSCATEL) term for a sweet wine which is made from MUSCAT grapes.

MUSCADELLE grape grown in the SAUTERNES region of France.

MUSCADET white-wine grape and AC grape for wines of the Muscadet district of Brittany in northern France. Good quality Muscadet wines come from **Muscadet de Coteaux de la Loire** in the LOIRE valley in Brittany, but the best come from **Muscadet de Sèvre-et-Maine** from the central part of Muscadet, also on the Loire. In a similar system to BEAUJOLAIS NOUVEAU **Muscadet Primeur** are the season's new wines rushed to the markets by Christmas. They should be drunk soon.

MUSCADINE sub-genus of the VITIS VINIFERA vine grown in the southern US. Varieties include the JAMES, the Mish and the Scuppernong.

MUSCAT sweet white-wine grape varieties used in the production of dessert wines. They include: **Muscat à Petits Grains**, a variety widely planted throughout Europe. Known in Italy as **Muscat Bianco**, it is used there to produce Asti Spumante. Its wine is often blended with others to increase flavour. **Muscat of Alexandria** is a multipurpose grape planted extensively in many countries. Known as **Muscat de Setúbal** in Portugal, **Muscatel de Málaga** in Spain, *Zibbibbo* in Italy and **Muscat Gordo Blanco** in Australia, it produces intensely flavoured fruity wines which are possibly the most 'grape'-like in taste.

MUSCAT D'ALSACE dry and fruity wine produced in the ALSACE region of northwest France. It has a SWEETNESS RATING of 3.

MUSCAT DE BEAUMES-DE-VENISE sweet dessert wine with a SWEETNESS RATING of 9, produced in the MIDI region of France; (2) a varietal grape grown in California.

MUSCAT DE FRONTIGNAN (1) VIN DOUX NATUREL produced in the MIDI region of France; (2) a varietal grape grown in California.

MUSCAT DE LUNEL VIN DOUX NATUREL and VIN DE LIQUEUR produced in the MIDI region of France.

MUSCAT DE MIREVAL a dessert wine produced near Frontignan in the MIDI region of France.

MUSCAT DE RIVESALTES sweet fortified wines from the RIVESALTES area of France, producing well-known wines.

MUSCAT DE SAINT-JEAN-DE-MINERVOIS VIN DOUX NATUREL and VIN DE LIQUEUR produced in the MIDI region of France.

MUSCATEL *see* MUSCADEL.

MUSCAT OF SAMOS well-known sweet white wine from the Greek island of SAMOS.

MUSCAT OTTONEL White-wine grape used in Austria, Luxembourg, Romania and Yugoslavia.

MUSIGNY GRAND CRU vineyard of the CHAMBOLLE-MUSIGNY commune in the CÔTE DE NUITS district of

BURGUNDY. Produces fine, delicate red wine and a small quantity of white.

MUSKAT OTTONEL *see* MUSCAT OTTONEL.

MUSKOTALY (YELLOW MUSCAT) Hungarian MUSCAT grape, used in the making of TOKAJI wine.

MUSSBACH town of GROSSLAGE Meerspinne in the BEREICH of MITTELHAARDT in the RHEINPFALZ region of Germany producing red and white wines. There is a large cooperative.

MUST the mixture of grape juice, skins and seeds before fermentation has been completed.

MUTIGNY CHAMPAGNE vineyard of the Canton d'Ay in the Champagne region of France. Classified 93 percent in the CIVC rating for black grapes.

N

NACKENHEIM village of GROSSLAGE Gutes Domtal in the BEREICH of NIERSTEIN in the RHEINHESSEN region of Germany. Produces some very good white wines.

NAGYBURGUNDI Hungarian Pinot Noir grape.

NAHE important wine-producing region of northwest Germany comprising the BEREICHEN of BAD KREUZNACH and SCHLOSSBÖCKELHEIM. The best wines of the region come from the villages of Niederhausen, Bad Kreuznach and Schloss Böckelheim (the latter two not to be confused with the Bereichen of the same names).

NAIRAC, CHÂTEAU deuxième GRAND CRU BARSAC wine from BORDEAUX.

NAOUSSA district of central Macedonia in Greece, producing mainly red wines. *See also* MAVRO.

NAPA VALLEY famous California wine region to the north of San Francisco, producing a wide range of styles from many producers, the best of which can rival the world's finest wines.

NARBAG red table wine from Turkey.

NASCO DI CAGLIARI DOC dry whites and also sweet, slightly bitter dessert white wine from the island of Sardinia.

NATURAL WINE wine with no additives.

NATURE French term for unsweetened wine. When applied to CHAMPAGNE the term may refer to still wine or unsweetened champagne.

NAVARRA region of northern Spain, near the Pyrenées, comprising the districts of Baja Montana, Ribera Alta, Ribera Baja, Valdizarbe, and Tierra de Estella. Red wines from Navarra have a TASTE RATING of B, and white wines a SWEETNESS RATING of 2.

NAVARRO VINEYARDS vineyards in the MENDOCINO region of California producing varietal wines, including CHARDONNAY, RIESLING and CABERNET SAUVIGNON.

NÉAC district of BORDEAUX in southwest France which has now been incorporated in LALANDE DE POMEROL.

NEBBIOLO excellent red-wine grape grown widely in the PIEMONTE region of Italy where it is used for the famous wines of BAROLO, BARBARESCO, GATTINARA and GHEMME and also regional wines such as the dry DOC **Nebbiolo d'Alba**. Other Italian regions with plantings include VALLE D'AOSTA and the VALTELLINA area of LOMBARDY where it is used to make Valtellina Superiore. It is also planted in California, and to some extent in Argentina and Uruguay. It produces full-bodied robust wines which can last for decades.

NEBUCHADNEZZAR large champagne bottle with a capacity equal to twenty ordinary bottles.

NEEF village of GROSSLAGE Grafschaft in the BEREICH of ZELL in the MOSEL-SAAR-RUWER region of Germany.

NÉGOCIANT buyer of wine from other growers who matures and bottles it in his own cellars. Also a term applied to a wine shipper, in the sense of being a small distributor.

NÉGOCIANT MANIPULANT *see* NM

NEGROAMARA red-wine grape used in the PUGLIA region of Italy in the production of red and rosé wines.

NEMEA town and dry red wine from the PELOPONNESE district of Greece.

NERVEUX French term used to describe a lively, vital and 'tight' wine.

NEUBURGER grape used in some Austrian wines and also in Romania.

NEUCHÂTEL city and wine region of Switzerland producing light, dry white wines and also the red CORTAILLOD made from PINOT NOIR grapes. More red is produced than whites.

NEUMAGEN-DHRON village of GROSSLAGE Michelsberg in the BEREICH of BERNKASTEL in the MOSEL-SAAR-RUWER region of Germany.

NEUSIEDLERSEE wine-producing area of BURGENLAND in Austria producing red and white wines.

NEUSTADT village of GROSSLAGE Meerspinne Rebstockel in the BEREICH of MITTELHAARDT in the RHEINPFALZ region of Germany.

NEUTRAL tasting term for a wine lacking distinctive or recognizable character. Related to VINOUS.

NEW SOUTH WALES important wine-producing state of Australia whose main wine-producing regions include the

HUNTER VALLEY, MUDGEE, Corowa, and Murrimbidgee Irrigation Area. Numerous other areas have minor plantings. Hunter Valley is the most famous region, renowned for a unique SEMILLON.

NEW ZEALAND island country in the Pacific Ocean situated to the east of Australia. Approximately 5,000 hectares are under vine in the major regions of Auckland, Bay of Plenty, Gisbourne, Hawkes Bay, Marlborough and other smaller areas in the South Island. The grapes grown are VITIS VINIFERA varieties including CHARDONNAY, SEMILLON, SAUVIGNON BLANC, RIESLING, GEWÜRZTRAMINER and MÜLLER-THURGAU for whites, and MERLOT, CABERNET SAUVIGNON and PINOT NOIR for reds. To date, great success has been had with Chardonnay and Sauvignon Blanc.

NIAGARA (1) wine-growing region of eastern US and Canada producing mostly table wines; (2) American white-wine grape with a FOXY taste.

NICOLAS large French commercial wine merchants.

NICORESTI village and wine region in eastern Romania producing white table wines and red BABEASCA wine.

NIEBAUM-COPPOLA estate in the NAPA VALLEY region of California producing varietal wines including CABERNET SAUVIGNON and ZINFANDEL.

NIEDERHÄUSEN village of GROSSLAGE Burgweg in the BEREICH of SCHLOSSBÖCKELHEIM, in the NAHE region of Germany.

NIEDERMENNIG *see* MENNIG.

NIEDERÖSTERREICH German term for Lower Austria, the largest wine region of the country.

NIERSTEIN BEREICH of the RHEINHESSEN region of Germany. Niersteiner wines are the best of the region, particularly the RIESLINGS. The majority of grape plantings are of MÜLLER-THURGAU.

NM (abbreviation of *Négociant Manipulant*) on a CHAMPAGNE label, shows that the producer bought in the wine from various growers and blended it. All the major champagne houses are NMs so the letters are a mark of quality.

NOBILE DI MONTEPULCIANO *see* VINO NOBILE DI MONTEPULCIANO.

NOBILO wine producers in the Huapai Valley in Auckland, New Zealand, producing distinctive red and white varietal wines: specializing in reds, including CABERNET SAUVIGNON and PINOT NOIR.

NOBLE term for outstanding, consistent and enduring quality. May be applied to a wine or a grape variety.

NOBLE ROT (*Botrytis cineria*) a fungus which attacks grapes in warm, moist climatic conditions and forms a mould which hastens the fermentation process and concentrates the sugars. It is of major importance in the production of sweet wines, its presence detectable by a honeyed taste on the nose and palate. Examples include SAUTERNES, BARSAC, and German wines of AUSLESE or higher classification. Similar styles are produced worldwide, usually of good to excellent quality. Known as *pourriture noble* in France, *Edelfäule* in Germany, and 'botrytised' in Australia.

NOBLING grape variety grown in the BADEN region of Germany, a cross of SILVANER and Gutedel.

NONVINTAGE (NV) term for a wine which is a blend of wines from different years. This is done to give continuity of flavour.

NORHEIM village of GROSSLAGE Burgweg in the BEREICH of SCHLOSSBÖCKELHEIM in the NAHE region of Germany.

NORIEN *see* PINOT NOIR.

NORTON good quality American red-wine grape.

NOSE tasting term for the characteristics of wine as assessed by the sense of smell. Similar to BOUQUET.

NOSING the practice of sniffing a wine to assess its quality, used during the production process and by the final consumer. The wine is swirled in a glass to agitate and aerate it and intensify its aromas and bouquet so that these can be detected by the nose.

NOSTRANO red-wine grape grown in the TICINO district of Switzerland.

NOUVEAU French word for 'new', used of wine to describe the current harvest's wine. Selling *nouveau* wines has become a popular marketing ploy, e.g. BEAUJOLAIS NOUVEAU, MUSCADET PRIMEUR.

NOVAL producer making quality PORT wines in the DOURO region of Portugal.

NOVITIATE WINERY winery in the SANTA CRUZ area of California, producing fortified dessert wines and some good table wines.

NOZET, CHÂTEAU DU wine-producing firm of POUILLY in the upper Loire in western France producing Pouilly-Fumé-de Ladoucette, Sancerre Comte Lafond and Pouilly-Fumé Baron de L.

NOZZOLE wine producers in Florence in the TUSCANY region of northwest Italy. Their DOC is CHIANTI CLASSICO.

NUITS-SAINT-GEORGES famous town and highly reputable vineyard area of the CÔTE DE NUITS district of BURGUNDY. Its best vineyards include Les Cailles, Les Porets, Les Pruliers, Les Saint-Georges and Les Vaucrains. Predominantly red wines but some good whites are made.

NURAGUS white-wine grape grown in Sardinia. It makes the DOC wine **Nuragus di Cagliari**, a good white table wine.

NÜSSBRUNNEN great EINZELLAGE vineyard of GROSSLAGE Deutelsberg in the RHEINGAU region of Germany. Produces excellent RIESLING wines.

NUSSDORF (1) village of GROSSLAGE Bischofskreuz in the BEREICH of SÜDLICHE WEINSTRASSE in the RHEINPFALZ region of Germany; (2) important town near Vienna in Austria, producing quality white wines.

NUTTY tasting term for the characteristic pungent flavour of SHERRY, due in part to wood age. Also found occasionally in dry table wines.

NV abbreviation for NONVINTAGE.

O

OBEREMMEL village of GROSSLAGE Scharzberg in the BEREICH of Saar-Ruwer in the MOSEL-SAAR-RUWER region of Germany, producing fine wines.

OBERMOSEL BEREICH of the MOSEL-SAAR-RUWER region of Germany comprising the GROSSLAGEN GIPFEL and KONIGSBERG. Produces good quality wines.

OCKENHEIM village of GROSSLAGE Sankt Rochuskapelle in the BEREICH of BINGEN in the RHEINHESSEN region of Germany. Both red and white wines are produced here.

OCKFEN village of GROSSLAGE Scharzberg in the BEREICH of SAAR-RUWER in the MOSEL-SAAR-RUWER region of Germany. Produces the best wines of the region, its best vineyard being BOCKSTEIN.

ODOBESTI vineyard area located in the centre of Focsani region, Romania.

OECHSLE scale of measurement used in Germany for measuring the specific gravity of MUST and hence the potential alcoholic content of a wine. The specific gravity when divided by 8 gives the approximate alcohol content, e.g. a wine of 110 degrees Oechsle has a potential alcohol content of 13.75 percent if fermented to dryness.

OENOLOGY the study of the chemical science of wine.

OESTERREICHER see ÖSTERREICHER.

OESTRICH see ÖSTRICH.

OFFLEY FORRESTER PORT producers in Vila Nova de Gaia in Portugal.

OGER CHAMPAGNE vineyard of the Canton d'Avize in the Champagne region of France. Classified 99 percent in the CIVC rating for white grapes.

OGGAU important town of the Austrian lake district in the BURGENLAND region. Produces top quality wines.

OIRY CHAMPAGNE vineyard of the Canton d'Avize in the Champagne region of France. Classified 99 percent in the CIVC rating for white grapes.

OLARRA wine producers in the RIOJA ALTA region of northern Spain producing red and white wines.

OLASZ RIZLING Hungarian term for the Italian Riesling with root stock from Italy. Dry white wines made from it have a SWEETNESS RATING of 3 and medium-dry wines 4.

OLD TRIANGLE brand name of wines made in the BAROSSA VALLEY, Australia, by Hill Smith.

OLIFANTS RIVER one of the demarcated WINES OF ORIGIN areas of South Africa.

OLIVIER, CHÂTEAU CRU wine from the GRAVES district of BORDEAUX.

OLOROSO full-bodied SHERRY with a deep golden colour and a strong RANCIO character on the nose and palate. May be dry or slightly sweetened. Olorosos are fortified with brandy up to 17-18 percent of alcohol by volume. Sherry naturally tends towards either a FINO or Oloroso type, depending on whether a FLOR is formed on it. Sherry without a flor, or with very little, is then developed into Oloroso.

OLTREPÒ PAVESE red and white DOC wines from the province of Pavia in the LOMBARDY region of Italy.

OLYMPIA demarcated wine district of Greece controlled for type and standard of grape.

OPOL rosé wines produced in DALMATIA, Yugoslavia.

OPORTO town at the mouth of the River DOURO in Portugal from which, by law, all fortified PORT wines are shipped. Its name is the origin of the word Port.

OPPENHEIM village of GROSSLAGE Guldenmorgen in the BEREICH of NIERSTEIN in the RHEINHESSEN region of Germany. **Oppenheimer** is one of the two best wines of the region, the other being Niersteiner.

OPTIMA white-wine grape variety grown in Germany. A cross of RIESLING, SYLVANER and MÜLLER-THURGAU.

OPUS ONE brand name of wines produced by MONDAVI.

ORDINAIRE French word for 'ordinary', used of wine to describe inexpensive, everyday table wine.

OREGON wine-producing state of northwest US, producing a modest amount of wine.

ORJAHOVIZA *see* ORYAHOVICA.

ORLANDO major commercial winemaker in the BAROSSA VALLEY area of South Australia making quality wines. One of the pioneers of the WINE BOX.

ORMES-DE-PEZ, CHÂTEAU LES cru GRAND BOURGEOIS wine from the SAINT-ESTÈPHE commune in BORDEAUX.

ORTENAU BEREICH of the BADEN region of Germany, producing some of its best wines. Highly regarded vineyards include Durbach, Neuweier and Ortenberg.

ORVIETO sweet and dry white wine produced in UMBRIA in central Italy. The best wines are the DOC Orvieto wines. **Orvieto Secco** (dry) has a SWEETNESS RATING of 2, and **Orvieto Abboccato** (sweet) has a SWEETNESS RATING of 4.

ORYAHOVIZA (ORJAHOVIZA) major Controliran wine-growing area of BULGARIA, producing CABERNET SAUVIGNON and MERLOT wines.

OSANN-MONZEL village of GROSSLAGE Kurfürstlay in the BEREICH of BERNKASTEL in the MOSEL-SAAR-RUWER region of Germany. Produces good quality wines.

OSBORNE Y CIA SHERRY producers in the JEREZ region of southern Spain producing a range of styles.

OSTHOFEN village of GROSSLAGE Gotteshilfe in the BEREICH of WONNEGAU in the RHEINHESSEN region of Germany. Produces good quality wines.

ÖSTERREICH German name for AUSTRIA.

ÖSTERREICHER another name for the SYLVANER grape.

ÖSTRICH village of GROSSLAGE Honigberg in the BEREICH of JOHANNISBERG in the RHEINGAU region of Germany.

OSTUNI light, dry, red and white DOC wines from PUGLIA in southern Italy. Grapes used are Ottavianello for red and Impiona and Francavilla for white.

OTHELLO well-known dry red wine produced in Cyprus.

OUDE LIBERTAS brand name of a wine produced by SFW in South Africa.

OXIDATION the contact of the oxygen in air with wine. This is undesirable as it results in wines going brown in colour and becoming flat and unpleasant to the palate.

OXIDIZED tasting term for a wine which has been exposed to too much oxygen, resulting in loss of flavour and development of coarseness. Oxidized wines usually contain higher levels of acetaldehyde.

P

PAARL district of Cape Province in South Africa producing light table wines.

PACHERENC DU VIC-BILH sweet white AC wine produced in the French Pyrenées.

PAILLARD BRUNO CHAMPAGNE firm in the Champagne region of France producing vintage and nonvintage champagnes.

PAIS red-wine grape and ordinary wine of the same name, grown and made extensively in Chile.

PALACIO DE BREJOEIRA superior estate-bottled VINHO VERDE wine which is made in the northernmost Minho wine region of Portugal.

PALATE the sense of taste detected by the mouth, tongue and throat. The tip of the tongue detects sweetness, the sides nearest the tip saltiness, the sides farther back sourness, and the centre of the tongue at the back bitterness. Fruit flavours are experienced by the front palate, the body or weight by the middle palate, and the finish or aftertaste by the back palate.

PALATINATE ancient English name for RHEINPFALZ.

PALE CREAM style of SHERRY, a sweetened FINO with a SWEETNESS RATING of 7.

PALETTE AC area of the PROVENCE district of southern France producing white and good red wines, the best known of which is Château Simone.

PALMA term used for a high quality fino SHERRY and a trade name for exported sherry (Tres Palmas).

PALMER, CHÂTEAU troisième GRAND CRU wine from the MARGAUX commune of BORDEAUX. Often regarded as being of better quality than its given classification.

PALO CORTADO SHERRY style with the bouquet of AMONTILLADO and palate similar to OLOROSO Sherry with the bouquet of a FINO. The name is often used loosely for wines of a similar type but the real wine is rare, taking twenty years to mature.

PALOMINO an important Spanish white-wine grape variety which provides large percentages of the grapes for SHERRY production. Widely planted in other countries including Australia, Argentina, California, Mexico and New Zealand, where it is used for table wines, but at its best in Sherry and other fortified styles. Known in California as Golden Chasselas.

PALOMINO & VERGARA SHERRY producers in the JEREZ region of southern Spain producing a range of Sherries mainly for domestic use.

PALUS French term for reclaimed alluvial marshland. Palus-grown wines are not of very high quality and are not usually AC classified.

PAMID red-wine grape used in Bulgaria in the production of table wines for local consumption.

PANISSEAU, CHÂTEAU DE estate of BERGERAC in southwest France producing some good dry white wines.

PAPAGNI VINEYARDS vineyards in the SAN JOAQUIN VALLEY, California, producing good varietals.

PAPE-CLÉMENT, CHÂTEAU GRAND CRU wine from the GRAVES district of BORDEAUX.

PARDUCCI WINERY well-known winery in the MENDOCINO district of California.

PARIGOT-RICHARD producers of CRÉMANT DE BOURGOGNE at Savigny-les-Beaune in eastern France.

PARRAS important wine-making region of Mexico. Its best-known winery, producing table wines, is the Vinicola del Marques de Aguayo.

PARRINA red and white DOC wines produced in the TUSCANY region of northwest Italy.

PASQUIER-DEVIGNES merchants in the BEAUJOLAIS district of BURGUNDY selling 'Les Marquisat' Beaujolais, VINS DE PAYS and VDQS wines.

PASSE-TOUS-GRAINS red BURGUNDY made from a blend, minimum 33 percent PINOT NOIR and GAMAY grapes, but not by the best communes. *See also* BOURG-OGNE-PASSE-TOUS-GRAINS.

PASSITO Italian term for wine made from dried grapes; usually dessert wine. The grapes shrivel on the vine, reducing water content and concentrating the sugars.

PATÂCHE D'AUX, CHÂTEAU CRU GRAND BOURGEOIS wine from the MÉDOC district of BORDEAUX.

PATERNINA wine producers of RIOJA ALTA in northern Spain. Brand names include Banda Azul, Banda Dorada, Conde de Los Andes and Vina Vial.

PATRAS town and wine-cooperative in the PELOPONNESE region of Greece producing good, mainly white, wines.

PATRIARCHE large growers and merchants in BURGUNDY and owners of Château de MEURSAULT and BEAUNE PREMIERS CRUS. They also produce a range of AC wines.

PATRIMONIO red and rosé AC wines from Corsica.

PAUILLAC town and commune of the HAUT-MÉDOC region of BORDEAUX and home to three of the five PREMIER GRAND CRU of Bordeaux: Châteaux Lafite, Latour and Mouton-Rothschild. Many other excellent châteaux make superb wines in Pauillac.

PAULSEN VINEYARDS vineyards in the SONOMA region of California producing SAUVIGNON BLANC.

PAVEIL-DE-LUZE, CHÂTEAU CRU BOURGEOIS wine from the MARGAUX commune of BORDEAUX.

PAVILLON-CADET, CHÂTEAU GRAND CRU wine from the SAINT-EMILION district of BORDEAUX.

PAVLIKENI wine town in northern Bulgaria producing CABERNET and GAMZA wines.

PAZO one of the best-selling wines from the Galicia region of Spain.

PÉCHARMANT AC estate in the BERGERAC district of southwest France producing full-flavoured red wines.

PECOTA WINERY winery in the NAPA VALLEY region of California, producing the Beaujolais-style Georges Duboeuf.

PECS town in the MECSEK district of Hungary producing sweet RIESLING wines.

PEDESCLAUX, CHÂTEAU cinquième PREMIER CRU wine from the PAUILLAC commune of BORDEAUX.

PEDRO XIMINEZ white-wine grape variety used in Spain in the production of SHERRY to help make the sweeter styles. The grapes are spread out on mats and left in the sun to increase their sugar content. Also grown in other countries for sweet wines.

PEDRONCELLI WINERY winery in the SONOMA region of California producing generic and varietal wines.

PELOPONNESE largest wine-growing region of Greece producing mostly dry white wines, MUSCAT and MAVRODAPHNE dessert wines.

PENAFIEL subregion of the Minho region of Portugal producing mainly white VINHO VERDE wine.

PEÑAFLOR largest wine growers and shippers in Argentina. Their Andean and Trapiche brands are particularly good.

PENDLETON WINERY winery in the SANTA CLARA region of California producing varietal wines.

PENEDÈS large DO district of CATALONIA in northeastern Spain producing mainly red and white table wines and sparkling wine made by the CHAMPAGNE METHOD. The red wines have a TASTE RATING of D and the whites a SWEETNESS RATING of 2.

PENFOLD'S winemakers with vineyards throughout Australia's winegrowing regions, considered to produce the country's finest reds, including GRANGE HERMITAGE.

PEPE, EMILIO family winery in the ABRUZZI region of Italy producing DOC wines. Grapes are still crushed by foot and wines are aged only in the bottle. Their wines include TREBBIANO D'ABRUZZO and MONTEPULCIANO.

PERELADA wine-town in northwest Spain producing red, white and rosé wines, the best being the rosés. Also produces a famous CAVA.

PER'E PALUMMO grape variety from the island of Ischia off the coast of the CAMPANIA region of southern Italy.

PÉRIGNON, DOM *see* DOM PÉRIGNON.

PERIQUITA brand name of a red table wine produced by FONSECA in Portugal.

PERLA DE TIRNAVE blended semi-sweet white wine from Romania.

PERLAN dry white CHASSELAS wine from the MANDEMENT district of Switzerland.

PERLANT French term for slightly sparkling wine. *See also* PÉTILLANT.

PERLWEIN name of a German carbonated sparkling wine.

PERNAND-VERGELESSES commune of the CÔTE DE BEAUNE in BURGUNDY producing red and white wines. Its lesser wines are normally sold as Pernand-Verglesses AC Côte de Beaune, and its better ones have the vineyard name added to the commune name. These include the PREMIER CRU Ile des Hautes Vergelesses, Les Basses Vergelesses, Creux de la Net, Les Fichots and En Caradeux.

PERRIER, JOSEPH CHAMPAGNE firm at Châlons-sur-Marne in northeast France producing a high quality range of vintage and nonvintage wines.

PERRIER, LAURENT CHAMPAGNE firm making good vintage and nonvintage wines in the traditional style.

PERRIER-JOUET CHAMPAGNE firm of Épernay in the Champagne region of northeast France.

PESSAC commune of the GRAVES district of BORDEAUX. Includes Châteaux Haut-Brion, La Mission and Pape-Clément.

PETALUMA modern winery in Adelaide Hills region of South Australia producing excellent wines. Now part owned by Bollinger.

PÉTILLANT French term for slightly sparkling wine, the sparkle being due to the presence of CARBON DIOXIDE. The term PERLANT is sometimes used as an alternative.

PETIT-CHABLIS lesser wines produced in the CHABLIS district of BURGUNDY at cheaper prices.

PETITE-SIRAH red-wine grape variety grown in California. Also known as Shiraz in Australia.

PETIT-FAURIE-DE-SOUTARD, CHÂTEAU GRAND CRU wine from the SAINT-EMILION district of BORDEAUX.

PETIT ROUGE red-wine grape used in the Valle d'Aosta district of PIEMONTE region of northwest Italy in the production of the DOC wine ENFER D'ARVIER.

PETITS CHÂTEAUX lesser châteaux and vineyards of BORDEAUX producing good red wines at more affordable prices.

PETIT-VERDOT red-wine grape variety used for red

wines in BORDEAUX and also for blending with CABERNET SAUVIGNON for top quality wines in MÉDOC. This quality variety helps fill the palate and adds complexity to a wine.

PETRUS, CHÂTEAU the leading château of the POMEROL region of BORDEAUX making superlative and rare wine which commands fabulous prices.

PEZ, CHÂTEAU DE CRU BOURGEOIS wine from the SAINT-ESTÈPHE commune in BORDEAUX.

PFALZ *see* RHEINPFALZ.

PHÉLAN-SÉGUR, CHÂTEAU CRU GRAND BOURGEOIS EXCEPTIONNEL wine from the SAINT-ESTÈPHE commune in BORDEAUX.

PHELPS VINEYARDS vineyards in the NAPA VALLEY region of California producing good varietal wines.

PHYLLOXERA parasitic disease of the vine caused by *Phylloxera vastatrix*, a root-eating louse indigenous to the eastern US. The disease, less harmful in eastern US itself, caused considerable damage to vines in California during the 19th century and devastated many vineyards in Europe, where imported vines spread the disease to most countries. The disease is nowadays avoided by grafting VITIS VINIFERA varieties on to native American root stocks.

PIAN D'ALBOLA wine producers in the TUSCANY region of northwest Italy. Their DOC is CHIANTI CLASSICO.

PIAT large merchants in MÂCON in eastern France selling BEAUJOLAIS and Mâcon wines and **Piat d'Or** table wines.

PIAVE dry red and white DOC wines produced in the VENETO region of northwest Italy.

PIC, ALBERT label of Reynard and Fils, NÉGOCIANT of CHABLIS in central France.

PICCARDAN one of the 13 grape varieties used in the production of CHÂTEAUNEUF-DU-PAPE.

PICOLIT grape variety grown at Colli Orientali del Friuli in the FRIULI-VENEZIA-GIULIA region of northern Italy, used in the making of dessert wines.

PICPOUL white-wine grape used commonly in southern France. It is an authorized grape for the production of CHÂTEAUNEUF-DU-PAPE and Armagnac and is also found in the CATALONIA region of Spain where it is called Avillo.

PIEDMONT English name for PIEMONTE.

PIEDROSSO (PIEDIROSSO) red-wine grape used in the CAMPANIA region of southwest Italy.

PIEMONTE famous wine-producing region of northwest Italy, on the eastern side of the French Alps. The main wine-producing areas are centred on the towns of ASTI and ALBA, the names featuring in many of the wine labels from the region, but the area of Oltrepò Pavese in the south of the region also produces good DOC wines. Various grape varieties are used, principally BARBERA, DOLCETTO, FREISA, MOSCATO and SPANNA (the Piemontese name for the NEBBIOLO) to make many DOC wines and the DOCG BAROLO and BARBARESCO.

PIEROPAN wine producers in the VENETO region of northern Italy. Their DOC is Soave-Recioto.

PIEROTH large firm of wine growers and merchants in Germany.

PIERRY CHAMPAGNE vineyard of the Canton d'Épernay in the Champagne region of France. Classified 90 percent in the CIVC rating.

PIESPORT village of GROSSLAGE Michelsberg in the BEREICH of BERNKASTEL in the MOSEL-SAAR-RUWER region of Germany. Produces some fine wines, the best vineyards being Goldtropfchen and Schubertslay.

PIGATO white-wine grape grown in the LIGURIA region of northern Italy. Produces full-bodied, flavoursome wines.

PIKETBERG official WO district of South Africa.

PILTON MANOR estate in Somerset, England, producing dry white wine and Marsac sparkling wine made by the CHAMPAGNE METHOD.

PINDEFLEURS, CHÂTEAU GRAND CRU of SAINT-EMILION in BORDEAUX, producing quality wines.

PINEAU D'AUNIS red-wine grape grown around ANJOU in the Loire Valley region of France where it is used in the production of red and rosé wines.

PINEAU DE LA LOIRE *see* CHENIN BLANC.

PINEAU DES CHARENTES strong, sweet white and rosé apéritif wines from the Charente and Charente-Maritime areas of the Cognac region in southern France. Made by the addition of a small amount of Cognac to new wine.

PINE RIDGE WINERY vineyards in the NAPA VALLEY region of California producing varietal wines from CHARDONNAY and CABERNET SAUVIGNON grapes.

PINOT family of grapes used extensively in France, particularly in Burgundy and in Champagne. Also widely planted throughout the world. Commonly used varieties include PINOT NOIR, PINOT LIEBAULT and PINOT MEUNIER for red wines and PINOT GRIS and PINOT BLANC for white.

PINOTAGE red-wine grape variety, a cross between PINOT NOIR and HERMITAGE (Syrah) grapes, originally developed in South Africa and now used also in New Zealand to make peppery red wines.

PINOT BIANCO (BORDOGNA BIANCO) grape variety used to make dry white wines of the same name in the TRENTINO-ALTO ADIGE and FRIULI-VENEZIA-GIULIA regions of Italy.

PINOT BLANC quality white-wine Burgundian grape variety which is overshadowed by CHARDONNAY in popularity. It is used extensively in BURGUNDY and CHAMPAGNE, and also Australia, Austria, California, Chile, England, Germany, Hungary, Italy and Luxembourg. It is a permitted grape of ALSACE where it makes **Pinot Blanc d'Alsace**, a white wine with a SWEETNESS RATING of 3. Other names include Weissburgunder, Klevner and Feherburgundi.

PINOT CHARDONNAY incorrect naming of the CHARDONNAY grape.

PINOT GRIGIO white-wine grape grown in northeast Italy to make mild white wines.

PINOT GRIS white-wine grape used extensively in France and also used in Algeria, Germany, Mexico, Rumania, Russia and Switzerland. It is possibly at its best in ALSACE, where it is a permitted grape, but also makes good quality wine in Italy. Alternative names include Auxerrois Gris, Fauvet, Malvoisie, Pinot Beurot, Rulander, Tokai, Tokayer and Tokay d'Alsace.

PINOT LIEBAULT red-wine grape used in France, particularly in Burgundy.

PINOT MEUNIER red-wine grape variety used for the production of CHAMPAGNE but as it is not of the same class as the other champagne varieties, the white CHARDONNAY and red PINOT NOIR, its plantings there are decreasing. A relative of the Pinot Noir, it is also used in the LOIRE Valley for rosé wines, and in Lorraine and New Zealand. Known as Mullerrebe in Germany.

PINOT NERO Italian name for the PINOT NOIR grape. It makes **Pinot Nero del Trentino**, a light, red, bitter DOC wine in the Alto Adige area of TRENTINO-ALTO ADIGE.

PINOT NOIR the classic red-wine grape variety of BUR-GUNDY where it produces some of the world's finest red wine. It is also used for the bulk of CHAMPAGNE production. It does not travel well, and outside Burgundy tends to lack both colour and depth although there have been some notable exceptions; Tyrell's 1976 from Australia won the first prize in 1979 at the Paris Wine Olympiad, and Tasmania and Oregon are making strides in developing quality wines. It is also found in California, Canada, Chile, England, Germany, Hungary, Italy, Mexico, Portugal, Rumania, Switzerland, Tunisia and Yugoslavia. Alternative names include Blauburgunder, Cortaillod, Elbling, Klevner, Nagyburgundi, Norien, Pineau, Pinot Nero, Savagnin and Spätburgunder.

PINOT ST GEORGES Californian red-wine grape.

PIO CESARE producers of good red wines in the PIEMONTE region of northern Italy. Wines include BAROLO BARBARESCO, Barbera d'Alba, DOLCETTO D'ALBA and NEBBIOLO D'ALBA.

PIPER-HEIDSIECK wine firm based at Reims in the Champagne region of France.

PIPER-SONOMA vineyards in the SONOMA region of California producing champagne-type wines.

PIQUANT French euphemism for wine which is unpleasantly sharp and acidic to the taste.

PIQUE French term used of wine with a vinegary taste caused by excessive acetic acid levels.

PIRES, JOÃO major producer of wines in Portugal, associated with FONSECA, making quality wines including a dry MUSCAT.

PITRAY, CHÂTEAU DE estate of CÔTES DE CASTILLON in the SAINT-EMILION district of BORDEAUX.

PITSILIA vineyard region of Cyprus producing red and white wines.

PLAVAC-MALI red-wine grape grown extensively in Yugoslavia.

PLAVIŇA light, dry red wine from DALMATIA in Yugoslavia.

PLEASANT VALLEY WINE CO. wine firm at Hammondsport in the FINGER LAKES district of New York State, US. Produces blended wines from a wide variety of grapes including good sparkling wines.

PLETTENBERG, VON estate in the NAHE region of Germany with interests in a range of good vineyards, the best being in BAD KREUZNACH.

PLINCE, CHÂTEAU wine from the POMEROL district of BORDEAUX.

PLONK term for cheap wine, possibly a corruption of *vin blanc*.

PLOVDINA red-wine grape grown in the region of Serbia in Yugoslavia to make a mild wine.

PODENSAC commune in the Gironde area of BORDEAUX making ordinary red wines and quality whites similar to those of the adjoining CÉRONS under which name they generally appear.

PODERE Italian word for an estate or farm. On a wine label it means that the grapes come from a particular estate or vineyard.

POGGIO AL SOLE wine producers in the TUSCANY region of northwest Italy. Their DOC is CHIANTI CLASSICO.

POINTE, CHÂTEAU LA quality wine from the POMEROL district of BORDEAUX.

POLCEVERA light white wine produced in the region of LIGURIA in Italy.

POLIGNY important wine-producing commune of the JURA region of France, making notable white wines, VIN JAUNE and VIN DE PAILLE.

POL ROGER largest family-owned CHAMPAGNE firm based at Épernay in the Champagne region of France, producing top quality champagne.

POMEROL district of BORDEAUX producing red and white wines. The vineyards of Pomerol are not classified. The best of its red wines is Château PETRUS, which ranks among the best wines of the world.

POMINO red and white DOC wines produced in the TUSCANY region of northern Italy.

POMMARD famous commune of the CÔTE DE BEAUNE district of BURGUNDY producing good to excellent full-bodied red wines. All its wines bear the name of the town and the better ones carry the vineyard name as well. All the vineyards have a PREMIER CRU classification.

POMMERY & GRENO wine firm based at Reims in the Champagne region of France.

PONNELLE, PIERRE NÉGOCIANT in BEAUNE in BURGUNDY with interests in a number of reputable vineyards in the CÔTE DE BEAUNE district.

PONTET-CANET, CHÂTEAU cinquième GRAND CRU wine from the PAUILLAC commune of BORDEAUX.

PONZI VINEYARDS vineyards in the Williamette Valley, Oregon, producing good white varietal wines. Grape varieties planted include RIESLING, CHARDONNAY, and PINOT NOIR.

POOR tasting term for a wine which is not faulty but of little merit.

POPE VALLEY WINERY winery in the NAPA VALLEY region of California producing varietal wines.

PORRÓN glass drinking vessel used in Spain which has a long spout from which the wine is poured directly into the mouth.

PORT rich, sweet fortified dessert wine produced in Portugal, which takes its name from the city of Oporto. It is made from a blend of grapes, including Bastardo, Mourisco, Donzelino Tinto, Touriga, Francesa, Tinta Roriz, Tinto Cao, Tinta Francisca and Touriga Nacional, grown on steep slopes along the banks of the DOURO river in the Alto Douro region. The MUST is not allowed to ferment until dry. Instead, when it has approximately 6-7 percent sugar left, the juice is run off into vats and fortified by the addition of brandy to an alcoholic strength of around 20 percent. After a period of maturation in the Port warehouses of Oporto, the length of which depends on the style of wine, bottling takes place. Port production is carefully controlled, and there are several styles: WHITE PORT, RUBY, TAWNY, CRUSTED, LATE BOTTLED VINTAGE, LATE BOTTLED OR VINTAGE CHARACTER, SINGLE QUINTA and VINTAGE. Wines of the latter two categories need to be kept for several years to mature and realize their full potential.

PORTUGAIS BLEAU *see* PORTUGIESER, BLAUER PORTUGIESER.

PORTUGAL European country famous for fortified PORT and MADEIRA wines. Over recent years Portuguese table wines have become increasingly popular in the UK, particularly rosé wines which have a SWEETNESS RATING of 4 and are good summer wines, and the VINHO VERDE, 'green wines', which are young wines both red and white. There is a *Denominacão de Origen* or DO appellation system which has 10 demarcated regions: ALGARVE, BAIRRADA, BUCELAS, CARCAVELHOS, COLARES, DÃO, DOURO, ESTREMADURA, MOSCATEL DE SETÚBAL and

VINHO VERDE. Within these, the major wine-producing areas are Minho, Tras-Os-Montes, Beira Alta, Beira Baixa, Beira Literal, Ribatejo, Aletenjo, and Setúbal. The reds in particular have great merit, with wines of character and depth of flavour available at bargain prices. Although quality white wines are produced, the standard does not rival that of the reds. This could change rapidly. The potential for excellent wines is currently restrained by outdated winemaking techniques, but the more progressive companies are introducing new technologies which will have a dramatic effect on white wine quality.

PORTUGIESER red-wine grape widely used in the AHR region of northwest Germany and in RHEINHESSEN. Also found in Czechoslovakia. *See also* BLAUER PORTUGIESER.

PORT-VENDRE commune of the Pyrénées Orientales, France, producing wines similar to those of BANYULS.

POSIP white-wine grape grown in the region of DALMATIA in Yugoslavia.

POT small wine bottle with a capacity of half a litre, used in cafés etc, for holding wine, mostly BEAUJOLAIS, poured directly from the cask.

POTENSAC, CHÂTEAU CRU BOURGEOIS wine from the MÉDOC district of BORDEAUX.

POUGET, CHÂTEAU quatrième GRAND CRU wine from the MARGAUX commune of BORDEAUX.

POUILLY-FUISSÉ full-bodied AC dry white wines of good quality produced in the adjoining communes of Pouilly and Fuissé in the MÂCONNAIS area of BURGUNDY. The best of the region although their prices are hard to justify.

POUILLY-FUMÉ dry white wine with a SWEETNESS RATING of 1, produced at POUILLY-SUR-LOIRE in the Loire Valley region of France.

POUILLY-LOCHE AC commune and vineyards of the MÂCONNAIS district of BURGUNDY producing a lesser dry white wine, similar in character to the POUILLY-FUISSÉ.

POUILLY-SUR-LOIRE (1) town in the LOIRE Valley region of France producing dry white wines, the best of which is POUILLY-FUMÉ; (2) a lesser dry white wine produced at Pouilly-sur-Loire.

POUILLY-VINZELLES vineyard of the MÂCONNAIS district of BURGUNDY producing a lesser dry white wine, similar in character to POUILLY-FUISSÉ.

POUJEAUX, CHÂTEAU wine from the MOULIS district of BORDEAUX.

POULSARD red-wine grape used in the ARBOIS district of the Jura Mountains in France for both red and rosé wines.

POURRITURE NOBLE French term for NOBLE ROT.

PRADEL wine merchants in the PROVENCE district of southern France.

PRÄDIKAT German term meaning special quality. *See* QMP.

PRECIPITATION crystalline deposit which forms on some young wines when they have been exposed to temperatures below freezing point. The crystals consist of potassium bitartrate and although unsightly are not harmful.

PRECOCIOUS tasting term for a wine which appears to have developed too rapidly.

PREISS ZIMMER, JEAN wine producers in the ALSACE region of northeast France producing fine wines including RIESLING and GEWÜRZTRAMINER.

PREMIAT high quality export Romanian wines.

PREMIER CRU second highest ranking in the French appellation contrôlée rankings, coming after GRAND CRU. Particularly noteworthy in BORDEAUX rankings.

PREMIÈRES CÔTES DE BLAYE district of BORDEAUX producing mostly red and some white wines. The reds are improving in quality.

PREMIÈRES CÔTES DE BORDEAUX district of BORDEAUX producing dry-medium sweet white wines with a SWEETNESS RATING of 7, and fruity red wines. Plantings of red-wine grapes now outnumber the white.

PRESLAV wine-producing area of BULGARIA which produces RIESLING wines under the Controliran system.

PRESTON WINE CELLARS large winery in the Yakima Valley, Washington State, US, producing a range of good varietal wines including CHARDONNAY, CHENIN BLANC, SAUVIGNON BLANC, CABERNET and MERLOT.

PRESTON VINEYARDS vineyards at Dry Creek in the SONOMA region of California producing varietal wines, including very good SAUVIGNON BLANC.

PREUSES, LES one of the seven GRANDS CRUS vineyards of the CHABLIS region of central France producing some very fine white wines.

PRICKED tasting term for a wine with excess volatile acidity, being sour and vinegary to taste.

PRIEURE, CHÂTEAU LE GRAND CRU wine from the SAINT-EMILION district of BORDEAUX.

PRIEURÉ-LICHINE, CHÂTEAU quatrième GRAND CRU wine from the MARGAUX commune of BORDEAUX.

PRIMEUR French term for wine produced for drinking shortly after harvest. e.g. Beaujolais Primeur.

PRIMITIVO DI APULIA good dry red wine from the PUGLIA region of southern Italy.

PRIORATO demarcated DO district of CATALONIA in northeastern Spain producing strong red wines, some with RANCIO character.

PROKUPAC the most widely used red-wine grape in Yugoslavia.

PROPRIÉTAIRE French term for vineyard owner.

PROPRIÉTAIRE-RÉCOLTANT French term for vineyard owner-manager.

PROSECCO Italian white-wine grape. In the VENETO region it makes the DOC wines **Prosecco di Conegliano di Valdobbiadene** in dry, semi-sweet, sweet fruity, and semi-sparkling styles.

PROSEK sweet dessert wine produced in the district of DALMATIA in Yugoslavia, made by cooking semi-dry grapes, MUST or grape juice and wine concentrate.

PROVADYA white-wine-producing area near SUMEN in eastern Bulgaria making good white wines, e.g. CHARDONNAY.

PROVENCE region of southern France producing red, white and rosé wines, the rosés being the most common and well-known. The AC areas of the region include BANDOL, BELLET, CASSIS, CÔTES DE PROVENCE and PALETTE. Wines from this region are steadily improving in quality.

PRÜFUNGSNUMMER *see* AMTLICHE PRÜFUNGS-NUMMER.

PRÜM renowned wine-making family of WEHLEN in the MOSEL-SAAR-RUWER region of Germany and owners of the exceptional Wehlener Sonnenuhr vineyard.

PUGLIA (APULIA) major wine-growing region of southeast Italy, producing large quantities of strong, heavy red wines and indifferent whites, with some exceptions, notably CASTEL DEL MONTE and MOSCATO DI TRANI.

PUISIEULX CHAMPAGNE vineyard of the Canton de Verzy in the Champagne region of France. Classified 100 percent in the CIVC rating for white grapes.

PUISSEGUIN-SAINT-EMILION village and commune of the SAINT-EMILION district of BORDEAUX producing full-bodied red wines.

PULIGNY-MONTRACHET world-renowned commune of the CÔTE DE BEAUNE district of BURGUNDY producing red and white wines, the dry whites being among the greatest of France. Its best vineyards, of GRAND CRU status, are MONTRACHET, BÂTARD-MONTRACHET, CHEVALIER-MONTRACHET and BIENVENUE-BÂTARD-MONTRACHET.

PÜNDERICH village of GROSSLAGE Vom Heissen Stein in the BEREICH of BERNKASTEL in the MOSEL-SAAR-RUWER region of Germany. Produces good RIESLING wines.

PUNGENT tasting term for a wine which is very aromatic, often earthy.

PUNT term for the indentation in the bottom of wine bottles which was originally the result of hand-blowing. Now it is useful for collecting sediment or using as a thumb-hold when pouring.

PUPILLIN village of the JURA region of France near ARBOIS, making white wines and in good years VIN JAUNE.

PUTTONYO bucket used in Hungary for measuring the quantities of grapes used for TOKAJI wines. The grapes are specially selected, and the number of puttunyos indicated on the bottle label is an indication of quality.

PUY-BLANQUET, CHÂTEAU GRAND CRU of SAINT-EMILION in BORDEAUX.

PX *see* PEDRO XIMENEZ.

PYRENÉES-ORIENTALES VIN DE PAYS area of Roussillon in southern France producing large amounts of red and white wines of good value.

Q

QbA abbreviation for *Qualitätswein Bestimmter Anbaugebiete*, a German category of quality wines from a particular area. It comes above Tafelwein and Landwein but below QmP. To qualify for the legal QbA appellation, wines must be of fine quality and reflect the character of their region of origin and of the grape from which they are made. They must also have a minimum level of 7.5 degrees alcohol content and come from one of the 11 official ANBAUGEBIETE of Germany. They have a SWEETNESS RATING of 4. Qualifying wines are tested and then labelled with an official control number (AMTLICHE PRÜFUNGSNUMMER).

QmP abbreviation for *Qualitätswein mit Prädikat* (literally 'quality wine with special attributes or distinction'), the top category of German wines. QmP wines are subjected to strict quality control in the vineyard and the winery. No adding of sugar to ferment to higher alcohol levels (CHAPTALIZATION) is allowed, and the wines are categorized according to sweetness/potential alcohol determined by the OECHSLE scale under six designations: KABINETT, SPÄTLESE, AUSLESE, BEERENAUSLESE, TROCKENBEERENAUSLESE and EISWEIN. QmP wines also carry an AMTLICHE PRÜFUNGSNUMMER.

QUADY WINERY winery in Madera, California, producing vintage Port-type wine and dessert wine under the Essensia label.

QUALITÄTSCHAUMWEIN German term for the highest grade of Schaumwein (sparkling wine).

QUALITÄTSWEIN German term for quality wines, the QbA and QmP wines from the 11 ANBAUGEBIETE. Quality wines come above Tafelwein.

QUALITÄTSWEIN BESTIMMTER ANBAU-GEBIETE *see* QBA.

QUALITÄTSWEIN MIT PRÄDIKAT *see* QMP.

QUARLES HARRIS & CO. producers of fine vintage PORT in Vila Nova de Gaia in Portugal.

QUARTOUZE small VDQS wine-growing area of LANGUEDOC in the Midi district of southern France.

QUARTS DE CHAUME important vineyard of the COTEAUX DE LAYON district of the LOIRE Valley in western France producing light, sweet white wines with a fairly high alcohol content.

QUINCY AC commune of the LOIRE Valley region of western France producing dry white wines, mainly from SAUVIGNON BLANC.

QUINTA Portuguese word for a farm, used in wine terms to mean a vineyard or wine estate.

QUINTA DE BACALHOA small vineyard at SETÚBAL owned by Joao PIRES.

QUINTA DO CORVAL vineyard belonging to Real Companhia Vinicola do Norte de Portugal, PORT producers in the DOURO region.

QUINTA DO NOVAL vineyard and company of the DOURO region of Portugal producing PORT.

R

RABAUD-PROMIS, CHÂTEAU GRAND CRU sweet white SAUTERNES from BORDEAUX.

RABIGATO grape variety used in Portugal in the production of WHITE PORT.

RABLAY-SUR-LAYON commune of the COTEAUX DE

LAYON district of the **LOIRE** Valley in western France producing white wines.

RABOSO red wine from the Raboso grape, produced near Venice in the **VENETO** province in Italy.

RABOSO DEL PIAVE astringent red wine from the **VENETO** region of northern Italy.

RACKING process performed during winemaking and ageing, in which the wine is drained from one barrel to another, leaving behind the sediment. Racking may be performed several times.

RADGONSKA RANINA sweet white wine from Yugoslavia, sold under the Tigrovo Mljeko (Tiger's Milk) label.

RAFANELLI WINERY small winery in the **SONOMA** region of California producing good varietal wines, including **CABERNET SAUVIGNON**, **ZINFANDEL** and **GAMAY**.

RAHOUL, CHÂTEAU wine from the **GRAVES** district of **BORDEAUX**. Château to watch as wines are improving.

RAINWATER term for a type of light, blended **MADEIRA**.

RAMISCO grape variety used in the **COLARES** district of southern Portugal.

RAMONET-PRUDHON domaine producers of **CHASSAGNE-MONTRACHET** commune in **BURGUNDY**, known particularly for their good white Burgundies. They also produce fine red wines.

RANCIO term having various meanings, all referring to a quality of taste associated with **SHERRY**-type wines caused by slow oxidation in large oak barrels not filled to capacity. In California it refers to food cooked in sweet dessert wines and in Spain to the nutty flavour of Sherry. It also refers to the strong taste of **MADEIRA**-type wines and in France it specifically refers to certain sweet dessert wines produced in **BANYULS** and at **CHÂTEAU-CHALON**.

RANDERSACKER village of GROSSLAGE Ewig Leben in the BEREICH of MAINDREIECK in the FRANKEN region of Germany. One of the best wine-villages of the region.

RAPOSEIRA quality producers of good, dry sparkling wines made by the CHAMPAGNE METHOD in the Dão and DOURO regions of northern Portugal.

RASTEAU village in the southern RHÔNE VALLEY in southern France producing both fortified sweet dessert wines and CÔTES DU RHÔNE wines including good red wines.

RATAFIA DE CHAMPAGNE sweetened apéritif.

RATTI producer in the PIEMONTE region of Italy making BAROLO wines by modern methods.

RAUENTHAL important village of GROSSLAGE Steinmacher in the BEREICH of JOHANNISBERG in the RHEINGAU region of Germany. Produces very high quality wines.

RAUSAN-SEGLAS, CHÂTEAU deuxième GRAND CRU wine from the MARGAUX commune of BORDEAUX.

RAUZAN-GASSIES, CHÂTEAU deuxième GRAND CRU wine from the MARGAUX commune of BORDEAUX.

RAVELLO village in the CAMPANIA district of southern Italy producing red, white and rosé wines.

RAVENEAU producer of CHABLIS wines, making several good GRAND CRU and PREMIER CRU wines.

RAYA designation found only in Spain, indicating a coarse kind of OLOROSO Sherry.

RAYAS, CHÂTEAU estate of CHÂTEAUNEUF-DU-PAPE in the Rhône Valley area of eastern France. One of the best Châteauneufs.

RAYMOND VINEYARDS winery and vineyards in the NAPA VALLEY region of California producing varietal wines including CHARDONNAY, ZINFANDEL and CABERNET SAUVIGNON.

RAYNE-VIGNEAU, CHÂTEAU PREMIER GRAND CRU SAUTERNES from BORDEAUX in southwest France.

RCATZITELI Russian white-wine vine used in northern Bulgaria to make dry wines.

RD abbreviation for (1) REGIÃO DEMARCADA; (2) *Récemment dégorgé*. These initials on a CHAMPAGNE label show it is a wine in which the yeast sediment deposited during the second fermentation has been left for some time to produce a richer wine.

REBELLO VALENTE brand name of VINTAGE PORT shipped by Robertson Bros. of Vila Nova de Gaia in Portugal.

RÉCEMMENT DÉGORGÉ *see* RD.

RECIOTO Italian term for wine produced from the ripest grapes, often dried.

RECIOTO DELLA VALPOLICELLA red DOC wines produced in the VENETO region of northeast Italy from partially dried selected grapes. They have a TASTE RATING of E. The *Amarone* style is dry and the *Amabile* style sweet.

RECIOTO DI GAMBELLARA sweet still, semi-sparkling and sparkling DOC white wines produced in the VENETO region of northeast Italy.

RECIOTO DI SOAVE white sweet DOC wine produced in the VENETO region of northeast Italy.

RÉCOLTANT MANIPULANT *see* RM.

RÉCOLTE French term for wine crop or vintage.

REDBROOK brand name of wines produced by Evans and Tate in the Swan Valley area of Western Australia.

RED INFURIATOR brand name of a strong red wine from Algeria.

RED WINE type of WINE made from black grapes which are fermented with the skin and pips. The longer these are in contact with the wine the stronger the COLOUR and the TANNIN will be.

REFOSCO full-bodied dry red DOC wine from the FRIULI-VENEZIA-GIULIA region of northeast Italy.

REGALEALI brand name of a range of good red and white wines produced by Conte Tasca d'Almertia in Sicily.

REGIÃO DEMARCADA (RD) Portuguese term for a demarcated region, part of the DO system and similar to an AC area.

RÉGNIÉ village hoping to become the tenth BEAUJOLAIS CRU. Because of its lower status, its wines represent good value for money.

REH, FRANZ leading export merchants in the MOSEL-SAAR-RUWER region of Germany.

REHOBOAM large CHAMPAGNE bottle with a capacity equivalent to six normal bottles.

REICHENSTEINER hybrid white-wine grape grown in England.

REIL village of GROSSLAGE Vom Heissen Stein in the BEREICH of BERNKASTEL in the MOSEL-SAAR-RUWER region of Germany.

REIMS capital of the Champagne region of northwest France which, along with ÉPERNAY, is at the centre of the CHAMPAGNE industry. Many leading houses, e.g. Pommery, Piper-Heidsieck, Taittinger, Ruinart and Mumm have their headquarters there.

REINE PÉDAUQUE, LA NÉGOCIANTS of BEAUNE in BURGUNDY and owners of Domaine de la Juvinière in the CÔTE DE NUITS district.

REMOISSENET PÈRE & FILS NÉGOCIANTS and owners of a small PREMIER CRU estate in BEAUNE in BURGUNDY.

RÉMY PANNIER leading NÉGOCIANTS and growers in the LOIRE Valley in western France.

RESERVA term used on the labels of Spanish wines to show they have been aged for a certain period depending on the style of wine and the area. In RIOJA red wine will have been aged for a minimum of three years. The same term is used in Chile for wines aged for four years.

RÉSERVE term often found on French wines, often in conjunction with *Spéciale*. It has no legal meaning.

RESIDUAL SUGAR tasting term for wines which are not quite dry. Sugar above about 5 grams per litre can usually be tasted.

RESS BALTHASAR growers and merchants in the RHEINGAU region of Germany with interests in a large number of good vineyards.

RETSINA white and rosé wines from Greece to which pine resin has been added. They have an unusual resinous taste which goes well with some Greek cuisine.

RETZ important wine-making centre of the WEINVIERTEL district of Austria.

REUILLY AC district of the LOIRE, France, producing mostly light dry white wines and some reds and rosés.

REYNELLA town and wine region of the Southern Vales area near Adelaide in South Australia producing a wide range of varietal wines. **Château Reynella** is a leading winery producing quality varietal wines and Australia's finest VINTAGE PORT.

RHEIN German spelling of Rhine.

RHEINART, ADOLF wine-growers of the MOSEL-SAAR-RUWER region of Germany. Part-owner of the Ockfener-Bockstein, Geisberg, Herrenberg and Feils vineyards, Ockfener-Bockstein being the top vineyard.

RHEINBURGENGAU BEREICH of the MITTELRHEIN region of Germany.

RHEINGAU one of the 11 officially designated ANBAU-GEBIETE of Germany on the right bank of the River Rhine, west of Frankfurt and south of Wiesbaden. It produces a few red wines and the finest white wines of the country, the whites being characteristically heavy and fruity. The major grape variety is RIESLING and great wines come from the villages of RAUENTHAL, ERBACH, HATTENHEIM, HALLGARTEN and RUDESHEIM and the vineyards of SCHLOSS VOLLRADS and Hasensprung, amongst others in the BEREICH of JOHANNISBERG.

RHEINHESSEN German ANBAUGEBIET lying between the Rivers Nahe and Rhine, south of RHEINGAU. It is the second largest of the 11 wine regions, with Alzey, Bingen, Mainz and Worms being the major centres. A wide variety of grapes is used to produce mainly fruity, floral, medium-bodied and medium-sweet wines. Most wines of the region also carry a GROSSLAGE or EINZELLAGE name.

RHEINPFALZ German ANBAUGEBIET bordering France on its west and RHEINHESSEN to the north. Home of some of Germany's finest vineyards, the area is famous for its very fruity, floral wines which have body and good depth of flavour. Known in English as the Palatinate.

RHEINRIESLING Austrian variety of the RIESLING grape. Also grown in Czechoslovakia and Hungary, and in Australia and New Zealand where it is called **Rhine Riesling** and makes wines with a SWEETNESS RATING of 4.

RHINE WINES general English term for wines grown along the River Rhine in Germany.

RHODES Greek wine-producing island in the Aegean Sea, off the coast of Turkey, its best known wine being a dry white named LINDOS.

RHODT village of GROSSLAGE Ordensgut in the BEREICH of SÜDLICHE WEINSTRASSE in the RHEINPFALZ region of Germany.

RHÔNE VALLEY region of southeast France along the River Rhône. Some excellent wines are produced, including CÔTE ROTIE, CONDRIEU, CROZES-HERMITAGE, HERMITAGE, CORNAS, CHÂTEAUNEUF-DU-PAPE, GIGONDAS, VACQUEYRAS and BEAUMES DE VENISE. The majority of wines in this large region are blended and sold as CÔTES DU RHÔNE. The region is highly regarded for its robust reds, delicate rosés and full-bodied whites which have a SWEETNESS RATING of 2. The southern location ensures plenty of sunlight throughout all but the worst vintages, and consequently the region is more consistent in quality than most other French vineyard areas. Rhône Valley wines usually represent good value.

RIBATEJO area of Portugal to the north of Lisbon, producing strong, full-bodied red wines and a large quantity of white.

RIBEAUVILLE commune and wine town in the region of ALSACE in northeast France producing RIESLING wines.

RIBEIRO DEL DUERO DO region of GALICIA in northern Spain producing sparkling VINHO VERDE-type wines. Its long-established cooperative makes good reds with a TASTE RATING of D.

RIBOLLA GIALLA white-wine grape grown in the FRIULI-VENEZIA-GIULIA region of northeastern Italy.

RICEYS, ROSÉ DES AC rosé produced in small quantities in the south of the CHAMPAGNE region of France and made only from PINOT NOIR grapes.

RICH tasting term for a full-bodied, fruity, rounded wine with intense flavour.

RICHE French word for 'rich'. When used of CHAMPAGNE it describes the sweetest category.

RICHEBOURG, LE GRAND CRU vineyard of the VOSNE-ROMANÉE commune in the CÔTE DE NUITS district of

BURGUNDY. Produces full and velvety red wines, one of Burgundy's finest.

RIDGE VINEYARDS vineyard in the SANTA CRUZ area of California producing excellent ZINFANDEL and CABERNET SAUVIGNON wines.

RIECINE wine producers in the TUSCANY region of northwest Italy. Their DOC is CHIANTI CLASSICO.

RIED Austrian term for a good single vineyard.

RIESLANER white-wine grape variety, a cross between RIESLING and SYLVANER, used extensively in Alsace in France and in the Mosel and Rhine regions of Germany. Also grown in many other countries.

RIESLING the noble white-wine grape variety of Germany but also planted the world over, often with different names, e.g. Rhine Riesling in Australia, Riesling Renano in Italy, Johannisberg Riesling in the US. The most famous Rieslings come from Germany where the variety accounts for over 20 percent of all vines planted, and also produces good wines with a SWEETNESS RATING of 2 in ALSACE. Riesling has a distinctive, delicate, fruity flavour and can be made in many styles, ranging from dry wines to NOBLE ROT-infected dessert wines.

RIESLING ITALICO white-wine grape variety grown in Italy. Despite the name, it is not the same as the German Riesling which is called Riesling Renano.

RIESLING RENANO fine white DOC wine produced in the FRIULI-VENEZIA-GIULIA region of northern Italy from German RIESLING grapes.

RIEUSSEC, CHÂTEAU PREMIER GRAND CRU sweet white SAUTERNES from BORDEAUX.

RILLY-LA-MONTAGNE CHAMPAGNE vineyard of the Canton de Verzy in the Champagne region of France. Classified 94 percent in the CIVC rating for black grapes.

RIOJA DO region of northern Spain producing red, white and rosé wines. The region consists of the districts RIOJA ALTA, RIOJA BAJA, and RIOJA ALAVESA. Rioja's red table wines are arguably the best in Spain and have a lovely oaky flavour. Rioja reds have a TASTE RATING of C, while RESERVA reds aged for three years have a TASTE RATING of D. Rioja whites have a SWEETNESS RATING of 2.

RIOJA ALAVESA one of the three subregions of RIOJA to the northwest of the region. Along with RIOJA ALTA it produces the best wines.

RIOJA ALTA northwest subregion of the RIOJA in northern Spain. Produces some of the best of the region's wines.

RIOJA BAJA largest subregion of RIOJA, producing ordinary, sometimes rough table wines. The reds are fairly strong and the whites, both sweet and dry, are of lesser quality than the reds. Wines in bottles labelled RESERVA or Reserva Especial are good but may be over-aged, when they tend to dry out, losing their fruit flavours.

RIOJANAS BODEGAS wine producers in the RIOJA ALTA region of Spain producing a range of wines including the RESERVA wines Viña Albina and Monte Real, and Albina (sweet white), Medieval (dry white) and Conchales (red).

RIOJA SANTIAGO wine-producers in the RIOJA ALTA region of northern Spain producing red and sweet or dry white wines under the name Yago.

RIO NEGRO province of Argentina, southwest of Buenos Aires and south of Mendoza, producing light dry and sparkling white wines.

RIPEAU, CHÂTEAU GRAND CRU wine from the SAINT-EMILION district of BORDEAUX.

RIQUEWIHR town and commune in ALSACE in northeast France producing white wines, the RIESLING wines being the best.

RISERVA Italian term for DOC wines which have been aged for a specified number of years, usually three.

RIUNITE very large group of cooperatives and exporters of the EMILIA-ROMAGNA region of northern Italy. Their DOC is LAMBRUSCO REGGIANO.

RIVANER name used in Luxembourg for the MÜLLER-THURGAU grape.

RIVAZ village and vineyard area of the Lavaux region of Switzerland.

RIVESALTES district of Haut-Roussillon near Perpignan in southwest France producing sweet fortified wines from the Muscat and Malvoisie grapes. *See also* MUSCAT DE RIVESALTES.

RIVIERA DEL GARDA red and rosato DOC wines produced in the LOMBARDY region of northern Italy.

RM abbreviation for *Récoltant Manipulant.* These initials on a CHAMPAGNE label show that the producer of the wine is also the grower of the grapes. When accompanied by the terms GRAND CRU or PREMIER CRU they indicate definite quality.

ROBERTSON (1) wine district of the Little Karoo region of South Africa, officially classified as a WO area. (2) vintage PORT shippers of Vila Nova de Gaia in Portugal. VINTAGE ports are sold under the Rebello Valente label and TAWNY Ports under the Game Bird, Privateer, Pyramid, Izaak Walton and Imperial labels.

ROBOLA *see* ROMBOLA.

ROCCA DELLE MACIE wine producer in the TUSCANY region of Italy making excellent CHIANTI and GALESTRO wines.

ROCHE-AUX-MOINES, LA important vineyard of Savannières in the COTEAUX DE LA LOIRE in western France producing fine strong, dry white wines.

ROCHEFORT-SUR-LOIRE commune of the COTEAUX DU LAYON in ANJOU, western France.

RODET, ANTONIN NÉGOCIANTS and growers of MERCUREY in the CÔTE CHALONNAISE in BURGUNDY. Their estate, Château Chamirey, includes most of the PREMIER CRU vineyard Clos du Roi. Both red and white wines are produced.

ROEDERER, LOUIS CHAMPAGNE firm based at REIMS in the Champagne district of France. Produces the superlative Cristal brand.

ROMANÉE, LA (1) PREMIER CRU vineyard of the CHASSAGNE-MONTRACHET commune in the CÔTE DE BEAUNE district of BURGUNDY producing white and red wines; (2) GRAND CRU vineyard of the VOSNE-ROMANÉE commune in the CÔTE DE NUITS district of BURGUNDY producing full-bodied red wines.

ROMANÉE-CONTI, LA famous GRAND CRU vineyard of the VOSNE-ROMANÉE commune in the CÔTE DE NUITS district of BURGUNDY producing very high quality red wines. Regarded as Burgundy's first wine.

ROMANÉE-SAINT-VIVANT GRAND CRU vineyard of the VOSNE-ROMANÉE commune in the CÔTE DU NUITS district of BURGUNDY producing outstanding red wines.

ROMANIA Central European country which is a large producer and exporter of wines. Wine production was nationalized following World War II. The drive for foreign currency has led to state subsidies for wine exports which are controlled by the state-run export company, Vinexport. Strict quality standards are maintained for exported wines, ensuring that only the best wines are shipped. Combined with the subsidies, this has led to the availability of reasonable quality wines at competitive prices. Main grape varieties used include CABERNET SAU-VIGNON, PINOT NOIR and CADARCA for reds and RIESLING, ALIGOTÉ, FETEASCA, MUSCAT and CHARDONNAY.

ROMBOLA (ROBOLA) dry white wine from the Greek island of CEPHALONIA.

ROMER-DU-HAYOT, CHÂTEAU deuxième GRAND CRU sweet white SAUTERNES from BORDEAUX.

RÖMERLAY GROSSLAGE of the BEREICH of SAAR-RUWER in the MOSEL-SAAR-RUWER region of Germany. Includes the wine villages of KASEL, MERTESDORF, TRIER and WALDRACH.

RONCHI, UMANI wine-producers in the MARCHE region of east-central Italy. Their DOC wines include ROSSO CONERO, ROSSO PICENO and VERDICCHIO DEI CASTELLI DI JESI.

ROODEBERG brand name of a blended red wine produced by KWV in South Africa.

ROPITEAU NÉGOCIANTS and growers of MEURSAULT in the BURGUNDY region producing red and white wines. They have interests in a number of top class vineyards, including several PREMIERS CRUS.

ROSADO Spanish term for rosé wine.

ROSATO Italian term for rosé wine.

ROSATO DEL SALENTO rosé wines produced in the Salento peninsula in the PUGLIA region of southern Italy from mainly MALVASIA and NEGROAMARO grapes.

ROSÉ pink or amber-coloured wine, made from red-wine grapes by keeping juice and skins together during fermentation until the required degree of colour has been obtained. True rosés are not a mixture of red and white wine. *See also* VIN GRIS.

ROSÉ CHAMPAGNE style of dry CHAMPAGNE once produced by allowing the juice of red grapes to remain in contact with the skins to extract colour. Nowadays usually made by blending in a red wine.

ROSÉ D'ANJOU type of rosé wine produced in the ANJOU-Saumur district of the LOIRE Valley, France, made from Cot, GAMAY, GROSLOT, and Pineau d'Aunis grapes.

ROSÉ DE BÉARN VDQS rosé wine produced in the Madiran region of the Basse-Pyrénées district of southwest France.

ROSÉ DE LOIRE general appellation of dry rosé wines produced in the LOIRE Valley in eastern France.

ROSÉ DE RICEYS *see* RICEYS, ROSE DE.

ROSEMOUNT winery in the HUNTER VALLEY area of New South Wales, producing a wide range of quality wines.

ROSENTHALER RIESLING brand name of a sweet MISKET wine produced in the KARLOVO region of Bulgaria.

ROSETTE region producing good white wines in the BERGERAC district of southwest France.

ROSEWEIN German term for rosé wines made from skinless red grapes. They are very light in style.

ROSSESE red-wine grape grown in Italy. It produces the rich and fruity DOC wine **Rossese di Dolceacqua** in the LIGURIA region of the Italian Riviera.

ROSSO Italian word for red. Refers to the dry red wines of Italy and also, in the US, to a sweet red wine.

ROSSO CONERO dry, fruity and acidic red DOC wine produced in the MARCHE district of east-central Italy from MONTEPULCIANO and SANGIOVESE grapes.

ROSSO DELLE COLLINE LUCCHESI firm full-bodied red DOC wine produced in the TUSCANY region of northwest Italy. Some white is also produced.

ROSSO PICENO the main red DOC wine produced in the MARCHE district of east central Italy. It is made from MONTEPULCIANO and SANGIOVESE grapes.

ROTGIPFLER Austrian white-wine grape variety, used in the GUMPOLDSKIRCHNER wines.

ROTHBURY ESTATE wine estate in the HUNTER VALLEY district of New South Wales in Australia. Produces good CHARDONNAY, SHIRAZ and SEMILLON wines.

ROTHENBERG EINZELLAGE in the GROSSLAGE Burgweg of the RHEINGAU region of Germany.

ROTLING German term for a rosé wine produced from red and white grapes mixed before crushing and fermentation.

ROTWEIN German term for red wine.

ROTY, JOSEPH growers of GEVREY-CHAMBERTIN in BURGUNDY. Their holdings include PREMIER CRU GEVREY-CHAMBERTIN and CHARMES-CHAMBERTIN.

ROUDON-SMITH VINEYARDS vineyards in the SANTA CRUZ region of California producing varietal wines. Good ZINFANDEL and also CHARDONNAY and CABERNET SAUVIGNON.

ROUGE French word for 'red'.

ROUGE HOMME brand of varietal CABERNET SAUVIGNON, CHARDONNAY and PINOT NOIR wines produced by Lindeman in the HUNTER VALLEY area of New South Wales, Australia.

ROUGET, CHÂTEAU wine from the POMEROL district of BORDEAUX.

ROUGH tasting term for the astringent coarse TANNIN taste in red wines, indicating lack of balance and maturity.

ROUNDED tasting term for a well-balanced wine showing body and fruitiness. Term used of balanced and harmonious wine.

ROUND HILL CELLARS winery in the NAPA VALLEY region of California producing varietal wines. Good CHARDONNAY and CABERNET SAUVIGNON wines.

ROUSSANNE white-wine grape grown in the PROVENCE and RHÔNE VALLEY regions of France.

ROUSSELET DE BÉARN VDQS district of the Pyrenées in southern France.

ROUSSETTE white-wine grape, used in the SEYSSEL wine of the Haut-Savoie district of the upper RHÔNE VALLEY.

ROUSSETTE DE SAVOIE white wines produced from the ROUSSETTE grape in an area of southeast France which includes Ains, SAVOIE, Haut-Savoie and Isère.

ROUSSILLON *see* GRAND ROUSSILLON.

ROZOVA DOLINA Controliran wine area of BULGARIA making mainly white MISKET wines.

RUBBERY tasting term for a wine with a peculiar aroma resulting from HYDROGEN SULPHIDE.

RUBESCO DI TORGIANO red DOC wine produced in the UMBRIA region of Italy.

RUBINO DI CANTAVENNA fresh fullish dry red DOC wine produced in the PIEMONTE region of northwest Italy from mainly BARBERA and GRIGNOLINO grapes.

RUBY CABERNET American hybrid grape developed from the CABERNET SAUVIGNON and CARIGNAN grapes. Grown in California, Australia, Mexico and Israel.

RUBY PORT basic category of PORT, a young, blended wine which is rich, sweet and fruity. Its TASTE RATING is D.

RUCHOTTES-CHAMBERTIN GRAND CRU vineyard of the GEVREY-CHAMBERTIN commune in the CÔTE DE NUITS district of BURGUNDY. Produces some outstanding red wine.

RÜDESHEIM-NAHE famous village of GROSSLAGE Rosengarten in the BEREICH of SCHLOSSBÖCKELHEIM in the NAHE region of Germany. Produces some of the best wine of the region.

RÜDESHEIM-RHEINGAU village of GROSSLAGE Burgweg in the BEREICH of JOHANNISBERG in the RHEINGAU region of Germany producing **Rüdesheimer Berg** RIESLING wines from the slopes of the nearby Rüdesheimer mountain. The vineyards include Berg Rottland, Berg Roseneck, Berg Schlossberg, Bischofsberg and Klosterberg. These wines are among the best of the region in good years.

RUEDA town in the Old Castile-León region of central Spain producing strong, white, aromatic DO wines with a SWEETNESS RATING of 2.

RUFFINO wine producers in the TUSCANY region of north-west Italy. Their DOC wines include CHIANTI, Chianti Classico and ORVIETO.

RUFINA subregion of the CHIANTI region of TUSCANY east of Florence, producing good quality wines.

RUINART CHAMPAGNE firm based in REIMS in the Champagne region of France.

RUIZ-MATEOS ZOILO SHERRY producers in the JEREZ region of southern Spain producing a range of fine Sherries under the Don Zolio label.

RULÄNDER German name for the PINOT NOIR grape. Also known as Tokay Grauerburgunder and Tokaier. Also grown in Austria, Australia, France (in Alsace), Italy, Luxembourg, Switzerland and Romania.

RULLY commune of the CHALONNAIS district of BURGUNDY producing red and white, still and sparkling wines of good value, the whites being superior to the reds. Rully has its own AC.

RUMASA large group which owns a number of SHERRY-producing firms in Spain.

RUPPERTSBERG village of GROSSLAGE Hofstuck in the BEREICH of MITTELHAARDT in the RHEINPFALZ region of

Germany. Produces outstanding strong fruity **Ruppertsberger** wines. Its best vineyard is that of Hoheburg.

RUSSIA *see* USSR.

RUSSIAN RIVER VALLEY subdistrict of SONOMA in California producing quality table wines. Growing in importance as quality improves.

RUST important wine area of BURGENLAND in southeastern Austria making good quality **Ruster Ausbruch**, a very sweet white wine.

RUTHERFORD HILL WINERY vineyards in the NAPA VALLEY region of California producing varietal wines including CHARDONNAY and GEWÜRZTRAMINER.

RUTHERFORD AND MILES MADEIRA wine shippers.

RUTHERGLEN region of Victoria in southern Australia producing some red table wines and good fortified and dessert wines including excellent liqueur MUSCAT and TOKAY wines.

RUWER *see* MOSEL-SAAR-RUWER, SAAR-RUWER.

RUZICA rosé wine produced in Yugoslavia.

S

SAARBURG village of GROSSLAGE Scharzberg in the BEREICH of SAAR-RUWER in the MOSEL-SAAR-RUWER region of Germany.

SAAR-RUWER BEREICH of the MOSEL-SAAR-RUWER region of Germany including Trier and the Saar and Ruwer river valleys. Produces light, and, in good years, great wines. The best come from the village of OCKFEN and from the SCHARZHOFBERG vineyard near Wiltingen.

SABLANT brand name of a dry CRÉMANT DE LOIRE wine.

SABLES DU GOLFE DU LION Vin de pays area of Provence making good wines sold under the Listel name. It contains the largest vineyard in France.

SACK old English name for sweet Sherry.

SACRAMENTO VALLEY wine-growing region of California producing mostly table and dessert wines.

SADOVA town in southwestern Romania producing a medium-sweet rosé wine.

SAINT-AMOUR one of the nine Beaujolais cru villages producing light, fruity wines, best drunk when young.

ST-ANDRÉ CORBIN, CHÂTEAU estate of Montagne-Saint-Emilion in Bordeaux.

SAINT-AUBIN commune of the Côte de Beaune district of Burgundy producing mostly white wines. They are good value for money, and the bulk of them are sold as Saint-Aubin, Saint-Aubin Côte de Beaune or Côte de Beaune-Villages. Its premier cru vineyards include Les Champlot, En Remilly and La Chatenière.

SAINT-AUBIN-DE-LUIGNE commune of the Coteaux du Layon in the Anjou district of the Loire Valley in France producing dry white wines.

SAINT-BRIS village of the Chablis region of central France producing excellent Sauvignon Blanc wines.

SAINT CHINIAN good VDQS table wine from the Coteaux du Languedoc in southern France.

SAINT CLEMENT VINEYARDS vineyards in the Napa Valley region of California producing varietal wines including good Chardonnay and Cabernet Sauvignon.

SAINTE-CROIX-DU-MONT district of Bordeaux producing sweet white wines.

SAINTE CHAPELLE VINEYARDS large vineyards and winery in Idaho State, US, producing Riesling, Gewürztraminer, Chardonnay and Merlot wines.

SAINT-EMILION famous wine village and region situated close to the Dordogne river in the eastern area of BORDEAUX, east of the city of Bordeaux, the two being separated by the ENTRE-DEUX-MERS region. Saint-Emilion is celebrated for its full, rich, powerful wines which have complexity and finesse. MERLOT is the major grape with varying amounts of MALBEC, CABERNET SAUVIGNON and Cabernet Franc making up the blends. Some of the best châteaux include Magdelaine, La Gaffelière, Pavie, Cheval Blanc, and Ausonne.

SAINT-ESTÈPHE commune of the HAUT-MÉDOC district of BORDEAUX producing good to excellent red wines, characteristically full, fairly heavy and fruity. The best vineyards are Châteaux Cos-d'Estournel, Montrose and Calon-Ségur.

SAINT-FOY-LA-GRAND district at the eastern extremity of BORDEAUX producing sweet white wines similar to those of MONBAZILLAC.

ST-GALL label of the Union Champagne cooperative in Avize in the CHAMPAGNE region of France.

SAINT-GEORGES-SAINT-EMILION commune of the SAINT-EMILION district of BORDEAUX producing wines similar to those of Saint-Emilion itself.

ST HENRI CLARET good red wine from PENFOLD'S in South Australia.

ST JEAN, CHÂTEAU winery at Kenwood in the SONOMA region of California, producing mostly still and sparkling white wines.

SAINT-JEAN-DE-MINERVOIS, MUSCAT DE sweet fortified AC wines produced in the region of MINERVOIS in the south of France.

SAINT-JOSEPH full-bodied red and white AC wines produced in the CÔTES DU RHÔNE district of southern France.

SAINT-JULIEN important commune of the HAUT-MÉDOC district of BORDEAUX. Its best vineyards include Châteaux Leóville-Poyferre, Leóville-Barton, Durfort Vivens and Gruaud-Larose.

SAINT-LAMBERT-DU-LATTAY commune of the COTEAUX DU LAYON district of ANJOU in the Loire Valley in France producing sweet white wines.

SAINT LAURENT (1) commune of the HAUT-MÉDOC district of BORDEAUX. Its best vineyards include Châteaux la Tour-Carnet, Belgrave and Carmensac; (2) red-wine grape grown in Austria, Czechoslovakia and Germany.

SAINT-MICHAEL (SANKT MICHAEL) GROSSLAGE of the BEREICH of BERNKASTEL in the MOSEL-SAAR-RUWER region of Germany.

SAINT-NICOLAS-DE-BOURGUEIL AC area of the TOURAINE district of the Loire Valley in France producing red and rosé wines.

ST PANTELEIMON sweet white wine produced in Cyprus.

SAINT-PÉRAY AC district of the RHÔNE VALLEY in France producing sweet and dry white wines and full-bodied sweet and dry sparkling wines, sold as Saint-Peray Mousseux.

SAINT-POURÇAIN small subregion and commune of the upper LOIRE, producing red, white and rosé wines.

SAINT-ROMAIN village of the CÔTE DE BEAUNE district of BURGUNDY producing good-value red and white wines. Some of its output is sold as CÔTE DE BEAUNE-VILLAGES.

SAINT-SAPHORIN important village and vineyards of the LAVAUX district of Switzerland.

SAINT SAUVEUR village and commune of the HAUT-MÉDOC region of BORDEAUX.

SAINT-SEURIN-DE-CADOURNE commune north of SAINT-ESTÈPHE in the MÉDOC district of BORDEAUX.

SAINT VÉRAN AC commune of the MÂCONNAIS district of BURGUNDY producing white wines similar to POUILLY-FUISSÉ. If not as good, the wines are certainly much cheaper.

SAKAK Controliran wine area of BULGARIA producing MERLOT wines.

SAKAR Controliran wine area of BULGARIA making CABERNET SAUVIGNON wines.

SALES, CHÂTEAU DE wine from the POMEROL district of BORDEAUX.

SALICE SALENTINO red and rosato DOC wines produced in the PUGLIA region of southern Italy, made from NEGROAMARO grapes.

SALMANAZAR large glass bottle equivalent to 12 ordinary bottles, normally used for CHAMPAGNE.

SALON LE MESNIL small CHAMPAGNE firm in Le Mesnil-sur-Oger in the Champagne region of France producing only vintage BLANC DE BLANCS wines of excellent quality.

SALTA wine-producing province of northern Argentina.

SALVAGNIN generic name for the fruity red wines produced in the VAUD district of Switzerland.

SAMOS Greek island and controlled name for wines grown on the island, notably the sweet MUSCAT.

SAMPERI *see* MARSALA.

SAMPIGNY-LES-MARANGES vineyard of the commune of Sampigny in the CÔTE DE BEAUNE district of BURGUNDY producing red and white wines. Most are sold as CÔTE DE BEAUNE, but the better wines are labelled with the vineyard names Sampigny-les-Maranges or Sampigny-les-Maranges-Clos du Roi.

SAN BENITO COUNTY area of California, south of Santa Clara, producing varietal wines.

SANCERRE district of the LOIRE Valley in France producing quality dry white wine with a SWEETNESS RATING of 1 from the SAUVIGNON BLANC grape.

SANDALFORD important vineyard of the SWAN VALLEY in Western Australia.

SANDEMAN large Port and Sherry growers and shippers of Vila Nova de Gaia in the DOURO region of Portugal.

SANDWEIN wine from the SEEWINKEL district of BURGENLAND in Austria. So called because the vines are grown in sandy soil.

SANFORD & BENEDICT VINEYARDS vineyards in the SANTA BARBARA region of California producing varietal wines. Their PINOT NOIR and CHARDONNAY are excellent.

SANGIOVESE quality red-wine grape variety with large plantings throughout central Italy. It is used for the production of VINO NOBILE DI MONTALCINO and is a major constituent of CHIANTI. It is also used to make the DOC wines **Sangiovese d'Aprilia**, red and rosé wine from the LATIUM region, and **Sangiovese di Romagna**, a red wine from the EMILIA-ROMAGNA region.

SANGRE DE TORO brand name of a rich red wine made by TORRES in Spain.

SANGRIA Spanish punch consisting of red wine and fruit juice with added sugar and soda or water and decorated with fruit slices.

SANGUE DI GIUDA sparkling sweet red DOC wine produced in OLTREPÒ PAVESE in the LOMBARDY region of northern Italy.

SAN JOAQUIN VALLEY *see* CENTRAL VALLEY.

SAN JUAN wine-producing province of Argentina.

SANKT MAGDALENER German name for SANTA MADDALENA.

SANLÚCAR DE BARRAMEDA important wine-town in the JEREZ region of Spain where MANZANILLA is produced.

SAN LUIS OBISPO vineyard area of California south of Santa Clara producing VARIETAL wines.

SAN MARINO tiny wine-producing country within Italy producing sweet, sparkling Moscato dessert wine, and red table wine from SANGIOVESE grapes.

SAN MARTIN WINERY winery of the SANTA CLARA district of the central coast region of California producing varietal wines, some of them internationally acclaimed. Also produces varietal dessert wine.

SAN PASQUAL VINEYARDS vineyards in the San Diego area of California producing varietal wines.

SAN SADURNI DE NOYA Spanish town in CATALONIA where CAVA sparkling wines are produced.

SAN SEVERO dry white, red and rosé DOC wines from the PUGLIA region of southeast Italy.

SANTA BARBARA district of southern California, northwest of Los Angeles, producing quality varietal wines.

SANTA CLARA district of California south of San Francisco Bay producing mostly table wines.

SANTA CRUZ district of the central coast area of California, south of San Francisco, producing good VARIETAL wines.

SANTA CRUZ MOUNTAIN VINEYARD vineyards in the SANTA CRUZ district of California producing varietal wines, especially PINOT NOIR.

SANTA MADDALENA (SANKT MAGDALENER) good red DOC wine produced in the TRENTINO-ALTO ADIGE region of Italy.

SANTAREM-JOÃO SANTAREM grape grown in the COLARES district of Portugal.

SANTA YNEZ VALLEY WINERY vineyards in the SANTA BARBARA region of California producing varietal wines, particularly whites. The best is SAUVIGNON BLANC.

SANTENAY commune of the CÔTE DE BEAUNE district of BURGUNDY producing mostly red and some white wines.

SANTORIN sweet and dry wines from the Greek island of **Santorini**, the sweet wines sometimes being labelled Vino Santo, and the dry white Thira.

SAPERAVI Russian red-wine grape, also grown in Bulgaria.

SAPPY term for a wine tasting of the sap from wooden barrels.

SARDINIA Italian island producing red, white and rosé wines which are strong and mostly sweet. A great deal of dessert wine is also produced. DOC wines include Cannonau di Sardegna, Malvasia di Bose, Nuragus di Cagliari, Vermentino di Gallura and Vernaccia di Oristano.

SASSELLA red DOC wine produced in the VALTELLINA district of LOMBARDY in northern Italy, made from NEBBIOLO grapes.

SASSICAIA very good CABERNET SAUVIGNON from Bolgheri in the TUSCANY region of northwestern Italy. Regarded by many as Italy's finest wine.

SAUMUR district of ANJOU in northwest France producing still and sparkling wines. The still wines are of good quality and range from dry to slightly sweet. Sold either as Saumur or Coteaux de Saumur. Reds have a TASTE RATING of B and whites a SWEETNESS RATING of 1. The best red is **Saumur-Champigny**.

SAUSAL WINERY winery in Alexander Valley in the SONOMA region of California producing VARIETAL wines.

453

SAUSSIGNAC, CÔTES DE AC white wines produced in the Dordogne region of southwest France. The better wines of the area may be labelled BERGERAC.

SAUTERNES region in southern BORDEAUX producing the world's finest sweet white wines made from a blend of SEMILLON, SAUVIGNON BLANC and MUSCADELLE grapes, usually affected by NOBLE ROT. Sauternes wines have a SWEETNESS RATING of 8. They are rich, full, luscious and complex and require many years of keeping to show at their best. The top château is the remarkable Château d'Yquem which has its own classification of GRAND PREMIER CRU. Other excellent producers include Châteaux Rieussec, Guiraud, de Rayne Vigneau and Suduiraut.

SAUVIGNON BLANC high quality white-wine grape grown in Bordeaux, Graves and the Loire Valley in France and also in California, Chile, New Zealand, Israel and Australia. It is used for dry, medium-sweet and sparkling wines, among them the renowned SANCERRE and POUILLY FUMÉ wines. It is quite easy to detect because of the crisp 'grassy' high-acid character it imparts to its wines. Its strong varietal character is even more concentrated when vines are grown in a cool-climate region. The style produced in the US and Australia is called Fumé Blanc to describe its 'smokey' flavour.

SAUVIGNON-DE-ST BRIS VDQS white wine from the Yonne district of BURGUNDY, made from Sauvignon Blanc grapes.

SAUVION ET FILS growers of Anjou-Saumur in the LOIRE Valley, France, and owners of Château du Cleray, growing mostly Muscadet.

SAUZET ETIENNE estate of PULIGNY-MONTRACHET in BURGUNDY with holdings in some excellent vineyards, including PREMIER CRU Puligny.

SAVAGNIN Swiss name for the white-wine grape Traminer (Gewürztraminer). Also grown in Alsace and the Jura in France and in Germany.

SAVENNIÈRES village of the Anjou-Saumur district of the LOIRE Valley in France producing strong dry wines; the best of the region. Its best vineyards include La Coulée de Serrant and La Roche-aux-Moines.

SAVIGNY-LES-BEAUNE commune of the CÔTE DE BEAUNE district of BURGUNDY producing red and white wines. Most are sold as Savigny-les-Beaune or Savigny-Les-Beaune-Côtes de Beaune and the best are labelled with the vineyard name, the PREMIERS CRUS being Dominode, Jarrons, Lavières, Marconnets and Vergelesses.

SAVOIE Alpine area of France bordering Italy and Switzerland and producing the dry light wines typical of a cooler region. Its wines include SEYSSEL and ROUSETTE.

SAVUTO strong red DOC wine from the CALABRIA region of southern Italy, made from the Arvino grape.

SCHAFFHAUSEN wine-producing canton of Switzerland, its best wines being produced in the Stein-am-Rhein district.

SCHAFISER wines from Schafis, one of the best vineyards of the Neuchâtel district of western Switzerland.

SCHARLACHBERG vineyard of BINGEN in GROSSLAGE Sankt Rochuskapelle in the BEREICH of Bingen in the RHEINHESSEN region of Germany. Produces very good white wines.

SCHARZBERG vineyard of OBEREMMEL in the BEREICH of SAAR-RUWER in MOSEL-SAAR-RUWER Germany.

SCHARZHOFBERG wine-estate at WILTINGEN in GROSSLAGE Scharzberg in the BEREICH of SAAR-RUWER in the MOSEL-SAAR-RUWER region of Germany. Produces some of the best Saar wines.

SCHAUMWEIN German term for low-price sparkling wine.

SCHEUREBE hybrid white-wine grape developed from the SYLVANER and RIESLING. Grown in Germany and England.

SCHIAVA red-wine grape grown mostly in the ALTO ADIGE area of the TRENTINO-ALTO ADIGE region of Italy.

SCHILCHER red-wine grape used for rosé production in the Styria district of southern Austria.

SCHILLERWEIN rosé wine produced in the WÜRTTEMBERG region of Germany, made from red and white grapes.

SCHLOSS German word for a castle or wine-estate, equivalent to the French CHÂTEAU.

SCHLOSSABZUG German term meaning 'bottled at the SCHLOSS'.

SCHLOSSBÖCKELHEIM BEREICH of the NAHE region of Germany; includes the well-known village of **Schloss Böckelheim** in GROSSLAGE Burgweg which produces some of the best wines of the region.

SCHLOSS JOHANNISBERG great vineyard of the RHEINGAU region of Germany, situated in BEREICH Johannisberg. Produces the region's best and most expensive wine which is graded with a yellow seal for estate-bottled Qualitätswein; a red seal for QMP average KABINETT; an orange seal for higher quality Kabinett; a green seal for average SPÄTLESE; a white seal for high quality Spatlese; a pink seal for average AUSLESE; a light blue seal for higher quality Auslese; and a gold seal for BEERENAUSLESE and TROCKENBEERENAUSLESE.

SCHLOSS REICHARTSHAUSEN castle and small vineyard near HATTENHEIM in GROSSLAGE Gottesthal in the BEREICH of Johannisberg in the RHEINGAU region of Germany.

SCHLOSS REINHARTSHAUSEN estate in Erbach of GROSSLAGE Deutelsberg in the BEREICH of JOHANNISBERG in Germany's RHEINGAU region.

SCHLOSS SCHÖNBORN large producers in HATTENHEIM in the RHEINGAU region of Germany with a big range of wines and interests in a number of vineyards.

SCHLOSS STAUFENBERG wine producers in DURBACH in the BADEN region of Germany, mostly producing dry Rieslings and also some sweet wines.

SCHLOSS VOLLRADS estate of GROSSLAGE Honigberg in the BEREICH of JOHANNISBERG in the RHEINGAU region of Germany producing some of the best Rhine wines. These are graded according to their foil bottle top coverings: green for Qualitätswein; blue for QMP Kabinett; pink for SPÄTLESE; white for AUSLESE; gold for Beerenauslese; and gold with a neckband showing a castle for Trockenbeerenauslese. The higher grades of each category have two gold stripes on the foil covering as well as the above colours.

SCHLUCK (1) light, dry wine produced in the WACHAU area of Austria; (2) brand name of a VELTLINER wine made by LENZ MOSER.

SCHLUMBERGER (1) growers and merchants in the ALSACE region of northeast France producing rich, sweet, wood-aged wines; (2) producer of sparkling wine made by the CHAMPAGNE METHOD in Vienna, Austria.

SCHMITT, FRANZ HERMANN producer in NIERSTEIN in Germany's RHEINHESSEN, producing very good RIESLING wines.

SCHMITT, GUSTAV ADOLF wine producers in NIERSTEIN in the RHEINHESSEN region of Germany with a wide range of wines: mostly RIESLING, some QMP but mostly commercial wines.

SCHMITT, H., SOHNE large growers and merchants in the MOSEL-SAAR-RUWER region of Germany producing wines under various brand names.

SCHOLTZ, HERMANOS wine producers of MÁLAGA in southern Spain producing a range of wines. The best-known is the sweet dessert wine Solera Scholtz.

SCHÖNHELL EINZELLAGE in HALLGARTEN, GROSSLAGE Mehrmolzchen, in good years producing some of the best wines of the RHEINGAU region of Germany.

SCHOPPENWEIN German term for rough wine sold by the glass in the RHEINPFALZ region.

SCHORLEMER, FRIEHERR VON wine estate of the MOSEL-SAAR-RUWER region of Germany whose properties include some of the best growths of BRAUNEBERG and ZELTINGEN.

SCHRAMSBERG VINEYARDS well-known winery in the NAPA VALLEY region of California producing sparkling wines.

SCHRÖDER & SCHYLER merchants in BORDEAUX. Owners of Château KIRWAN.

SCHWABSBURG village of GROSSLAGE Auflangen in the BEREICH of NIERSTEIN in the RHEINHESSEN region of Germany.

SCHWEIGEN village of GROSSLAGE Guttenberg in the BEREICH of SÜDLICHE WEINSTRASSE in the RHEINPFALZ region of Germany.

SEBASTIANI VINEYARDS vineyards in the SONOMA region of California with a reputation for good wines.

SEC French word for 'dry' and usually applied to sparkling wines which contain a small but detectable quantity of sugar.

SECCO Italian word for 'dry'.

SÈCHE French term for harsh wines which have been excessively oxidized.

SECO Spanish word for 'dry'.

SECOND WINES wines from many top BORDEAUX châteaux which although good are not their very best and are sold at cheaper (but still not cheap) prices.

SEDIMENT (LEES) solid, harmless particles deposited in wine bottles as the wine ages. Remove before serving by DECANTING.

SEEWEINE (LAKE WINE) wines produced at Lake Constance in the BEREICH of BODENSEE in the BADEN region of Germany.

SEEWINKEL area of the Austrian Lake District producing SANDWEIN.

SEGARCEA vineyard in Romania producing red and white wines, mainly in a sweeter style.

SÉGUR, CHÂTEAU CRU GRAND BOURGEOIS wine from the HAUT-MÉDOC district of BORDEAUX.

SEGURA VIUDAS wine producers in CATALONIA in northeast Spain producing a range of wines including Jean Perico, a sparkling wine sold by Gonzalez Byass. Their best wine is Reserva Heredad.

SEKT German term for sparkling wine of good quality. *See also* DEUTSCHER SEKT.

SÉLECTION DE GRAINS NOBLES term used in ALSACE, northeast France, for wines produced from selected grapes with NOBLE ROT.

SÉLECTION SPÉCIALE French term found on wine labels. It has no legal significance.

SELLA & MOSCA large wine producers in Sardinia producing a variety of wines. They have one of the largest wine estates in Europe.

SELZEN village of GROSSLAGE Gutes Domtal in the BEREICH of NIERSTEIN in the RHEINHESSEN region of Germany.

SEMELI good red wine from Haggipavlu in Cyprus.

SEMILLON white-wine grape widely used in southwest France and also grown in Argentina, Australia, California, Chile, Israel, Japan, Mexico, Portugal, Tunisia, Uruguay and Yugoslavia. It is famous for the part it plays in the production of SAUTERNES, in conjunction with the SAUVIGNON BLANC grape, when it is frequently affected with NOBLE ROT. It also produces excellent dry wines in many regions including the HUNTER VALLEY region of New South Wales. Semillon wine from here improves for many years in the bottle and develops great character and complexity. It is the red-wine drinker's white wine.

SEMI-SECO Spanish term for medium dry.

SÉNÉJAC, CHÂTEAU CRU BOURGEOIS wine from the HAUT-MÉDOC district of BORDEAUX.

SEÑORIO DE SARRIA wine producer in the NAVARRA region of Spain, making good red wines.

SEPPELT large winery in the BAROSSA VALLEY area of South Australia and in Victoria.

SERBIA second-largest wine-producing region of Yugoslavia producing mostly ordinary wines for local consumption.

SERCIAL approved grape used in the production of high quality **Sercial Madeira**, an almost dry wine with a SWEETNESS RATING of 2, excellent as an apéritif.

SERRADAYRES dry red table wine from the RIBATEJO area of southern Portugal.

SERRIG village of GROSSLAGE Scharzberg in the BEREICH of SAAR-RUWER in the MOSEL-SAAR-RUWER region of Germany producing some good wines.

SETÚBAL barrel-aged MUSCAT wine produced near Lisbon in Portugal.

SEVILLE ESTATE highly regarded estate at Seville in Victoria, Australia. Their CHARDONNAY and RIESLING wines are considered to be their best.

SÈVRE-ET-MAINE area of the MUSCADET district of Brittany in northern France, in which the best and the most of the district's wine is produced.

SEYSSEL light fruity white from the SAVOIE region of France. Sparkling Seyssel is made by the CHAMPAGNE METHOD.

SEYVAL BLANC hybrid grape developed from French and American vines.

SFORSATO good, strong red table wine from the LOMBARDY region of northern Italy. Those labelled RISERVA have been aged for four years.

SFW (STELLENBOSCH FARMERS' WINERIES) large wine-producers of STELLENBOSCH in the Cape region of South Africa producing dry and semi-sweet red and white wines under a range of trade names.

SHAFER VINEYARDS vineyards in the NAPA VALLEY region of California producing VARIETAL wines.

SHARP tasting term for an agreeable and harmonious wine, the opposite of astringent, harsh or rough.

SHERRY renowned fortified wine produced in the Andalusia region of Spain around the city of JEREZ de la Frontera. Its production is controlled by the government quality DO laws which classify wines according to the region of production and type of soil. Areas with white chalky Albariza soil produce the finest wines. Soils with Barros soil produce fuller, less delicate Sherry, and the sandy Arenas soils produce a lesser product in great quantity. Two major grape varieties are used, PALOMINO and PEDRO XIMINEZ. Palomino makes the finest Sherry and Pedro Ximinez is dried on straw mats after picking to concentrate the sugar and flavour as a sweetener for sweeter styles. Brandy is added to the base wine and the mix is put into barrels for blending by the SOLERA system. In the barrel some wines develop a FLOR yeast which causes the characteristic flavour of flor Sherries. Barrels that do not attract this yeast are used for less delicate, fuller styles. Different vintages are blended, allowing a consistent style and level of quality. The styles of Sherry are AMONTILLADO, AMOROSO, CREAM, FINO, MANZANILLA and OLOROSO. Sherry is one of the best wine bargains.

SHIRAZ noble red-wine grape variety grown in South Africa and Australia where it produces wines with a TASTE RATING of E. See SYRAH.

SHOWN VINEYARDS vineyards in the NAPA VALLEY region of California producing varietal wines.

SHUMEN see SUMEN.

SICHEL owners of Château Angludet and part owners of Château Palmer in the HAUT-MÉDOC district of BURGUNDY.

SICILY wine-producing Italian island producing red and white wines and dessert wines. Sicily's DOC wines include Alcamo, Cerasuolo di Vittoria, Corvo di Casteldaccia, Etna, Malvasia di Lipari, Mamertino, Marsala, Moscato di Noto, Moscato di Pantelleria and Moscato di Siracusa.

SIEVERING wine-village near Vienna in Austria producing HEURIGEN wines.

SIGALAS-RABAUD, CHÂTEAU PREMIER GRAND CRU SAUTERNES from BORDEAUX.

SILLER WINE Hungarian red wine made from a mixture of red and white grapes; similar to rosé but more richly coloured. See also SCHILLERWEIN.

SILLERY CHAMPAGNE vineyard of the Canton de Verzy in the Champagne region of France. Classified 100 percent in the CIVC rating.

SILVANER *see* SYLVANER.

SILVERADO CELLARS winery in the NAPA VALLEY region of California producing varietal wines.

SILVER OAK CELLARS winery in the NAPA VALLEY region of California producing a CABERNET SAUVIGNON which is aged for three years in the wood and for a further two in the bottle.

SIMI WINERY winery in the SONOMA region of California producing varietal wines.

SIMONE, CHÂTEAU wine producers of PROVENCE in southern France producing red and white AC wines.

SIN CRIANZA Spanish term meaning a wine has not been aged in wood. *See also* CRIANZA.

SINGLE QUINTA PORT second-highest style of PORT after VINTAGE, made from grapes from one estate. It is matured for two years before bottling, and needs some years in the bottle.

SION centre of the VALAIS district of Switzerland, well-known for white FENDANT wines.

SIPON (CHIPON) white-wine grape variety grown in SLOVENIA in Yugoslavia. Sometimes found on LJUTOMER wine labels.

SIRAH (SYRAH) red-wine grape grown in the RHÔNE district of France and elsewhere. Known in Australia as SHIRAZ. *See* SYRAH.

SIRAN, CHÂTEAU CRU BOURGEOIS SUPÉRIEUR wine from the MARGAUX commune of BORDEAUX.

SITGES town in the PENEDÈS district of Spain, near Barcelona, producing mostly strong, sweet wines.

SIZZANO dry red DOC wine produced in the PIEMONTE region of northwest Italy.

SLOVENIA major wine-growing region of Yugoslavia producing red, white and rosé wines, the white LJUTOMER table wines being the best-known outside Yugoslavia. The best-known red wine is KRASKI from the ISTRIA district of Slovenia.

SMEDEREVKA white-wine grape grown in Yugoslavia and used in the better white wines of the Smederevo and Macedonia districts.

SMITH-HAUT-LAFITTE, CHÂTEAU GRAND CRU wine from the GRAVES district of BORDEAUX in southwest France producing top quality red and white wines.

SMITH-MADRONE VINEYARDS vineyards in the NAPA VALLEY region of California producing good varietal wines.

SMITH WOODHOUSE PORT producers in Vila Nova De Gaia in the DOURO region of Spain, producing VINTAGE wines. They also ship under the Gould, Campbell label.

SOAVE dry, smooth white DOC wine produced in the Verona district of the region of VENETO in northeast Italy. *See also* RECIOTO DI SOAVE.

SOCIANDO-MALLET, CHÂTEAU CRU GRAND BOURGEOIS wine from the HAUT-MÉDOC district of BORDEAUX.

SODAP large SHERRY firm at the port of LIMASSOL in Cyprus.

SOFT tasting term for wine with a pleasing finish without being hard or aggressive. Usually applied to wines low in acid and slightly sweet. Wine may lose its hardness or roughness, either through ageing or as a result of the particular grape varieties used. Some soft wines may mature fairly quickly.

SOKAL BLOSSER WINERY large winery in the Williamette Valley, Oregon, producing varietals and blends.

SOLAR DI SAMANIEGO brand name of soft light red wines made by Bodegas Alavesas in RIOJA ALAVESA.

SOLERA the system of progressive blending in tiers of small casks used in the maturation of Spanish SHERRY and other fortified wines. The best wines are stored for very long periods. The young wine is stored in the top tier, and as the matured wine in the bottom tier is drawn off from time to time, the casks are topped up with wine from the tier above. In this way younger wines eventually acquire the characteristics of the older wine; thus the wines are periodically refreshed yet maintain their original high standard. MADEIRA and MÁLAGA may undergo the Solera process. The average age of a Madeira treated in this way is 80 years.

SOLOPACA red and white wines produced in the CAMPANIA district of northwest Italy.

SOMLOI registered wine district of the BALATON area of Hungary making excellent white wines from FURMINT and RIESLING grapes, designated 'outstanding quality'.

SOMMELIER French word for 'wine waiter'.

SONNENBERG (1) vineyard near Eltville am Rhein of GROSSLAGE Steinmacher in Germany's RHEINGAU region; (2) vineyard in the BEREICH of SAAR-RUWER in the MOSEL-SAAR-RUWER region; (3) vineyard near Norheim in GROSSLAGE Burgweg, BEREICH Schloss Bockheim in the NAHE region of Germany.

SONNENGLANZ important vineyard in ALSACE in northeast France producing good quality wines.

SONNENKÜSTE brand name of a medium-sweet white wine produced in the Black Sea area of Bulgaria.

SONNENUHR (1) vineyard of WEHLEN in the BEREICH of BERNKASTEL in the MOSEL-SAAR-RUWER region of Germany; (2) vineyard of ZELTINGEN-RACHTIG in the BEREICH of BERNKASTEL.

SONOMA wine-producing region of California, situated north of San Francisco, with the Mayacamas Mountains separating it from the NAPA VALLEY. Sonoma produces premium quality wines from mainly VITIS VINIFERA grape varieties. Emerging subregions producing some of the best wines include Russian River Valley, Alexander Valley, Sonoma Valley and Dry Creek.

SONOMA VINEYARDS large vineyard holdings in northern California, partly owned by Piper-Heidsieck. Its traditional-method sparkling wines are among the best in California.

SONSTIGE vine grown extensively in the BADEN region of Germany.

SOPRON registered wine-district of Hungary producing officially designated 'excellent quality' red wines.

SORNI red and white wine produced in the TRENTINO-ALTO ADIGE district of Italy.

SOUR tasting term for a wine which is disagreeably acid. The opposite is FLAT. It is used of wine which has turned vinegary due to excessive ACETIC ACID.

SOUSSANS commune of the HAUT-MÉDOC district of BORDEAUX producing red wines. Soussans has a right to the AC MARGAUX.

SOUTARD, CHÂTEAU GRAND CRU wine from the SAINT-EMILION district of Bordeaux.

SOUTO VEDRO dry, slightly sparkling wine from the AMARANTE district of the VINHO VERDE region of Portugal.

SOUVERAIN WINERY winery in the NAPA VALLEY region of California, producing varietal wines.

SPAIN European country which is the world's third largest producer of wine, with an ancient tradition. Wine production is widespread with most regions making some wines for local consumption and many exporting. Spain has been famous for its incomparable SHERRY wines for centuries but has only recently gained recognition for its outstanding table wines. The red wines of the RIOJA region with their characteristic oaky flavour and smooth texture have had an enormous impact in the UK and created much interest in Spanish wines generally. Wines from other regions such as NAVARRA and PENEDÈS are of very good quality and are now widely available. As new winemaking technology is introduced there will be rapid improvements in the quality of white wines which at present generally fall below reds for quality and consistency. The recent introduction of the *Denominación de Origen* (DO) appellation system on French lines should ensure ever-improving quality of wine throughout Spain.

SPANNA name used in the PIEMONTE region of northwest Italy for the NEBBIOLO grape. Also the name of a red wine produced in the region.

SPARKLING BURGUNDY red, white and rosé BURGUNDY wines of varying quality which have been rendered sparkling by the secondary fermentation method.

SPARKLING WINE wine containing CARBON DIOXIDE gas, introduced by secondary fermentation (*see* CHAMPAGNE METHOD), by bottling under pressure or by carbonating (*see* CARBONATED WINES).

SPÄTBURGUNDER German vine descended from the French PINOT NOIR and used extensively in the AHR region of northwest Germany. Also grown in the regions of BADEN, FRANKEN, RHEINGAU, RHEINHESSEN, RHEINPFALZ and WÜRTTEMBERG.

SPÄTLESE German term for naturally sweet QmP wines produced from late-picked grapes which have more concentrated sugar. They must have a minimum sweetness/potential alcohol level of 76 degrees OECHSLE. Made in Austria and the RHEINGAU, RHEINHESSEN and RHEINPFALZ regions of Germany.

SPÄTROT Austrian white-wine grape, also known as Zierfandler.

SPICY tasting term for a wine with a natural piquant taste, such as those made from GEWÜRZTRAMINER grapes.

SPINDLER vineyard owners with properties in FORST, DEIDESHEIM, RUPPERTSBERG and WACHENHEIM.

SPITZENWEIN Austrian term for fine wines.

SPRING MOUNTAIN VINEYARDS vineyard of the NAPA VALLEY region of California producing varietal wines.

SPRITZER German term for a mixture of HOCK and soda in the proportions 1:2. Used as a light refreshment.

SPRITZIG German term for a wine which causes a slight fizzing on the tongue, indicating the presence of some carbon dioxide bubbles but insufficient to produce any froth in the glass. The approximate French equivalent is PÉTILLANT, the Italian FRIZZANTE.

SPUMANTE Italian word for 'sparkling', used for sparkling wines.

SQUINZANO red wine produced in the PUGLIA region of southeast Italy.

STAATLICHER HOFKELLER vineyards in Würzburg in the FRANKEN region of Germany producing dry and semi-dry white wine.

STAATSWEINGUT German term for state-owned wine estate.

STAG'S LEAP WINE CELLARS vineyards in the NAPA VALLEY region of California producing varietal wines. Their Bordeaux-style CABERNET SAUVIGNON is particularly good.

STALKY tasting term for a wine with an unpleasant flavour and hardness caused by too much contact of the TANNIC stalks with the grapes during pressing.

STANLEY LEASINGHAM winery in the CLARE district of South Australia producing varietal wines.

STEEN local name for the CHENIN BLANC grape grown in the Cape region of South Africa. **Steendruif** is its Afrikaans version.

STEIGERWALD BEREICH of the FRANKEN region of Germany.

STEIN term used in South Africa for medium-dry white wines.

STEINBERG (1) vineyard of BAD DÜRKHEIM in the BEREICH of MITTELHAARDT in the RHEINPFALZ region of Germany; (2) famous vineyard of HATTENHEIM in the BEREICH of JOHANNISBERG in the RHEINGAU region. Produces some of the best RHEINGAU wines; (3) vineyard of DALSHEIM in the BEREICH of NIERSTEIN in the RHEINHESSEN region; (4) wine-producing area of the Danube region of lower Austria, properly called ZISTERSDORF.

STEINWEIN white wine from the FRANKEN region of Germany, properly from the Würzburger Stein vineyard.

STEIERMARK *see* STYRIA.

STELLENBOSCH official WO district of the Cape region of South Africa.

STELLENBOSCH FARMERS' WINERY *see* SFW.

STELLENRYCK range of wines sold by Bergkelder in STELLENBOSCH, South Africa.

STEMMY tasting term for the aroma and taste of red wines which have been in contact with stems damaged during crushing.

STERLING VINEYARDS winery in the NAPA VALLEY region of California, owned by Coca Cola. It makes a good range of varietal wines.

STIFT German word for a monastery or religious building.

STILL WINE non-sparkling table wine or non-sparkling CHAMPAGNE.

STONEGATE WINERY winery in the Napa Valley, California, producing varietal wines.

STONY HILL VINEYARD vineyard in the NAPA VALLEY region of California, producing high quality white wines.

STOP FERMENTATION process of adding alcohol to fermenting grape juice to prevent the completion of fermentation, resulting in wines with residual sugar.

STRAVECCHIO Italian term for very old wine.

STRAW WINE wine made from grapes which have been sun-dried on straw mats.

STUCK WINE wine which finished fermenting before the sugar was fully converted into alcohol. Extra yeast must be added to convert the remaining sugar to alcohol. If this is not done the wine will be sweeter than intended.

STURDY non-complimentary tasting term for robustness or heartiness in a wine.

STUTTGART wine town of GROSSLAGE Weinsteige in the BEREICH of Remstalstuttgart in the BADEN-WÜRTTEMBERG region of Germany.

STYRIA (STEIERMARK) wine-producing province of southern Austria. Its better-known vineyards include Deutschlandsberg (producing SCHILCHER wine), Feldbach, Furstenfeld, Hartberg, Hitzendorf, Ligist, Mureck, Radkersburg and Steinz.

SÜDLICHE WEINSTRASSE BEREICH of the RHEINPFALZ region of Germany. Its outstanding wine villages include DEIDESHEIM, FORST, KONIGSBACH, RUPPERTSBERG and WACHENHEIM.

SUDUIRAUT, CHÂTEAU PREMIER GRAND CRU SAUTERNES from BORDEAUX.

SUHINDOL wine town and cooperative in northern Bulgaria producing good CABERNET SAUVIGNON wines.

SULPHIDE *see* HYDROGEN SULPHIDE.

SULPHUR DIOXIDE *see* SULPHURIZATION, SULPHUROUS.

SULPHURIZATION practice of treating wine with sulphur dioxide to kill bacteria, slow down fermentation and prevent oxidation. If too much is added, an off odour can result.

SULPHUROUS tasting term for a wine with too much sulphur dioxide. It is detected at the back of the nose on the first or second sniffs and may be tasted if present in excessive quantity.

SUMEN (SHUMEN) town in eastern Bulgaria; large producer of white wines.

SUNGARLARE town and Controliran area of eastern BULGARIA, producing a dry MISKET wine.

SUPÉRIEUR(E) French word for 'superior', used particularly in BORDEAUX classification.

SUPERIORE Italian word for 'superior'. On a wine label it indicates extra alcohol but not necessarily superior quality.

SUPPLE tasting term for a quality of liveliness in a young, usually red wine.

SUR LIE French term (literally 'on the lees') for sediment allowed to remain in a wine before bottling to add extra flavour e.g. MUSCADET SUR LIE.

SÜSSDRUCK Swiss term for wine produced from selected grape bunches. Same as the German AUSLESE.

SÜSS RESERVE German term for grape juice which has not been fermented and is used to sweeten fermented wines.

SUTTER HOME WINERY winery in the NAPA VALLEY region of California.

SVISHTOV reputable winery in northern BULGARIA producing CABERNET SAUVIGNON wines under Controliran regulations.

SWAN, JOSEPH, VINEYARDS winery in the SONOMA area of California, producing varietal wines.

SWAN VALLEY major wine-production area on the northern edge of Perth, the first wine-producing area of Western Australia.

SWARTLAND demarcated WO district of Cape Province in South Africa.

SWEET tasting term for a wine which is more than fruity and distinctly sweet because of the presence of sugar.

SWEETNESS RATING series of codes devised by the Wine Development Board to categorize the sweetness level of white and rosé wines. It also covers fortified wines. The codes run from 1 to 9; the lower the number the drier the wine will be. Examples of wines from each code are 1 MUSCADET and SANCERRE wines; 2 CHARDONNAY wines, dry SHERRY; 3 AMONTILLADO Sherry, HALBTROCKEN German wines; 4 ANJOU Rosé, German KABINETT wines; 5 LIEBFRAUMILCH; 6 DEMI-SEC sparkling wines and German SPÄTLESE; 7 ASTI SPUMANTE and German AUSLESE; 8 SAUTERNES and BEERENAUSLESE; and 9 TROCKENBEERENAUSLESE and MÁLAGA. *See also* TASTE RATING.

SWEET WINES wines sweetened either artificially by the addition of sugar, juice or sweeter wines, or naturally, by stopping the fermentation process before all the sugar has been converted to alcohol. Some wines are made from specially selected overripe grapes with a concentrated sugar content. In Germany such wines are labelled AUSLESE, BEERENAUSLESE or TROCKENBEERENAUSLESE. In France they include the sweet wines of BARSAC and SAUTERNES. *See also* SWEETNESS RATING.

SWELLENDAM official WO area of South Africa.

SWITZERLAND European country producing wines of good quality. Because of strong home demand and relatively limited production small quantities are exported, and high land and production costs mean they are rather expensive. The CHASSELAS grape is used for the bulk of white-wine production, along with the SYLVANER, known in Switzerland as the Johannisberger. PINOT GRIS and Marsanne are also used to a lesser extent. Most red wines are produced from PINOT NOIR, GAMAY and MERLOT grapes. Wine is made in almost all the cantons, the main ones being VAUD, VALAIS, NEUCHÂTEL and TICINO.

SYCAMORE CREEK vineyards in the SANTA CLARA region of California.

SYLVANER German white-wine grape of merit and widely used, being grown in Argentina, Australia, Austria, Bulgaria, California, Czechoslovakia, France, Germany, Luxembourg, Switzerland, the USSR and Yugoslavia. It produces sound fruity wines in average vintages and excellent wines of great concentration and ripeness in the top years. Also known as Silvaner, Franken Riesling and Österreicher.

SYRAH excellent red-wine grape grown in Algeria, Australia, France, South Africa, Switzerland and the US. In its home area of the RHÔNE VALLEY it produces full-bodied wines with intense colour and wonderful, deep, complex flavours. It often has a distinct 'peppery' nose and palate. Although used for blending in CHÂTEAUNEUF-DU-PAPE, it is capable of fine-wine quality alone. Australian examples have created much interest recently in the UK because of the great depth of rich fruit at value-for-money prices. It is also grown with success in the US. The TASTE RATING of Syrah red wines is D. Also known as SHIRAZ, SIRAH.

SZEKSZARDI registered wine-district of Hungary producing officially designated 'excellent quality' full-bodied red wines mainly from KADARKA grapes.

SZURKEBARAT white-wine grape grown in Hungary, related to the PINOT GRIS.

T

TABLE WINE ordinary still wine normally drunk with meals. In the US a table wine must have less than 14 per cent of alcohol per volume. *See also* TAFELWEIN, VIN DE TABLE, VINO DA TÀVOLA.

TÂCHE, LA superlative GRAND CRU vineyard of the commune Vosne-Romanée in the CÔTE DE NUITS district of BURGUNDY. The La Tâche name also incorporates the neighbouring Les Gaudichots, and La Grande Rue.

TAFELWEIN German term for table wine, as distinct from QUALITATSWEIN. The lowest level of the German APPELLATION system, it must have in excess of 8.5 per cent alcohol and is labelled after the name of the river near which it is made. Tafelwein may also be blended from wines from other EEC countries.

TAGLIO Italian term for blended wine.

TAHBILK, CHÂTEAU vineyard in Victoria, southern Australia, producing excellent red and white table wines. Many Australian wineries have copied the French vineyard house name.

TAITTINGER CHAMPAGNE firm based at Reims in the Champagne region of France.

TALBOT, CHÂTEAU quatrième GRAND CRU wine from the SAINT-JULIEN commune in BORDEAUX.

TALTARNI vineyard and winery in Victoria, Australia, producing varietal wines. The reds are considered the best.

TAMIANKI sweet white dessert wine from Bulgaria.

TAMIIOASA white-wine grape variety grown in Romania.

TANNAT red-wine grape grown in Madiran in southwest France.

TANNIC tasting term for a wine that is coarse or too astringent because of an excess of TANNIN.

TANNIN organic constituent of wine, found in greater quantities in reds than in whites. It has an important effect on the palate, giving fullness of body and astringency (grip) to dry reds while in sweet wine it helps to cover the sugar. An excess of tannin makes light dry white wines too big in body and too coarse and in reds creates a hard, overly astringent quality. It affects the length of maturation of wine: a full-bodied red high in tannin requires a longer period than a lighter-bodied wine in order to obtain the same degree of improvement.

TARGOVICHTE non-state winery in Bulgaria producing sweet and medium-sweet white wines.

TARIK red blended wine from North Africa (Tunisia, Algeria and Morocco).

TARRAGONA demarcated area of the CATALONIA region of eastern Spain producing dry and dessert red and white wines, including **Tarragona Port**.

TART tasting term for a wine too high in acid.

TARTARIC ACID the principal acid in wine, derived from the grape, which helps to prevent bacterial formation, preserve stability and colour and give the wine an element of sharpness.

TASKELDER range of wines sold by SFW in South Africa.

TASMANIA wine-producing island state of Australia. At present, production is on a small scale, and weather conditions may prove not to be ideal for consistently good wines. However, some superb CHARDONNAY and CABERNET SAUVIGNON wines and quality PINOT NOIR are currently being produced.

TASTE RATING series of five codes devised by the Wine Development Board to categorize the level of body, the colour and TANNIN content of red wines. The codes run from A to E, the lightest bodied wines being A, and the fullest E. Examples of wines from each code are A BEAUJOLAIS red, French VIN DE TABLE, Italian VINO DA TAVOLA; B BEAUJOLAIS CRU, PINOT NOIR wines, VALPOLICELLA; C RIOJA reds and Bulgarian CABERNET SAUVIGNON; D BAIRRADA and CHÂTEAUNEUF-DU-PAPE; and E BAROLO and SHIRAZ wines from Australia and South Africa. *See also* SWEETNESS RATING.

TASTEVIN French term for a flat silver cup with raised indentations used for wine tasting, particularly in Burgundy. Silver reflects more light than glass in the dim surroundings of wine cellars.

TAURASI strong red wine produced in the CAMPANIA region of southwest Italy.

TAVEL area of the RHÔNE VALLEY in France producing well-known full-bodied rosé wine with a SWEETNESS RATING of 1.

TAWNY (1) tasting term for wines which have turned from red to brownish during maturation; (2) top quality LATE-BOTTLED style of PORT matured in wood casks for up to ten years.

TAYLOR old-established PORT-shipping company.

TAYLOR CALIFORNIA CELLARS winery in MONTEREY, California, producing VARIETAL and generic wines.

TAYLOR WINE COMPANY wine company owned by Coca Cola in the FINGER LAKES district of New York State, producing blended wines.

TEARS *see* LEGS.

TEDESCHI wine producer of the VENETO region of Italy, producing red and white wines including good quality VINI DA TÀVOLA and RECIOTO wines.

TE MATA ESTATE winery in HAWKE'S BAY, New Zealand, producing good varietal wines. It is the oldest winery in New Zealand.

TEMPERATURE an important factor when serving wine. Ideally, wines should be served at the temperature in which they were stored and tasted by the bottler, i.e. 9 degrees C (48 F) for white wines and 13 degrees C (55 F) for red. The reduction in temperature of white wines may be hastened by an ice bucket or fridge, but red wines should be left in room temperature for as long as necessary and not be warmed quickly.

TEMPRANILLO red-wine grape variety grown in the RIOJA region of Spain and in Argentina.

TENUTA Italian word for a farm or estate. On a wine label it indicates that a wine comes from a particular vineyard or estate.

TENUTA DI CAPEZZANA major wine producer of CAR-MIGNANO in the TUSCANY region of Italy.

TERAN red-wine grape grown in Yugoslavia. Used in the making of Kraski Teran in Istria.

TERLANER white DOC wines produced in the TRENTINO-ALTO ADIGE region of northeast Italy. The best wines also carry the name of the grape. The village of **Terlano** is one of the best white-wine areas of the region.

TERMENO D'AVIO white Traminer wine produced in the TRENTINO-ALTO ADIGE region of Italy.

TEROLDAGO good red DOC wines produced in the TRENTINO-ALTO ADIGE region of northeast Italy. The best red wines of the region. **Teroldago Rotaliano** wines are dry, full-bodied, slightly bitter red and rosé wines.

TERRA ALTA demarcated area of the CATALONIA region of Spain producing strong red and white wines.

TERRACINA town in the LATIUM region of Italy, best known for a MUSCAT wine.

TERRE DI BAROLO large cooperative producer in the PIEMONTE region of Italy making DOC wines including BARBERA D'ALBA and BAROLO.

TERROIR French word for 'earthy', used particularly of the flavour of wine. *See also* GOÛT.

TERTRE, CHÂTEAU DU cinquième GRAND CRU wine from the Médoc district of BORDEAUX.

TERTRE-DAUGAY, CHÂTEAU GRAND CRU wine from the SAINT-EMILION district of BORDEAUX.

TÊTE DE CUVÉE French term for the best wines of a producer in a given area or appellation.

THALLERN village near Gumpoldskirchen in Austria producing good wines of the same name.

THANISCH wine producers in the MOSEL-SAAR-RUWER

region of Germany. Their holdings include the famous Doktor vineyard.

THIN tasting term for a wine lacking in body, almost watery, being low in body, flavour and strength.

TICINO southern canton of Switzerland producing red and white wines of moderate quality. *See also* VITI.

TIERRA DE BARROS DO area of EXTRAMADURA in Spain.

TIGER'S MILK (TIGROVO MLJEKO) *see* RADGONSKA RANINA.

TIGNANELLO dry red wine produced in the TUSCANY region of northwest Italy.

TINTA family of vines used in the making of PORT.

TINTARA vineyard and winery in South Australia producing dry red and PORT-type wines.

TINTILLO Spanish term for red wine, used in Argentina.

TINTO Spanish and Portuguese term for red wine.

TIO PEPE brand name of a dry SHERRY, a world leader in consumption.

TIRAGE *see* LIQUEUR DE TIRAGE.

TIRED tasting term for a wine past its peak for drinking.

TIRNAVE vineyard along the river Tirnave in Romania producing good quality wines, including the well-known Perla de Tirnave, made from a blend of grapes.

TIRNOVO sweet red dessert wine produced in Bulgaria.

TISDALL wine producers in Victoria, Australia, producing varietal wines under the Mount Helen and Picolla Estates labels.

TOCAI (1) white-wine grape varieties used in northern Italy. They include **Tocai Friuliano**, used in FRIULI-VENEZIA-GIULIA; (2) wines made from Tocai grapes. They include **Tocai di Lisona**, a good, light, slightly bitter DOC white wine from VENETO, and **Tocai di San Martino**

della Battaglia, a slightly bitter dry white DOC wine produced in LOMBARDY.

TOKAJI (TOKAY) very fine dessert wine produced in Hungary, in 29 approved villages, and also partly in Czechoslovakia. Hungarian Tokaji is made only from Furmint and Harslevelu grapes affected by NOBLE ROT. When the grapes are dried out, they are known as ASZU grapes and these are selected from the vines for wine-making by several different methods.

TOKAJI ASZU top quality TOKAJI wine, with a SWEETNESS RATING of 7, made by treading dried-out ASZU grapes into a paste and blending it with a MUST of ordinary pressed grapes and stalks. The resulting free-run juice is matured for six or seven years in lightly bunged casks that allow oxidation by a fungus. The wine is graded and labelled according to the number of buckets (PUTTANYOS) of mashed grapes which are added.

TOKAJI ESSENZ TOKAJI wine made by a process in which raisins of the FURMINT grape are drained of some of their juice by heaping them and allowing their own weight to crush the liquid out. The juice is a very rich syrup which is stored in casks for many years. Now used to blend and fill the body of lighter bodied wines.

TOKAJI FORDITAS TOKAJI wine which is made by performing the TOKAJI ASZU process twice, adding fresh MUST to the mashed pulp left over from the original mixture.

TOKAJI MASLAS TOKAJI wine made by racking TOKAJI ASZU or TOKAJI SZAMORODNI wine and filling the barrel with ordinary Tokaji wine.

TOKAJI SZAMORODNI TOKAJI wine made by a process similar to TOKAJI ASZU, except that the grapes are not selected but are 'as grown', i.e. the wine is made according to the degree of ripeness the grapes achieve. Sweet styles have a SWEETNESS RATING of 6.

TOKAJI SZARAZ dry Hungarian TOKAJI wine.

TOKAY (1) English name for TOKAJI wine; (2) white-wine grape grown in Australia for producing ordinary white and dessert wines.

TOKAY D'ALSACE name for the PINOT GRIS grape.

TOLLOT-BEAUT highly respected growers of BEAUNE in BURGUNDY. They have holdings in CHOREY-LES-BEAUNE and in several PREMIERS CRUS of Beaune, Savigny and Aloxe-Corton.

TORBATO DI ALGHERO dry white wine produced on the Italian island of Sardinia.

TORGIANO red and white DOC wines from the UMBRIA region of central Italy.

TORO red wine produced in the Spanish province of Zamora.

TORREMILANOS brand of red wine produced by Bodegas Lopez Penalba in the Old Castile region of northern Spain.

TORRES wine-exporting family based at Villafranca de Penedès in the district of Barcelona in Spain. Torres Gran Coronas and Coronas are widely known brands.

TORRES VEDRAS area of Portugal producing mostly ordinary red and also white and sweet dessert wines. The better whites include Cadaval and Alenquer.

TOSCANA Italian name for TUSCANY.

TOURAINE district of the LOIRE Valley of France, producing red, white and rosé wines, but best known for its whites, especially VOUVRAY. Sparkling wines are labelled **Touraine Mousseux** and slightly sparkling wines **Touraine Pétillant**. The red wines have a TASTE RATING of A, the whites a SWEETNESS RATING of 1. Subdistricts are BOURGUEIL, CHINON, MONTLOUIS, SAINT NICOLAS-DE-

BOURGUEIL, **Touraine-Amboise**, which produces red, white and rosé wines, **Touraine-Azay-Le-Rideau**, which produces good dry white wines from CHENIN BLANC grapes, **Touraine-Mesland**, which makes red, white and rosé wines, and Vouvray.

TOUR-BLANCHE, CHÂTEAU LA PREMIER GRAND CRU sweet white SAUTERNES from BORDEAUX.

TOUR-CARNET, CHÂTEAU LA quatrième GRAND CRU wine from the HAUT-MÉDOC district of BORDEAUX.

TOUR DE BY, CHÂTEAU LA CRU GRAND BOURGEOIS wine from the MÉDOC district of BORDEAUX.

TOUR-DU-PIN-FIGEAC, CHÂTEAU LA GRAND CRU wine of SAINT-EMILION in BORDEAUX.

TOURIGA red-wine grape grown in the DÃO region of Portugal and used in the production of PORT. Also grown in California and Australia.

TOUR-HAUT-BRION, CHÂTEAU LA CRU wine from the GRAVES district of BORDEAUX.

TOURS, CHÂTEAU DES estate of MONTAGNE-SAINT-EMILION in BORDEAUX.

TOURS-SUR-MARNE CHAMPAGNE vineyard of the Canton d'Ay in the Champagne region of France producing red and white wines. Classified 100 percent (red) and 90 percent (white) in the CIVC rating.

TRABEN TRARBACH two villages of GROSSLAGE Schwarzlay in the BEREICH of BERNKASTEL in the MOSEL-SAAR-RUWER region of Germany.

TRAISEN area of the NAHE region of Germany producing very fine Rieslings.

TRAISKIRCHEN wine town near Gumpoldskirchen south of Vienna in Austria, producing spicy wines.

TRAKIA light table wine from Bulgaria.

TRAMINER white-wine vine grown mainly in Alsace in France and in Germany. Also grown in Australia, Austria, California, Czechoslovakia, Hungary, Italy, Luxembourg, New Zealand, Romania, Russia, South Africa, and Yugoslavia. Produces wines with a spicy taste.

TRAMINER AROMATICO DE TRENTINO dry white DOC wine from Gewürztraminer grapes, produced in the TRENTINO-ALTO ADIGE region of Italy.

TREBBIANO the most widely planted white-wine grape variety in Italy, producing vinous rather than fruity wines. Occasionally Trebbiano is blended with red wines because of its high natural acidity. Also known as UGNI BLANC in France. Three dry white DOC wines made from it are **Trebbiano d'Abruzzo** from the ABRUZZI region, **Trebbiano d'Aprilia** from LATIUM, and **Trebbiano di Romagna** from EMILIA-ROMAGNA.

TREFETHEN VINEYARDS vineyard in the NAPA VALLEY region of California, producing excellent varietal wines, including superlative CHARDONNAY and good PINOT NOIR, and a good quality cheaper range of wines, e.g. Eshcol White and Red.

TRENTADUE VINEYARD winery and vineyards in the SONOMA region of California producing dry, strong, full-bodied wines.

TRENTINO-ALTO ADIGE region of northern Italy bordering Austria in the north, Switzerland in the east and Lombardy in the south. Trentino, the southern part of the region, produces the best reds; Alto Adige to the north contains part of the Tyrol and makes good red and white wines from German and Italian grape varieties. The DOC system names grapes rather than regions and Alto Adige wine labels are often in German as well as Italian.

TRENTO city on the Adige river in northern Italy, giving its name to the Trentino district of the TRENTINO-ALTO ADIGE region. It produces the best red wines of the region.

TRÉPAIL CHAMPAGNE vineyard of the Canton de Verzy in the Champagne region of France. Classified 95 percent in the CIVC rating.

TREPPCHEN EINZELLAGE of GROSSLAGE Michelsberg in the BEREICH of BERNKASTEL in the MOSEL-SAAR-RUWER region of Germany.

TRIER largest wine city of the MOSEL-SAAR-RUWER region of Germany, producing reasonable quality white wines. Trier is in GROSSLAGE Römerlay in the BEREICH of SAAR-RUWER.

TRIMBACH, F.E. growers and NÉGOCIANTS in the ALSACE region of northern France producing fine dry wines, their Rieslings being particularly good. Their wines are classified, in ascending order: Standard, Reserve and Reserve Personnelle.

TRIMOULET, CHÂTEAU GRAND CRU wine from the SAINT-EMILION district of BORDEAUX.

TRITTENHEIM village of GROSSLAGE Michelsberg in the BEREICH of BERNKASTEL in the MOSEL-SAAR-RUWER region of Germany. Its best vineyards include Apotheke and Altarchen.

TROCKEN German word for 'dry' and the official name for wines with less than nine grams of unfermented sugar per litre. These wines have a SWEETNESS RATING of 2.

TROCKENBEERENAUSLESE German term for wine made from grapes that have been allowed to dry on the vine and are then individually selected. Sweetest of the six QMP categories, its wines must have a sweetness/potential alcohol level of more than 150 degrees OECHSLE. The SWEETNESS RATING is 9.

TROLLINGER red-wine grape grown in the WÜRTTEM-BERG region of Germany. Also called Blauer Malvasier in RHEINPFALZ.

TRONQUOY-LALANDE, CHÂTEAU CRU BOURGEOIS wine from the SAINT-ESTÈPHE commune in BORDEAUX.

TROPLONG-MONDOT, CHÂTEAU GRAND CRU wine from the SAINT-EMILION district of BORDEAUX.

TROUSSEAU red-wine grape grown in California and in the JURA district of France.

TUALATIN VINEYARDS winery in the Williamette Valley, Oregon, specializing in white wines and good PINOT NOIR.

TULBAGH wine-producing district of the Cape region of South Africa producing dry and semi-sweet table wines.

TULLOCH wine estate in the HUNTER VALLEY region of New South Wales in Australia.

TUNISIA wine-producing country which has seen a major reduction of acreages under vines in recent years. State-run cooperatives are endeavouring to raise the standards of wine exported. Tunisia is best known for sweet muscat styles, but agreeable reds and good rosés are also produced.

TURCKHEIM wine town in the region of ALSACE in north-east France. Its best vineyard is Brand.

TURGEON & LOHR wine producers of SANTA CLARA in California. Their RIESLING is particularly good.

TURKEY country with vast acreages under vine, with most of the produce sold as table grapes for both home and export markets. The wines produced are of fair to good quality and represent excellent value. A country to watch, par-ticularly if it joins the EEC. Tekel is the biggest wine pro-ducer and Dolucais is one of the most respected.

TUSCANY (TOSCANA) major wine-producing region of

northern west-central Italy. The CHIANTI hills, home of the famous DOCG wine, lie in the central part of the region between Florence and Siena, and southwest of Siena are Montalcino and Montepulciano, around which are grown two more DOCG wines, the superb BRUNELLO DI MONTALCINO and VINO NOBILE DI MONTEPULCIANO. Good white DOC wines, such as GALESTRO and VERNACCIA DI SAN GIMIGNANO, are also produced, and the region also makes the foritified VIN SANTO.

TYRRELL'S vineyard in the HUNTER VALLEY region of New South Wales, Australia, producing a wide range of good to excellent wines. One of the oldest wineries in the state, it produces excellent SEMILLON and CHARDONNAY wines.

U

UGNI BLANC white-wine grape grown in south of France, Algeria, Argentina, California, Italy, Mexico and Tunisia. Also known as TREBBIANO and SAINT-EMILION.

ULLAGE term for the space between the top of a bottle or cask and the wine contained in it. When used as a tasting term it may indicate a faulty cork and damage to the wine.

ÜLVERSHEIM village of GROSSLAGE Krotenbrünnen in the BEREICH of NIERSTEIN in the RHEINHESSEN region of Germany producing quality strong full-bodied wines.

UMBRIA region of central Italy bounded by TUSCANY, LATIUM and MARCHE, producing mostly white wines. Its best-known wine is ORVIETO from the north of the region, and other good wines include the DOC wines COLLI DEL TRASIMENO and TORGIANO.

UNGSTEIN village of Grosslage Honigsackel in the Bereich of Mittelhaardt in the Rheinpfalz region of Germany.

UNIDOR abbreviation for *Union des Coopératives Vinicole de la Dordogne*, a union of 13 cooperatives in Bergerac and Lot-et-Garonne in southwest France, producing red and white wines.

UNION WINE producers and merchants of Paarl in the Cape region of South Africa producing Bellingham and Culemborg wines.

UNITED KINGDOM *see* English wine.

UNITED STATES major wine-producing country with vineyard regions widespread throughout many of its states, growing a wide variety of both Vitis vinifera and native varieties. To date the best wines have come from the west coast states of California and recently Oregon and Washington. However, many other states are rapidly improving quality and further plantings of *Vitis vinifera* will reduce the gap in quality.

ÜRZIG village of Grosslage Schwarzlay in the Bereich of Bernkastel in the Mosel-Saar-Ruwer region of Germany producing spicy wines.

US abbreviation for United States.

USSR (RUSSIA) wine-producing country producing vast quantities of mainly sweet white and red wine. In addition to its own production, Russia draws on its neighbouring satellites for more wine. The main Russian regions are around the Black Sea and also in Georgia and the Crimea.

UTIEL-REQUENA DO subdistrict of the Valencia region of central Spain where black grapes are grown and used in the production of *Vino de Doble Pasta*, a heavily coloured wine fermented with double the normal amount of grape skins. Rosé wines are also produced.

V

VACCARÈSE red-wine grape variety used in the RHÔNE VALLEY in France, one of the 13 varieties used in the production of CHÂTEAUNEUF-DU-PAPE.

VACQUEYRAS commune of the VAUCLUSE district of the CÔTES DU RHÔNE in southern France producing strong red, white and rosé wines. One of the RHÔNE VALLEY's better communes.

VAILLONS PREMIER CRU vineyard of the Chablis commune in the CHABLIS district of BURGUNDY.

VALAIS vineyard area of the upper Rhône in Switzerland. Its better wines include strong from the white-wine AMIGNE and Arvine grapes, strong white and some reds from the HUMAGNE grape, and the rare white Vin du Glacier matured high in the Alps.

VALBUENA town in the Old Castile region of Spain where the famous VEGA SICILIA wine is produced.

VALCALEPIO light red and white DOC wines produced in the LOMBARDY region of Italy.

VALDADIGE red and white DOC wines produced in the TRENTINO-ALTO ADIGE region of Italy.

VAL D'ARBIA light white DOC wine produced in the TUSCANY region of Italy.

VALDEORRAS demarcated DO region of the Galicia district of western Spain.

VALDEPEÑAS (1) grape used in the production of Californian 'Port'; (2) strong red and white wines produced in the La Mancha district of Spain. The reds have a TASTE RATING of B.

VALDESPINO SHERRY producers in the JEREZ region of

southern Spain. Their best wines include the FINO Ynocente and the AMONTILLADO Tio Diego.

VALEA CALUGAREASCA vineyard in Romania producing rich, smooth, sweet red wines.

VALENÇAY red and dry white VDQS wines from the upper LOIRE Valley in France.

VALENCIA town and demarcated DO area of the Levante region of eastern Spain, producing red wines with a TASTE RATING of B, and whites with a SWEETNESS RATING of 2.

VALGELLA red wines produced at Valtellina in the LOMBARDY region of northern Italy.

VALLE D'AOSTA wine-producing region of northern Italy between LOMBARDY and France. Donnaz and Enfer d'Arvier are original DOC wines but several other good quality wines are produced.

VALLE ISARCO light white DOC wine produced in the TRENTINO-ALTO ADIGE region of northern Italy.

VALMUR GRAND CRU vineyard of the CHABLIS region of BURGUNDY.

VALPANTENA wine-producing area of VENETO in northeast Italy, neighbouring VALPOLICELLA. It produces dry red wines.

VALPOLICELLA area of the VENETO region of northeast Italy producing the best red DOC wines of the region, including those of Fracia, Grumello, Inferno, Sassela and Valgella. They have a TASTE RATING of B. *See also* RECIOTO DELLA VALPOLICELLA.

VALTELLINA DOC area of northern LOMBARDY in Italy near the Swiss border, producing red wines, particularly **Valtellina Superiore**, made from NEBBIOLO grapes.

VARICHON & CLERC NÉGOCIANTS and specialists in sparkling wines in the SAVOIE district of the Rhône in France.

VARIETAL term for wine labelled with the name of the grape variety or varieties used in its production, e.g. Cabernet Sauvignon or Semillon/Chardonnay. This practice is common in the US, Australia and New Zealand and is becoming more widespread in Europe. In the US such wines must be made from at least 51 percent of the named European grapes, e.g. Napa Gamay. A wine is said to have good varietal characteristics when its odours and flavours are consistent with those normally found in a wine from that particular grape. *See also* individual grape names.

VARNA Controliran wine area of the coastal region of BULGARIA, producing CHARDONNAY wines.

VASSE FELIX winery in the MARGARET RIVER district of Western Australia producing varietal wines including very good CABERNET SAUVIGNON.

VAT container in which wines are fermented and blended, usually made of oak or stainless steel.

VAUCLUSE area of the CÔTES DU RHÔNE in southern France, mostly producing rosé wines. VACQUEYRAS is one of its best communes.

VAUCOUPIN PREMIER CRU vineyard of the CHABLIS region of BURGUNDY.

VAUD large wine-producing region of Switzerland to the north of Lake Geneva, consisting of two subregions: Lavaux and La Côte.

VAUDÉSIR one of the seven GRANDS CRUS vineyards of the CHABLIS district of BURGUNDY, which, like its neighbours, produces a superb dry gold Chablis wine.

VAUDEVEY PREMIER CRU vineyard of the CHABLIS district of BURGUNDY.

VDN abbreviation for VIN DOUX NATUREL.

VDP abbreviation for VIN DE PAYS, the category of French wines below VDQS and AC but above unclassified wines.

VDQS abbreviation for *Vin Délimité de Qualité Supérieure*, classification of French wines applied to those which are of superior quality to VIN DE PAYS but of lesser quality than those with an AC classification.

VECCHIO Italian word for 'old'. This term may be used for some DOC wines which have been aged for a certain time.

VEGA SICILIA famous vineyard in the Old Castile region of northern Spain, producing Bordeaux-style red wines which are aged for a minimum of five years prior to bottling. Bottles of an older vintage are labelled *Reserva Especial Unica*. Many believe Vega Sicilia to be Spain's finest wine.

VELDENZ village of GROSSLAGE Kurfürstlay, in the BEREICH of BERNKASTEL in the MOSEL-SAAR-RUWER region of Germany producing minor white wines.

VELHO Portuguese term for matured red wine.

VELLETRI red and white DOC wines produced in the LATIUM region of central Italy.

VELTLINER most widely planted white-wine grape in Austria.

VENDANGE French term for grape harvest or vintage.

VENDANGE TARDIVE French term for late vintage, indicating a higher concentration of sugar in the grapes.

VENDEMMIA Italian term for grape harvest or vintage.

VENDIMIA Spanish term for grape harvest or vintage.

VENEGAZZU-CONTE   LOREDAN-GASPARINI estate in the VENETO region of northern Italy producing good red and white wines. The reds in particular are of interest as the blend used is the same as in BORDEAUX: Cabernet Sauvignon, Merlot and Malbec.

VENETO region of northeast Italy stretching from the Austrian border to the Adriatic Sea. It produces good red and white wines, the best known being BARDOLINO, SOAVE,

VALPANTENA and VALPOLICELLA, and from the east of the region, near Venice, VERDUZZO and PROSECCO.

VENTANA VINEYARDS vineyards and winery in the MONTEREY district of California producing varietal wines.

VERDE *see* VINHO VERDE.

VERDELHO (1) white-wine grape grown in Portugal and used in the production of white PORT. When grown in cool regions, it can have a grassy nose with flavours similar to SAUVIGNON BLANC; (2) type of sweet dry MADEIRA wine produced from the Verdelho grape. **Verdelho Madeira** has a SWEETNESS RATING of 5.

VERDICCHIO white-wine grape grown in UMBRIA and other districts of central Italy and used in the production of ORVIETO. In the MARCHE region it makes the white dry and semi-sweet DOC **Verdicchio dei Castelli di Jesi** and the DOC **Verdicchio di Matelica**.

VERDIGNAN, CHÂTEAU CRU GRAND BOURGEOIS wine from the HAUT-MÉDOC district of BORDEAUX.

VERDISO white-wine grape used in northern Italy for dry wines.

VERDUZZO white-wine grape grown in the FRIULI-VENEZIA-GIULIA region of northern Italy, used for dry, often RECIOTO-type wines.

VEREINIGTE HOSPITIEN hospital in Trier in the MOSEL-SAAR-RUWER region of Germany which owns part of a number of vineyards including Piesporter Schuberstlay.

VERMENTINO DI GALLURA dry, amber DOC wine produced on the Italian island of Sardinia.

VERMENTINO LIGURIA light, white often sparkling wine produced in the Liguria district of the Italian Riviera.

VERMOUTH slightly fortified wine containing aromatic herbs and other flavourings of different porportions according to the recipe of the producer. Originally made in Italy, it is now produced in many countries in various styles: dry white, with a SWEETNESS RATING of 3; medium dry, 3 and 4; and *bianco*, rosé and *rosso*, 7.

VERNACCIA white-wine grape grown in central Italy and the island of Sardinia. On Sardinia it makes **Vernaccia di Oristano**, a well-known dry white DOC wine with a SWEETNESS RATING of 3. Those labelled *Riserva* have been aged for four years before bottling. In TUSCANY it produces the DOC **Vernaccia di San Gimignano** near Siena, a strongly flavoured wine with an almondy taste. Its *Riserva* is aged for one year.

VERTUS CHAMPAGNE vineyard of the Canton de Vertus in the Champagne region of France. Classified 93 percent in the CIVC rating.

VERZENAY CHAMPAGNE vineyard of the Canton de Verzy in the Champagne region of France. Classified 100 percent in the CIVC rating for black grapes.

VERZY CHAMPAGNE vineyard of the Canton de Verzy in the Champagne region of France. Classified 99 percent in the CIVC rating for black grapes.

VESPOLINA red-wine grape grown in the PIEMONTE region of northwest Italy.

VEUVE CLIQUOT-PONSARDIN CHAMPAGNE firm based at Reims in the Champagne region of France.

VEVEY town in the centre of the Lavaux district of VAUD in Switzerland and host to the international wine festival, *Fête des Vignerons*.

VICCHIOMAGGIO wine producers in the TUSCANY region of northwest Italy. Their DOC is CHIANTI CLASSICO.

VICHON WINERY winery in the NAPA VALLEY region of California producing VARIETAL wines.

VICTORIA wine-producing state of southern Australia. Its vineyards are situated in areas with climates ranging from very cool to extremely hot. The styles of wines produced are also varied, ranging from the intense rich liqueur MUSCAT wines of Rutherglen in the northeast to the elegant varietal styles of the Yarra Valley, Geelong and the Western Pyrenees regions.

VIDAL WINE PRODUCERS wine company in Hawke's Bay, New Zealand, making 100 percent CABERNET SAUVIGNON and lovely sparkling wines.

VIDAL-FLEURY, J. large grower and NÉGOCIANT in the CÔTE ROTIE district of the RHÔNE VALLEY in France, selling under the La Rolande and other labels.

VIDE Italian term which appears on the collar label of a bottle to show that the wine has passed the strict tests of a producers' association.

VIEILLES VIGNES French term for old vines, the ones which produce the best wines.

VIEJO Spanish word for 'old'. Often used of SHERRY but with no legal significance.

VIENOT CHARLES reputable growers and merchants of NUITS-SAINT-GEORGES in BURGUNDY.

VIEUX-CHÂTEAU-CERTAN outstanding full-bodied red wine of POMEROL in BORDEAUX.

VIEUX-CHÂTEAU-LANDON CRU BOURGEOIS estate of the MÉDOC district of BORDEAUX.

VIGNA (VIGNETO) Italian term for a vineyard. On a wine label it indicates that the grapes came from a particular vineyard or estate.

VIGNAMAGGIO wine producers in the TUSCANY region of northwest Italy. Their DOC is a good, light CHIANTI CLASSICO.

VIGNE French term for (1) an individual grape vine; (2) a section or parcel of a vineyard.

VIGNERON French word for 'wine grower'.

VIGNETO *see* VIGNA.

VIGNOBLE French word for a vineyard.

VILA NOVA DE GAYA city on the left bank of the River Douro in Portugal, across from OPORTO. Many PORT shippers have their stores here.

VILANY red-wine area of the BALATON district of Hungary.

VILLA Italian word for a country house. On a wine label it indicates that the grapes came from a particular vineyard or estate.

VILLA BANFI major wine producer in the US and Italy. It owns vinyards at Strevi in PIEMONTE and Montalcino in TUSCANY (Castello Banfi) and imports enormous quantities of Italian wine into the US.

VILLA MARIA wine producers in Auckland, New Zealand, producing white and light red VARIETAL wines.

VILLA MOUNT EDEN estate in the NAPA VALLEY region of California producing good VARIETAL wines.

VILLANY KISBURGUNDI quality red wine made in southern Hungary from PINOT NOIR grapes.

VILLANY-PECS important wine-producing area of southern Hungary near the city of Vilany.

VILLA SACHSEN wine estate in the BEREICH of BINGEN in the RHEINHESSEN region of Germany.

VILLAUDRIC cooperative producers of the CÔTES DU FRONTON in southwest France, producing red and rosé wines and Villaudric VIN DE TABLE.

VILLEGORGE, CHÂTEAU CRU GRAND BOURGEOIS EXCEPTIONNEL wine from the HAUT-MÉDOC district of BORDEAUX.

VILLEMAURINE, CHÂTEAU GRAND CRU wine from the SAINT-EMILION district of BORDEAUX.

VIN French word for wine.

VIÑA Spanish word for a vineyard. Also used in various brand names.

VIN BLANC French term for white wine.

VIN BOURRU French term for wine newly drawn from the barrel, still with suspended material, prior to filtration. *See also* VIN DE PRIMEUR.

VIN CHAUD French term for MULLED WINE.

VIN CLASSÉ second lowest classification of LUXEMBOURG wines.

VIN DE BÉARN VDQS red, white and rosé wines from the Madiran district of the Haut-Pyrénées region of southwest France.

VIN DE BLANQUETTE still white wine produced at Limoux in southwest France.

VIN DE CONSOMMATION COURANTE French term for ordinary, everyday wine.

VIN DE CORSE appellation of wines from CORSICA.

VIN DE COULE French term for wine produced from the first pressing of the grapes.

VIN DE CUVÉE French term equivalent to VIN DE COULE but used of CHAMPAGNE.

VIN DE GARDE French term for wine which should be kept to improve.

VIN DE GOUTTE French term for wine produced from the last pressing of the grapes.

VIN DE LA MOSELLE *see* LORRAINE.

VIN DE LA MOSELLE LUXEMBOURGEOISIE ordinary wine produced in Luxembourg.

VIN DE L'ANNÉE French term for wine of the year, i.e. from this year's crop.

VIN DÉLIMITÉ DE QUALITÉ SUPÉRIÉURE *see* VDQS.

VIN DE LIQUEUR French term for (1) very sweet wine; (2) CHAMPAGNE mixed with wine which has been fortified with brandy.

VIN DE MARC French term for wine produced from grape residue and water, sweetened with added sugar. *See also* VIN DE PRESSE.

VIN DE MARQUE wine bearing a brand name, normally an ordinary wine.

VIN DE PAILLE French term (literally 'straw wine') for wine produced from grapes dried on a bed of straw and having a straw colour.

VIN DE PAYS (VDP) tertiary category of French wines, below VDQS and AC but better than unclassified ordinary wines. Red vins de pays have a TASTE RATING of B.

VIN DE PLAINE French term for wine from a vineyard on a plain, generally not as good as wine from hillside vineyards.

VIN DE PRESSE French term for wine produced from grape residue. *See also* VIN DE MARC.

VIN DE PRIMEUR French term for young wine. *See also* VIN BOURRU.

VIN DE QUEUE French term for wine produced from pressed vine stalks.

VIN DE TABLE French term for table wine.

VIN DE TÊTE French term used in SAUTERNES for wine produced from the first pressing.

VIN DE THOURSAIS white VDQS wine from the LOIRE region of France.

VIN DOUX French term for grape juice which has not yet fermented.

VIN DOUX NATUREL strong sweet red or white wine fortified with brandy, produced mostly in the GRAND ROUSSILLON and FRONTIGNAN areas of southern France.

VIN DU GLACIER *see* VALAIS.

VIN DU HAUT-POITOU sound VDQS wines from the southern LOIRE Valley, produced by a large cooperative.

VIN DU TURSAN VDQS wine produced by a cooperative in the Madiran region of southwest France.

VIN FIN French term for quality wine. The term often has more promotional than accurately informative value.

VIN GRIS pink wine (literally 'grey wine') produced in LORRAINE and JURA. It is made from red-wine grapes, but unlike rosé wine it is pressed before fermentation.

VINHO CLARO Portuguese term for unfortified wine.

VINHO DE CONSUMO Portuguese term for everyday table wine.

VINHO DO RODO *see* VINHO SPUMOSO.

VINHO ESTUFADO Portuguese term for MADEIRA wine matured in an ESTUFA.

VINHO GENEROSO (VINHO LIQUOROSO) Portuguese term for fortified wine other than PORT.

VINHO LIQUOROSO *see* VINHO GENEROSO.

VINHO MADURO Portuguese term for wine which has been matured, the opposite of VINHO VERDE.

VINHO SPUMOSO (VINHO DO RODO) Portuguese term for sparkling wine.

VINHO VERDE 'green', light, slightly astringent wines produced in the Minho area of northwest Portugal. They are not in fact green but young, made from early-picked grapes. The best include Agulha, Alvarino de Moncao, Avelada, Casa da Calcada, Casa da Seara, Casa de Vilacetinho, Casalmendes, Casal Miranda, Casalinho, Gamga,

Gatão, Lagosta, Meireles, Mirita, Moura Basto, Souto Vedro and Tres Marias. Vinho Verde wines have a SWEET-NESS RATING of 4.

VIN JAUNE yellow wine produced in the JURA region of eastern France. Made from late-picked grapes, it is sometimes matured in the bottle for up to 50 years.

VINÍCOLA DE CASTILLA wine firm in the LA MANCHA district of Spain, selling a range of wines under the Castillo de Manza and Gran Verdad labels.

VINÍCOLA DEL MARQUES DE AGUAYO winery in the PARRAS region of Mexico. Established in 1593, it is the oldest winery in America.

VINIFERA *see* VITIS VINIFERA.

VINIFERA WINE CELLARS vineyard in Hammondsport, New York State, producing varietal wines.

VINIFICATION term meaning wine making.

VINIMPEX name of the state wine authority of BULGARIA which controls the export of wine. *See also* VINPROM.

VIN MOUSSEUX French term for sparkling wine.

VIN NATURE French term for unsweetened or unfortified wine.

VIN NON-MOUSSEUX French term for still wine.

VIN NOUVEAU French term for any fermented wine less than a year old.

VINO Italian and Spanish term for wine.

VINO BIANCO Italian and Spanish term for white wine.

VINO CORRIENTE Spanish term for ordinary table wine.

VINO DA PASTO Italian term for table wine.

VINO (VINI) DA TÀVOLA Italian term for non-DOC table wines. Red *vini da tàvola* have a TASTE RATING of A.

VINO DE ARROSTO Italian term for a wine with power and depth of flavour which needs keeping. Suitable for drinking with heavy meats.

VINO DE CUARTE rosé wine from the VALENCIA district of Spain.

VINO DE LA TIERRA Spanish term for local wine.

VINO DELLA RIVIERA wines from the Lake Garda area of LOMBARDY in Italy.

VINO DE MESA (VINO DE PASTO) Spanish term for table wine.

VINO DE PASTO *see* VINO DE MESA.

VINO DI LUSSO Italian term for a deluxe dessert wine.

VINO ESPUMOSO Spanish term for sparkling wine not of the best quality.

VINO FRIZZANTE Italian term for lightly sparkling or cheap fizzy wine.

VINO LIQUOROSO Italian term for dessert wine.

VINO NOBILE DI MONTEPULCIANO famous red wine, also known simply as Montepulciano, produced at Montepulciano in the TUSCANY region of Italy.

VINO MAESTRO Spanish term for a very sweet strong wine used for blending with weaker acidic wines.

VIN ORDINAIRE French term for ordinary wine.

VINO ROSATO Italian term for rosé wine.

VINO ROSSO Italian term for red wine.

VINO SANTO sweet white dessert wine produced on the Greek island of Santorini and also in parts of Italy. Made from grapes dried on the vine. *See also* VIN SANTO.

VINO SANTO DEL TRENTINO sweet white DOC dessert wine produced in the TRENTINO-ALTO ADIGE region of the Italian Tyrol.

VINOSITY the characteristic of wine made from grapes but not exhibiting VARIETAL character.

VINO SPUMANTE Italian term for sparkling wine.

VINO SPUMOSO Spanish term for sparkling wine.

VINOT brand name of a red Beaujolais Nouveau-style wine produced by Angelo Gaja in the PIEMONTE region of northern Italy.

VINO TINTO Spanish term for red wine.

VINO TIPICO Italian term for standard wine.

VINOUS tasting term for a wine which has VINOSITY and no VARIETAL character.

VINPROM official state organization of BULGARIA which controls the Bulgarian wine trade. *See also* VINIMPEX.

VIN ROSÉ French term for rosé wine.

VIN ROUGE French term for red wine.

VIN SANTO strong, sweet, amber DOC dessert wine produced all over Italy, especially in TUSCANY. It is made from grapes concentrated by a lengthy drying process and the fermented wine is aged in the cask for many years then held in bottle for further maturation.

VINSANTO DI GAMBELLARA sweet white DOC wine produced in the VENETO region of northern Italy.

VINSOBRES village in the Drome district of the Rhône Valley in France producing CÔTES DU RHÔNE-Villages wines.

VINTAGE time of year when grapes are harvested and also the basis for labelling and dating bottled wine. Wine from the 1987 vintage is labelled as such.

VINTAGE CHAMPAGNE CHAMPAGNE made from the wines of one year. To maintain standards of quality, vintage wines are made only in very good years, 'declared' by the producers.

VINTAGE PORT PORT made from the harvest of a single, very good year and aged in wood for two years. Vintage Port should be matured in the bottle for many years and decanted before serving.

VIN VERT crisp white wine from the Midi region of southern France.

VIOGNIER a leading white-wine grape grown in the RHÔNE VALLEY in France.

VIRÉ *see* MÂCON-VIRÉ.

VIRGIN HILLS vineyard in Victoria, southern Australia, producing VARIETAL wines.

VISAN (1) village of the CÔTES DU RHÔNE producing quality wine at reasonable prices; (2) wine producers in LA MANCHA, central Spain. Their wines include Castillo de Mudela and Viña Tito.

VITI official quality label found on some wines from the TICINO district of Switzerland.

VITICOLTORE Italian term for a vine-grower.

VITICULTEUR French term for a vine-grower.

VITICULTURE the science of grape growing.

VITIS LABRUSCA genus of vines native to North America. *V. labrusca* vines produce wines with an unpleasant 'foxy' odour and taste and are banned in Europe in favour of VITIS VINIFERA.

VITIS VINIFERA main wine-making vine species used throughout the world. Literally means 'the wine-making vine' and is the origin of most of the best grapes.

VIURA white-wine grape grown in the Rioja region of northern Spain.

VOGÜÉ, COMTE GEORGES DE estate in BURGUNDY whose holdings include Bonnes Mares, Chambolle-Musigny, Le Musigny and PREMIER CRU Les Amoureuses.

VOJVODINA wine-growing area of Serbia in Yugoslavia comprising the districts of Fruska Gora, Suboticka Pescara and part of the Banat.

VOLNAY commune of the CÔTE DE BEAUNE district of BURGUNDY producing elegant, well-balanced red wines. Its PREMIERS GRANDS CRUS vineyards include Les Angles, Les Brouillards, Les Caillerets, Les Caillerets-Dessus, Clos des Ducs, Les Mitans and L'Ormeau.

VOLNAY-SANTENOTS red wines grown in Meursault in the CÔTE DE BEAUNE district of BURGUNDY, in the vineyard area adjoining VOLNAY.

VOSE WINERY winery in the NAPA VALLEY region of California producing VARIETAL wines.

VOSGROS PREMIER CRU vineyard of the Chichée commune in the CHABLIS region of France.

VÖSLAU important winegrowing area of the Danube region of Austria, producing still and sparkling red wines.

VOSNE-ROMANÉE great commune of the CÔTE DE NUITS district of BURGUNDY producing particularly good soft red wines of great finesse. Its GRAND CRU vineyards are La Romanée-Conti, Les Richebourg, La Tâche, La Romanée and La Romanée-Saint-Vivant. Some wines sold as Vosne-Romanée come in fact from the two grands crus vineyards of the neighbouring FLAGEY-ECHÉZEAUX commune: Grands-Echézeaux and Echézeaux.

VOUGEOT commune of the CÔTE DE NUITS district of BURGUNDY producing red and white wines. Its famous GRAND CRU vineyard is Clos de Vougeot.

VOUVRAY famous light, dryish, still, semi-sparkling and sparkling white wines produced in the TOURAINE district of the LOIRE Valley in France. Dry Vouvray has a SWEETNESS RATING of 2 and Vouvray Demi-Sec a rating of 5.

VQPRD abbreviation for *Vini di Qualità Prodotti in Regioni Delimitate*, an Italian quality wine classification to satisfy EEC regulations. The equivalent of DOC. There is a separate VSQPRD for sparkling wines.

VRANAC vine grown in the Montenegro district of Yugoslavia to produce strong red wines with keeping potential.

VRAYE CROIX DE GAY, CHÂTEAU wine from the POMEROL district of BORDEAUX.

VSQPRD *see* VQPRD.

W

WACHAU district of lower Austria producing fine RIESLINGS.

WACHENHEIM village of GROSSLAGE Mariengarten in the BEREICH of MITTELHAARDT in the RHEINPFALZ region of Germany, producing fine wines. Its best vineyards are Altenburg, Bachel, Gerümpel and Rechbachel.

WALDRACH village of GROSSLAGE Römerlay in the BEREICH of SAAR-RUWER in the MOSEL-SAAR-RUWER region of Germany.

WALLUF village of GROSSLAGE Rauenthaler Steinmacher in the BEREICH of Johannisberg in the RHEINGAU region of Germany.

WALPORZHEIM-AHRTAL BEREICH of the AHR region of Germany, producing red wine from Spätburgunder and PINOT NOIR grapes.

WÄLSCHRIESLING white-wine grape variety cultivated widely in BURGENLAND, Austria, and also in Bulgaria, Hungary and Yugoslavia.

WARRE large English PORT firm in Vila Nova de Gaia in Portugal, producing good vintage Port wines.

WAWERN village of GROSSLAGE Scharzberg in the BEREICH of SAAR-RUWER in the MOSEL-SAAR-RUWER region of Germany. Its best wines are produced in the Golberg and Herrenberg vineyards.

WEEPER term for a wine bottle showing signs of a leaky cork.

WEGELER-ERBEN large and reputable estate in the RHEINGAU region of Germany. Their interests include Geisenheimer-Rothenberg, Oestricher-Lenchen, Rüdesheimer Berg and Winkeler-Hasensprung. They export under the DEINHARD label.

WEHLEN village of GROSSLAGE Munzlay in the BEREICH of BERNKASTEL in the MOSEL-SAAR-RUWER region of Germany producing exceptionally fine white wines. Its best vineyard is that of SONNENUHR, and **Wehlener Sonnenuhr** is considered among the finest wines of the Mosel.

WEIBEL vineyard in the MENDOCINO district of California, producing bottle-fermented champagne-style wines and varietal wines.

WEIGHT tasting term for the fullness of a wine. Equivalent to BODY.

WEIL, DR R. estate of Kiedrich in the RHEINGAU region of Germany. Their interests include Graafenberg, Kiedricher-Sandgrub, Klosterberg and Wasseros.

WEIN German word for 'wine'.

WEINBAUORT *see* GEMARKUNG.

WEINBERG town in the WÜRTTEMBERG region of Germany and home of the state viticultural institute, an excellent training ground for students of wine.

WEINGUT German term for a wine estate.

WEINGUTESIEGEL ÖSTERREICH Austrian quality wine seal, consisting of a red, white and gold disc.

WEINKELLEREI German term for wine cellar or winery.

WEINSTRASSE German term for tourist wine route through a wine-growing region. Originally a road through a vineyard.

WEINVIERTEL (literally 'wine quarter') district north of the Danube in Lower Austria producing mostly light white wines. Its important wine-producing areas are Eggenburg, Falkenstein, Haugsdorf, Hollabrun, Mailberg, Matzen, Polysdorf, Ravelsbach, Retz, Paulkau, Wolkersdorf and Zistersdorf.

WEISSBURGUNDER leading grape variety produced in the district of STYRIA in Austria and also grown in Czechoslovakia and Germany. Also known as Weisser Burgunder and Pinot Blanc.

WEISSHERBST full-bodied rosé wine produced in the BADEN region of Germany.

WENTE BROTHERS WINERY winery in the LIVERMORE VALLEY district of California, producing high quality VARIETAL wines.

WESTERN AUSTRALIA *see* AUSTRALIA.

WESTHOFEN village of GROSSLAGE Bergkloster in the BEREICH of WONNEGAU in the RHEINHESSEN region of Germany.

WEST VINEYARDS, MARK vineyards in the SONOMA region of California producing VARIETAL wines, including sparkling wine.

WHITE BEAUJOLAIS *see* BEAUJOLAIS BLANC.

WHITE PORT PORT produced from white-wine grapes. Both dry and sweet white Ports are available. The sweet has a SWEETNESS RATING of 7, the dry a rating of 5.

WHITE WINE type of WINE made from black or white grapes or a combination of the two, the juice of the grapes being fermented without the skins. If only white grapes are used it is BLANC DE BLANCS; if only red, BLANCS DE NOIRS.

WIDMER'S WINE CELLARS wine firm in the FINGER LAKES district of New York State, producing VARIETAL wines, some of which are vintage wines, and fortified Sherry-type wines.

WIEDERKEHR WINE CELLARS large winery at Altus, Arkansas, producing a range of still and sparkling wines.

WIEMER, HERMANN J., VINEYARDS vineyards in the Dundee district of FINGER LAKES in New York State producing VARIETAL wines, especially Rieslings.

WIEN German name for Vienna, capital and wine-growing district of Austria.

WIENERWALD-STEINFELD wine-growing region of Austria, around the town of Baden, south of Vienna.

WILLIAMS & HUMBERT SHERRY producers in the JEREZ region of southern Spain. Brand names include As You Like It, A Winter's Tale, Canasta Cream, Cedro, Dry Sack, Pando and Walnut Brown.

WILTINGEN village of GROSSLAGE Scharzberg in the BEREICH of SAAR-RUWER in the MOSEL-SAAR-RUWER region of Germany. Its best-known vineyard is SCHARZHOFBERG.

WINE the fermented juice of ripe grapes. Grapes are crushed immediately after harvesting to release the juice. During FERMENTATION the sugar content of the juice is converted to alcohol. Generally speaking, sweeter grapes will produce stronger wines, and the longer the fermentation the drier the wine will be. For SWEET WINE styles STOP FERMENTATION is used. After RACKING, the wine is allowed to settle and mature for a period depending on its style before FINING and FILTRATION. It is then bottled and aged, again according to style. Young styles such as Beaujolais Nouveau, rosés or delicate whites are best drunk as soon as possible after bottling while others, like CHAMPAGNE, MADEIRA, SHERRY or PORT can mature for many years in the bottle.

WINE BOX method of storing wine in airtight bags packaged in cardboard containers. Invented in the early 1970s in Australia, they were effective in removing Australia's wine lake of the time by increasing consumption. The quality of Australian wine sold in this way is better than European or American wines. Also known as bag-in-box wines and bladder packs.

WINE OF ORIGIN *see* WO

WINKEL village of GROSSLAGE Honigberg in the BEREICH of JOHANNISBERG in the RHEINGAU region of Germany. Its best vineyards are Hasensprung, JESUITENGARTEN and SCHLOSS VOLLRADS.

WINNINGEN village of GROSSLAGE Weinhex in the BEREICH of Zell in the MOSEL-SAAR-RUWER region of Germany.

WINTRICH village of GROSSLAGE Kurfürstlay in the BEREICH of BERNKASTEL in the MOSEL-SAAR-RUWER region of Germany.

WINZERGENOSSENSCHAFT German term for winegrowers' cooperative.

WINZERVEREIN German term for wine-growers' cooperative.

WIRRA WIRRA vineyard and winery in McLaren Vale, South Australia, producing VARIETAL wines including good RIESLINGS.

WISSELBRUNNEN vineyard of HATTENHEIM in GROSSLAGE Deutelsberg in the BEREICH of JOHANNISBERG in the RHEINGAU region of Germany producing a great white wine.

WITTLICH village of GROSSLAGE Schwarzlay in the BEREICH of BERNKASTEL in the MOSEL-SAAR-RUWER region of Germany.

WO (WINES OF ORIGIN) demarcated wine-growing areas of South Africa under official jurisdiction for standards of wine produced.

WONNEGAU BEREICH of the RHEINHESSEN region of Germany.

WOODBURY WINERY winery in Marin County, California, producing Port-type wines.

WOODY tasting term for the presence of oak aroma and flavour in a wine, the result of ageing in wooden barrels. Sometimes hardwoods are used which leave an undesirable character.

WOOTTON vineyard in Somerset, England, producing fruity, good quality wines from Schonburger, Seyval Blanc and MÜLLER-THURGAU grapes.

WORCESTER wine-producing district of Cape Province in South Africa.

WORKING term for wine which is still in the process of FERMENTATION.

WORMS city of GROSSLAGE Liebfrauenmorgen in the BEREICH of WONNEGAU in the RHEINHESSEN region of Germany. Includes the vineyard of LIEBFRAUENKIRCHE.

WÜRTTEMBERG vineyard region of Germany surrounding the Neckar river. Württemberg produces the most red wine of any German region, using Spätburgunder, Mullerrebe, Trollinger, Lemberger and Portugieser vines. White-wine varieties include Riesling, Sylvaner, Müller-Thurgau, Traminer and Kerner. Both whites and reds are very fruity with good body. Stuttgart is the major city.

WÜRZBURG city in the BEREICH of MAINDREIECK in the FRANKEN region of Germany. Franken STEINWEIN is produced at Würzburg.

WYNN'S large wine company in Nunawading, Victoria, Australia. Vineyards are located in Coonawarra, Southern Vales and Padthaway regions of South Australia. Excellent CHARDONNAY and CABERNET SAUVIGNON wines are produced.

WYOMING BENTONITE *see* BENTONITE.

XYZ

XERES *see* JEREZ.

XYNISTERI white-wine grape grown in Cyprus and used in the production of COMMANDARIA.

YALUMBA large family-owned wine company in South Australia. Its best-known wine is the white Carte d'Or.

YARRA VALLEY wine-growing district of Victoria, Australia.

YEAST single-cell micro-organism which converts sugars to alcohol during fermentation.

YEASTY tasting term for a white wine with a taste of yeast, particularly acetaldehyde, following fermentation.

YECLA wine-producing area of the LEVANTE in eastern Spain producing wines of DO standard.

YELLOW MUSCAT *see* MUSKOTALY.

YON-FIGEAC, CHÂTEAU GRAND CRU wine from the SAINT-EMILION district of BORDEAUX.

YONNE wine-growing department of BURGUNDY, the home of CHABLIS.

YORK MOUNTAIN WINERY winery in the San Luis Obispo region of California.

YQUEM, CHÂTEAU D' PREMIER GRAND CRU SAUTERNES from BORDEAUX in southwest France. Generally regarded as the world's finest sweet white wine.

YUGOSLAVIA country with old traditions of wine production and currently among the world's largest producers. Each of the six different regions produces a variety of wine styles. The regions of Serbia and Croatia produce the majority of the wine, with Slovenia, Macedonia, Montenegro and Bosnia-Herzegovina all producing smaller quantities.

YVORNE very good white CHABLAIS wine produced in the Vaud district of Switzerland.

ZACA MESA WINERY winery in the SANTA BARBARA region of California producing VARIETAL wines.

ZACCAR wine subregion of Algeria and the name given to its red and white table wines, the stronger ones having a VDQS classification.

ZACO white wine produced in the RIOJA region of Spain.

ZAGAROLO dry or sweet white DOC wine produced in the LATIUM region of Italy.

ZBW abbreviation for *Zentralkellerei Badischer Winzergenossenschaften*, very large cooperative in the BADEN region of Germany producing a large range of wines from around 100 smaller cooperatives.

ZD WINES winery in the NAPA VALLEY region of California producing VARIETAL wines including excellent CHARDONNAYS.

ZELL BEREICH in the MOSEL-SAAR-RUWER region of Germany.

ZELTINGEN-RACHTIG outstanding village of GROSSLAGE Munzlay in the BEREICH of BERNKASTEL in the

Mosel-Saar-Ruwer region of Germany. Its production is extremely large and includes many ordinary as well as outstanding wines. The best vineyards are Deutschherrenberg, Himmelreich, Schlossberg and Sonnenuhr.

ZENTRALKELLEREI German term for a large wine cooperative. There are six of these in the major wine regions of Germany, including Europe's largest cooperative, ZBW, and **Zentralkellerei Baden-Wurttemburg**.

ZIBBIBO see Muscat.

ZIERFÁNDLER see Spätrot.

ZILAVKA white-wine grape native to Yugoslavia, used in the making of strong wines.

ZINFANDEL excellent widely used classic red-wine grape variety of California. It has a unique 'raspberry' flavour, vibrant colour and intense spicy fruit on the nose.

ZISTERSDORF wine-producing area of the Weinviertel in Austria. Also called Steinberg.

ZOLDSZILVANI Hungarian green Sylvaner grape, grown around Lake Balaton.

ZONIN wine producers in the Veneto region of northern Italy. Their DOC wines include Bardolino, Gambellara, Recioto di Gambellara and Valpolicella.

ZONNEBLOEM brand name of a range of red wines produced by SFW in South Africa.

ZOOPIYI village in Cyprus producing Commandaria.

ZUPA red and rosé table wines from east-central Yugoslavia.

ZWICKER term used on bottle labels in the Alsace region of northern France to indicate wines made from a mixture of grape varieties.